Beyond Contract: Work, Power and Trust Relations

SOCIETY TODAY AND TOMORROW

General Editor: A. H. Halsey

MARXIST SOCIOLOGY IN ACTION: *A Sociological Critique of the Marxist Approach to Industrial Relations*
by J. A. Banks

CONSTITUENCY POLITICS: *A Study of Newcastle-under-Lyme*
by Frank Bealey, J. Blondel and W. P. McCann

BRITISH MODERN POLITICS
by Samuel Beer

WINCHESTER AND THE PUBLIC SCHOOL ELITE
by T. J. H. Bishop and Rupert Wilkinson

TELEVISION IN POLITICS
by Jay G. Blumler and Denis McQuail

LSD, MAN AND SOCIETY
by Richard C. De Bold and Russell C. Leaf

PEOPLE AND PLANNING: *The Sociology of Housing in Sunderland*
by Norman Dennis

PUBLIC PARTICIPATION AND PLANNERS' BLIGHT
by Norman Dennis

THE FAWLEY PRODUCTIVITY AGREEMENTS
by Allan Flanders

EXPERIMENT IN INDUSTRIAL DEMOCRACY: *A Study of the John Lewis Partnership*
by Allan Flanders, Ruth Pomeranz and Joan Woodward

THE BRITISH ACADEMICS
by A. H. Halsey and Martin Trow

IS SCIENTIFIC MANAGEMENT POSSIBLE?
by Joe Kelly

SOCIAL CLASS AND DELINQUENCY
by Lynn McDonald

ART STUDENTS OBSERVED
by Charles Madge and Barbara Weinberger

CRIME AND THE SOCIAL STRUCTURE
by John Barron Mays

TECHNOCRACY
by Jean Meynaud

POLITICAL MOBILIZATION
by J. P. Nettl

INTERNATIONAL SYSTEMS AND THE MODERNIZATION OF SOCIETIES: *The Formation of National Goals and Attitudes*
by J. P. Nettl and Roland Robertson

PROFESSIONAL EMPLOYEES: *A Study of Scientists and Engineers*
by Kenneth Prandy

THE REVOLUTION OF THE DONS: *Cambridge and Society in Victorian England*
by Sheldon Rothblatt

EDUCATION AND MODERNIZATION
by M. D. Shipman

THE ELITE IN THE WELFARE STATE
by Piet Thoenes

THE YOUNG WORKER AT COLLEGE: *A Study of a Local Tech.*
by Ethel Venables

Beyond Contract: Work, Power and Trust Relations

ALAN FOX

FABER AND FABER LIMITED
3 Queen Square, London

First published in 1974
by Faber and Faber Limited
3 Queen Square London WC1
Printed in Great Britain by
Western Printing Services

ISBN 0 571 10469 x

For Margaret

Acknowledgements

My thanks are due to Dr. A. H. Halsey, of Nuffield College, Oxford, and Dr. R. Martin, of Trinity College, Oxford, who read this book in draft and made many valuable suggestions. I alone am responsible for the final outcome. Most of it was written during sabbatical leave granted me by the University of Oxford, a privilege greatly appreciated.

Department of Social and Administrative Studies, University of Oxford

ALAN FOX

Contents

1 · Discretion, Status, and Rewards in Work

This book seeks to explore fundamental principles implicitly informing the ways in which men organize, regulate, and reward themselves for the production and distribution of goods and services, and the significance of these principles for their wider social relations. For all the talk of the coming 'age of leisure' the theme is likely to remain a central one for modern man. As Everett Hughes wrote: 'In our particular society, work organization looms so large as a separate and specialized system of things, and work experience is so fateful a part of every man's life, that we cannot make much headway as students of society and of social psychology without using work as one of our main laboratories' (1952: 426). His perspective is apposite, since it will be argued here that the principles by which we organize work not only have 'fateful' consequences in this field for our individual experience, for our relations with others, and for relations between social groups, but also have profound significance for the study of institutions and interactions throughout the wider social setting beyond work.

These principles concern relationships of trust and distrust between men and between groups in work situations. On the level of familiar everyday usages, trust is a familiar talking point for managers, administrators, and indeed rulers of all kinds. 'Trust the company!' is an appeal frequently addressed to its employees, just as 'Trust my leadership!' is a frequent appeal of political rulers to their subjects. In personal, face-to-face relationships, too, the manager is keenly aware of trust or distrust in the attitudes of subordinates, and their effect on work performance and cooperation. Trust is increasingly seen, indeed, as a key factor in organizational wellbeing.

But these everyday usages, large as they loom for those in positions of command, take us only part of the way towards understanding the full nature of trust and distrust, the forms they take in the affairs of men, and the dynamics of change which they generate in those affairs. For men manifest trust and distrust towards others – and perceive others as doing the same towards themselves – not only in personal terms but also in terms of the roles, rules, and relations which they impose on those others – or have imposed on themselves. When we bind a man with rules which minimize his discretion in a particular sphere of behaviour he may, to be sure, accept the constraints willingly as legitimate, and it is important to work out under what conditions this is likely to be so. But he may perceive the constraints as indicating that we do not trust him, in which case he is likely to reciprocate with distrust towards us. This reciprocated distrust can take many behavioural forms, ranging from evasion of obligations to attempts at imposing similar controls on those who seek to dominate him. Nowhere are these dynamics more abundantly displayed than in the field of work, where the few make decisions about job design, technology, and organization structure in attempts to shape the experience of the many. By their very nature, these decisions seek to determine who make other decisions – not only about the technical day-to-day conduct of the organization but also about objectives, the types of means employed, and the distribution of financial rewards, status, and other things men value. In respect of each of these issues, some men are included in, and others are excluded from, the more important decision-making processes. Some, as a consequence, see themselves as trusted; others see themselves as distrusted. In the creation of these categories, and in the changes which they generate, power is the essential agency. Power enables the few to minimize their dependence on the many. It enables the few to minimize the discretion of the many in the making of decisions deemed by the few to be important for their purposes. It enables the few, in other words, to manifest distrust of the many by imposing upon them work roles and rules which leave little scope for important choices – including those determining the whole pattern of rewards, status, and privilege. The reciprocation of this distrust by the many has had massive consequences not only for the work organization, in modifying decision-making structures and creating problems of motivation which increasingly preoccupy its managers, but also for society at large, in shaping the nature of intergroup conflict and throwing up issues of the utmost profundity concerning the principles on which men should base their social institutions and relations with each other.

Here, then, can be found patterns of trust and distrust generated by men's exercise of power over others in the pursuit of their own purposes. Here can be traced dynamics which inform behaviour not only in the work organization but also outside it. Both categories raise fundamental issues of social cooperation and conflict. They cover, at one extreme, the manager's relations with his subordinates and colleagues and, at the other, major problems relating to the stability of the whole society. They raise the issue which has been, and remains, one of the most searching that men can put to themselves – the issue of what principles they should follow in relating themselves to each other in the pursuit of their interests and purposes. This problem of how men should live together, essentially one which raises all the important questions of what meanings are to be given to such concepts as community, justice, and respect, has emerged in many different ways from many different types of analysis. It emerges here from the analysis of industrial society in terms of trust relations. This analysis demonstrates that, in discussing the principles by which men live, we must look not only at the principles by which they act and treat each other within the *existing* social institutions, patterns, and processes, but more fundamentally at those which are embodied in the institutions, patterns, and processes themselves, for these, too, are devised, supported, and operated by men who are capable of choosing differently.

This and the succeeding chapters apply this approach to an analysis of current patterns of work organization, of how they developed from earlier patterns, of how they are differentially perceived by the various participant groups, and of how they have changed and are changing under many diverse pressures – including pressures from groups conscious of deprivation. The analysis opens out from a micro-level focus on the nature of work to the macro-level of societal power relations, income distribution, perceptions of justice, and the whole nature of the social bond. This requires a close concern at the outset with what may strike some readers as an excessively technical examination of work in its many diverse forms. The purpose is to lay a necessary foundation for what follows. The reader is asked to bear with it in the hope that he will find it to have been justified by subsequent stages of the argument.

Prescribed and Discretionary Work: Specificity and Diffuseness

John Kenneth Galbraith, the American economist, has described as 'one of the oldest and most effective obfuscations in the field of social science' the assertion 'that all work – physical, mental, artistic, or managerial – is essentially the same. . . . To economists it has seemed a harmless and, indeed, an indispensable simplification' (1962: 273–4). In precisely what respect this obfuscation has been effective will be examined later; for the moment it is enough to say that from many other perspectives this simplification is harmful and dispensable. An argument of this book will be, in fact, that it conceals differences of the utmost relevance not only to the individual's experience in work, to the structure of rewards, and to the dynamics governing the nature and growth of rules and relations generally in the work situation, but also to group and class relations and to the nature of the social bond.

The starting point from which subsequent analysis will be developed is the distinction elaborated by Jaques between 'prescribed' and 'discretionary' work (1956, 1967).* This has much in common with the notions of 'specificity' and 'diffuseness' as applied to what the sociologist might call work role definitions, or the industrial engineer 'job specifications'.

Work roles can be specific or diffuse in two different senses, however, which are sometimes confused. In what might be called the 'task-range' sense, a role limited to one task could be seen as having the quality of specificity, whereas a role embracing a wide range of different tasks has the quality of diffuseness (Hoselitz 1963:18). In the second, the 'discretionary-content' sense, the behaviours called for by the role may be either specifically defined, thereby offering little choice, or diffusely defined, thereby requiring the exercise of discretion. In terms of measurement, the task range may be narrow or wide – a lateral conception – whereas discretionary content might be more appropriately assessed as low or high – a vertical conception.

Some roles are highly specific in both senses, as in the case of the assembly line operator confined to the repetition of one simple and undemanding task; others are diffuse in both, as on the highest

* Although I use Jaques's distinction and quote him in this opening section he must not be taken as necessarily agreeing with my elaboration of his argument, still less with the use to which I put it in subsequent chapters.

managerial level where the exercise of discretion over a wide range of issues and activities is required. But a role may be specific in the first sense and diffuse in the second, as with a surgeon who specializes in one highly skilled operation, or diffuse in the first and specific in the second, as in the case of an odd-job man performing a wide range of tasks all of which call for only minimal discretion. In practice the narrowing of a job's task range may well result in the creation of jobs of increased specificity also in the sense of reduced discretion. There are three possibilities. First: a high-discretion task may be hived off and leave the role composed only of low-discretion tasks. Second: the 'wide task-range' role often endows its occupant with the discretion of deciding when to turn from one task to another and how much time and other resources to devote to each. If the role is narrowed by being differentiated into separate tasks, each performed by a different person, these decisions will have to be taken by a superior exercising a coordinating function. Thus even if the tasks are of equal discretion and remain unchanged, those occupying the newer, more specific roles are being denied an element present in the older, more diffuse one: namely the discretionary judgement involved in combining and coordinating them. It may of course be the case that the occupant of the old wide range role enjoyed no such discretion anyway, but was constrained by personal supervision or technology in respect of how much resources he directed to each task. In such a case, there is no loss of discretion when the role is differentiated. Third: an increase of specificity in terms of a narrower task range has often brought change, too, to the differentiated tasks in terms of discretionary content. Situations have been frequent where the narrowing of task range has been followed by, or introduced expressly to accommodate, a simplification of tasks by machinery or new methods, thereby transferring discretion upwards to machine designers, coordinative managers,and a range of other specialists.

This book is concerned with specificity and diffuseness in the sense of discretionary content. It is for this reason that we take up the distinction as developed by Jaques, who defines 'employment work' as 'the application of knowledge and the exercise of discretion within the limits prescribed by the immediate manager and by higher policies, in order to carry out the activities allocated by the immediate manager, the whole carried out within an employment contract for a wage or salary' (1967:77). Embodied within this definition are the notions of prescribed limits, which seek to specify precisely some of the required patterns of behaviour, and the discretionary content of responsibility, which grants the role occupant a certain freedom of choice of action within those prescribed limits – an area of the role definition characterized by diffuseness as against the specificity of the prescribed aspects.

Every work role contains both. When the employer or manager or their representative defines a job, he does so partly in prescribed terms: 'that is to say, in such a manner that his subordinate will be in no doubt whatever when he has completed his task, and completed it as instructed'; and partly in discretionary terms: 'that is to say, in such a manner that his subordinate will have to use his own discretion in deciding when he has pursued the particular activities to the point where the result is likely to satisfy the requirements of his manager' (*Ibid*: 77). Jaques offers these examples of prescribed terms: 'follow this routine; get such-and-such records out each Friday; use British standards in drawing; keep double-entry books; use the Matrix intelligence test; travel via trunk road A3; keep below the speeds, as shown on a speedometer, specified for each curve on a railway: confine yourself to air ejector systems in designing these machine tools; advertise only in the national daily newspapers; see that a random ten per cent of all goods is inspected before despatch; visit all customers with more than a given turnover at least once a month.' Examples of discretionary terms are: 'make sure you buy enough stamps; use the best method in the circumstances; design advertisements with public appeal; keep a satisfactory standard of finish; select the most capable of the applicants' (*Ibid*: 78).

It is clear that the prescribed terms are objectively defined in the sense that they lay down external and independent standards to which reference can be made when judging performance. Did or did not the subordinate follow this specified routine; travel via trunk road A3; advertise only in the national dailies? By contrast, the discretionary terms tell the subordinate only that he must do *something* about stamps, best methods, appealing advertisements. In the absence of any objective reference the meaning of the instruction and the sense of what constitutes appropriate performance are left for the time being to the subordinate's discretion.

The fact that objective standards are embodied in the prescribed terms enables us to say that what is demanded of the subordinate in these aspects of his job is obedience, conformity. Certainly he must be trained, indoctrinated, or educated in the appropriate ways. Given this, however, the requirement is that he adhere to the prescribed procedures and instructions laid down for him in the form of specific external controls. These take many different forms. Machinery may itself constitute a control by constraining the subordinate in terms of method and possibly quality and pace as well. Other physical controls include jigs, railway tracks, automatic temperature regulators, and signals such as lights or bells which require no interpretation. Prescriptive controls may also be administrative in nature, as when rules lay down specific procedures to be followed; or technical, when rules specify certain techniques to be employed; or policy-defining, in specifying particular markets or customers or categories of customers with whom business is to be done. The prescriptive limits need not originate from management even though it may have to bear the responsibility for enforcing them. External agencies may call upon management to apply certain prescriptive rules; as with fire, safety, and insurance regulations, requirements under factory and welfare legislation, the rulings of certain professional associations, or, in some societies, the planning edicts of governmental departments or bureaux.

By contrast, performance of the discretionary content requires, not trained obedience to specific external controls, but the exercise of wisdom, judgement, expertise. The control comes from within – it is, in the literal sense, self-control. The occupant of the role must himself choose, judge, feel, sense, consider, conclude what would be the best thing to do in the circumstances, the best way of going about what he is doing.

The investigation of these characteristics of work roles must begin with the recognition that no role can be totally diffuse or totally specific. It is easy to accept the former – that no work role can be totally discretionary. The occupant of the most elevated post has to operate within prescribed limits, usually a great many. It may be more difficult, however, to accept that all jobs contain discretionary as well as prescriptive elements. Surely many jobs in our kind of industrial society are *totally* prescribed; totally without discretion? Such a view cannot be sustained. However elaborate the external controlling structure of mechanical, administrative, technical, or policy prescriptions, some residual element of discretion always remains. Jaques himself demonstrates the point. 'When an adding machine operator – the same analysis would apply to copy-typing and, indeed, to the operation of all machines – is at work, much of what is going on is under his own control; it is not prescribed or regulated. He himself controls the way he sits, the movement of his arms, hands, and fingers, how hard he strikes the keys, the number of times and the way he refers to the columns of figures he is transcribing, his sizing up of how much work there is to be done, his adjustment of his pace of work in order to complete so much by, say, lunch-time or by the end of the day, or before the regular midweek rush comes in the following afternoon. This control may not be wholly conscious; it is being exercised all the same' (*Ibid*: 80). In other words, just as no job is without some prescription, so no job is without some discretion.

We may express these propositions in the language of decision-making. Carrying out the prescribed aspects of the role does not involve the incumbent in making decisions between alternative choices of action, for the choice has already been made by someone else. He is required only to use his training in conforming to that prior choice. In using discretion, however, choice is of the essence. A decision has to be made as to which of the perceived alternatives is to be pursued. Since all jobs contain some degree of discretion it follows that all jobs involve decision-making. Simon, in a reference which broadens the discussion by distinguishing between the factual premises and the value premises of a decision, describes the degree of discretion as being 'determined by the number and importance of the premises which are specified, and the number and importance of those which are left unspecified' (1965: 223).

There is ample scope for theoretical and empirical research into the wide variations of discretion with which work roles in our society are endowed. Jaques and others of his school have expounded and applied his 'time-span of discretion' technique, which seeks to measure the discretionary content of a job by the period of time for which 'it would be possible to exercise inadequate discretion before that fact would come to the attention of the immediate manager' (1967:96).* Jaques asserts his technique to be 'objective' and to have

* This gives but the barest indication of the time-span notion. Jaques, 1967, not only gives a full exposition both of theory and practical technique but also includes a bibliography (345–8). Jaques links his time-span theory with wage and salary fixing; a different set of arguments altogether which will be touched on briefly later. Critical appraisals of this aspect are offered by Fox, 1966a;

'been tested independently in many countries' (*Ibid*: 9,15). In so far as it does prove to yield similar results for different researchers it could serve as a valuable device for rendering operational one of the key concepts used in developing the argument of this book.* Whether or not, however, the varying degrees and types of discretion in different jobs can be precisely measured, the fact of variations will hardly be disputed; a fact which enables us to postulate for theoretical purposes a continuum ranging from low to high discretion, and thereby to speak in relative terms of low and high discretion work roles.

Before we start to explore these differences a point must be raised of considerable importance for our theoretical framework. Do men perceive their work role in terms which accord with the assessments of independent observers? How men react to their role is determined by *their* experience and perceptions, not those of independent observers. If we are going to draw upon such independent reports for information about different types of work it is important to be confident that they appear in much the same form to those who have to perform them. Hackman and Lawler offer reassurance on this point. They report of an empirical sample that 'Employee perceptions of their jobs have substantial convergence with the assessments of objective job characteristics made by the researchers and by company supervisors' (1971, in Davis and Taylor 1972: 285).

Low-Discretion and High-Discretion Work

Even if personal observation failed to alert us to wide differences of discretion in work, the literature would remedy the omission. References to these distinctions begin at least as early as 1776 with Adam Smith's observations that 'in the progress of the division of labour, the employment . . . of the great body of the people comes to be confined to a few very simple operations; frequently to one or

Hellriegel and French, 1969; and Milkovitch and Campbell, 1972. But see also Richardson, 1971.

* Hellriegel and French 'feel one of the major contributions of Jaques has been the development of an operational means for *measuring discretion* in jobs . . . It is likely that a great deal of initial training will be necessary, but our own experience indicates the system can be made operational' (1969: 269–79, their italics). Richardson likewise, after conducting his own experiments, concluded that 'the time-span of discretion technique has shown promise of being a workable and reliable measuring device . . .' (1971: 77).

two. . . . The man whose whole life is spent in performing a few simple operations . . . has no occasion to exert his understanding, or to exercise his invention in finding out expedients for removing difficulties which never occur' (1904, vol. 2: 267). Marx and Engels asserted in 1848 that 'owing to the extensive use of machinery and to division of labour, the work of the proletarians has lost all individual character. . . .' The workman 'becomes an appendage of the machine, and it is only the most simple, most monotonous, and most easily acquired knack, that is required of him' (1967: 87). Veblen's analysis of 'the machine process' in 1904 saw the workman as taking 'thought of the machine and its work in terms given him by the process that is going forward. His thinking in the premises is reduced to standard units of gauge and grade. If he fails of the precise measure, by more or less, the exigencies of the process check the aberration and drive home the need of conformity. . . . The machine process . . . requires close and unremitting thought, but it is thought which runs in standard terms of quantitative precision. Broadly, other intelligence on the part of the workman is useless; it is even worse than useless, for a habit of thinking in other than quantitative terms blurs the workman's quantitative apprehension of the facts with which he has to do' (1958: 147).

These few examples, which of course could be multiplied from nineteenth and twentieth century literature, indicate only a general awareness that much work – allegedly an increasing quantity – contained relatively little of what is being described here as discretion. They are characteristic of many conventional broad-brush generalizations about the effects of the Industrial Revolution in that they focus selectively on certain aspects of current novelty and leave unmentioned the many diversities in the division of labour which continued to survive. Nor do they refer to the ways in which industrialization, besides breaking down some high-discretion into low-discretion work, was also creating new high-discretion work. For our purposes a fuller picture is needed of the range found in work organizations today.

Among many others, Blauner recapitulates the effects of machine technology, 'which generally reduces the control of the employee, over his work process. Workers are rarely able to choose their own methods of work, since these decisions have been incorporated into the machines' very design and functioning.' Operatives simply respond to the rhythms and exigencies of the technical system instead of initiating activity and exerting control. The extreme case of the assembly line and conveyor belt system reduces the worker's control to a minimal level – it 'dictates most movements of the operative and pre-empts many of his potential choices and decisions' (1964: 170). Prominent among comparatively recent writers in celebrating these extreme applications of the division of labour was Frederick Winslow Taylor, the pioneer of modern Scientific Management. Taylor's writings are useful in bringing out that, given the necessary training, all that is required of the performer by the prescribed elements in his job is obedience. 'The management must think out and plan the work in the most careful and detailed way, demanding of the worker "not to seek to increase production by his own *initiative*, but to perform punctiliously the orders given down to their slightest detail"' (Friedmann 1961: 34, quoting Taylor).

This extreme limitation of discretion is by no means confined, of course, to manual workers. There are situations where 'the mechanization and rationalization of office work has proceeded to the extent that relatively large groups of semi-skilled employees are concentrated together, separated from managerial and supervisory staffs, performing continuous, routinized and disciplined work', and where clerical work becomes 'extremely like that of the factory operative' (Lockwood 1958: 92). But this trend is easy to exaggerate. 'In the large firm, as in the small', much clerical work is non-repetitive and requires 'a modicum of skill and responsibility and individual judgement' (*Ibid*: 78).

If minimal discretion is not confined to manual workers, neither are all manual workers subject to minimal discretion. Craft activities offer a different picture. Here, while the presumption would have to be that discretion falls far short in range and quality of that enjoyed at the managerial and professional levels, the worker has some freedom to control his immediate socio-technical environment; freedom which 'is almost a technological necessity for the work to get done' (Blauner 1964: 98). 'The interconnection between traditional manual skill and control is so intimate that theoretical distinctions between the two concepts become blurred: the very definition of traditional skill implies control over tools, materials, and pace of work'. Work discipline 'in craft industries is . . . essentially self-discipline' (*Ibid*: 170, 175).

Increasingly studied in the contemporary world, moreover, are employee groups in so called science-based or advanced-technology industries whose work verges on 'whitecoat' status. The technology tends to be of the continuous process or automated kind where, in place of 'physical effort and skill in the traditional, manual sense, the major job requirement for production workers . . . is responsibility' (*Ibid*: 133); responsibility which 'demands thinking in terms of the collective whole rather than the individual part' (*Ibid*: 173). 'Traditional manual skill and "non-manual" responsibility differ in their basic qualities, but both require considerable discretion and initiative' (*Ibid*: 168). A similar view of this type of work situation is presented by Touraine. 'Whether or not the worker is qualified for the job depends now on his capacity to integrate himself into the social group and to take responsibility' (1955: 429).

As we look still higher in the occupational status scale the discretionary content of jobs tends to enlarge further in scope and importance.* The work of functional, technical, and professional specialists often contains such a high degree of discretion as to call attention to the differences between *specialists* of this kind and the *specialized* worker whose minimal discretion is often seen as a symbol of industrialized work. Referring to the former, Friedmann (whose terms these are) observes that the narrowing of their range of activity may be 'based upon a previous professional training of which it is the prolongation and crown'; in contrast to the latter, 'who carries out a fragmentary job into which he is initiated (in the case of the semi-skilled worker it is one wholly concerned with motions) without having received, or usually receiving later, any general training such as would form a background explaining or illuminating his "unit of work" by connecting it with the whole process' (1961: 88).† Generally speaking, 'the higher the degree of

* The emphasis must be on the word 'tends'. Goodman, examining empirically in one industrial company some implications of Jaques's concept of time span, found 'a large number of high time span [i.e. high-discretion] jobs' at 'the lower organizational levels' (1967:163). The discretionary content of a given role cannot, therefore, be inferred from its location in the hierarchy and must always be subject to empirical inquiry. However, the generalization that discretion rises with position in the hierarchy is sufficiently widely based to serve us for this exposition.

† Often only the context enables us to judge how a writer intends us to interpret his use of words like 'specialization' and 'specialism'. Loose usage often reflects a failure to distinguish the two senses of specificity (and diffuse-

professional training, the more discretion employees will exercise in performing their tasks' (Bell 1966: 451). Finally, of course, we have to think of the executive line of management, with a presumption, subject always to empirical verification, of an ever enlarging sphere of discretion as one moves upwards.

The foregoing sketch of received notions about the degree of discretion exercised at different organizational levels illustrates the earlier theoretical exposition. It suggests that, given an accepted method of measuring discretion, occupational categories could be ranked in a graduated scale along that dimension. For the purposes of this book, however, it will be convenient to think not in terms of a graduated scale of small differences but in terms of three broad categories of low, medium, and high discretion roles. Indeed, for the most part attention is directed to the opposing extremes of the scale. This is not from failure to recognize that fine gradations exist, but from the wish to sharpen theoretical tools of analysis by emphasizing certain differences.

In pursuit of this aim it is necessary now to move from our statement about low-discretion and high-discretion work to the postulation of two syndromes of defining features which may be seen as characterizing two sharply contrasting work patterns. These will be referred to as the low-discretion and high-discretion syndromes. They carry the potential weaknesses as well as the potential usefulness of all such analytical constructs. While they offer a selective emphasis and grouping of ideas which seems useful given our present awareness of empirical probabilities, they may prove, as more data appear, to have too many exceptions to be of value. They certainly make assumptions to which there are important exceptions. These will be identified later and their implications explored. Moreover, these assumptions and exceptions will never be lost sight of in the subsequent arguments of the book.

Work Role Patterns (a) The Low-Discretion Syndrome

The syndrome of characteristics which will be taken as defining, for our purposes, the highly prescribed, low-discretion work role

ness) noted in the opening of this chapter. Friedmann's specialist role is specific in task range but diffuse in discretionary terms; his specialized worker role is specific along both dimensions.

pattern comprises five items. The first is fundamental and basic in the sense of explaining the others. The role occupant perceives superordinates as behaving as if they believe he cannot be trusted, of his own volition, to deliver a work performance which fully accords with the goals they wish to see pursued or the values they wish to see observed. Their 'behaviour', in this context, refers to the ways in which they design, for example, his task rules and the supervisory, inspection, and other control systems which govern him. It excludes verbal protestations designed for public relations or shareholders' meetings. We may note in passing, since it will emerge as important later, that if we perceive others as systematically demonstrating doubts as to whether we can be trusted we are likely to deduce that their goals or values diverge at some points from our own.

The remaining items of the syndrome elucidate certain consequential tendencies stemming from this basic disposition. Not only are the job activities themselves specifically defined: the incumbent is also subjected to close supervision* and/or hedged about with impersonal rules or procedures designed to check and monitor his performance (Day and Hamblin 1964). 'We would expect policing activities and mutual suspicions to be more prevalent in organizations with a preponderance of routinized jobs than in more dynamic organizations.' We must 'expect an aura of distrust on both sides, of organizations by members in prescribed jobs and of the latter by organizations' (Thompson 1967: 122). 'The rationalization and routinization of work and the disciplined impersonality of the superordinate and subordinate relationship go together' (Lockwood 1958: 79). Gouldner argues that the 'extreme elaboration of bureaucratic rules is prompted by an abiding distrust of people and of their intentions. Quite commonly, such rules serve those whose ambitions do not generate the ready and full consent of others; they diminish reliance upon and withhold commitment to persons who are viewed as recalcitrant and untrustworthy.' From this point of view, 'rules are a form of *communication* to those who are seen as desirous of evading responsibilities, of avoiding commitment, and of withholding proper and full performance of obligations' (1955: 163, 179).

* Some definitions include in the notion of close supervision the highly specific designing of the job itself, as when Hopper describes it as one end of the continuum that describes the degree to which a supervisor 'specifies the roles of the subordinates and checks up to see that they comply' (1965: 189).

This approach is central to the Scientific Management tradition. 'Classical management theories emphasize that the particular job and work cycle for each rank-and-file employee is to be clearly specified, and that he should be closely supervised to be sure that he adheres to the task as specified' (Likert 1961: 20). Some researchers have found that 'as closeness of supervision increases, the extent of rule-usage also increases' (Bell 1965: 445); others that in some organizations they may be seen as alternatives (Ingham 1970: 36). Rushing has emphasized that, with an increase in organizational size, control through such impersonal mechanisms as 'the routinization of performance in formal rules and by keeping written records of work performance', or 'administration based on the files' as it is sometimes known, increases faster than control through personal surveillance procedures of the kind usually referred to as 'close supervision' (1965: 432–40).*

It is a feature of the low-discretion syndrome that close supervision and bureaucratic rules generate a mutually reinforcing circle. In the situation documented by Gouldner, 'the supervisor perceived the worker as unmotivated; he then carefully watched and directed him; this aroused the worker's ire and accentuated his apathy, and now the supervisor was back where he began' (1955: 160). Given this situation of declining mutual trust, higher authority sees further intensification of supervision or rules as necessary.

The third item in the syndrome of the highly prescribed, low-discretion role relates to another aspect of control – the coordination of the occupant's activities with those of others. The nature of the interdependence of such roles is such that close coordination has to be imposed, either by specific, standardized 'routines or rules which constrain action . . . into paths consistent with those taken by others in the interdependent relationship', or by 'the establishment of schedules for the interdependent units by which their actions may

* There is no space here for a review of the growing research on such structural dimensions of organizations as 'complexity', 'formalization', 'centralization' etc. There is room, however, for a minimal warning – large size is not the infallible indication of organizational complexity and formalization that it is in popular imagination, any more than the fact that an organization is small can 'be taken as evidence that a *gemeinschaft* sort of social system is operating' (Hall, Haas, and Johnson 1967: 911). Those wishing to follow up this line of work might begin with Woodward 1965 and 1970; Pugh *et al.* 1963; Hinings and Lee 1971; and Aiken and Hage 1971, all of whom offer many more references.

then be governed' (Thompson 1967: 56). This need for imposed and standardized coordination carries implications for the whole pattern of interaction and communication. A 'free flow of suggestions and criticisms' facilitates certain kinds of problem solving but 'impedes coordination' (Blau and Scott 1963: 125). In low-discretion work structures the problems are considered to have been foreseen and planned for already by higher authority through the means of technological and workflow design and/or of bureaucratic discipline. The need for coordination which then becomes predominant therefore calls for highly restricted interaction and communication patterns between lower and higher ranks (*Ibid*: 124–8).

The fourth item concerns the official response to failures or inadequacies of performance. The assumption is that they result from careless indifference to job rules and organizational goals, calling for punishment and an intensification of supervision or more rules or both (March and Simon 1958: 44–6). This assumption comes readily to higher authority with respect to occupants of highly prescribed roles since, as was noted earlier, the prescriptive elements of a job require only obedience to ensure the appropriate performance. Inadequate performance creates the presumption that, through negligence, dereliction, or insubordination, the incumbent failed to obey the rules laid down by higher authority. Thus in the large, impersonal, machine technology plant 'social control rests less on consensus and more on the power of management to enforce compliance to the rule system. . . .' Technological constraints and monetary rewards are seen as more important 'than internalized standards of quality performance or an identification with organizational goals in providing the discipline that gets work done in an orderly fashion' (Blauner 1964: 177–8).

The fifth and last item in the syndrome relates to the way in which conflict between role occupants and their superior is handled. In the case of low-discretion role occupants conflict is handled on a group basis through bargaining processes. This draws attention again to the perceived lack of full consensus. 'Where bargaining is used, disagreement over goals is taken as fixed. . . . We can identify a bargaining process by its paraphernalia of acknowledged conflict of interests, threats, falsification of position, and (in general) games manship' (March and Simon 1958: 130). The extreme form of this mode of conflict resolution is analysed by Walton and McKersie

(1965) as 'distributive bargaining' and by Chamberlain and Kuhn (1965) as 'conjunctive bargaining'. The latter present the process as one where 'the parties agree to terms as a result of mutual coercion and arrive at a truce only because they are indispensable to each other. . . . It provides no incentive to the parties to do more than carry out the minimum terms of the agreement which has temporarily resolved their divergent interests' (*Ibid*: 424–35). This behavioural acceptance of divergent purposes does not exclude the possibility that superiors may continue verbally to assert the shared nature of goals, not so much in the belief that these assertions describe reality as in the hope of persuading subordinates to accept, wholly or partially, this view of their situation. To the extent that such a view is accepted top management is provided with a technique of control, though if subordinates are irreversibly convinced that goals in fact diverge then these ideological efforts by management may well be counterproductive in terms of its own purposes (Fox 1966b).

In sum, therefore, the low-discretion syndrome presents a picture sketched by Strauss when he contrasts the rank and file production worker with what is often called the 'professional' in the looser sense of that word. The former, he argues, has little sense of being an expert; of commitment to a calling; of autonomy on the job; or of obligation to produce high quality work; in other words, of being a professional.* In addition, he has little or no sense of identification with the organization (1963a). These characteristics would certainly be regarded as widespread among low level employees in most large organizations in industry, business, and commerce. Crozier's description of work in a large public clerical agency in Paris, for example, includes all the items of the syndrome– simple, repetitive, prescribed routines; close supervision and personal pressure by supervisors; harsh discipline; careful checks on performance and punitive responses towards mistakes (1964). Davis, Canter, and Hoffman, in a study covering twenty-four large American companies, found that prevailing practice with respect to the design of manual jobs adheres 'to the very narrow and limited criteria of minimizing immediate cost or maximizing immediate productivity'. It 'designs jobs based entirely on the principles of specialization, repetitiveness, low skill content and minimum impact of the worker on the production

* For a critical analysis of the conventional concept of professionalism see Johnson 1972.

process' (1955, in Davis and Taylor 1972: 81). The 'organization strives for maximum interchangeability of personnel (with minimum training) to reduce its dependence on availability, ability, or motivation of individuals' (Davis 1966, in Davis and Taylor 1972: 302). These and their associated practices 'are consistent with the principles of rationalization or scientific management' (Davis and Taylor 1972: 80). Any adverse effects are thought to be adequately controlled by selection, training, incentives, and supervision.

Work Role Patterns (b) The High-Discretion Syndrome

These defining characteristics may now be contrasted with those of the high-discretion work pattern. The first is that occupants of these roles are deemed to have commitment to, and 'moral involvement'* in, a calling and/or 'organizational' goals and values. March and Simon assert that 'the more participation in making policy decisions, the stronger the tendency . . . to identify with the organization'(1958: 74). Since we have seen that the exercise of discretion lies in making decisions as against conforming to prescriptive rules, it follows that high-discretion roles encourage their occupants to make this identification. Similarly, Perrow observes that 'lengthy training and specialized skills appear to be associated with higher morale and greater commitment to organizational goals . . . Organizations which must deploy members to places where they cannot be under close surveillance . . . have the choice of proliferating rules and reporting procedures to keep control, or "professionalizing" such personnel so they can be trusted to act in the organization's interests' (1970: 61–2). Blau and Scott apply the same idea of managerial choice to the design of work at lower levels. 'A professionalized labor force that can exercise initiative and is motivated to do so by opportunities for advancement would sharply reduce the need for hierarchical supervision and control through directives passed down the pyramid of authority.' Professionalization in this context is defined as 'the redesigning of the division of labour to . . . permit the exercise of considerable discretion' (1963: 249). Stinchcombe had earlier contrasted 'bureaucratic' and 'craft' administration of production. The latter differed from the former 'by substituting professional training of manual

* The term is Etzioni's. It designates 'a positive orientation of high intensity' (1961:10).

workers for detailed centralized planning of work' – a strategy which might be more efficient in situations of marked uncertainty (1959: 175). The commitment sought by these means is of a diffuse kind which matches the diffuse high-discretion nature of the role. 'On the side of commitment to the organization, the symbolic output consists of diffuse loyalty to the organization as such', by virtue of which the individual 'tends to develop a sense of organizational responsibility and to accept, as the occasion demands, responsibilities beyond any specific contracted function' (Parsons and Smelser 1956: 116).*

The choice between bureaucratic discipline and professional expertise in 'coping with areas of uncertainty' – a discipline which operates 'by reducing the scope of uncertainty' and a professional expertise 'by providing the knowledge and social support that enables individuals to cope with uncertainty and thus to assume more responsibility' – is conditioned by many factors, among which is technical possibility. 'When the over-all responsibility of the organization cannot be broken down into fairly routine specialized tasks . . . expert judgements of professionals rather than disciplined compliance with the commands of superiors must govern operations in the interest of efficiency' (Blau and Scott 1963: 247).

The postulation of a link between high-discretion roles and a belief that their occupants can be assumed to offer a high degree of moral involvement in the organization has to meet the frequently canvassed opinion that the goals and values of professionals such as scientists tend to clash with those of industrial or commercial organizations which employ them (Kornhauser 1962). Such situations have been assumed by many theorists to evoke from top management the view that although high professional discretion generates commitment it is in the wrong direction, being to the profession instead of to the organization. Recent research among a British sample of industrial scientists, however, shows that a majority 'do not experience high levels of dissatisfaction and strain' from this alleged conflict, which appears to be far less marked than had been supposed (Cotgrove and Box 1970. See also Ellis 1969). In any case, the very fact that professionals do offer commitment ensures that

* The reference to 'specific contracted function' draws attention to the difference – to be explored later – between the work role and the employment contract legalizing occupancy of it.

even when it takes forms inconvenient for top management the relationship remains profoundly different from that between top management and low-discretion employees, who are usually seen as offering no commitment whatever and as being, at best, passive and indifferent, and, at worst, actively hostile and disaffected. Divergencies of policy and opinion between top management and professionals are usually defined as disagreements about 'the organization's best interests'. Tensions may become considerable, but the two groups continue overtly to define each other as responsible agents doing their honest best in a difficult shared situation. Such mutual compliments are rarely exchanged between top management and low-discretion employees.

The same factors determine supervisory patterns. Along with high-discretion work goes the belief that close supervision and/or detailed regulation by specific impersonal rules would be inappropriate – indeed a contradiction in terms. 'Disciplined compliance with orders of hierarchical superiors entails a fundamental conflict with professionalism. In the absence of direct hierarchical supervision, genuine professional work can be and, indeed, frequently is carried out in otherwise bureaucratized organizations' (Blau and Scott 1963: 209). The same applies to many functional staff specialists in such fields as accounting, research, and engineering who aspire to professional autonomy. Among the latter, for example; 'to the extent that the engineer is professionally oriented he feels that all questions should be open to free discussion by qualified professionals, with the final decision made on the basis of logical proof.' He does not want 'to be fettered by precise rules' and 'the boss, he thinks, should be no more than a senior colleague who provides help when asked, but who does not give orders' (Strauss 1963a: 25). 'Permitting each individual to control decisions on the job indicates a trend toward a colleague rather than a hierarchical relationship (Litwak 1961: 178).

The model for these aspirations is that of the 'pure' science research laboratory or some similar group of autonomous professionals. Juniors feel free to challenge the opinions of older colleagues; the highest ranks are expected to behave as supportive seniors but not as overseers; and the concept of 'management' or 'supervision' is alien (Strauss 1963a: 13). 'The ethics governing colleague relationships demand behaviour that is cooperative, equalitarian, and supportive'

(Greenwood 1957: 213). In Litwak's words: 'Individuals faced with non-uniform events which are not clearly covered by rules are insecure. In such situations, they must be able to call on colleagues in whom they put great trust if they are to perform efficiently' (1961: 179). All these characteristics indicate a pattern of interaction in which communications are open, free, and unfettered by hierarchical status distinctions; the emphasis being on 'problem solving' rather than on externally imposed coordination (Blau and Scott 1963: 124–34). Such relationships prevail also within senior management and administrative groups. As men move into this stratum the less they expect to be subject to direct discipline and the more they expect to be treated by seniors as equal colleagues who may be consulted and given advice but not directions or orders.

The whole aspect of control over high-discretion work reveals such significant differences from that exercised over low-discretion work as to bring out the essence of the distinction. As compared with a situation where 'we are able to break a skill down into component elements, prescribe sequences of tasks in a performance, leaving little to the judgement and understanding of the worker', there is in the sciences, professions and kindred work an element of tacit knowledge which 'helps explain their achievement of exclusive jurisdiction; it also helps explain their traditionalism. The client public sees a mystery in the tasks to be performed, a mystery which it is not given to the ordinary man to acquire. Since tacit knowledge is relatively inaccessible, it is also less subject to direct criticism and quick change' (Wilensky 1964: 148–9).* The means by which a profession enforces observance of its code 'constitute a case study in social control'. Self-discipline is achieved informally through 'the subtle and the not-so-subtle pressures that colleagues exert upon one another', and formally through 'the professional associations, which possess the power to criticize or to censure, and in extreme cases to bar recalcitrants' (Greenwood 1957: 213–14).

Many new occupational groups coming into business organizations who 'deal with ideas and not their hands' and who 'consider themselves to be professionals' likewise present control problems

* Wilensky refers at another point to 'the scores of engineering specialities in the Soviet Union where the régime finds it easy to train and control its technicians by continual narrowing and re-division of traditional engineering curriculums' (*Ibid*:157).

different from those relating to manual workers. 'A withdrawal of effort on their part is much less visible', thus obliging the organization to require 'a different kind of commitment from them than it did from manual workers' (Goldner 1965: 80). Alderfer makes a similar point with respect to 'complex' jobs generally (1967: 457). A great deal of managerial performance, too, 'cannot be objectively evaluated', with the result that in assessments by their superiors 'subjective criteria tend to predominate, such as degree of loyalty to the objectives of the organization. The value placed on organizational loyalty is due . . . to the need for a principle to insure the recruitment of trustworthy managers who will participate in critical decision-making or in the execution of decisions . . .' (Evan 1961: 541–2). The meaning of loyalty here is that invoked by Parsons and Smelser as the acceptance of 'responsibilities beyond any specific contracted function' (1956: 116).

The nature of coordination among the occupants of work roles like these differs from that among occupants of low-discretion roles. The need is more for problem solving relations than for standardized, externally imposed coordination. This results in what Thompson calls 'coordination by mutual adjustment', which 'involves the transmission of new information during the process of action' and 'may involve communication across hierarchical lines' (1967: 56). The implications for interaction and communication become apparent in the emphasis on the free flow of ideas, suggestions, criticisms, advice and consultation characteristic of high-discretion work structures.

Clearly the whole texture of these situations is likely to generate an official response towards inadequacies of performance which is markedly different from that evoked by failures in low-discretion roles. As we have seen, the latter lend themselves to the diagnosis that the occupant has simply failed to observe the specific rules laid down for his behaviour. On the assumption that he is adequately trained, punitive measures may be considered appropriate. Such a diagnosis is the more likely since, despite exhortatory references to shared goals and team spirit, much managerial behaviour can be interpreted as manifesting a belief that low-discretion employees cannot be trusted since their identification with management goals is doubtful.

Attitudes towards the occupant of the high-discretion role are different on all counts. His loyalty, support, and goodwill are taken for granted. Failures and inadequacies are regarded as due not to wilful deviance, dereliction, or neglect, but to substandard exercise of discretion. '. . . questions of negligence or insubordination or dishonesty simply do not arise as they do in the case of failure to conform to prescribed regulations. All that can be said is that substandard work has been done. The subordinate . . . has not done as well as he was expected or called upon to do. Such occurrences are everyday matters. Niceness of judgement is always a relative matter – a matter of more or less good, rather than of clear-cut right or wrong' (Jaques 1967: 84). If the superior assumes the subordinate to be doing his best then punishment will seem futile since he cannot be coerced into making better decisions. He may of course be replaced but this, by definition, is not punishment aimed at improving his role performance. These contrasting treatments produced by differences in the degree of discretion give rise to a popular impression of the double standard. Substandard performers in the lower ranks are punished; in the upper ranks they are quietly replaced, retired on pension or kicked upstairs.*

This brings us to the fifth and final item: the way conflict is handled. In the case of conflict involving low-discretion role occupants there is a behavioural acceptance (though not necessarily an ideological acceptance) by superiors that goals to some extent diverge and that bargaining is the appropriate mode of resolution. Where high-discretion roles are concerned the assumption is that goals are shared, thus making it impossible to legitimize bargaining and its accompanying tactics of threats, falsification of positions and general gamesmanship. The mode adopted has to be either that of 'problem solving', with stress on the importance of assembling information, increasing search behaviour, and evoking new alternatives; or that of persuasion based on the assumption that '*at some level* objectives are shared and that disagreement over subgoals can be mediated by reference to common goals' (March and Simon 1958: 129). Between problem solving and bargaining there is not a dichotomy but a continuum which matches the continuum of discretion. Some theorists refer to the problem solving end of the continuum, in fact,

* Moreover, those who administer the fate of others have a personal interest, perhaps, in not treating failed occupants of high-discretion roles too harshly. They themselves may be judged some day to have failed.

as a mode of bargaining. Walton and McKersie (1965) use the term 'integrative bargaining' to describe situations where goals are not perceived as being in fundamental conflict and where the preferences of the parties can be integrated either to benefit both or to benefit one without disadvantage to the other.

Such, then, is the high-discretion syndrome suggested as an appropriate model for studying the work situations of, for example, senior managers, functional specialists, doctors in hospitals or partnership practice, university teachers, research scientists, lawyers, architects, small élite military units, and top administrative groups. Along with these characteristics of high-discretion patterns go certain associated features which differ significantly from those associated with low-discretion patterns. First, there is an expectation bearing upon occupants of high-discretion roles that they will feel a strong commitment to the social and economic system which has endowed them with their superior position and supports them in their privileges. Just as, at the level of the organization, only occupants of high-discretion roles are presumed to be capable of really caring about the organization 'as a whole', so it is expected that only they are capable of full 'responsible' commitment to the master institutions of the wider society. Kohn and Schooler have described relationships between class position and orientations which they consider 'substantially attributable to class-correlated variations in the degree to which jobs allow and require self-direction' – where self-direction means the use of 'initiative, thought, and independent judgement in work' (1969: 676). The higher men's class position, the more likely they are to see themselves as competent members of 'an essentially benign society'; the lower their class position, the more likely they are to see themselves as less competent members of 'an essentially indifferent or threatening society' (*Ibid*: 676). Occupants of low-discretion roles are thus perceived as likely to have a more tenuous, less informed, and less reliable commitment both to the formal organizational values and objectives and to the structures and mechanisms of the wider social setting. Given these tendencies, any equivocal attitude by a high-discretion group towards the master institutions of the system may appear to other high-discretion groups – some of which may have power or influence over rewards and privileges – as a rejection of the beliefs 'appropriate' to such groups. This rejection might call in question whether the group concerned could be viewed as deserving full membership of the high-discretion fraternity.

Second, certain types of high-discretion role are linked with professional associations and their familiar trappings of graded status, codes of conduct, assertions of public service, qualifying examinations and aspirations to self-government. Those engaging in such activities are apt to allege certain contrasts with trade unions. These, it is said, are narrowly sectional bodies which stress the material advantage of their members to the virtual exclusion of vocational commitment and public responsibility.

Third, high-discretion roles are accompanied by certain distinctive styles of life as manifested in such features as dress, vocabulary, demeanour, housing, leisure occupations, and expectations for one's children. By virtue of their association with high-discretion roles, such features acquire symbolic importance as indicating membership of these groups or a strong affinity for and desire to join them. An occupational group occupying high-discretion roles may find its claim to high status and the associated rewards and privileges marginally strengthened if certain appropriate attitudes, behaviours, and trappings of these kinds are adopted. Random individual deviations are not what matter here, but the characteristics of the group as a whole. Individual deviations may be thought, however, to weaken the group's public presentation of itself, and sanctions of a formal and/or informal kind may be brought to bear on them.

The Middle Range of Discretion

Between the high-discretion levels and the very large number of low-discretion roles lie a number of intermediate groups exercising a degree of discretion greater than the latter but less than the former. They include some craftsmen; technicians; draughtsmen; supervisors; clerks; minor specialists; nurses; and many similar groups. The work situations of such roles as these display characteristics drawn from both the low- and the high-discretion syndromes. Although in many cases subjected to ideological pressure designed to promote perception of shared goals with their superiors, the structure of their work situation often appears to reveal a conviction on the part of higher authority that they cannot wholly be trusted to behave in the desired ways and must therefore be hedged about with rules, controls, checks, monitoring devices, or discipline. They are likely to be made aware of subordination and of social distance from the higher ranks. Many of them seek to resolve conflict through group bargaining processes. Yet all wield a degree of discretion greater than do the groups described under the low-discretion syndrome, though to be sure there are important differences among them in this respect.*

This is the appropriate stage at which to emphasize that such general industrial or occupational categories as, for example, 'steel workers', 'craftsmen', 'technicians', 'managers' and others used in the exposition serve only as approximate guides and are no substitute for empirical inquiry into the actual amount of discretion vested in the roles concerned in particular situations. A given category may contain significant differences. For an example we may refer to a research report which compares a number of chemical plants located on one site and employing wage earners who might all be designated chemical operatives (Wedderburn and Crompton 1972). As between Works A and Work C, differences of overall task, technology, and work organization were accompanied by differences in the degree of discretion vested in wage-earning work roles. In Works A, each control-room operator had a number of monitoring tasks to perform and 'some discretion as to when, and in which sequence, these tasks were carried out. Moreover when all was going well . . . he had great freedom to vary the pace of work, and to move about . . .' (*Ibid*: 80). The nature of quality control 'broadened the responsibility of the operator and encouraged a "teamwork" relationship between supervisors and men because they worked together to solve the technical problems posed by the system' (*Ibid*: 226); the supervisor being as likely to be required to offer advice as to give orders. Moreover, there

* The differences between the crafts and other manual occupations can easily be, and often are, exaggerated. Caplow writes of the former that 'All involve determinate operations which, once learned, are not much affected by individual talent. It is assumed . . . that all passed craftsmen in the same craft are perfectly interchangeable, that any journeyman, put to a given job, will perform the same quantity of work of the same quality as another' (1964: 111, 166). This contrasts with assumptions made about professionals who, with their far greater discretion, are seen as 'perfectly non-interchangeable. The work of each is considered to be his individual expression, not capable of direct substitution. . . . It is assumed as a matter of course that the service is unique . . . ' (*Ibid*: 171). How far this is true of any given professional is of course a matter for empirical investigation.

was relatively high interaction between operatives and management. Within this pattern of work organization, 72 per cent found their jobs interesting (a finding which 'seemed to be related to the ability to exercise discretion on the job' (*Ibid*: 52)); 81 per cent saw their work situation in 'teamwork' terms; and there was relatively high consciousness of identity as chemical workers. In Works C many of the employees exercised but little discretion and freedom of movement; quality control in certain major departments involved supervisors in direct personal intervention, close supervision and increasing pressure on the operators; and there was relatively little interaction between operatives and senior management. Of the workers in this context, only 26 per cent found their work interesting; 57 per cent saw their situation in teamwork terms; and there was relatively low consciousness of identity as chemical workers.

Thus even among chemical workers employed by the same company on the same site there were differences in discretion accompanied by observable differences in attitudes and behaviour. However, these differences must be kept in perspective. All the plants concerned were organized by trade unions which negotiated highly prescriptive collective agreements with management, thereby manifesting a characteristic of the relatively low-discretion syndrome. Inquiry would almost certainly reveal that the discretion differences among operatives were smaller than between operatives and top management.

We return now, then, to those greater and far more significant differences expressed in the two syndromes or models. In the rest of this chapter our purpose will be to show in what ways the models accord with other recent theorizing about work and management, and to note certain of their implications with respect to the definition of work, status, and rewards.

Theoretical Convergence: Recent Contributions

Many pieces of research and theorizing carried out in recent decades can be assimilated within the framework offered above. Again and again a two-model framework emerges which can easily be translated or extended to accord with the present approach. Hickson (1966: 225) notes that much theorizing about organization structure 'has converged upon the specificity (or precision) of role prescription and its obverse, the range of legitimate discretion' (a convergence which, it should be added, he finds in certain respects 'disconcerting').

Gouldner presents the contrast in terms of a distinction (implicit in Weber's theory of bureaucracy) between 'punishment-centred' and 'representative' bureaucracy. The former is 'administration by authoritarian discipline' backed up by 'blame and punishment', where superiors and subordinates are conscious of conflicting values and interests. The latter is 'administration by experts' on the basis of knowledge, 'a consensus on ends or values', and shared control (1955: 220–1).

Burns and Stalker contrast 'mechanistic' with 'organic' systems. The former are marked by 'the specialized differentiation of functional tasks', with 'precise definition of rights and obligations and technical methods attached to each functional role'; a hierarchical structure of control, authority, and communication; the assumption that knowledge resides at the top; a tendency for interaction to be vertical, i.e. between superior and subordinate, and to consist predominantly of instructions and directives; and an emphasis on obedience. The organic system is characterized by a emphasis on 'special knowledge', which for the particular task in hand may be 'anywhere in the network'; 'the adjustment and continual redefinition of individual tasks through interaction with others'; a tendency for the individual to be motivated by a sense of commitment and common objectives with others rather than by 'a contractual relationship between himself and a non-personal corporation, represented for him by an immediate superior'; a relatively non-hierarchical lateral structure of control and communication in which consultation, information, and advice play a prominent part; and by a tendency to value commitment to the common tasks and shared ethos more highly than obedience (1961: 120–1).

McGregor's Theory X postulates organization structures and job definitions based on assumptions that men are passive, indolent, resistant to responsibility, and indifferent if not hostile to 'organizational needs'. They must therefore be 'programmed', directed, manipulated, and controlled, even though meaning becomes eliminated from work as a result. Theory Y, McGregor's preferred alternative, assumes men to have the potentiality for accepting responsibility and actively directing their efforts towards 'organizational goals'. Organization structures and work roles inspired by this approach are designed to release this potential; remove obstacles to 'personal growth'; rely on self-control and self-direction as against external control; encourage creativity; and promote participation in decision-making (1960).

Argyris operates with a similar set of ideas. Most organizations are designed on the assumptions that men are passive, dependent, and subordinate; have only a short span of interest and restricted time perspective for the meaning of their actions; and are limited in their awareness of themselves as individuals. These assumptions are said to inform the work designs of industrial engineers operating on the Scientific Management principles of Frederick Taylor and his successors, resulting in many tasks being 'fractionized', closely supervised, and drained of opportunity for judgement, challenge, and responsibility. Argyris elaborates the alternative perspective which designs work on the assumption that men actively seek independence, autonomy, and personal growth; resulting in roles and structures characterized by challenge, responsibility, and openness of communications and interaction (1957, 1964).

Shepard contrasts an ideal type characterized by coercion and compromise with one characterized by collaboration and consensus. In the first, superordinate power is used to control behaviour, and forces are generated 'that divide men, that isolate and alienate them from one another'. The organization structure is power-based; stressing authority and obedience or, if these fail, bargaining, with all the attendant features of gamesmanship, win-lose and bluff behaviour, mutual suspicion and threat. In the second, 'control is achieved through agreement on goals, coupled with a communication system which provides continuous feedback of results, so that members can steer themselves'. The structure is 'task-based rather than power-based'; the 'concept of multigroup membership is substituted for the concept of supervision in coercive-compromise systems'; and differences are handled by problem solving methods based on mutual confidence and trust (1965: 1117–31).

These are only a few examples of the many instances of convergence upon similar distinctions and contrasts.* They differ widely in how far they emphasize the constraints upon work designers of task and

* Similar ideas emerge in, e.g. Likert 1961; Barnes 1960; Litwak 1961; Herzberg 1968; Guest 1962; Pym 1968; Stinchcombe 1959. For introductory reviews and discussions: Strauss 1963b; and Spencer and Sofer 1964.

technology in the shaping of roles and structures, and how far they stress free choice and purely personal orientations and attitudes in determining which pattern or combination of patterns is operated. No satisfactory theory of organization can ignore either, as (for example) March's mammoth *Handbook of Organizations* (1965) and the files of the *Administrative Science Quarterly* will soon reveal for those wishing to pursue this aspect further.

Theorists who stress the nature of the task usually emphasize the importance of such characteristics as 'uncertainty', 'unpredictability', 'non-uniformity' or 'conditions of rapid change', in influencing work designers towards roles and structures described as 'organic', 'problem solving', 'open', 'Theory Y', 'participative', and the like. What emerges as the common element is that the work role is seen as desirably embodying a high degree of discretion. It is easy to appreciate that the definition of a task as involving widely varying or rapidly changing problems and decisions which are difficult to programme in advance may well dispose work designers to establish high-discretion roles (which will hopefully evoke loyalty and commitment), rather than attempt to rely on low-discretion roles accompanied by close supervision and/or detailed impersonal rules. There might, indeed, be situations in which the latter alternative could be pursued only at high cost and low efficiency; situations in which 'if a general rule is developed for each situation, the rules would be so numerous as to defy learning . . . The individuals concerned might do better to internalize the values of the organization and reach *ad hoc* . . . decisions . . .' (Litwak 1961: 178. See also Bell 1966).

The choice made by the relevant superordinate depends, however, upon his priorities and the costs and benefits of the alternatives as he sees them, and here personalities can be specially important, as too can be organizational tradition. Other aspects of this problem will be examined later: meanwhile it will be sufficient to note, as illustration, that a manager who is himself being called punitively to account may limit the discretion of subordinates to a degree which encroaches on the adaptiveness and creativity of his department, preferring this to the threat of more visible disasters which may occasionally result from their greater autonomy. A stronger man might behave differently. This point alone draws our attention to the factor of superordinate choice, variable though its scope is from one situation to another.

This, as we have seen, means that such considerations as, for example, the authoritarian characteristics of the superordinate's personality or his attitudes and ideologies must enter into the analysis as well as considerations of task and technology.* There is no simple determinism by which task and technology dictate structure.

The argument so far can be summed up as pointing the contrasts between work roles and structures which are highly specific in nature and those which are highly diffuse, and as suggesting that the contrasts are linked with differences of discretion embodied in the roles themselves. The intention has been to trace the connections between, on the one hand, the degree of discretion conferred by the role and, on the other, important characteristics of the work situation which bear upon goals, authority structures, communication systems, and the nature of relations generally.

We may summarize with a passage by Argyris which further stresses the convergence of much work in this field. Reviewing the points made by many writers, he concludes that the mechanistic organization is characterized by '(1) decision making and control at the top levels . . . , (2) an emphasis on unilateral management action, based on dependency and passive conformity, (3) the specialization of tasks so that the concern for the whole is broken down, (4) the centralization of information, rewards and penalties . . . , (5) the management being responsible for developing and maintaining the loyalty, commitment, and responsibility of all the participants on as high a level as possible, and (6) an emphasis on social status, intergroup and individual competition and rivalry'. The organic organization is characterized by '(1) decision making widely done throughout the organization, (2) an emphasis on mutual dependence and cooperation based on trust, confidence, and high technical or professional competence, (3) a constant pressure to enlarge tasks and inter-relate them so that the concern for the whole is emphasized, (4) the decentralization of responsibility for and use of information, rewards and penalties . . ., (5) participants at all levels being responsible for developing and maintaining loyalty and commitment at as high a level as possible, and (6) an emphasis on status through

* Much of the literature stresses the superordinate's personal attitudes; hence the interest in 'sensitivity' or 'T-group' training, which aspires to change them in more 'open', 'participative', and 'trusting' directions (Schein and Bennis 1965, for an introduction).

contribution to the whole and intergroup and interindividual cooperation' (1964: 184–5).

Although none of the theorists whose work has been briefly reviewed draws out his analysis from the factor of discretion, as is done here, the similarity of the resultant models is apparent. These same theorists also agree, along with others, that the two models differ sharply in their impact upon the individual in terms of intrinsic work satisfactions and personal growth and development. All have concluded that the organic model tends to develop greater moral involvement and responsibility among its participants and provide them with greater intrinsic rewards. 'The higher up the organizational ladder and/or the greater the professionalization, the higher the probability that people will report intrinsic work satisfaction. The lower one goes down the organizational ladder and the less skilled the work, the lower the probability that people will report intrinsic work satisfaction' (Argyris 1964:53, 185–6).

In referring to personal growth and intrinsic rewards the writers concerned are using criteria far more complex than are often implicit in the use of such concepts as 'job satisfaction'. These criteria embody controversial definitions of such notions as 'the self', 'identity', and 'mental health'. It can be no part of our present purpose to explore them,* but the link with the discussion of work roles and structures is demonstrated by Argyris's assertion that 'the psychologically healthy individual strives to be self-responsible, self-directed, self-motivated, aspires towards excellence in problem solving, strives to decrease his defensive and compulsive behaviour, to be fully functioning, and so on' (1964: 162). This is no recipe for a life of bovine contentment, and the doctrine of positive mental health and pyschological growth accepts that striving and a certain amount of stress are inevitable features, as we can see by applying the doctrine to the kind of work situation reported as yielding major intrinsic rewards. Exercising a high degree of discretion, with its attendant efforts of evaluating alternatives, making a considered judgement between them, and accepting responsibility for one's choice, involves activities which are not without strain. However, the point must not be exaggerated. The intrinsic rewards of such roles can be satisfying in a way that leads the occupant to value the work for its

* One way into this discussion is via Argyris 1964; another, via Herzberg 1968. Strauss, 1963b, offers a sceptical review.

own sake. Moreover, in the debate on the effects of work experience upon experience in other aspects of life, research suggests rather that high-discretion work broadens, deepens and generally nourishes the personality in ways which enlarge the capacity for rewarding experience outside as well as inside the work situation (Parker 1971; Meissner 1971). It would indeed be surprising if the effect of significant decision-making, choice, and responsibility did not, to some degree at least, carry over into non-work spheres of activity.

Separate and distinct, however, from the debate about the effects of different kinds of work upon personality development is the debate about what men seek from their work. These are separate issues in the sense that men might be enlarged and enriched by a certain type of work experience yet not actively aspire to that state. In this context, some writers are eager to insist that many, perhaps most, men do not want work to play a central role in their lives, and are content that it offer only instrumental, extrinsic rewards (Strauss 1963b). If we examine men as they currently are, shaped in their aspirations and adaptations by family, school, job, and subculture, it is clearly true that many do not include intrinsic rewards among their priority work aspirations (Goldthorpe *et al.*, 1968). If men were incapable of adapting their aspirations to the lot which they see as inevitable the mental hospitals would be even busier than they are. What we do not know is the proportion of men who would find intrinsic work satisfaction nourishing to the personality and spirit were their early socializing experiences and current opportunities to be different. A guess that the proportion is small is, of course, just as much an expression of the beliefs and philosophy of the guesser as one that the proportion is large. Theories of personality development are involved. No doubt some of what follows in this book reflects the writer's belief that the proportion is much larger than the hard-headed school supposes. Meanwhile we may note the curious vehemence with which some middle-class academic members of this school accuse other middle-class academics of imposing their values on others (Strauss 1963b: 47–8; Perrow, reported in Argyris 1972: 39). Perhaps those conscious of being members of a minority lucky enough to enjoy intrinsic work satisfaction prefer to believe that this is not privilege since the majority do not want it anyway.

The position taken up in this book, in so far as it is relevant, is that such concepts as psychological growth and self-actualization embody a central notion of Western liberal culture – the importance attached to the development of the individual personality. The accord is not simply a verbal one resting on use of the term 'development', for development is defined by the relevant psychologists in terms which echo deeply rooted and continuing themes in Western history (for a discussion and analysis, Argyris 1957: Chap. 2; 1964: Chaps. 1 and 2). Western liberalism asserts man to be the measure of all things and urges that institutions and societies be judged in terms of what they mean to and for the individual human being. In Hobhouse's words, the liberal's concept of the common good 'is founded on personality, and postulates free scope for the development of personality in each member of the community' (1911: 130). Work is seen here as one of the major sets of roles, relations, and structures which provide, or fail to provide, the individual with scope for the development of his personality. Since one way of evaluating a society is in terms of how it distributes opportunities for access to what is culturally valued, the facts relating to the highly unequal location of discretion in work are clearly relevant to such judgements.

Work as 'Disutility'

These wide differences in the degree to which work roles afford experiences defined by the culture as enriching bring us back to the point with which this chapter began: the 'obfuscation' purveyed by many economists that 'all work – physical, mental, artistic, or managerial – is essentially the same. . . .' This refers to the doctrine that all work is a painful burden for which men must be compensated by money, status, and other extrinsic benefits. The tradition goes back at least as far as Adam Smith, with his proposition that 'The real price of every thing, what every thing really costs to the man who wants to acquire it, is the toil and trouble of acquiring it' (1904, Vol. 1: 32). Jevons, in his presentation of marginal utility analysis in 1871, defined labour in terms of disutility – as 'any painful exertion of mind or body' undergone 'to ward off pains of greater amount, or to procure pleasures which leave a balance in our favour' (1970: 188–9). Marshall, in 1898, modified this in such a way as to admit more explicitly than Jevons the possibility of deriving intrinsic rewards from work, by defining labour as 'any exertion of mind or body undergone partly or wholly with a view to some good other than the pleasure derived directly from the work' (1898: 124). Marshall's definition obviously recognizes a category of persons for whom work is a reward in itself. However, this category played little or no further part in his analysis and Galbraith asserts that 'It has played almost no formal role in economic theory since' (1962: 274, fn). The concept of work as 'disutility' thus 'became expressive of a subjective sacrifice' (Roll 1945: 374).

To this day, theories which stress market as against social and conventional factors in determining money rewards usually set much store by the concept of work as disutility. Even Phelps Brown, a labour economist exceptionally alert to the many available perspectives on human behaviour, refers to doctors' pay in the context of 'the arduous training, the long years of sustained mental effort as students in which they earn little or nothing' (1962: 149). And, indeed, it would be absurd to suppose that in an acquisitive and competitive society they would not demand and receive more than, say, street cleaners. Of course the market theory looks to the number who are not only willing but also able to undertake this arduous training and sustained mental effort. We can certainly understand why the marginal supply price embodies a differential over that of the street cleaner, especially when we remember the inequality of opportunity for acquiring both aspirations and capacities. But were the differential of money reward to take into account the vastly different intrinsic rewards afforded by the two occupations it could hardly fail to be smaller than it is now – especially if all other occupations were evaluated in the same way.

Understandably, therefore, the assertion that all work is subjective sacrifice has evoked eager support from otherwise widely differing groups. 'The president of the corporation is pleased to think that his handsomely appointed office is the scene of the same kind of toil as the assembly line. . . . The communist office-holder cannot afford to have it supposed that his labour differs in any significant respect from that of the comrade at the lathe. . . . In both societies it serves the democratic conscience of the more favoured groups to identify themselves with those who do hard physical labour' (Galbraith 1962: 274). Galbraith might have pushed his analysis further by pointing out the logical implications of this definition of work for the distribution of money rewards. When, for example, the money rewards of high-discretion work come up for decision or justification, it is such characteristics as expertise, knowledge, responsibility, and skill said to require long and gruelling education, arduous training, or hardwon experience (all of which tend to be defined in terms of personal sacrifice), which are usually selected for emphasis as calling for compensation (Davis and Moore 1945). The intrinsic satisfactions and their effects on human personality which, by our society's definitions, are thought to deepen and enrich experience, are either ignored or redefined so as to bring them within the category of burdens and sacrifices (Tumin 1953). Far from being seen as requiring, in equity, a downward adjustment of extrinsic rewards relative to those offered for low-discretion work, they are usually accompanied by substantially higher compensations in money and status.* Were the intrinsic satisfactions to be recognized as part of the total rewards accruing to high-discretion roles, the threat to the established pattern of wages and salaries would be considerable, for low-discretion roles would then deserve compensating for the lack of them.

The notion that all work is the same in being 'disutility', 'painful exertion', 'toil and trouble' is therefore convenient for occupants of high-discretion roles in helping to justify the system which favours them. As a leading historian of economic thought observes: 'It cannot be doubted that there is an apologetic strain in modern [economic] theory. In its origins the utility school was strongly influenced by a desire to strengthen the potentially apologetic character of economics. The classical theory was not strong enough to withstand the attacks of the growing working-class movement.' The strengthening was effected by 'the introduction of a subjectivism which absolved economists from concerning themselves with the social order at all. . . . Theorems which had been developed on a basis of equal individuals undertaking abstinence and toil and trouble could have nothing to say about the real social differentiation of these individuals' (Roll 1945: 376).

The 'equitable payment' approach of Jaques and his school embodies, no doubt unconsciously, the same apologetic strain.

* Wootton observed that there was no 'sign at all of an inverse relationship between the monetary and the non-monetary attractions of different jobs. If the entire structure of earned incomes is treated as a single whole, it is apparent that the more agreeable and more responsible posts win on every count, (1955: 66).

Posing the question: 'What constitutes the effort in work?', Jaques replies that 'the essence of the effort in work is to be found in the anxiety engendered by the uncertainties which are part and parcel of the exercise of discretion' (1967: 89). Since he then proceeds to argue that differences in rates of pay should correlate with differences in degrees of discretion, measured according to time-span theory, it follows that financial rewards are seen as compensating for the burdensome effort of work which increases with the discretion it embodies. The intrinsic satisfactions derivable from high-discretion work are not allowed to enter into the account. Thus a theory of pay-fixing which is presented as a contribution to an objective way of handling industrial relations proves to contain ideological implications favouring those in high-discretion roles. Apart from registering this point – and noting that all job evaluation systems and principles for fixing rewards are culturally and ideologically based in some way – we are not concerned further with the attempt by Jaques to apply his technique of discretion-measurement to the fixing and justification of monetary compensation. We turn instead to develop certain propositions with respect to money and status rewards generally which are relevant to the foregoing analysis.

Discretion, Status, and Rewards

Barnard describes status in formal organizations as 'that condition of the individual that is defined by a statement of his rights, privileges, immunities, duties, and obligations . . . and, obversely, by a statement of the restrictions, limitations, and prohibitions governing his behaviour. . . . Status becomes systematic . . . when the conditions of the status of all individuals are published by means of differentiating designations, titles, appellations, insignia, or overt patterns of behaviour' (1946: 207–43). The organizational apparatus by which status is established and maintained therefore includes ceremonies of induction and appointment, titles, insignia and other symbols, and emoluments and perquisites.

What does not come over in Barnard's account is the element in status of social honour, prestige or esteem, which is differentially bestowed upon occupations and for which men may be expected to compete. They compete not only because prestige and esteem are pleasant in themselves, but also because to have one's role esteemed highly by society helps to legitimize one's claim to superior treatment and rewards.* Some occupants of high-discretion roles do not need to establish a claim in any literal sense, since their role includes the discretion to fix their own rewards. Employers, company directors, proprietors, and the Fellows of Oxbridge colleges are among this fortunate company. They will nevertheless feel their hand to be strengthened if their occupation ranks high in the scale of social honour, prestige, and esteem. Many high-discretion roles, however, depend for their rewards upon the decisions of others, thereby giving their occupants a more direct interest in establishing and maintaining their role as one of high status.

But by what criteria is the status of occupations to be judged, and who lays down those criteria? Some accounts treat the latter question as unproblematical, or assume a consensus spontaneously emerging from, or 'unconsciously evolved' by, 'society' (Davis and Moore 1945). More convincing is the supposition that ruling groups use their power and influence to promote wide acceptance of a status ranking which puts themselves at the top of it. This requires them to select as the qualifying criteria for high status what they see as the essential distinguishing characteristics in their own work roles.† For Barnard, status accords with the *ability* to do *difficult* work of *importance* – all three features being subject to degree. Allocation of status by such criteria would be likely to produce a ranking in accord with that produced by Jaques's time span of discretion. In other words, individuals and groups enjoying major power and influence support as criteria for high status the salient characteristics of their own roles, which tend to be those described here as comprising the high-discretion syndrome.

Having selected high-discretion roles as qualifying for high status, power-holders seek to have this principle legitimized by others in order to secure their own privileges. One of the ways in which they can help to maintain the principle firmly established is to avoid weakening it by transgressing it themselves; in other words to be careful to use it in the decisions they make about the rewards and

* Relevant here is Thompson's proposition that 'Acquiring prestige is the "cheapest" way of acquiring power' (1967: 33).

† Barnard strikes a very different note with the apologetical proposition that 'the possession of titles and of other indicia of rank certifies that those in the best position to have responsible judgement acknowledge and publish the status indicated. . . .'

privileges of others. This means that in so far as they perceive in other work roles those status-qualifying features that they seek to have recognized and rewarded in their own, they must be prepared to bestow, or approve the bestowing of, the same pay prospects, career opportunities, and privileges that they consider appropriate for themselves.* In so far as roles lack these features they must be evaluated accordingly. Ruling groups have had considerable success in promoting acceptance of their preferred status scale. One leading labour economist refers to the widespread belief that 'different, jobs have inherently different statuses, some superior, some inferior, and that the structure of pay should conform to this structure of esteem' (Phelps Brown 1962: 130). True, changes take place in the structure, and the hierarchy of pay does not wholly conform to the hierarchy of esteem (as in the cases of the cleric, the *nouveau riche*, and the impoverished aristocrat), but the correlation is considerable and it 'is widely felt to be just . . . that a given occupation should be paid less than those of higher and more than those of lower status'. A man cannot 'usually keep his rightful rung on the ladder if he is known to earn less than one whose rightful place is below him', and therefore one criterion for 'fair' pay is that 'it shall enable the recipient to keep up a position in the class to which his job assigns him' (*Ibid*: 131).† Wootton, too, notes that while 'high pay itself confers high prestige . . . there is nothing in that to invalidate the converse proposition . . . In an acquisitive society those who enjoy large salaries are also, as a rule, accorded high social prestige; and the prestige of these callings in turn requires that their standard of pay should be correspondingly generous' (1955: 70). The consequence is that the structure still, 'as a whole honours more than anything else the rule that to him that hath shall be given. The well-paid jobs

* When, for example, a high-ranking enemy officer is captured in war, the government and military authorities usually ensure he is treated with something approaching the same kind of respect and privilege that they accord to their own equivalent ranks. Quite apart from prudent calculations of reciprocity, if an enemy general were to be treated by lower-rank captors as a private who could be sure where such a dangerous precedent might not lead?

† 'O! when degree is shak'd,
Which is the ladder to all high designs,
The enterprise is sick'
(*Troilus and Cressida*, Act 1, Scene 3).

Such is the belief, at any rate, among top leaders in most organizations, certainly not least the business enterprise.

are those in which satisfaction is to be found in the work itself . . .' (*Ibid*: 165).

Among the complex forces determining money rewards in industrial society, therefore, are not only the various supply positions (as shaped by social factors) of the marketable skills and aptitudes, relative to the demand for them (likewise shaped by social factors), but also the principle, which occupants of high-discretion roles seek to have widely accepted, that work of their high status deserves greatly superior rewards. How far this principle works against so-called market forces and results in a reward structure different from the one which would prevail in its absence is of course a major issue in its own right. Wootton implies that the difference is significant, arguing that 'the spread from top to bottom far exceeds the range of differences that can credibly be ascribed to variations in inborn aptitudes. It is also greater than can be accounted for by the cost of acquiring the necessary training' (1955: 66). Taken along with the concept of work as disutility, the principle would certainly seem to exemplify the opportunity open to groups with power and influence to shape the belief-structure of society in ways which help to sustain their own privileges.

Given such a principle, an aspiring occupational group may perceive a need to consider its strategy and tactics in the light of their bearing on status. Are there policies available which could enhance the group's status by enlarging the work discretion of its members, or defend it by preventing a reduction of discretion? Other factors may be seen as relevant besides central job characteristics. As was noted earlier, occupants of high-discretion roles frequently see themselves – and expect to see fellow occupants – as the reliably committed members both of the organization and of the wider society; and may assume they can identify each other through the display of this commitment – and perhaps through such symbolic trappings as membership of associations, style of life, demeanour, and vocabulary. The members of a group on the fringes of the high-discretion world – a position from which they might easily move, by their own decision or top management's, into the low-discretion world where they could take up an overtly oppositional conflict stance and rely solely on their effectiveness as an organized pressure group – may aspire instead to cling to the benefits of high status by stressing such characteristics as these, hoping that for top management they will tip the scales marginally in favour of the group continuing to be accorded some, at least, of the privileges of the high-status fraternity. And, indeed, in the absence of positive pressures impelling top management otherwise, a group whose roles have been gradually slipping down the discretion scale may, through management inertia, succeed through the display of these 'secondary' characteristics in retaining some high-status benefits.

Some groups of clerical workers fit this picture. In the earlier days of the 'counting-house' tradition, the division of labour was slight and the 'relationship between clerk and employer was . . . in most cases a personal and particular one, strongly characterized by the exhibition of mutual trust in the form of unwritten, tacit expectations of conduct' (Lockwood 1958: 29). The clerk's dress 'approximated that of the master class'; he was often 'entrusted with confidential matters and delegated authority over other employees' (*Ibid*: 34). Both functionally and environmentally, he worked in 'proximity to authority' (Bain and Price 1972:337). It has been suggested that a process of 'assimilation by association' was at work. 'A group whose work possesses characteristics which have become symbolically associated with the possession of, or proximity to, authority may become assimilated to the white-collar group by its association with those symbols' (*Ibid*: 338) High status had in many cases, however, a solid functional underpinning of high discretion in the work role. On the basis of this relationship the clerk usually enjoyed 'permanency of employment, periodical increases of salary, payment of salary during sickness and holidays, comparatively reasonable hours of work, and in certain sections superannuation' (Lockwood 1958: 40, quoting *The Clerk*, 1916). The clerk reciprocated with loyalty, docility, and a total commitment to the social and economic *status quo*.

This situation has changed less than might be supposed. Bureaucratization and rationalization 'have by no means completely swept away the personal and particular relationships of the counting-house work environment' (*Ibid*: 95). Nevertheless, universal literacy, the influx of women, increased division of labour, and the growth of the 'office factory' have all wrought their changes in clerical work. Yet clerks long continued to cultivate their high-status characteristics of dress, loyalty to the organization, and commitment to social and political respectability. Although in many cases these symbols came to lose their functional underpinning as a consequence of bureaucratization and rationalization, the association with high status continued, in the absence of contrary pressures, to prevail among many employers. As a consequence, the clerk's privileges proved extremely resistant to change. Not until recent decades have financial rewards been overtaken by those for manual labour and although a gradual assimilation of hourly paid workers to 'staff conditions and status' is under way the process is slow and halting.

These mutual interactions between pay, status, and work roles pose delicate questions for many members of occupational groups in the middle or upper-middle ranges of the discretion and status hierarchy when they consider the best tactics for defending and advancing their own interests. Do they have a reasonable prospect of persuading the relevant decision-makers that their occupation manifests the qualifying criteria entitling them to high status and the rewards deemed fitting to that status? Can they successfully assert a claim to be full members of the high-discretion fraternity; a membership which guarantees that their interests will automatically be considered at every turn by top management, who will include them in the 'us' category? Would this claim be furthered or prejudiced by combining in an association? An association might be able to do a great deal to foster the status claims of its members. If association is chosen as an element in this strategy it must, however, work to an ideology of shared interests with top management, since to structure the situation in terms of divergent interests would tip the scales and transfer them, in the eyes of top management, from the 'us' to the 'them' category, thereby leaving them open to less favourable treatment.* Many an employer has made clear, not necessarily explicitly, to staff employees that their participation in trade union activities against him would automatically define them out of that community of shared goals and values which entitles them to the special consideration fitting to members of a privileged fraternity. They may have to accept that they would thereby relegate themselves to a relationship more distant and calculative in nature, where obligations and expectations become

* Despite a tendency to deplore the language and attitudes of 'them' and 'us' when manifested by lower-discretion employees, top management implicitly works to a similar distinction itself. This does not prevent it, in many cases, from urging such employees to abandon these attitudes, identify with management, and pull together for the joint effort.

less diffuse and more specific on both sides. They may nevertheless decide that this would now serve their interests and aspirations better than membership of the high-status fraternity. This drawing away, demonstrating as it does that they no longer define their position *vis-à-vis* superiors as one of shared interests or values, can be expected to evoke distrust from above, manifested perhaps in attempts to impose on them rules which seek to define their obligations more explicitly. Thus a sequence of reactions may be triggered off which were not necessarily foreseen by the initiating parties. At the very least it becomes clear that the choice of strategy by groups in this position calls for delicate calculation – so delicate in fact that marked differences and tensions may develop within the group as to the best choice.

Alliances, too, have to be chosen carefully. Links with manual worker unions or militant white-collar groups may convey the impression that the association is throwing in its lot with those who define the industrial scene in conflict terms. It may also be seen as important to avoid alliances which carry the taint of political hostility to high-discretion privileges. An ideology of shared interests has implications, too, for methods, which must lean towards the kind of problem solving approach suitable for status equals or near-equals who see the world in similar terms, rather than towards the implicit threats and bargaining pressures which develop between parties with divergent interests and values who are each seeking a power compromise at the other's expense. The bargaining, divergent-interests strategy may, however, be chosen if the other is seen as offering poor prospects of success. It is the choice of those who (a) see no real hope of winning or retaining membership of the high-discretion fraternity or (b) feel themselves to be members yet only marginally so in a way which does not fully protect their interests. We might expect both categories to be beset by doubt and debate as to the strategy which seems likely to pay off best.

These points can be illustrated from Strauss's analysis of the case of the professional engineer in the United States. On the one hand, he displays a strong interest in claiming professional status on the basis of specialized knowledge and skills; autonomy; commitment to a calling; and pretensions to a code of ethics. He probably feels some identification with management. 'His job usually gives him some discretion . . . ', and he aspires to get ahead by promotion through management ranks. On the other hand, the engineer in a large organization 'may feel neither like a manager nor a professional but much more like a factory worker. . . . He may be subject to factory-like discipline. . . . Also his discretion is called for much less than he would like. . . . He seeks to protect himself and his fellow engineers against arbitrary management acts; he asks pay rises, overtime payments, and the like.' The consequence is that many engineers' associations are 'torn by the conflict between professional and employee orientations', and the 'motivation of engineers (as well as of other professionals and quasi-professionals) who join unions is complex and ambivalent. They seek to win greater freedom to do work in their own way and to raise their status (and one form of status is to be considered a part of management), but explicitly and implicitly, they also seek economic advantages.' The position of groups conscious of being on the precarious fringes of the high-discretion fraternity could hardly be better exemplified (see also Roberts *et al.*, 1972). The strategy of seeking full acceptance within that fraternity is well expressed by the leaders of one union who 'felt that all problems could be solved on a friendly basis, with the company and union acting as "one big happy family" ' (Strauss 1964: 519–33).

These are questions which afflict neither those at the low-discretion end of the scale, who have no hope of using status as a method of defence, nor those at the high-discretion end, who see their status as secure enough to need no association or who have an association which has so far secured their interests without their having had to make too many overt and publicly visible assertions of power. From these complexities two points emerge. The tendency noticeable in the past to analyse the slow development of white-collar unionism in terms of staff employees' status snobbery embodies an assumption that status is being enjoyed simply for its own sake, whereas in fact status can be a means to the end of protecting or advancing monetary rewards and other privileges.* Second, there is no necessary antithesis between using status as a form of defence and resorting to pressure through association. Apprenticed craftsmen in the nineteenth century valued their status both terminally and instrumentally and used their organizations to protect it. There is not the space here to pursue this

* This is not intended as an explanation of the slow development of white-collar unionism.

field of inquiry.* Before we leave the subject of monetary rewards, however, we should note some further implications towards which the two models lead us.

Discretion and Inequalities

Wootton examines the explanations offered by economic theory for the characteristic features of our wage and salary structure and finds them wanting. '. . . little support can be found in economic considerations for the more conspicuous inequalities of our wage and salary system, and in particular, for the superior rewards of those who hold the more skilled, responsible or interesting jobs in any given industry' (1955: 181). There has already emerged from the present analysis one reason why occupants of high-discretion roles who fix other men's rewards are likely to be careful to offer those who establish a persuasive claim to high status such career and pay prospects as are congruent with their own. To do otherwise would weaken the principle on which their own privileges rest. But there is a further reason for their doing so.

In the earlier discussion of the prescriptive and discretionary, or specific and diffuse, rules comprising the work role, it was noted that, given the appropriate training, the prescribed elements call only for obedience, since these represent decisions, choices, preferences, or judgements already made by someone else and programmed into the role. The discretionary content, on the other hand, requires the necessary decisions, choices, preferences, or judgements to be made by the role occupant himself. The question at once presents itself: in the light of whose values, interests and goals is he going to make them? For his superiors or others to whom he is accountable, the question presents itself the more sharply the higher the discretionary content of his role. The greater the extent to which the occupant of a high-discretion role entertains values, interests, and goals which diverge from theirs, the greater the threat that he may use his discretion in ways of which they would disapprove if they became aware of them. Their problem is compounded by the fact that they will not become aware of them until considerable damage is done. The very fact of his long time span of discretion means that before

* For those seeking a way into it: Bain 1970; Strauss 1963a; Strauss 1964; Sturmthal 1966; Kassalow *et al.* 1965; Prandy 1965.

the consequences of his decisions start to become apparent he will have had time to make a good many of them. It is crucial for his superiors, therefore, to ensure that as far as possible he identifies himself with their purposes; that as far as possible his values, interests, and goals are integrated with theirs. There are various means by which they can try to achieve this. They can assimilate him socially; using approval and disapproval to tailor him into the desired ways of thinking, feeling, perceiving, and aspiring. They can try to arrange that he is trained, educated, socialized, and indoctrinated even before he enters their service, or at least during it. Most relevant for our purpose, they can offer a level of rewards, perquisites, opportunities, and prospects which make it clear that they see him as one of themselves; one of their community; one of the favoured fraternity whose rewards and prospects must, of course, match heavy 'responsibilities' now and heavier still to come. In these ways they can hope to ensure that he exercises his discretion along lines they would approve.* To repeat Goldner's proposition: the fact that a 'withdrawal of effort' by occupants of high-discretion roles 'is much less visible' requires top management to seek 'a different kind of commitment from them than it did from manual workers' (1965: 80). Evan, too, we noted as emphasizing the need, since high-discretion role performance 'cannot be objectively evaluated', for ensuring that occupants of such roles are loyal and trustworthy (1961: 541–2).

These considerations alone, quite independently of market factors, would lead us to expect top management to bring markedly different attitudes to bear upon the rewards of high-discretion as against those of low-discretion roles. Their dependence upon the goodwill, personal commitment, and identification displayed by occupants of the latter is far less than upon that displayed by occupants of the former. The emphasis in the case of the latter is likely to take the form of asking: what is the minimum level of rewards necessary to induce people to take up and retain these low-discretion roles? To secure the appropriate level of performance once the role is taken up, management will be relying, not on internal commitment and identification, but on external controls built into

* The rewards and prospects offered must, to be effective, be in terms of what the role occupant values. Top management's assumptions in this respect may or may not be correct.

technology, supervision, administrative rules, immediate financial incentives, and a range of penalties and deterrents. Thus whereas in the case of high-discretion roles top management is having to buy identification, commitment, and loyalty; its main need in the case of low-discretion roles is to buy only a continuing physical presence, obedience, and response to external stimuli. Experience demonstrates that the former is the more expensive.* We have to expect top management to manifest a keener alertness to the needs and aspirations of those upon whose identification, commitment, and loyalty they are more heavily dependent. Their approach to the needs and aspirations of those occupying low-discretion roles can be expected to be somewhat different. Apart, perhaps, from promoting an ideology of common interests which seeks to bend even minimal discretion in their favour, they do not seriously seek to welcome occupants of low-discretion roles into their own fraternity of values, thought, and action. In much of their behaviour, in such respects as work planning and organization design, there lies implicit an assumption that, almost irrespective of the financial rewards offered, low-discretion members cannot be expected to manifest the same concern, interest, and conscientious involvement which is expected of high-discretion members. They are perceived as an alien group whose needs and aspirations must be met, at best with grudging compromise, at worst with flat resistance.

Compromise will, however, often be necessary. The fact that discretion can never be completely programmed out of any work role means that, quite apart from strike action, there is always some minimal quantum of power available if the role occupant has the aspiration to use it, either individually or – more probably in the case of low-discretion roles – collectively with others. 'Practically . . . the system can never be so tight as it can theoretically. There is always some possibility of play within the framework delimited by the rules, and therefore dependence relations and bargaining are

* The fact that *all* work roles have *some* discretionary content prompts many managers to retain the hope, often forlorn, that appropriate indoctrination will induce people even at this level to use their small discretion actively to further managerial purposes. Propagation of the unitary ideology of shared goals and mutual trust is, at this level, an attempt to secure from low-discretion roles the responses characteristic of high-discretion roles. The conditions under which these efforts become, for management, counterproductive will be examined later.

never completely suppressed. The curious practice of the *grève du zèle* – striking by slowing down the work flow and paralysing the functioning of the organization just by observing, to the letter, all the required prescriptions – has been repeatedly used in many sectors of French public administration, precisely as a way of expressing the fact that management must rely on workers' support and must therefore bargain for it' (Crozier 1964: 189). The reference reminds us that the perception of divergent goals in the low-discretion situation tends to promote the bargaining mode of settling disagreements. We can now note an important social consequence of the contrast between this mode and that employed in determining rewards for high-discretion roles.

In elucidating it we shall elaborate the point just made with respect to power. To speak of top management's heavy dependence upon the occupants of high-discretion roles is to refer to the fact that roles vested with a high degree of discretion are endowed with a corresponding degree of power, for a dependence relationship is a power relationship. When top management takes care to supply the rewards and privileges considered appropriate to the status of these roles, lest the occupants misuse their discretion or leave the organization altogether, it is manifesting an awareness of that power relationship. There is likely to be little overt demonstration of their power by the role occupants. No open threats may be uttered. They rarely need to be. Consciousness even of a purely implicit threat that remains unspoken bends the mind towards whatever pattern of behaviour is required to prevent the threat being made manifest. It is where the consciousness of power is greatest, in fact, that its active exercise is least necessary. So far as the third-party observer is concerned, however, it is also true that where power least needs to be visibly deployed it is least likely to be noticed. Response to a source of power which remains silent and invisible is unlikely to be perceived by the casual observer as a power relationship at all: the effects of power on behaviour are often not registered unless it is being overtly exercised. The fact remains, however, that the occupants of high-discretion roles assume that top management's dependence on their discretion will induce it spontaneously to ensure that their rewards, privileges, and prospects are those appropriate to members of the high-trust fraternity.

The case is very different for occupants of low-discretion roles.

They cannot sell for a high price their commitment and identification in the exercise of discretion, for what discretion they have is relatively unimportant. They need not, therefore, be expensively wooed. Since they cannot rely individually on their discretionary role to induce top management to reward them generously, they must bring collective pressure to bear if their interests are to be secured. Collectively they can force top management to do reluctantly and on a far lower level of concession what the individual occupant of a high-discretion role can rely on top management to do spontaneously and relatively generously. But this requires overt collective mobilization and a visible and usually well-publicized exercise of pressure upon the management concerned. This is the kind of power relationship which fully registers with the public, unlike that arising from high-discretion roles, which passes unnoticed. Not surprisingly, it is the former which the more readily becomes identified as 'sectional greed'. If members of the higher echelons do not themselves initiate these identifications they are hardly likely to strain every nerve to set the record straight even if they see it straight themselves, which is unlikely, their need for self-justification being as strong as it is in everyone else.

The upshot is therefore that occupants of high-discretion roles can feel confident of seeing their interests secured while still subscribing to, and remaining within, a conformist culture and ideology – conformist, that is, with those who command their destinies – whereas the occupants of low-discretion roles are obliged in some respects to break out of that culture and ideology and enter into a visible power contest in which they are seen to challenge high-status members of society. It is hardly surprising that such of these high-status members as choose to do so can easily fasten upon trade unions a reputation for 'sectional activities' against 'the public interest'; a reputation which does not attach to members of their own fraternity who can secure their interests more effectively yet with far less publicity.

Since the designing of work roles in terms of high discretion involves top management in heavy dependence upon the goodwill of others and in the high costs of evoking and maintaining it, we might postulate among the drives of economic rationality a disposition on top management's part to seek or be receptive towards ways of reducing discretion in order to reduce this dependence and its attendant costs. Such a postulate would prompt us to explore the reasons why high-discretion roles remain. Among them is inertia; possibly a factor too little emphasized in the social sciences. Unless pressed by circumstance or motivated by specially high aspirations towards economic rationality, top management will accept many work roles as traditionally defined. We must not mistake for inertia, however, two very different reasons which may be operative. The first relates to the nature of the task to be done and the possibilities it offers or fails to offer for redefinition and restructuring in low-discretion terms. It may be that, after a careful appraisal of the comparative costs and benefits of structuring and defining certain roles in different ways, the balance of advantage is perceived in terms of maintaining them as high-discretion roles. The other possibility is that top management may see benefits in reducing the discretion vested in certain roles but is deterred by the resistance that would be encountered. For these reasons the redefining of roles in terms of reduced discretion probably tends to be as often applied to those where discretionary content is already low as to those where it is high. Doubtful of the personal commitment of those in low-discretion roles, management is frequently disposed, provided there is not too much costly resistance, to reduce that discretion still further. Hobson noted in 1894 that 'a great part of modern inventiveness . . . is engaged in devising automatic checks and indicators for the sake of dispensing with detailed human skill and reducing the spontaneous or thoughtful elements of tending machinery to a minimum' (1926: 347).

These points will be further explored later. Meanwhile the arguments just presented can be illustrated, albeit expressed in somewhat different terms, from a current manual on company remuneration policy (McBeath 1969). Unskilled and semi-skilled work is described as offering 'very limited scope for recognising variations in performance or personal merit', though there is 'the possibility of simple merit awards limited to defined work standards'. For skilled manual workers there is 'greater scope for individual performance adjustments'. Salaries for charge hands and foremen should be 'based on differentials over the operatives they supervise, with generally small salary ranges within which personal merit may be recognized'. For clerical and other office personnel the basic structure consists of a series of steps linked to age or service, with perhaps a narrow merit band which acknowledges seniority as much as differences in performance. Finally, 'the further one goes into more and more complex jobs in which individual approach, ability, capacity, etc., influence what is done, the greater the need for individual valuation . . .' (*Ibid*: 80, 85).

Discretion, Individuality, and Identity

Implicit in these notes are statements not only about differences in discretion and their implications for status and rewards, but also about the *individual* nature of discretionary work. It is the discretionary element of the work role which gives its occupant the opportunity to express *his* decisions, choices, preferences, judgements. By contrast, the prescribed elements embody decisions, choices, preferences, and judgements already made by others. This minimizing of the individual's own contribution in the low-discretion role renders such roles highly 'generalized' in the sense that they call for human qualities and characteristics which are widely available, cultivable or enforceable. Obedience, regularity, conformity to relatively simple prescribed routines and programmes – precisely because these require and evoke no contribution that is specifically individual in terms of choice or judgement they are the very stuff of anonymity. 'It is often urged', wrote Hobson in 1894, 'that the tendency of machinery is not merely to render monotonous the activity of the individual worker, but to reduce the individual differences in workers. This criticism finds expression in the saying: "All men are equal before the machine" ' (1926: 348–9). Selznick offers empirical evidence in making the same point. On the shop floor of the factory 'it is the job that is important. Individuals are interchangeable. In the offices, drafting rooms, and laboratories of modern industry, on the other hand, individual capabilities and characteristics become quite important. Men come and go in these salaried positions, but because of the importance of initiative, creativity, and specific technical skills, each new employee is likely to have considerable influence on his job and on the jobs of those around him. . . . Unskilled and skilled manual workers tend strongly to believe that the duties of their jobs would be the same, regardless of who filled the job, while managerial, professional, and technical persons are more likely to emphasize the contribution of the individual' (1969: 188). Gouldner, too, after registering that a 'technologically advanced civilization reduces and standardizes the skills required for wanted performances: it simplifies and mechanizes many tasks', adduces as one of the consequences the fact that 'men are becoming more interchangeable, more replaceable, and removable at lower costs' (1971: 277).

This tendency of low-discretion roles to induce in their occupants a sense of anonymity, contrasted with the sense of individual contribution that is evoked by the exercise of high discretion, can be related to the themes of personal identity and personal responsibility. It is not difficult to argue that the individual's sense of responsibility within a given social context is closely bound up with whether or not he has a sense of identity in that context. There is the familiar illustration of the person who 'loses himself' (a significant choice of words) in the anonymity of the mob and thereby becomes capable of acts from which as a separate individual he would shrink. There is no reason to think the same mechanism is not operative in the work situation. The absence of commitment or moral involvement which the manager so often deplores in the lower ranks of the organization is, in considerable measure, a consequence of the low-discretion roles that he and his forerunners have designed for them and for earlier generations of employees who have bequeathed their low expectations and responses to their children.

Once again, then, we find ourselves linking differences in the degree of discretion vested in the work role with differences in the whole syndrome of features which characterize the role and its relations with superordinates. The cumulative impression conveyed by the data and arguments of this chapter is that low-discretion role relations with superordinates tend to embody, by comparison with high-discretion role relations, a lower level of mutual support, mutual confidence, open communications, concern for each other's interests, expectations of good faith and, basic to all these, consciousness of shared interests and values. The reason why a reduced consciousness of shared interests and values is basic is that it generates the distrust of which the other syndrome characteristics are expressions. Indeed, no small part of the data and argument in this field tends to be expressed in terms of trust relations – the word itself and synonyms such as 'reliance' and 'confidence' (or words connoting the lack of these sentiments) appear frequently in both empirical descriptions and theoretical discussions. Relationships of trust and distrust appear, in fact, to be central to the issues with which we are concerned.

So far, however, no attempt at a comprehensive integrated analysis grounded in the concept of trust has been put forward. In the belief that such an analysis has something to offer the understanding of social structures and dynamics, an attempt will be made in the succeeding chapters to offer one. The development of the argument soon brings out connections and implications which extend far beyond work organizations to class relations and the very texture of much social interaction within industrial societies. This suggests that trust might be seen as an integrating notion which can be used to link, within a coherent pattern of thought, a wide range of data, concepts, and ideas which at present tend to be fragmented among a number of sub-disciplines or specialist fields of interest. Should the concept of trust prove to be capable of carrying this kind of weight it might not be surprising. Mutual trust and distrust could hardly fail to be among the central characteristics of social interaction; being generated within, and in turn reacting back upon, the various structured forms of human association. The surprise is rather that these concepts tend, when they are used, to be used only as descriptive rather than analytical tools. Trust and distrust appear as symptoms rather than as a source of social dynamics in their own right which might be useful in analysis. It is in the belief that they can offer this more significant explanatory use that the ensuing argument is put forward.

But before even the present exploratory essay in this direction can begin, certain essential preliminaries must be undertaken. How is the concept of trust to be defined in this context? How can it be related to degrees of discretion in work roles? And where lies the usefulness of introducing such a concept? It is to such questions that we turn in the next chapter.

2 · Exchange and Trust Dynamics

Institutionalized Trust

An examination of the prescribed and discretionary aspects of work in terms of trust relations calls for clarification of how the word is going to be used. The *New English Dictionary* defines it in such terms as 'confidence in or reliance on some quality or attribute of a person or thing'; 'confident expectation of something'; 'to have faith or confidence in'; 'to have faith or confidence that something desired is, or will be, the case'. To *distrust* is 'to have no confidence in, or suspect the actions, intentions, motives of'. In reporting research on small problem solving groups among management, Zand follows Deutsch's definition whose principal terms describe 'trusting behaviour' as 'consisting of actions that (a) increase one's vulnerability, (b) to another whose behaviour is not under one's control . . .' (Zand 1972: 230).

These definitions may seem at first sight to accord closely with all our everyday usages. Yet there is one paradoxical form which escapes these categories and which needs to be noted because the process of unravelling the paradox later will bring out a factor of importance for certain arguments of this book. While the essence of trust is presented in the definitions as consisting in having faith and confidence in a person or thing, the word is sometimes used in situations where clearly very little faith or confidence is involved. Two examples will make the point. The parents of a young girl are discussing her announced determination to go on holiday with acquaintances about whom the parents entertain some moral suspicions. Finally they decide: 'We'll just have to trust her.' In the second example, the girl is kidnapped and the parents agree to pay ransom money, but ask the kidnapper: 'How do we know you'll return her safe and sound?' He replies: 'You don't; you'll just have to trust me.'

In both these examples the word is being used to describe a relationship from which faith and confidence are conspicuously absent, and which might be more appropriately described as distrust. The situation is one which the parents might wish to describe in such terms as: 'We don't really trust our daughter/the kidnapper but feel constrained by circumstances to submit to her/his discretion.' A similar mood inspired Thomas Jefferson to write: 'Free government is founded in jealousy and not in confidence, it is jealousy, and not confidence, which prescribes limited constitutions, to bind down those whom we are obliged to trust with power . . .' (Selznick 1969: 18).

The significance of this for work roles and relations will emerge later. Meanwhile we need to register three more points about trust relations before applying them to the theory of work. First, the essential character of all trust relations is their reciprocal nature. Trust tends to evoke trust, distrust to evoke distrust.* The more X is perceived as manifesting a trust in Y, the easier Y will find it to trust X, for X's behaviour suggests to Y a belief that they share certain relevant values or interests. If X shows what is deemed by Y to be distrust, Y is likely to deduce (provided he believes X to have all the relevant facts) that X perceives their values or interests to be different, thus giving Y good reasons for distrusting X.

The second point is that the perceived decline of trust on the part of X towards Y does not leave, as it were, a gap; a disposition of neutrality. To say that X does not trust Y is to say that he distrusts him. As trust shrinks, distrust takes over. This is a crucial consideration with respect to the third point, which concerns the forms through which trust and distrust are manifested in social relations. They are usually thought of as being expressed in purely personal terms. I trust my friends; distrust my enemies; start by trusting colleague X but come to distrust him, or *vice versa*. But we shall be concerned in this book with 'institutionalized' trust; with the notion that trust and distrust – or, to express the same idea in different words, differing degrees of trust – are perceived as being embodied in the rules, roles,

* Noting the findings of small group research, Zand writes: 'When others encounter low-trust behaviour, initially they will hesitate to reveal information, reject influence, and evade control. This short cycle feedback will reinforce the originator's low-trust . . .' (1972: 230). Thus 'mutual trust or mistrust, among members of a group, are likely to be reinforced, unless there is marked or prolonged disconfirming behaviour' (*Ibid*: 238). Zand offers a diagrammatic interaction model of this 'spiral reinforcement' process (*Ibid*: 232–3).

and relations which some men impose on, or seek to get accepted by, others.

Limited though our concern is to the world of work, these rules, roles, and relations nevertheless cover a wide range of behaviour and interaction. They regulate the actions of men in their task activities; the rewards and punishments brought to bear upon them; and their relations with others in terms of interdependence, communication, inspection, supervision, and authority. They range far beyond the explicit and formal promulgations by those in superordinate positions (who may in some cases be applying rules laid down by the law and other external agencies such as government departments and insurance companies). They include explicitly enunciated rules formulated and articulated by subordinate groups. A further category comprises informal understandings, customs, and conventions. We must also include formal rules and informal understandings that are concerted and jointly sponsored by superordinate and subordinate groups. What is more, we are interested not in rules, roles, prescriptions, and procedures as these may be laid down in job manuals, organization charts, or collective agreements, but as they are actually applied by the people involved. Rules and prescriptions do not apply themselves, and there enter into their application individual differences of personality and orientation which have their own social consequences. It is individual men who interpret, observe or apply roles and rules and if their individualness is ignored a major dynamic in their behaviour and their relations with others is ignored along with it.

When men design roles and rules of these diverse kinds for each other, those being regulated perceive them as expressing, by their very nature, either a high or low degree of reliance, confidence, and faith in the behaviour of those for whom they are made. The degree of trust is not an objective characteristic of the rules, for as we shall see later men may perceive the same rules differently, depending on their frame of reference or ideological perspective. In speaking of institutionalized trust relations we are referring to the perceptions men have of the trust reposed in their behaviour as it is expressed and embodied in the rules and relations which others seek to impose on them. The fact that we are concerned, not with personal feelings between people as individuals, but with relationships which are structured and institutionalized in the form of roles and rules, means that the terms 'trust' and 'distrust' do not carry the same overtones as they sometimes do in everyday usage. We follow Zand in using trust to mean 'not a global feeling of warmth or affection, but the conscious regulation of one's dependence on another . . .' (1972: 230). Trust used in this sense is compatible with personal dislike of the person trusted; distrust with personal liking and respect for him.

The importance of the frame of reference must await subsequent exploration, but for the moment the convenience of exposition will be served by making certain assumptions which are justified by a high degree of empirical probability. We shall assume that the occupants of high-discretion roles perceive themselves as the recipients of high trust which is institutionalized in the rules and relationships laid down for them. Conversely, occupants of low-discretion roles will be assumed to perceive themselves as the recipients of institutionalized low trust. That an association is likely to emerge between one's allocation of discretion and one's perceptions of being trusted or distrusted is plausible enough. To be endowed with high discretion suggests a belief on the part of superordinates that one can be trusted to exercise choice between alternative possible decisions in ways which, on balance, meet with their approval. Conversely, to be severely limited in discretion may lead one to deduce that they do not have this confidence and that, to safeguard their interests, they feel driven to define one's role and its surrounding rules accordingly.

If this mode of displaying what is perceived as institutionalized trust (high or low) is referred to, for the sake of convenience, as discretionary trust, we might identify another mode as prescriptive trust. Not only can it be asked how far a subordinate is trusted to exercise discretion; it can also be asked how far he is trusted to obey, conform to, and honour the prescribed rules which limit his discretion. There is scope for great variations in the frequency, rigour, and punitiveness with which these rules are policed and infractions penalized. Two very different questions can therefore be posed of the occupant of a work role. First, is he conforming to the prescribed limits which superiors bring to bear upon his behaviour? Second, what is the quality of the discretion which he exercises within those prescribed limits? On both questions he will perceive himself as the recipient of high or low trust. Checks on the prescribed aspects of his performance may be infrequent and infractions visited only with mild reproof, possibly even sympathetic understanding. Alternatively they may be frequent and strongly punitive. The same range of possibilities applies to his exercise of discretion. Bearing in mind the nature of his job and all the characteristics of its setting, we may ask Jaques's question; how long a period of time would elapse before any substandard exercise of discretion on his part came before the considered attention of his immediate superior?

To elucidate these points we may take one aspect of the train-driver's role – the prescribed rule to 'keep below the speeds, as shown on a speedometer, specified for each curve on a railway' (Jaques 1967: 78). Checks may or may not be applied to police this rule. There is the further question: what is the quality of his discretion in judging when to slacken speed for these curves? To do so too early will cause the train to run behind time, which may evoke a reprimand. To do so too late will require the heavy application of brakes and possibly a tumble for a standing passenger who may formally complain. In either case the driver is conscious that the nature of his role does not permit him to exercise substandard discretion for very long before the fact is noted. If we tease out the implicit as well as the explicit features of this example, we may suppose the employing body to be saying, in effect: 'We trust you to use your judgement in such a way as to keep to the prescribed speeds on curves without running late or causing injury to passengers. However, we shall maintain a complaints department and a pattern of internal communications such as will enable criticisms of your judgement to pass to your relevant superior.' A conceivable though unlikely alternative would be for the employing body to declare instead: 'We shall maintain no apparatus for enabling us to evaluate your judgement. We shall trust you totally.'* In terms of practical probabilities, of course, what is suggested by the low-discretion syndrome is that roles which enjoy little discretionary trust are likely to meet with little prescriptive trust. The tendency is for them to be closely monitored and sanctioned in a manner rarely imposed on the occupants of high-discretion roles.

Economic and Social Exchange

Given this preliminary elucidation of how trust becomes perceived as being institutionalized in the roles and rules which some men make

* The elaboration of this example is the present author's.

for others, we can carry the analysis forward by drawing upon what has become known as exchange theory (Heath 1971). This deals, in certain of its formulations, with concepts which can readily be used to illuminate the social nature of work in terms of trust relations.

The starting point here is the distinction drawn by Blau between economic and social exchange. Exchange itself consists in the voluntary actions of individuals that are motivated by the returns they are expected to bring and typically do in fact bring from others (1964: 91). 'The basic and most crucial distinction' between the two 'is that social exchange entails *unspecified* obligations'. The prototype of an economic exchange, on the other hand, is a transaction resting on a 'formal contract that stipulates the exact quantities to be exchanged'. Social exchange 'involves the principle that one person does another a favour, and while there is a general expectation of some future return, its exact nature is definitely *not* stipulated in advance'. It involves 'favours that create diffuse future obligations, not precisely specified ones. . . '. This very diffuseness; this absence of a specifically defined reciprocity; 'requires trusting others to to discharge their obligations'. Economic exchange, by contrast, prescribes specifically the nature and extent of the favours exchanged. They are not left, as in social exchange, to the discretion of the parties. Thus neither is trusting the other. Moreover, since the favours exchanged are being specifically defined in advance, the way is open for bargaining over the terms, whereas in social exchange, involving as it does 'diffuse future obligations, not precisely specified ones', the 'nature of the return cannot be bargained about but must be left to the discretion of the one who makes it'. In social exchange 'there is no binding contract that can be enforced, in contrast to the contractual obligations in economic exchange, which can be enforced through legal sanctions'.

The consequences of the distinction extend further. 'Only social exchange tends to engender feelings of personal obligation, gratitude, and trust; purely economic exchange as such does not.' Social exchange therefore tends to generate a spiral of rising trust. 'By discharging their obligations for services rendered, if only to provide inducements for the supply of more assistance, individuals demonstrate their trustworthiness, and the gradual expansion of mutual service is accompanied by a parallel growth of mutual trust.' This 'mutual trust between committed exchange partners encourages them to engage in a variety of transactions – to exchange advice, help, social support, and companionship – and these diffuse transactions give the partnership some intrinsic significance. Only impersonal economic exchange remains exclusively focused on specific extrinsic benefits; in social exchange the association itself invariably assumes a minimum of intrinsic significance' (*Ibid*: 93–8, 315). If the tendency of social exchange is to promote a spiral of rising trust, the tendency of economic exchange must be to promote a spiral of falling trust. Blau does not pursue this symmetry but the logic of the argument speaks for itself. The specific nature of the exchange, embodying little trust by each in the other's discretion, generates a probability that each will watch the other with increasing vigilance, both to secure for himself an acceptable bargain and to ensure the full observance of its terms. Relations are therefore low in trust to the extent that they approach the wholly contractual form postulated by economists as pure economic exchange, with precisely defined and specific obligations on both sides, and with each party watching the other for infractions; jealously guarding concessions; and refusing any request for extra-contractual favours unless precisely defined reciprocation is guaranteed.*

At this point it need only be added that social and economic exchanges are presented here as polar extremes simply to sharpen the contrast for theoretical purposes and to simplify the exposition. Between the extremes lies a continuum along which relative diffuseness of obligation and relationships of high trust shade off into relative specificity of obligation and relationships of low trust. This parallels the scale of high-to-low discretion noted in Chapter 1 with respect to work roles. In the exposition which follows, complications will be avoided by limiting it, for the most part, to the extremes of high and low discretion and trust, on the understanding that these are relative terms on a graduated scale.

Exchange and Trust

In applying these concepts to work roles and relations, economic exchange can be shown to accord with the low-discretion, low-trust

* It may be noted that reciprocation can be measured along two dimensions: that of short/long term and that of specific/diffuse. The lowest trust point would be characterized by short-term specific reciprocation; the highest trust point by long-term diffuse. In between come long-term specific and short-term diffuse.

model, and social exchange with the high-discretion, high-trust model. Inevitably, the presentation of such opposed ideal types creates an impression of unrealistic extremes, especially when they involve such value-laden terms as trust and distrust. They suggest a world of Panglossian felicity on the one hand and a Hobbesian nightmare on the other. The necessary corrective has to be applied by seeing them as standards of reference to which real-life situations more or less approximate; as analytical constructs with which to explore certain selected qualities of social relations.

It will be recalled that the low-discretion syndrome associates roles of this kind with (a) a perceived disposition on the part of superordinates to behave as if the role occupant cannot be trusted, of his own volition, to perform according to their goals and values; (b) the imposition, as a consequence, of close personal supervision, specific impersonal rules, or other forms of systematic control; (c) the imposition, too, of tight coordination through externally applied standardized routines and schedules, thereby ruling out the open unrestricted communication and interaction patterns more appropriate for certain kinds of problem solving; (d) an assumption that failures or inadequacies of performance result from negligence or insubordination; and (e) a tendency for conflict to be conducted on a group basis through bargaining, with an acknowledged divergence of interests and the exercise of threats, gamesmanship and other characteristics of negotiation.*

This model can be shown to manifest the conditions of economic exchange. In return for a specific extrinsic reward, in the form of a wage or salary, the occupant of the role performs certain services of a predominantly specific nature. Both sides, therefore, bring to this relationship expectations of a highly specific reciprocation. Hopes by either that the other can be brought to go beyond the prescribed terms without guaranteed specific reciprocation prove forlorn. This makes it likely that mutual vigilance will increase rather than diminish. More and more aspects of the relationship are brought under prescription as bargaining develops to handle what are

* At the small group level, Zand suggests that 'One who does not trust others will conceal or distort relevant information, . . . will resist or deflect the attempts of others to exert influence . . . will be suspicious of their views, and not receptive to their proposals of goals . . . will try to minimize his dependence on others . . . will try to impose controls on their behaviour . . . but will resist and be alarmed at their attempts to control his behaviour' (1972: 230).

increasingly conceded to be divergent interests. At the level both of the individual employee's work performance and of the implementation of a jointly negotiated collective agreement, failure or insufficiency are interpreted as negligence, dishonesty, or bad faith; behaviours thought to call for compulsion and enforcement. Here we are reminded of the 'contractual obligations in economic exchange which can be enforced through legal sanctions'. In relations of this kind we are familiar, too, with another facet of the spiral of falling trust when close punitive supervision aggravates the very motivational difficulties it is intended to solve, thus appearing to create the need for more of the same treatment.

Chamberlain and Kuhn's analysis of conjunctive bargaining brings out major features of relations at this low-trust extreme of the continuum. '. . . the parties agree to terms as a result of mutual coercion and arrive at a truce only because they are indispensable to each other. . . . It provides no incentive to the parties to do more than carry out the minimum terms of the agreement which has temporarily resolved their divergent interests. The obligations which each has assumed to the other . . . and the advantages . . . which each has wrested from the other are fixed. For one party to give a superior performance by cooperating more effectively with the other is not likely to win it any further concession because concessions are predetermined. Conjunctive bargaining allows the minimum required cooperation of each with the other, which tends to become the maximum actual cooperation as well. Indeed, there sometimes arises a fixed determination on the part of owner-managers or union member-employees not to meet their obligations in any greater degree than what the other party can exact. The result sometimes takes the form of "getting away" with as much as possible' (*Ibid.*: 424–35). The meaning of low-trust relations could hardly be conveyed more unmistakably – even to the tendency for *prescribed* terms of the relationship to come under default.

The specific short-term reciprocations characteristic of these low-discretion relations leave little scope for mutual long-term diffuse obligations. The employee displays few manifestations of 'loyalty' which could not more convincingly be interpreted as habituated attachment. The attachment is of an extrinsic kind, based on financial rewards, security, convenience, or satisfying social relationships with fellow employees. Relationships with superiors do not 'engender feelings of personal obligations, gratitude, and trust'. For precisely the same reasons, superiors do not feel conscious of any long-term debt which they must discharge in the form of a concern with the subordinate's general welfare and future; a debt created by the diffuse loyalty and service which he offers them and expects to see returned. There is no development of mutual bonds of support expressive of reciprocated trust; only the calculated wariness and suspicion expressive of reciprocated distrust.

Little can be expected, therefore, in the way of a community of values and sympathies; a shared universe of meanings, understandings and attitudes. Indeed, perspectives may, at some points, diverge sharply. Kohn and Schooler have documented significant class difference of values and orientation that correlate with 'variations in the degree to which jobs allow and require self-direction' (1969: 676). 'In industrial society, where occupation is central to men's lives, occupational experiences that facilitate or deter the exercise of self-direction come to permeate men's views, not only of work and of their role in work, but also of the world and of self.' Those in higher class and occupational positions tend to emphasize self-direction, with its implication of the necessity for standards of personal responsibility; incline towards a more optimistic view of their ability to conduct themselves in the world; and are apt to take extrinsic rewards for granted and stress the importance of the intrinsic. Those in lower occupational positions are more aware of the pressures towards conformity to rules, seeing conformity in terms of the letter – not necessarily the spirit – of the rules; incline to be more socially pessimistic and distrustful; and stress the extrinsic rather than the intrinsic rewards of work (*Ibid.* See also Kornhauser 1965 and Inkeles 1960).

The occupant of the low-discretion role is not, therefore, being invited to join his superiors in a community of shared interests and values to which he is expected to contribute his moral involvement, commitment, judgement, creativeness, and problem solving abilities. Whatever the designers of his role may *say*, they demonstrate by the very nature of their design that they are not inviting this kind of contribution. Interesting in this context is the observation of a social anthropologist who, in a discussion of reciprocity and exchange in tribal societies, asserts that 'To refuse to give, or *to fail to invite*, is – like refusing to accept – the equivalent of a declaration of war; it is a refusal of friendship and intercourse' (Evans-Pritchard, in Mauss 1954: 11. Italics added). This explains why the characteristic top management exhortation to rank and file employees to 'trust the company' is often received with cynicism. In the very way it structures work, authority, and rewards it excludes them from its own high-discretion, high-trust fellowship, yet asks them to submit to its discretion in handling their interests and destinies. In other words: 'We do not trust you, but we ask you nevertheless to trust us.' Mere verbal exhortations or formulae cannot, in Western-type society, indefinitely disguise this imbalance of reciprocity though, as we shall see later, power may enforce it.

In exploring these qualities of low-discretion roles and relations the fact will have become apparent that little could be gleaned from the bare formal contract of employment. We have had to go far beyond this to discover the texture of these relations. We have found ourselves exploring what Schein has termed the 'psychological contract'. This 'implies that the individual has a variety of expectations of the organization and that the organization has a variety of expectations of him. These expectations not only cover how much work is to be performed for how much pay, but also involve the whole pattern of rights, privileges, and obligations between worker and organization. For example, the worker may expect the company not to fire him after he has worked there for a certain number of years and the company may expect that the worker will not run down the company's public image or give away company secrets to competitors. Expectations such as these are not written into any formal agreement between employee and organization, yet they operate powerfully as determinants of behaviour' (1965: 11). This is the context in which the individual formulates 'the decision of whether to join, the decision of how hard to work and how creative to be, feelings of loyalty and commitment, expectations of being taken care of and finding a sense of identity through one's organization role, and a host of other decisions, feelings, and expectations' (*Ibid*: 13).

In the case of the low-discretion role these mutual expectations are minimal except in so far as certain of them may enter into collective agreements which themselves become structured into the expectations. But then of course the expectations become prescriptive and not discretionary in nature. Yet however minimal, trust in some degree there has to be. We must not mistake a model for a description; the notion of a work relationship wholly without trust – or, for that matter wholly without distrust – is only a polar extreme of a theoretical construct and cannot be found in practice. As noted earlier, even the most rigorously prescribed work role requires *some* use of discretion, and to that extent is vested with a trust, albeit negligible. At the other end of the scale, no role exists which does not embody prescribed limits and which to that extent denies discretion to the occupant, thereby withholding trust. The differences are, however, fundamental and profound. In their structural forms they have been explored already, but the current purpose is to demonstrate the contrast in terms of trust relations. We turn now, then, to examine high-discretion roles in this light.

It will be recalled that the corresponding syndrome in their case comprises the following items: (a) an assumption by superordinates of personal commitment on the part of the role occupant to an occupational calling and/or to the goals and values of the organization (as superordinates define them). This commitment includes the notion of effort and application being freely offered rather than measured calculatively against a specific return. It expresses the Parsons and Smelser view of a 'diffuse loyalty to the organization as such' which prompts the individual 'to accept, as the occasion demands, responsibilities beyond any specific contracted function' (1956: 116); (b) freedom from close supervision and detailed regulation by specific impersonal rules; (c) a relatively open network of communication and interaction, with those in superordinate or leadership positions being seen as supportive colleagues; (d) a tendency for communication to take the forms of advice, information and consultative discussion, rather than of orders, commands, and directives; (e) an emphasis on problem solving through 'processes of mutual adjustment' rather than on externally imposed coordination through standardized routines; (f) a tendency for inadequacies of performance to be categorized as honest misjudgements rather than as derelictions of duty or insubordination, and (g) the handling of disagreements on a basis of 'working through' in the light of shared goals rather than on a basis of bargaining in the light of divergent goals.

This is demonstrably a high-trust syndrome.* If we begin the

* It accords closely with Zand's description of high-trust relations at the small group level. 'Persons who trust one another will provide relevant,

comparison with its low-trust counterpart by examining what is being offered by the employing body, marked differences are soon apparent. It consists of an invitation of no small order. The occupant of the high-discretion role is invited to participate in a fellowship of common values and beliefs; a fellowship within which he is invited and expected to exercise his discretion towards ends shared with the other members. Subject to such conventions as may prescribe respect for seniority and experience, he is free to express opinions, reasoned arguments, and criticism. He may, in the course of his career, make errors and misjudgements, but unless these are frequent and serious they will be categorized as honest mistakes of the kind to which even the best are prone. Should he fall into disagreement with seniors or colleagues this will be defined not in terms of his pursuing private interests which clash with 'organizational needs', but in terms of his interpreting those needs differently though in a manner open to change through discussion and persuasion if necessary. The problem solving approach to conflict resolution 'depends on the capacity for mutual identification. It is based on the assumption that a solution will not be satisfactory to one party unless it is also satisfactory to the other party. In short, the solution must be satisfactory to everyone involved' (Kahn and Boulding 1964: 134). Logically implied by this is that his loyalty be taken for granted. And, finally, as a member of this fraternal order of high-discretion, high-status colleagues he must, of course, be looked after. Relevant here are not only immediate monetary rewards, privileges, and perquisites, but also prospects in terms of career structure, along with a diffuse assurance that his general interests will be sympathetically nurtured.

Here, then, is an invitation of a highly diffuse kind to join a high-trust group of colleagues. To be sure, the texture of relations within the group will vary according to the personalities of its most influential members, and much literature in the 'human relations' tradition directs our attention to this factor and seeks to promote high-trust relations through 'sensitivity' or 'T-Group' training aimed at changing personal attitudes. It can safely be said, however, that

comprehensive, accurate and timely information . . . for problem-solving efforts . . . will have less fear that their exposure will be abused, and will therefore be receptive to influence from others . . . will accept interdependence . . . and therefore will have less need to impose controls on others. . . .' (1972: 230–1).

the range of contrasts among high-discretion groups in this respect is far exceeded by the contrast between these groups in general and occupants of low-discretion roles, who receive no invitation remotely comparable.

The occupant of the high-discretion role is expected to reciprocate with a correspondingly diffuse commitment to the occupational calling or to the organization as personified in its top leaders. His obligations to them are no more precisely specified than theirs to him. He is always ready to 'go the second mile' and sacrifice immediate personal interests and convenience, confident that this diffuse goodwill is reciprocal. He does not expect that reciprocation, diffuse or otherwise, will necessarily follow in the short run. He does assume, however, that in the long run dedicated commitment and loyal service will be recognized and rewarded.

Where this high-trust reciprocation is at its fullest, defensive behaviour by individuals and groups is at its minimum. The mutual support that both expresses and promotes high trust 'enables each member to be more himself, to feel less necessity for fighting to obtain his "rights"...' (McGregor 1967: 164). The contrast with those in low-discretion, low-trust situations is apparent. This, along with the other features just noted, suggests that there may well be more both sought and gained from membership of this fraternity than extrinsic rewards. The member may value for its own sake his part in this equality of peers from which he and his fellows draw self-respect, status, and identity. We do not have to look far for evidence that membership of this web of mutual respect and trust can be a profoundly satisfying experience.

Vertical and Lateral Trust

So far we have applied the concept of trust to the 'vertical' relations between subordinates and superordinates. This perspective must now be supplemented by a recognition of trust relations as they may develop 'laterally' among subordinates who share a similar work situation.

Societies on the Western model are of course familiar with the way in which those in low-discretion work roles (though not exclusively those) tend to combine for the purpose of seeking effective remedy or palliation of their deprivations and grievances. Out of these combinations have often come high-trust relations between those engaged in common struggles. Their extent and incidence are a matter for empirical appraisal. Relations between men in low-discretion roles may be competitive and suspicious if technology, work organization, product market, or ideology divide them or create obstacles to collective action. Relations between groups that have succeeded in organizing themselves can sometimes be as distrustful and narrowly self-regarding as any between employer and employee. Nevertheless the record shows individuals and groups enduring suffering for the sake of a wider brotherhood in a way which can only be described as a high-trust orientation. When, for example, men refuse badly needed employment on the grounds that its terms undercut and thereby weaken the standards fixed by their fellows as 'a living wage', they expect no immediate reciprocation by those thereby benefited, but feel rather that they are upholding a widespread network of highly diffuse obligation from which they themselves may need, somewhere, some day, to draw support. There is no calculation of a concrete exchange, but rather an assumption of a fund of fellowship to which all must contribute and from which each can draw if occasion demands. If the men in the situation just noted were to be convinced that none of their fellows elsewhere would sacrifice immediate personal interests for the more diffuse, long-term good of the group, their own readiness to do so would quickly decline. Conversely, the greater the extent to which they perceived the others to be holding – and manifesting – this sentiment of fellowship, the greater the likelihood of their finding the strength to bear such costs as it might require of them. What is being reciprocated, then, is not particular acts of help or support – which many may never require – but the shared conviction that a generalized sentiment of mutual help and support exists which can be drawn upon in need. A quotation from Nisbet strikes the correct note here. 'Did the good samaritan come to my rescue because of his desire for gratitude? Such an ascription would be too simple. But were I to reward his assistance to me with chilly indifference or hostility a vital exchange relationship would have been ruptured' (1970: 65).

Out of the strains and conflicts generated by low-trust vertical relations may therefore come high-trust lateral relations. It is a matter for empirical inquiry how far high-trust relations within the immediate work group extend to cover those similarly placed in work organizations elsewhere, and how far they also extend vertically through their own collective to include a top-level union leadership. The same analysis can be applied to intra-union trust relations as to intra-enterprise trust relations. Members of a work group may resist attempts by the union hierarchy to assert discretion over them just as it may resist similar attempts by management. At the time of writing, efforts are being made in Britain by the National Industrial Relations Court to gear workgroup spokesmen (elected by their fellow workers), firmly and unmistakably into the hierarchical authority structure of the union. If this bid to force a centralization of union power and reduce the discretion of shop-floor leadership evokes the same low-trust responses by employees towards their top level leaders as those they are apt to extend to management, the results may not serve what power-holders usually think of as 'good industrial relations'.

Lateral relations between occupants of high-discretion roles may likewise be marked by high trust, and display the same institutionalized patterns of mutual confidence and support as characterize the vertical relations. Alternatively they may reveal a low-trust pattern. This becomes a possibility when occupants of high-discretion, high-trust roles within an organization are competing for approval and preferment by superior authority. All are trusted, but all wonder who is nearest the throne. The consequent sidelong glances, jealousies, and manoeuvres are of course manifestations of distrust (Dalton 1959).

Those who enjoy high-trust relations both vertically and laterally are exceptionally favoured; those who enjoy them in neither are exceptionally deprived. Satisfaction in one direction, but one only, is perhaps the most common condition. Contrasting ideologies come to be constructed on men's differing experiences and help to perpetuate them. The combination of low vertical and high lateral trust lends itself to ideologies of collectivism, mutual aid, equality, solidarity, and the disparagement of individual striving as 'self-seeking'. The combination of high vertical and low lateral trust promotes ideologies of competitive individualism, opportunity, admiration for success, differential rewards for differential contributions to the team effort, and the disparagement of collectivism as 'the glorification of mediocrity'. These ideologies then become a political and social force in their own right, serving as a resource for justifying behaviour and styles of life, and as an inspiration or a warning when designing new forms of social organization.

Men's adaptations to particular combinations of trust relations, vertical and lateral, may become so strong as to render transfer to a different combination difficult for them. Industry is acquainted with the manual worker who refuses the promotion to foreman which would lose him the high-trust camaraderie of the shop-floor, and with the manager reared in a competitive low-trust atmosphere who disrupts the high-trust teamwork into which he may move in transferring to a different company or industry. Sometimes, of course, men transfer to a different combination out of restlessness with their existing one. Here and there a manual worker can be found who wants a high-discretion, high-trust role, accompanied though it be by low-trust lateral relations, far more than he values his existing position which combines a low-discretion role with high-trust lateral relations. Occasionally the occupant of a high-discretion role chooses to drop out of the 'rat-race' in which he feels it has involved him. At this point we move towards questions which would take us far beyond the scope of this book, such as the sorts of personal identity which men accept, choose, or cultivate for themselves. Instead we must retrace our steps to the mainstream of the argument.

Trust Relations and Alienation

The foregoing analysis of trust relations can be shown to accord closely with one usage of the alienation concept. The argument involves taking up again the distinction between social and economic exchange.

Both forms involve the discharge of a trust. In economic exchange, reciprocation lies in honouring terms which have been specifically defined. By definition, no exercise of discretion is called for, since the specificity of the terms excludes choice. Translated into the work context, the emphasis is on conformity to the prescribed elements which make up the greater part of the role. As we saw earlier, the fact that obedience is the crucial requirement invests the discharge of this kind of trust with the quality of anonymity. Nothing of the individual self is demanded. In other words, we can distinguish the person as an individual from the reciprocating act, since the nature of the act requires no contribution from him as an individual. Anyone capable of conformity to the prescriptive rules will do as well as any other. Here lies the significance of that consciousness among occupants of low-discretion roles of being interchangeable.*

By contrast, social exchange involves discharging a trust of a very different order. The obligation is diffuse, left to the interpretation of the role occupant in the light of *his* judgement, *his* knowledge, *his* capacity to evaluate consequences, *his* loyalty and dedication. The individual's own contribution is of the essence; we cannot distinguish the person from the reciprocating act, since it is his act, his choice. Relevant here is an observation by Caplow about the market for professional services. 'Professionals are, in theory, perfectly non-interchangeable. The work of each is considered to be his individual expression, not capable of direct substitution. . . . It is assumed as a matter of course that the service is unique . . . (1964: 171). This element of choice gives high-discretion work roles a moral character not shared by low-discretion roles. To the extent that discretion is excluded from work, therefore, a wedge is driven between the person as a unique individual and the reciprocating acts with which he discharges his trust; he is, as it were, alienated from those reciprocating acts. We thus arrive at the concept of alienation as self-estrangement. The low-discretion role alienates its occupant from the moral nature of work as it can be and is for a small number of privileged groups. We may briefly anticipate a later development of the argument by noting that, in this respect, the extreme division of labour characteristic of industrial society excludes considerable numbers of its citizens from a universe of action much valued by those who inhabit it, thereby demanding of them a price for their share of the relative affluence which is not demanded of the privileged minority, despite the fact that the minority's share is itself on a substantially higher scale.

We can note a further parallel between low-discretion work and the economic exchange of the market. The permeation of virtually every aspect of social life by economic exchange has been accompanied by a continuous growth of legislation designed to prevent fraud, deception, bad faith, and sharp practice. As prescriptive

* There is the same interchangeability of assets in the economic exchange of the market-place. In so far as it meets the prescribed terms, any batch of goods, any bank transfer, any reliable signature of endorsement, is as acceptable as another.

exchange takes over, thus driving out the moral character of the high-discretion, high-trust relationship, low-trust relations increasingly prevail, adversely affecting observance of the prescriptive elements themselves. A growing battery of controls, detection mechanisms, and punitive sanctions comes into existence to cope with this development. Similarly, low-discretion work roles tend to be accompanied by control mechanisms and sanctions designed to enforce conformity to the prescriptive rules which predominate. In both cases, a reduction in discretionary trust results in a decline in respect for the observance of the prescriptive element in the relationship. Characteristically, functionaries specially appointed to enforce prescriptive rules develop a distrust of those within their overview. Policemen, weights-and-measures inspectors, and food analysts are a few examples. In the field of work, where time study and methods engineering may be found 'closely interwoven with highly developed systems of cost control, checks on labour and machine utilization', the result can be an 'atmosphere where distrust was normal and confidence abnormal'; where operatives and work study engineers conduct a battle of wits, and where one engineer declares: 'I don't really trust anyone' (Klein 1964: x, 20). McGregor, too, notes that 'Staff groups often display an attitude of mistrust towards those who are effected by the control system that the staff have designed and are administering' (1967: 121).

Role Definition – The Spontaneous Consensus and Power Models

Given the growing contrast now emerging between low-discretion roles and low-trust relations on the one hand, and high-discretion roles and high-trust relations on the other, the question needs to be posed of how work roles come to be defined. In other words, how is the organization to be conceptualized from this point of view?

Once again use will be made of two models, both relevant as analytical tools for thinking about work roles and the high and low trust relations which they create. Here we shall find ourselves complicating the exposition by exploring more fully the significance of goals and by introducing new dimensions into the analysis; the dimensions of power and legitimacy. In the process the question will be posed: do low-discretion roles *necessarily* imply low-trust relations, and high-discretion roles high-trust relations? The answer soon emerges that they do not.

The two models may be referred to as the Spontaneous Consensus and the Power models. The former makes a starting assumption that the members of the organization share a spontaneous consensus on ends and means. By spontaneous is meant that the consensus is not the outcome of some members legitimizing organizational ends and means simply from having been socialized and indoctrinated as a consequence of their inferior position in a power structure – organizationally and societally viewed. This spontaneous consensus will be taken to include agreement on a division of labour which requires some members to accept low-discretion roles. The model assumes that the members concerned display willing and active compliance within these roles, and that the spiral of reciprocal distrust never begins. This represents a situation which, for want of a better term, might be labelled 'equilibrium'. By this is meant no more than that the participants acquiesce in the current definition of roles, with their differing degrees of discretion, and make no attempt, covert or overt, individual or collective, to redefine those roles, either their own or those of other participants. In other words, all members legitimize the existing distribution of discretion in the sense of accepting it and being prepared to work with and through it. To be sure, submission to a low-discretion situation does not necessarily derive from the will to play an active part in a team effort towards some common purpose. Some individuals have a psychological need for dependency and passive submission to direction – a further indication of the need to combine sociological with psychological variables in constructing theoretical models for organizational behaviour. It might also seem that, besides this category, there is another which comprises those for whom work is so marginal to their life interests that a totally passive attachment with minimal personal involvement is an ideal solution. Such individuals might surely be ready to legitimize their low-discretion roles and not perceive them in low-trust terms? The position taken here, however, is that this devaluing of work as a marginal passive concern is not a free spontaneous selection from a number of alternative attitudes to work, but an adaptive response to experience and subculture within an organizational and societal power structure which subjects them – and has subjected their forebears – to intrinsically unrewarding work. Individuals in this category are more convincingly considered in the context of the Power model to be examined shortly.

What is being recognized in the Spontaneous Consensus model, rather, is that men who share common goals are capable of allocating roles among themselves in the light of what they perceive as 'functional necessities', and that those allocated low-discretion roles may accept them willingly as their contribution to the joint effort. This is a high-trust situation in as much as the lower participants do not feel they are being used for purposes they do not share. They submit to the discretion exercised over them from above with no fear that it will be used to exploit them for someone else's advantage. Given this high trust in the leaders and the willing compliance it promotes, the linked characteristics of the low-trust syndrome, deriving as they do from a consciousness of divergent goals, do not emerge. Such safeguards and restrictions as leaders feel it necessary to impose are perceived by all as functionally necessary to protect the common effort against the occasional wilful deviant or temporary human weakness.

This pattern of organizational relations can exist where men are moved by a common cause or by some sustaining religious, political, or ethical conviction. Such frustrations and deprivations as they are aware of in their low-discretion role are pushed to the periphery of consciousness by the strength of their commitment. If we seek examples, perhaps approximations to this pattern might be found in the Israeli kibbutz, the self-supporting monastery, the cooperative production enterprise. Another can be found in the world of wartime military operations. A small American élite unit known as 'Carlson's Raiders' was 'characterized by mutual commitment to one another and to superordinate goals. . . . As a military group, they were legally structured as a hierarchical system of coercion. In actual practice, they used the command system (by consensus) only during the course of a raid, when it seemed the best form to achieve success. The planning process before a raid was a process that involved the joint deliberation of all members of the team' (Shepard 1965: 1130–1). These are, however, extreme examples and, as at earlier stages in this analysis, it is clear that we have to think rather in terms of a continuum along which differences of degree are possible and likely. The pattern characterized by these examples, where the occupants of even low-discretion roles are so committed to a common objective or idea that they bring to their task behaviour the same positive and active dedication as that displayed by top leaders, is not the only one which could be subsumed under this low-discretion, high-trust category. In another type of possible situation – the best which could be hoped for, perhaps, in an industrial society based on extreme division of labour – lower participants are not inspired to bring to their low-discretion roles that degree of commitment which generates total dedication even to humble and undemanding tasks, but they nevertheless feel able to extend to superordinates a readiness to trust their leadership, convinced that the ends being pursued and the means used to pursue them are such as they can endorse and respect. Policies proposed and arguments advanced by superordinates are received sympathetically, interpreted favourably, and given the benefit of any doubt – responses which justify us in locating such situations in the high-trust rather than the low-trust category.

The answer, therefore, to the first of our questions is that low-discretion roles do not necessarily imply low-trust relations. Does this not destroy the usefulness of the low-trust syndrome as a model? The low-trust syndrome assumes awareness by both parties that goals to some extent diverge, and it has just been argued that low-discretion roles need not be accompanied by such an awareness. Why, then, was the earlier analysis presented as if they are? The reason is that the Spontaneous Consensus model, while useful for explaining a certain limited range of organizational patterns, does not offer a convincing framework for understanding the great bulk of organized work activities as at present conducted in advanced industrial societies. In societies of this type it is totally implausible to think of groups voluntarily assembling for the purpose of pursuing certain commonly held work goals. The scene is dominated rather by concentrations of economic resources controlled by owners or their agents or by political appointees of the State. The large majority of citizens, being without ownership or control of resources, must seek employment within these concentrations, most of them in the lower rather than the upper reaches of the discretion range. They have no voice in the ends pursued and at best only a marginal influence on the means used to pursue them. It is a scene marked by great disparities of power as between, on the one hand, the low-discretion 'managed', and on the other, the high-discretion top managers and their supportive specialists and advisers. The latter bend their efforts to maximize the return on the labour of the former, which is seen as a commodity resource to be hired or discarded as required. Even the labour of middle managers and others at a similar level may also sometimes be treated by their superiors as a market commodity to a comparable degree. Where this is the case, the application of our models would indicate this to be a move in the economic-exchange, low-trust direction, and would alert us to possibilities suggested by that syndrome, such as that it would be followed, in turn, by symptoms of low-trust reciprocation by the middle managers and then by greater watchfulness on the part of superiors as they sensed the change in motivation.* In general, however, it remains true that expectations of being used as a commodity are significantly greater at low-discretion levels.

The implausibility of the Spontaneous Consensus model turns us, therefore, to the Power model. Resource controllers use their power to marshal the majority into work organizations designed by the controllers to serve their own purposes. This does not require us to imagine a continuous *direct* exercise of that power. The task of the controllers in handling their human instruments is greatly facilitated by the fact that long before men enter employment they have been socialized by a variety of agencies into accepting hierarchy, subordination, inferiority of status and rewards, and a general expectation of lacking control over large sectors of their work experience. This socialization includes a bias, which varies considerably in strength as between national cultures, towards such propositions as that the interests of management and of rank and file are fundamentally the same and that managerial prerogatives must be respected. The significance of this in promoting a higher rather than a lower trust syndrome makes its importance obvious. National, regional, and ethnic cultures may therefore play an important part in shaping men's attitudes to subordination, restriction of autonomy, and limitations to self-development.

When low-discretion employees take up their roles their superiors may be able to sustain and reinforce this ideological socialization to

* An advertisement in *The Times* some years ago by Mr. Clive Jenkins's union, the Association of Scientific, Technical and Managerial Staffs, depicting a managing director telling a lower-level colleague 'The Board and I have decided that we don't like the colour of your eyes', was clearly designed to appeal to those at this level who suspect that they are not being seen as full members of the high-trust fraternity – and to encourage them to make the appropriate low-trust response by looking around for friends, i.e. Mr. Jenkins.

a degree which ensures that high-trust relations prevail and that little or no resistance is offered to management's definition of roles, allocation of rewards, and general conduct of the organization's business.* For to say that employees fully legitimize managerial prerogative is to say that they are not conscious of having interests which can be legitimately opposed to the purposes of management, since that prerogative includes the right to define employee activities and behaviour. And if there is no consciousness of legitimate separate interests there will be no perception of management policies as low-trust behaviour. This function of ideologies is examined more fully in Chapter 6. Meanwhile it is sufficient to note that full and active legitimation of this kind by the rank and file produces the same combination as that envisaged under the Spontaneous Consensus model – that of low-discretion roles and high-trust relations – though of course in this case it comes about through power-holders using their superior strength and command over resources to bend men's ideologies and expectations in directions convenient to themselves.

National cultures and governments differ considerably in the support they give to management in this respect. In the Soviet Union, 'the rising level of skill and education associated with advanced industrialization would appear to be creating a system of social inequality', closely related to occupation, 'which, save for its ownership class component, is very similar to that of Western capitalist states' (Lane 1971 : 69). Through the State monopoly of communications, official ideology strives to induce perceptions of this system as a high-trust pattern in which inequalities of education and income are no more than are required by functional exigencies. 'Socialist society, as defined by Stalin, was a harmonious society based on comradely cooperation' (*Ibid*: 35). Soviet sociologists recognize as significant the division of labour and differential levels of consumption, but deny that the occupational structure gives rise to superior and inferior social status, implying thereby that it is perceived by all levels as a functional necessity upheld by shared goals and the absence of exploitation. 'The values of Soviet society they say are those of fraternal equality and the leaders of the Communist Party and factory labourers may regard each other as "comrades" ' (*Ibid*: 79). Ossowski,

* Some of the psychological processes involved in socialization of the kind relevant to organizational behaviour are examined in Presthus 1958.

the Polish sociologist, comments however that 'a charwoman or porter would be called "comrade" by those who had unlimited bank-accounts, could shop at special stores and had access to special social services for themselves and their children' (1963: 190). Soviet sociologists nevertheless argue that the special conditions of their society enable those doing even the humblest work to take what is described here as a high-trust perspective of the productive system and their own place in it. Naumova criticizes the view 'that the worker's attitude towards his labours depends, first and foremost, on the degree to which his job is of technical interest to him, i.e. on the nature of the equipment and technology at his disposal and on the level of his skill' (1971: 262). That there is a connection he does not doubt, but he sees it as 'refracted through the specific features of the society in which the given technical facilities function'. The technical nature of labour 'merely intensifies or weakens the effect of the basic, socio-economic factor'. Thus whereas some Western sociologists 'consider that the main cause of the workers' negative attitude towards their work is the fact that technical developments have broken jobs down into narrow, repetitive operations', the real causes are the exploitation, subordination, and dependence which characterize their location in the economic and social structure of Western enterprise and society. Transformation of these features, along with 'direct participation of all members of society in management and administration', has made possible a 'sense of duty' and 'the recognition that every worker's labour is essential for our society'. Naumova therefore conjures up a picture similar in essence to that of Carlson's Raiders. Men who feel that they are playing a respected part in a common endeavour and are not being used in the pursuit of purposes they do not share can submit to low-discretion roles without returning low-trust responses. Naumova is thus using a theoretical model similar in some respects to that developed here. What remains in doubt is how nearly Soviet society approximates to this model. Two considerations must suffice. The obstacles which block men's spontaneous commitment to a given set of ends and means appear to increase with the size and complex differentiation of the exercise, and on the scale of modern industrial society must be considered enormous. Second, commitment of a sort can be promoted through ideological indoctrination, especially given a monopoly of the relevant resources. Since the Soviet's use of this technique on a massive scale is hardly in doubt, any claim that it can be characterized in terms of the Spontaneous Consensus model is suspect.

Admirers of the philosophy satirized in Aldous Huxley's *Brave New World* might wonder whether it matters that the consensus which underpins stability and harmony is engineered rather than spontaneous. Even for the power-holders, however, there are important differences. Earlier it was stated that where ideological indoctrination succeeds in inducing 'full and active legitimation' by the occupants of low-discretion roles they return full high-trust responses. At this point we have to recognize the limitations to the effectiveness of ideological indoctrination of a given kind in situations where men's actual experience is open to a very different interpretation. Here the input of ideological resources may have to be considerable and yet still secure only a partial acceptance. Relevant here is the distinction noted by Mann between '*pragmatic* acceptance, where the individual complies because he perceives no realistic alternative, and *normative* acceptance, where the individual internalizes the moral expectations of the ruling class and views his own inferior positions as legitimate' (1970: 425). This distinction is none the less important for being difficult to operationalize. We can gain clues about the past by noting some subjected groups that were not slow in repudiating certain ruling-class values and norms (e.g. the rights of 'masters' to total prerogative over their 'servants'), as soon as a modicum of greater strength brought repudiation within the realm of possibility, despite the fact of these rights being preached incessantly from the counting house, the magistrate's bench, and the church pulpit. The nearer the acceptance of a given value to the pragmatic end of the continuum, the more vulnerable it is to shifts in power relations which benefit the subjected. We cannot tell, therefore, how far Naumova's respondents are voicing a genuine internalized conviction and how far a skin-deep acquiescence (born of a lack of perceived alternatives) which would quickly disappear were the power structure to change.

Even so, however, it would be a mistake to play down what can be achieved through indoctrination in this type of social structure. In advanced Western societies the ideological support enjoyed by employers, managers, and administrators is a good deal less than this. The difference must not be exaggerated; the socializing agencies of family, school, and communications media offer them, designedly or otherwise, considerable help. In some industrializing societies managers may derive great benefit from, and be able to mobilize and exploit, certain traditional values and orientations. The case of Japan will be examined later; Presthus has also documented relevant features in the Turkish coal mining industry (1961). Even in older centres of industrialization, managers can count on the greater part of the organization they design and many of the values and conventions informing it being accepted, in varying degrees, as legitimate by rank and file participants (Bendix 1963: 249) – though as we have noted this assessment would come up for test were rank and file participants to feel that they had the power to change it if they wished. Much of the acceptance is no doubt a low-key taking-for-granted – which gives point to Mann's argument that the 'most common form of manipulative socialization by the liberal democratic state' is the perpetuation of 'values that do not aid the working-class to interpret the reality it actually experiences' (*Ibid*: 437). But neither organizational leaders themselves nor their many friends enjoy a monopoly of ideological communication, and competing ideologies are disseminated which encourage those in subordinate positions to challenge managerial discretion and values in certain limited fields of decision-making. Neither does management enjoy State support to an extent which enables it forcibly to prevent low-discretion employees from comparing, mutually reinforcing, and collectively expressing their grievances. The absence of these advantages has important consequences for Western management, for it results in a situation where rank and file participants can be neither fully indoctrinated to endorse management's ends and means nor prevented from acting on the divergent orientations which result from this shortfall of indoctrination. For given such a shortfall, it is evident that no spontaneous commitment to a common purpose with management tends to develop among lower-rank members of large work organizations. The provision of goods and services for totally anonymous customers and consumers within a competitive acquisitive society does not, it seems, fire the spirit of those whose contribution to the process is itself anonymous and minuscule. Failing any sustaining and overriding corporate commitment, the frustrations and deprivations of the low-discretion role do not remain at the periphery of consciousness. On the contrary, they tend to occupy the centre of it. Allocated inferior rewards and status, and divorced from most decision-making even where it bears on their own immediate task, occupants of low-discretion roles see those roles not in terms of their being functionally necessary for a joint pursuit of an overriding common purpose, but in terms of their being designed by management to serve its own objectives. In the private sector, rank and file employees perceive their interests as being furthered by management only to the extent that this is compatible with the claims of profit, efficiency or growth; in the public sector, with the claims of the anonymous consumer, taxpayer, government, or some even more remote and unreal abstraction such as 'the national interest'.* Unable or undisposed to commit themselves to top management's objectives, they see their low-discretion roles as expressive of management's intent to use them as instruments towards ends they do not share. And given that managerial control over the propagation of ideology is far short of total, management finds it difficult – though not impossible – to induce them to believe otherwise. The consequence is that the whole panoply of low-discretion control, which would be legitimized as a high-trust pattern by the lower participants were they to see purposes and values as shared, becomes perceived instead in low-trust terms. This tendency has long been prevalent in the West in most medium and large scale work organizations. It explains why the low-discretion syndrome was presented in Chapter 1 as assuming that the occupants of these roles see the close prescription of their behaviour as embodying a management conviction that their work situation cannot be expected to generate identification with management goals.

None of this must be taken to suggest that rank and file participants react against the whole range of managerial discretion. Experience indicates that they usually legitimize, on some level, management's claim to exercise discretion over broad organizational objectives, structure, general strategy, and a high proportion of everyday operational activities. They have shown themselves likely, however, to define certain categories of decisions, such as those

* It is worth noting, however, that there are certain kinds of public service, such as social work, fire fighting, hospitals, armed forces, and the police which lend themselves more readily to attempts by top leaders to convince lower levels that they share a high common purpose which requires the latter to submit willingly to specific rules administered by the former. Even here, any assumption by the former that the latter have no legitimate private interests or constructive part to play in determining the rules may weaken the high-trust bond if the rank and file have aspirations of this kind.

relating to pay, working hours, working arrangements, and job security, as bearing so closely upon their own values and interests that, in the light of top management's divergent goals, they prefer not to vest their trust in management by conceding it full discretion over these decisions. In other words, they no longer fully legitimize the existing pattern of role definitions. The categories of decisions which they deem sufficiently relevant to their values and interests to deter them from legitimizing full managerial discretion show a tendency to increase with rising living standards and increasing education and literacy. Relatively to the total range of decision-making, however, their claims remain modest, and how rapidly they will grow in the future is a matter for conjecture.

It will be as true in the future, however, as it has been in the past, that the frame of reference brought to bear by rank and file upon mangement's 'rights', goals, and values must play a crucial part in shaping the extent and nature of these claims. And one of the major charges made against trade unions, radicals, and so-called 'agitators' by those who wish to promote among low-discretion participants a 'common interests' or high-trust view is that the former promote a 'divergent interests' or low-trust view. It is this latter view, they assert, which breeds attitudes, such as those expressed in phrases like 'them and us' and 'the two sides', that are so inimical to cooperation. Those making this charge are apt to inveigh against the 'ideological' or 'political' content of the perspective they criticize; unaware, presumably, of the ideological and political content of their own.

For all the existence of a low-trust perspective among subordinates, power relations may be such that management is able to enforce its own discretion even on those issues where its claim to prerogative is not legitimized by those affected. Low-discretion subordinates may hold a strongly developed conflict ideology which sees management goals and values as divergent from their own, and which gives rise, therefore, to low-trust perceptions, and yet be unable to express low-trust responses in ways they would prefer. Feeling in no position to mount an effective challenge, subordinates are constrained to acquiesce in the *status quo*. An equilibrium of a sort, therefore, prevails, albeit one characterized partly by a forced compliance underpinned by power.

As we have noted, it will be quite otherwise for the occupants of the high-discretion roles in this same organizational situation. They have been invited to join the fraternity of important decision-makers – the controllers and their specialist advisers and colleagues – and they are rewarded accordingly. In reciprocation of the diffuse invitation extended to them, they are expected to use their discretion to support the goals and values of this favoured high-trust group. Does this demonstrate, then, that the answer to our second question – whether high-discretion roles necessarily imply high-trust relations – must be yes? Again, the introduction of power into the analysis shows that this is not so.

We may start by noting that while the division of labour presided over by top management must, in a society which sets so much store by maximizing the return on resources, include a considerable measure of economic rationality, there has to be room in our framework for many forms of behaviour which do not serve economic values, including nepotism, sinecures, unquestioned assumptions, and sheer inertia. Of special significance for this context is that management may include certain work roles in its division of labour which it would prefer for economic reasons to redefine along different lines but does not. The reason is that the occupants of these roles are individually or, more probably, collectively powerful enough to deter management from redefining their roles. Some may object to having their discretion enlarged, but more often this situation arises when management wishes to reduce the discretion vested in a given role or set of roles, either because the loyalty, dedication, goals, or commitment of the occupant are suspect, or because some gain of efficiency through technological or organizational change presents itself. Except in a small minority of situations, management's power would be fully equal to the task of imposing a redefinition of roles upon recalcitrant occupants but its assessment may be that the benefits would not justify the costs of the illwill and dislocation likely to ensue. In these circumstances management feels it must tolerate the exercise of a significant degree of discretion by those whom it does not wholly trust or whose work role it would like, for efficiency reasons, to modify. Such a situation accords with the paradoxical usage described where one party feels constrained to submit to the discretion of another but has only a qualified confidence in the outcome; a usage in which the phrase 'We've got to trust them' means in fact: 'We don't trust them but feel constrained to submit to their discretion.' This simply describes, of course, a power relationship.

One example is that of manual craftsmen. Historically vulnerable to the rationalizing drives of mechanization and industrial engineering, they have long mobilized their highly solidaristic occupational subculture in a collective and frequently militant defence of their superior status and its attendant privileges. Many employers and managements have considered it less troublesome to acquiesce in the craftsmen's own role definitions rather than try to impose the lower-discretion roles which economic rationality might appear to suggest. Periodically some groups of employers have made different calculations and challenged the craftsmen to what have proved to be bitter and prolonged power struggles (Clegg, Fox, and Thompson 1964: Chapter 4).

The craftsmen's choice of this collective power strategy as the means of protection and advancement was made the easier for them by the fact that their role discretion was not sufficient to turn their thoughts, as individuals, towards possible membership of the favoured fraternity. They have been less racked than are some 'middle-range discretion' groups today by disagreements as to whether their best chance lay in militant collective action or in trying to gain or retain a place in the high-trust fraternity – a strategy which might be furthered by collective action but certainly not of the kind based on a conflict stance and an assertion of divergent goals.

Another example of the high-discretion, low-trust situation might be that of the scientist or other professional who has much to offer top management in terms of expertise but is thought to be less than wholeheartedly behind its goals and values, perhaps because, like craftsmen, he shares those of an independent, horizontally structured occupational or professional group. With its confidence in him thus qualified, top management may exclude him from its counsels and thereby structure an element of distrust into the relationship.

The upshot of these two sets of exceptions, therefore, is that the reason why low-discretion roles do not necessarily imply low-trust relations, nor high-discretion roles high-trust relations, has to do with whether goals are perceived as shared or divergent. In order that low-discretion work be accompanied by the full low-discretion syndrome, and thus susceptible of characterization as a low-trust pattern, the occupants of such roles must perceive their situation as being due to management's distrust of their ability or willingness to pursue management's goals. Conversely, for high-discretion work to be accompanied by the relevant syndrome as a high-trust pattern, superiors must not be conceding high discretion only under the pressures of power, for this implies that they believe their purposes would ideally be better served by other arrangements.

The initial exposition of the discretion syndromes in Chapter 1 therefore made certain assumptions which are justified for working purposes by the high probabilities inherent in Western industrial societies. Experience has shown a growing tendency for occupants of low-discretion roles to perceive superiors in low-trust terms of divergent goals, while occupants of high-discretion roles are usually perceived by superiors in high-trust terms. Yet it needs to be remembered that the alternative possibilities exist, for otherwise we cannot make sociological sense of patterns which existed in the past and survive today, in the West and elsewhere.

Both types of exception are of considerable theoretical interest in that they set us on the way to exploring the dynamics of trust relations. As a necessary prelude to this exploration the importance of power needs to be emphasized. The preceding analysis shows not only how power can enable top management to impose low-discretion roles despite the withholding of legitimacy by their occupants, but also how top management may feel constrained to acquiesce in certain roles wielding higher discretion than it would prefer; both of which situations imply low-trust relations. From this we can draw a general proposition. To the extent that role definitions are imposed by one party upon another, i.e., to the extent that the latter is conscious of accepting the given definition under constraint rather than extending to it the willing compliance implied in legitimizing it, the act of imposition will be perceived by the constrained party as evidence that goals are divergent, and will both express and aggravate low-trust relations. Two of the examples from which this proposition was drawn describe the assertion by *subordinates* of high-discretion definitions of their own roles; definitions in which their superiors feel constrained to acquiesce. Historically it is the reverse situation which has prevailed, and which prevails today. Superiors have been able to impose upon subordinates low-discretion roles which excluded them from participation in decision-making not only about objectives and the technological and organizational means employed to pursue them, but also about the allocation of rewards and privileges, including of course their own. Later we shall trace, *inter alia*, the dynamics by which trade unionism, collective bargaining, and much else besides have emerged as responses to this situation. Before this stage is reached, however, some elaboration is required not only of the concept of power but also of the concept of reciprocity which has appeared at various points in the exposition.

Reciprocity and Power

Many anthropologists, sociologists, and others have stressed the central importance in all social life, traditional and modern, of the principle of reciprocity (Gouldner 1960). Reciprocation of goods, services, favours or plain goodwill is seen as having a stabilizing, sustaining, and nourishing effect on social systems, and according to Gouldner can be hypothesized as being 'no less universal and important an element of culture than the incest taboo . . .' (*Ibid*: 171). What is less frequently noted in the literature is that there can be reciprocation of negative as well as of positive acts and sentiments. Along with spiralling trust there exists, as we have already seen, the possibility of spiralling distrust. Men reciprocate suspicion as well as confidence. It is only the latter that Gouldner has in mind when he asserts that 'Although reciprocal relations stabilize patterns, it need not follow that a lack of reciprocity is socially impossible or invariably disruptive of the patterns involved' (*Ibid*: 164). Elsewhere he notes that the less reciprocal the relationship the less likely it is to persist '*unless compensatory mechanisms are present*' (1959, his italics). Two such mechanisms which have emerged in the preceding analysis are first, power, and second, legitimacy derived from goal consensus or from a cultural value which bestows unquestioning acceptance on managerial rule. If we now apply these propositions to work roles the dynamics of their change and development begin to emerge.

The relationship between top management and the occupant of a high-discretion role can usefully be explored, as we have seen, with the aid of a model characterized as a reciprocal balance of high trust in which each bears towards the other a sense of diffuse long term obligation. The relationship between top management and the occupant of a low-discretion role, on the other hand, is one of imbalance of reciprocity. In the situation that exists before trade unions partially redress the balance, top management requires of the low-discretion subordinate a range of specific duties and obligations which it enforces by controls and sanctions, while at the same time it retains discretion over his rights and privileges. It refuses to place itself in trust to the employee's behaviour, but forces him to place himself in trust to management's. While specifically bound in what he is obliged to give, the employee is dependent on grace and favour for what he hopes to receive.

This situation of imbalance can be supported by either of the two compensatory mechanisms already mentioned. On the one hand, there may be a spontaneous commitment by subordinates to shared goals and a readiness on their part to comply willingly with the requirements of low-discretion roles. Even in the absence of spontaneous commitment in this sense there may be acceptance of a cultural value which unquestioningly legitimizes management rule and thereby accepts management definition of objectives and of the roles necessary for pursuing them. Alternatively, superior management power may be used to enforce an imbalance of reciprocity even where it is not legitimized. What may pass, on superficial observation, for an employee legitimation of such an imbalance may be no more than submission to *force majeure*. Historical retrospect may fall into the same error, lacking precise evidence. It is significant that when nineteenth century trade booms brought labour scarcity and a marginal shift in the balance of power, many employee groups were quick to manifest low-trust responses. This suggests that legitimation was either absent or only, to use Mann's term, pragmatic, and that when a little power came to hand it was promptly used in an effort to reduce the imbalance.

A decline in the strength of compensatory mechanisms of the first kind will throw a greater burden on those of the second if the intention is to maintain the imbalance. In other words, to the extent that the legitimacy of managerial prerogative in the eyes of the governed suffers a decline, an increased exercise of power will be required to enforce the imbalance of reciprocity. In arguing thus we are implying an hypothesis which must now be made explicit. The hypothesis is that, in the absence of shared goals or some other legitimizing principle which leads those subjected to an imbalance to offer willing compliance with it, they will be disposed to take steps to reduce the imbalance and will only be prevented from doing so by consciousness of superior power.*

* See also, in this context, Adams's discussion of the dynamics introduced

If we examine some probabilities in the situation where top management enjoys an imbalance of reciprocity against occupants of low-discretion roles, we see that there are two directions in which the latter can act. They can try to enlarge their own discretion and they can try to reduce that of top management. Both lines of action can be pursued on either an individual basis or through a collective effort along with others conscious of sharing a common position. Enlargement of their own discretion may or may not be accompanied by an effort to have this enlargement recognized and acknowledged by top management. The rewards to the individual or the group of an increase in discretion may not require knowledge of it by higher authority; indeed may require ignorance or at least connivance. The individual or group may thus set aside the formal rules, roles, and relations, and work to others which serve their purposes better. Prescriptive rules governing the pace and methods of work, for example, may be replaced by individual or group practices which embody greater autonomy. The rewards may be intrinsic, in giving greater satisfaction with the work itself, or extrinsic, in giving, for example, greater control on such issues as job security or the creation of more overtime at premium rates of pay. The rewards accruing from an enlargement of discretion may, however, require for their realization that top management make explicit acknowledgement of it. Here we return to the point made earlier that the greater the discretion vested in a role the more spontaneously and generously top management is likely to reward its occupant in the hope of winning him over to their goals and values. This is the essential truth of a theme explored by Crozier. 'Subordinates try to increase their amount of discretion and utilize it to oblige higher-ups to pay more for their cooperation' (1964: 111, 160).

This illuminates the significance of discretion as a source of power. '. . . workers who have been restricted by scientific work-organization to a completely stereotyped task use every available means to regain enough unpredictability in their behaviour to enhance their low bargaining power' (*Ibid*: 162). Crozier also illustrates the kind of strategy appropriate to a defence of existing discretion by examining the behaviour of maintenance workers in one particular plant. 'Their strategy is . . . to keep the area under their own control free from

into an exchange relationship by perceptions of inequity (Adams 1963, 1965; Telly *et al.* 1971; Goodman and Friedman 1971).

outside interference. For this purpose, they prevent both production workers and supervisors from dealing in any way with machine maintenance. . . . Maintenance and repair problems must be kept secret. No explanation is ever given. Production workers must not understand. Maintenance workers keep their skill itself as a rule-of-thumb skill. They completely disregard all blueprints and maintenance directions, and have been able to make them disappear from the plants. They believe in individual settings exclusively, and they are the only ones to know those settings' (*Ibid*: 153). A common element is apparent as between this strategy, which in essence if not detail is that of all craft groups, and the strategy of the professions, which seek to maintain a situation in which 'the client public sees a mystery in the tasks to be performed, a mystery which it is not given to the ordinary man to acquire' (Wilensky 1964: 149).

Besides seeking to enlarge their own discretion, individuals and groups trying to modify an imbalance of reciprocity can seek to limit the discretion of those in the superior position. In other words they try to bind the behaviour of superiors by inducing them to commit themselves to certain specified rules on matters important for those in the inferior position. Just as superiors seek to protect themselves against an unfavourable exercise of discretion on the part of subordinates by replacing part of that discretion with prescriptive rules, so subordinates may aspire to do likewise with respect to superiors. An agreement about a wage rate, in being a prescriptive rule, limits the discretion of top management and thereby protects those covered by it. Clearly their conviction that they need protection embodies a belief that top management is governing with other interests in mind than theirs. This belief we have seen to be specially characteristic of low-discretion roles, whether in the private sector or the public. The disposition to seek protection by limiting management's discretion extends to all those spheres of managerial action in respect of which subordinates feel they have values or interests which they are not prepared to entrust to unilateral management decision.

Disposition, however, is one thing; its expression in practical forms is another. Whether individuals or groups are able to reduce an imbalance of reciprocity upheld by power depends on their being able to mobilize sufficient counterpower. Top management may impose a low-discretion role on subordinates: can subordinates muster enough power to reduce the discretion of top management on matters important to them? Power becomes the more important with the tendency of the dynamics of this type of situation to generate a spiral of institutionalized distrust. This tendency we may term the low-trust dynamic.

The Dynamics of Low-Trust Relations

The low-trust dynamic appears most commonly in the relations between top management and the occupants of low-discretion roles. It begins with one party initiating a change in those relations in a low-trust direction. The other may accept and legitimize the change. More probably it counters with low-trust responses of its own provided it can mobilize whatever degree of power is necessary. The full range of possible low-trust responses is wide and some of them have already emerged. They can be made on either an individual or a collective basis. They include attempts to limit, by means of prescriptive rules, the discretion of the other party on matters deemed important; a disinclination to increase one's own contribution to the exchange without a guaranteed specific reciprocation; an extreme 'win-lose' or 'zero-sum' approach to this bargaining process; a tendency to perceive and interpret the behaviour, communications, policies, or values of the other side as being antipathetic to one's own interests and concerns; and such forms of behaviour as indifferent performance, clock-watching, and high absence, sickness, wastage or turnover rates, which may in varying degrees symptomize the individual's inability to see himself as participating in a fellowship of common purpose and shared endeavour.*

Our statement of the dynamic is as yet far from complete. We have to define, in theoretical terms, not only the mechanisms which initiate a given sequence but also those which bring it to an end – for the spiral of distrust develops intermittently rather than continuously. It is useful to begin with the notion of equilibrium as defined earlier; namely as prevailing when superiors and subordinates are, for the time being, acquiescing in the existing pattern of role definitions. Low-discretion subordinates may have their behaviour closely

* These symptoms are complex phenomena and are offered here simply as possibilities. Some workers may focus on earnings to the total exclusion of any interest or involvement in managerial purposes and for this very reason, should they be on piecework, for example, maintain high effort, attendance, and time-keeping.

prescribed by superiors but no scope for prescribing the behaviour of superiors – behaviour which includes the allocation of rewards as well as administration of all the other aspects of organizational functioning. This equilibrium may, as we have seen, be enforced by power which the subjected party lacks the ability or the motivation to challenge. It may, alternatively, be supported by sentiments of legitimation. The former can often, of course, promote the latter – a given pattern of division of labour and role relations which was imposed by power in the first place may come to be legitimized by employees. There may or may not in a given situation be joint regulation of certain issues by management and worker representatives. The existence of collective bargaining by no means precludes the kind of equilibrium stability to which we are referring. The area of regulation may remain constant if aspirations, the balance of power, the division of labour, and the pattern of work organization change only very slowly. In such a situation both sides may acquiesce in the prevailing pattern of discretion and decision-making.

One or more factors can disturb this equilibrium and trigger off a fresh sequence of low-trust dynamics. A disturbance in equilibrium occurs when one of the parties seeks to allocate discretion along different lines from those currently prevailing by securing a redefinition of work roles. Examples occur when management applies work study, controls, or mechanical devices in order to reduce further the discretion in manual roles, or when the discretion in its own role is reduced by having to submit to collective agreements and procedures for appeal against its decisions. One type of low-trust move by management specially liable to evoke retaliation occurs when specific rules which management has allowed to be laxly or diffusely applied are suddenly enforced in their full specificity. A degree of give and take in the application of rules is characteristic of most organizations and represents, of course, a measure of trust. Should management decide, suddenly and without consultation, to apply certain of the rules with rigorous precision, this will be seen as a hostile and aggressive act and countered accordingly. Management enjoys a public relations advantage, however, in the conflict that follows by being able to assert that it is doing no more than applying the rules. If the rules in question are included in a collective agreement its case may appear particularly strong to the uninformed eye, for the employees can be presented as perversely and anarchically resisting the application of jointly negotiated rules whereas management can rest on the cry: 'We are only trying to operate the agreement.'

It follows from the preceding arguments that any disturbance of equilibrium expressed through a reallocation of discretion must be due either to a shift in power relations or to a change in sentiments of legitimation, or to a combination of the two. A shift of power from management to the managed, whether fortuitous or engineered, may enable subordinates to offer a challenge that is inspired by sentiments which they have long cherished but hitherto been unable to manifest in action. It may also, of course, stimulate wholly new aspirations and sentiments which have not previously emerged simply because no prospect existed of realizing them. The same possibilities might lie for top management given a power shift in the other direction. Disturbance may also originate from a feeling by either subordinates or top management that they can no longer legitimize the existing distribution of discretion because it violates certain of their values or fails to secure certain of their interests.

What follows the disturbance of the equilibrium depends on whether the disturbance takes a low-trust or a high-trust direction. Since we are presently concerned with the former we shall assume that subordinates, no longer prepared to acquiesce in the prevailing degree of imbalance, try to limit the discretion of their superiors on certain matters important to them. In so doing they manifest an institutionalized distrust of management, thereby strengthening a management belief in a divergence of goals which disposes it to manifest counter-expressions of distrust towards subordinates. The forms which these can take are many, but all represent a further shift from the (diffuse) social exchange end of the continuum towards the (specific) economic exchange end. Further reciprocation of low trust by subordinates may impart another twist to the spiral.

Nothing in this analysis should be taken to imply that these moves and counter-moves necessarily follow each other quickly over a brief time scale. We are dealing here with broad shifts in social relations which may move slowly. Neither does the analysis suggest that the spiralling of distrust continues indefinitely. The party initiating the disturbance, having secured the particular enlargement of its own discretion or the particular limitation of the other party's discretion which it sought, may be happy to settle for the new equilibrium. To push further may be seen as not legitimate, or as involving a power struggle which threatens greater costs than benefits. Over the long term, however, a probability is created of a spiralling of distrust as subordinates aspire to contest managerial discretion over a widening range of organizational issues. Each side develops a frame of reference marked by suspicious vigilance towards the other. Within the terms of a given employment contract, no favour is granted unless a balancing favour is returned. The inclination is for each to measure both his own and the other's contribution with increasing precision. Such characteristics are of course the very stuff of economic as against social exchange.

How do these institutionalized low-trust relations interact with trust on the personal level, i.e., with high or low trust between specific individuals? A full treatment of this theme would be a major exercise which, important though it is, could only be a considerable diversion in a book concerned to explore institutionalized trust. We must limit ourselves here to noting certain salient points. Low or high trust on the personal level can affect men's structuring of behaviours and interactions at the institutionalized level. For example, a manager or supervisor may be determined, by his beliefs and assumptions not only about men in general but also about certain specific men in particular, in the way he structures their role and the rules and interactions he defines for them. Shop stewards may be determined by their distrust of a particular manager in the precision with which they seek to pin him down to specific rules and procedures. But these are complex phenomena and other possibilities would need careful exploration. The manager or supervisor may consider that although personally he trusts some subordinates and distrusts others, he would lose more than he gained by trying to discriminate and must extend to all the same degree of institutionalized trust or distrust. The personal trust felt by a shop steward or trade union officer towards an employer or manager may not mitigate the institutionalized distrust through which they seek to limit his discretion on issues important to them. The characteristic situation in industrial countries where collective bargaining is well developed is of confrontation between mutually suspicious hard bargainers who in personal terms respect, trust, and possibly even like each other.

It is certainly possible, however, for an organizational leader to inspire relationships of personal trust with occupants of low-discretion roles which mitigate the severities of the low-trust dynamic or even inhibit it altogether. In the extreme case of this sort, one might wish to define the situation as one where, through these personal high-trust relations, the leader is succeeding in maintaining among subordinates a sense of shared goals or full legitimation of managerial prerogative or both. This, as we saw earlier, describes a low-discretion high-trust situation. It is in contexts of this sort that the emergence of a low-trust dynamic can prove a severe shock for management. An example can be offered which illustrates this point and shows how the theoretical equipment presented here can suggest ways of interpreting practical situations. A paternalist family firm of long standing operates a pattern of high-trust relations with its low-discretion employees. Gradually, however, and perhaps unnoticed by management, its legitimacy becomes eroded by changing values, rising aspirations, and unfavourable comparisons by employees between their conditions of employment and those prevailing elsewhere. Management power nevertheless maintains the reciprocity imbalance by which it closely regulates employees' behaviour towards itself but retains full discretion over its own treatment of employees. Eventually a grievance common to all employees unites them in a dramatic repudiation of management authority and out of this crisis emerges stable union organization which, representing as it now does occupants of low-discretion roles in low-trust relationships with management, reciprocates by seeking to impose low-trust rules upon management. Demands are made that management commit itself to joint representative procedures for handling claims and grievances, and through them to agreed wage scales, working hours, overtime and holiday arrangements, and perhaps other features of the work situation. Employees come to view their employment relationship increasingly as one of economic exchange. They become increasingly disinclined to 'go the second mile' or to give management the benefit of any doubt. Less and less is the relationship one in which the employee extends to management some benefit or favour for which no short term specific reciprocation is made but for which he confidently expects some long term diffuse return.

Not all employees, to be sure, welcome these changes. There may in the earlier stages be something of a rift between those who want to push forward with the new low-trust regulation of management, seeing this as the pattern of the future, and those who feel a nostalgia for the past, regret the disappearance of the old régime when the current scion of the family dynasty took a personal interest, and dislike what they perceive as the formalistic impersonal flavour of the new order. Management, for its part, is likely to evince shock, disappointment, and resentment at what it sees as a retrogressive change in labour relations. It is likely to accuse the trade union of destroying long-established relationships of trust between itself and its employees. It is nevertheless likely to compound these changes with low-trust gestures of its own. The trend towards increasingly specific formalization of relations can take many different forms. Work may become more closely monitored and checked. Errors, misjudgements, or other inadequacies of performance come to be viewed more punitively. The diffuse 'slack' in the employment relationship gradually becomes tightened up. Small indulgences are eliminated; requests for 'time off' examined more critically; lateness and absence measured, recorded, and punished; applications for treatment over and beyond that required by the formal contract grudgingly received and decreasingly likely to be granted. The pound of flesh is weighed with increasing care. All these are signs that the low-trust dynamic is in operation.*

We need now, however, to note more systematically the sources of change which may initiate the sequence. The approach so far has been to assume the disturbance of equilibrium to come from the employees' side. Rising aspirations on their part may galvanize them into action stemming from unfavourable comparisons between their own rewards and those of others. Leadership from a union hierarchy outside the plant which is pursuing a policy of negotiating certain standardized practices throughout its membership domain may also

* An approximation to this sequence may be in process in one corner of the academic world. The stirrings among Oxbridge college 'servants' such as porters, scouts, and kitchen staff to unionize themselves will provide a test situation for the hypothesis of the low-trust dynamic. Their relations with college governing bodies have traditionally been highly diffuse, and reveal many examples of occupants of humble roles offering high-trust loyalty and dedication reciprocated by the colleges with paternalistic *ex gratia* help and support where needed. In so far as these employees come to perceive this pattern of relations as giving them inadequate protection they will move towards what is described here as a low-trust pattern. We would expect college governing bodies to reciprocate by reviewing, on a more calculative economic-exchange basis, such diffuse, *ex gratia* gestures as they have been wont to extend, and perhaps by tightening up relations more generally in some of the ways suggested above. We would also expect some members of both sides to deplore this trend.

provide the stimulus. But equally, of course, the disequilibrating factor may come from the management side. Technological or organizational innovation may result in increased division of labour and increasingly specific work roles. Growing size of organization may be thought by top management to need tighter coordination and control. Organizational leaders may come under stricter external accountability and feel that this requires, for their own protection, closer and more punitive internal accountability. Changing perceptions among top management may promote increased distrust of lower-rank motivations. Any one of these may disturb a prevailing acquiescence in the existing state of the reciprocity imbalance, and initiate a new twist to the spiral of institutionalized distrust.

When the organization has come to include procedures for collective bargaining and grievance settlement, along with new roles such as shop steward, union officer, and their managerial counterparts, there exists an additional area of social structure upon which the two sides can direct these institutional expressions of low-trust attitudes. Employee representatives may seek, for example, to bind managerial behaviour within these procedures more specifically and formally by precise formulation of the successive stages through which disputes must pass and of the maximum time allocation at each stage. They may try to limit management choices in day-to-day administration by insisting on the right to refer every proposed managerial departure from the *status quo* to the disputes procedure for negotiation. Conversely, management may try to prescribe the role of the steward or union officer more closely and formally, or to enlarge its own discretion by insisting that some areas of decision-making be recognized as within managerial prerogative and thereby free of procedural challenge.

Everything said so far in elucidating the low-trust dynamic has linked it with low-discretion roles. The same approach may also help, however, to cast light on certain situations higher in the status scale. 'The centralization of planful reflection and the consequent expropriation of individual rationality parallel the rationalization of the white-collar hierarchy as a whole. What a single individual used to do is now broken up into functions of decision and research, direction and checking up, each performed by a separate group of individuals. Many executive functions are thus becoming less autonomous and permitting less initiative. The centralization of reflection entails for many the deprivation of initiative: for them, decision becomes the application of fixed rules . . .' (Mills 1956: 140–1). Some middle managers, for example, are finding that as a consequence of computerization their roles have been 'greatly reduced in size and responsibility' (Mumford 1964: 30); others that the growing size of the management structure, or the absorption of their company in amalgamations and takeovers, perhaps by multinational concerns, has been followed by tighter controls and procedures for monitoring, checking, and sanctioning their performance. Even though events may not go this far, increasing size of the management team can promote a trend towards bureaucratizing managerial terms and conditions of employment which is itself a move in the low-trust direction. Managers may 'become so numerous that they constitute a work force of their own' and it becomes necessary 'to treat them as a category and not as individuals'. The organization has 'to create a bureaucratic set of rules in order to treat managers by standardized procedures'. This depersonalization tends to evoke low-trust reciprocation. 'Bureaucratic rules and standardized procedures call forth appeals from the application of these rules' (Goldner 1965: 79–80). This is another way of saying that the individual appealing is not prepared to accept higher management's exercise of its discretion – essentially a low-trust situation. If previously accustomed to high-trust relations where more diffuse and long-term expectations prevailed, managers may consider that these changes, representing as they do a reduction in the institutionalized trust embodied in top management policies, throws out of equilibrium the psychological contract they had with the company. Accustomed to an assumption that they are giving maximum performance in the service of company ends – an assumption promoting free and open confidence between colleagues who accept each other as equals – they now find themselves watched, measured, evaluated, and otherwise regulated by systematic, perhaps even quantitative, criteria. They reciprocate by reducing their commitment to the company and by weighing their contribution in a more calculating spirit. Should they come to feel excluded from the high-discretion fraternity altogether they may decide that to take up a conflict stance against the company by joining a militant white-collar union will damage their prospects less than union membership will improve them. Participation in militant union behaviour will, by defining their role on a 'divergent interests' basis, unquestionably disqualify them from fraternity treatment, but if the prospects of receiving such treatment already seem dim little may be lost.

Such responses are clearly not inevitable, since they depend on the nature of the psychological contract. Middle managers reared in a culture which teaches them to expect and approve top management efforts to promote efficiency and growth by closely monitoring performance at every level will more readily legitimize such practices when directed at themselves. This expectation becomes structured into their psychological contract and, when realized, does not trigger off low-trust dynamics of the sort just examined.

As in the case of low-discretion roles, however, high-discretion subordinates themselves may supply a disequilibrating impulse. Despite enjoying high-trust relations with superiors, they may come to compare their salaries unfavourably with those paid for work of a comparable kind in other industries or occupations. If their skills are transferable they may trickle away as individuals. If not they may decide that collective representations to top management are called for. The leaders of this movement may well include some of the most alert and ambitious. Depending on the strategy chosen, their relations with top management will either remain within the shared assumptions and understandings of the high-discretion fraternity or sharpen and break out into a conflict pattern, in which case one would expect top management to reciprocate this expression of low trust with similar manifestations of their own.

Increasing size of organization may cause professionals, too, in the middle and upper ranges of discretion to feel that their position as individuals has been weakened to a degree where they are no longer able to trust top management as before. The United Kingdom Association of Professional Engineers adduced, in its manifesto, the rationalization of firms through amalgamation and takeover as one major factor which was making the individual relationship with management increasingly unsatisfactory. '. . . with employing bodies becoming even larger and more remote, it is becoming increasingly difficult for the individual to negotiate from a position strong enough to secure fair treatment. His position is becoming more insecure. . . .' The Association could hardly have illustrated the low-trust dynamic more aptly than with its comment: 'Loyalty cannot persist indefinitely if loyalty is not offered in return . . .' (Dickens 1972: 14). Thus a consciousness that changing circumstances are nudging members of the occupation towards the outer fringes of the high-trust fraternity may result in collective action coming to seem the best strategy. Yet the uneasy mixture of tactics to which this may give rise is likewise illustrated by the U.K.A.P.E., which as yet clearly aspires to maintain its claim to membership of the high-trust fraternity. Strikes are seen as 'prejudicial to the public interest to which the professional engineer's code bids him have full regard'. The engineer has a duty to act in a 'fiduciary manner toward clients and employers, towards others with whom his work is concerned and towards other members'. The Association also refers to the loyalty that professional engineers instinctively feel for their employer'. It specifically eschews links with the Labour Party and the Trades Union Congress (Dickens 1972: 11–12).

Goldstein's analysis of the changing position and strategy of professional engineers in America likewise leads itself to interpretation in the light of the framework used here. He describes them as increasingly conscious of rationalization and division of labour. Their job role is becoming specialized and they may lose the capacity to do work 'involving the consistent exercise of discretion and judgement' (1955: 201). They are also beginning to recognize that their chances of moving up into the higher ranks of management are lessening. In short, one consequence of 'the large-scale employment of professionals in industry is that it becomes necessary for management to deal with them as but another part of the labor force – precisely what the professional is seeking to avoid' (*Ibid*: 200). But these sources of unease are usually, argues Goldstein, 'more than balanced by the basically pro-management orientation of the professional. He tends to accept the prevailing beliefs in individualism and free enterprise, conceives of his work as part of the managerial function, and may even envision himself in a management position at the end of his career line' (*Ibid*: 201). In other words, he still hopes, by manifesting the appropriate behaviours and beliefs, to retain high-trust fraternity status. This hope informs the strategy and ideology of his union. In situations of disagreement with higher authority the union emphasis is on the methods of problem solving and rational discussion between equals. 'The stronger the adherence to the professional component of the status as salaried employee, the greater the reluctance to see personnel policies and conditions of employment as grievances. In contract negotiations, the emphasis is on "acting like gentlemen" instead of "pounding the table", on placing the plain facts before management rather than relying on "emotion". . . . The emphasis is on educating management . . . to understand that better treatment will result in better work. The general strategy appears to be one of winning management over by reason, over a period of years, to the point where the engineer will be accorded the prestige and financial reward to which he feels he is entitled' (*Ibid*: 204). In a later study Goldstein shows even more clearly that they seek to define and conduct collective bargaining as a high-trust, problem solving integrative process. They see it 'as a process of exchange whereby two parties present facts that must be evaluated in an attempt to reach a mutually beneficial contract' (1959: 327). Their attitude to the strike weapon is consistent with this approach – the relationship with the employer should not be 'a power struggle'.

But, as Dickens observes, these careful repudiations of a conflict, low-trust stance are 'not necessarily a lasting characteristic of the professional union'. Higher authority may not choose to reciprocate these high-trust gestures. '. . . engineers will grant that the employer often behaves as though' the relationship *were* a power struggle (Goldstein 1959: 327). Persistence by the employer in these low-trust policies and attitudes is likely eventually to evoke a revision of strategy by the professional union. Dickens notes that since this moderate approach has come to be seen by professional unions as failing them they have begun to resort to strike action, and that similar tendencies are visible in Britain and, for example, Israel (1972a: 7).

We would expect to find low-trust responses of one kind or another emerging, too, from certain changes in some (certainly not all) situations of scientific teamwork as described by Hagstrom (1964). The two traditional forms of such teamwork, the free collaboration of peers and the professor-student group, both have 'elements of technical irrationality'. In the terms of the present analysis, both are highly diffuse, high-trust structures. But 'just as the modern corporation has supplanted free partnership and apprenticeship in industry, so a more complex form of organization may be supplanting free collaboration and the professor-student association in science. Both changes involve the development of a more complex division of labour, the separation of the worker from the tools of production, and greater centralization of authority' (*Ibid*: 251). Prominent among these developments is the emergence of the salaried specialist technician who is expected neither to choose the research goals, nor to make research decisions, nor to be committed to the solution of scientific problems. He solves technical difficulties in return for specific money rewards instead of for diffuse professional recognition; is capable of alienating himself from his work; and is not expected to 'be strongly committed to the norms and goals of science since he is paid not to have commitments which get in the way of others' (*Ibid*: 254). Here, then, we see the introduction into scientific teamwork of a low-trust element.

In some situations the occupants of relatively high-discretion roles come under external pressure, along with management, to accept trade unionism and collective bargaining. Industries and services in Britain's public sector, for example, have to meet statutory requirements in this respect – the 'density of white-collar unionism in the public sector of the economy is over 80 per cent while in the private sector it is just slightly over 10 per cent'; a fact due principally to government encouragement and the favourable climate it produced (Bain 1970: 39, 181). Staff departments in organizations newly brought under public ownership may therefore undergo significant changes in their institutionalized trust relations. If previously non-union, they probably operated on a pattern of diffuse, high-trust, give and take relationships between superiors and subordinates. Brought by union organization and joint regulation within an ambit of increased specificity and formalization of rights and obligations, they may become caught up willy-nilly in the low-trust dynamic, with both sides moving towards more measured and calculative attitudes. To identify such a trend, if indeed systematic research as against casual impressions prove it to exist, would not by itself imply any overall judgement that a change for the worse had occurred, any more than the increasingly low-trust relations created by industrialization could in themselves be seen as evidence for an overall deterioration in the social condition. Many other factors would enter into the assessment – such as whether the original high-trust situation had approximated more to the Spontaneous Consensus or to the Power model; what men were conscious of gaining and losing by the change; and what values were represented by group self-determination.

The Dynamics of High-Trust Relations

We have examined the dynamics of low-trust relations, seen as a process by which an imbalance of reciprocity is redressed by one side in a low-trust direction, leading to low-trust counter-moves by the other provided it has the necessary power and no reason for legitimizing the new pattern. We now have to ask whether the reverse process can occur. There is ample evidence that it can. Management may introduce technological or organizational change which significantly enlarges the discretionary element in certain roles or categories of roles. In accordance with the tendencies implied in the high-trust syndrome, this is likely to be accompanied by additional changes which we have characterized as a movement towards a high-trust work design. On the assumption that this trend is legitimized by the role occupants, they are likely to offer high-trust reciprocation, thus promoting a spiral towards diffuse as against specific obligations; social as against economic exchange. This is the same effect, of course, as is created by promoting a given individual through a series of posts each vested with greater discretion than the one before. It is usual for an individual moving thus up the hierarchy to display an increasing intensity of commitment to, and identification with, the organization and its imputed interests.

In the situation with which we are concerned here, however, we may suppose top management, for purely economic reasons and without thought of the social and behavioural implications, to introduce certain technological or organizational changes which vest some roles with a significantly higher degree of discretion than before. Certain implications then emerge which we have examined in the context of the high-discretion syndrome. It becomes apparent that high-discretion roles call for a set of high-trust rules, relations, and modes of conduct on top management's part that are quite different from those deemed appropriate to low-discretion roles. If they are not observed the full potentialities of high-discretion work will not be realized. Thus the low-trust rules and modes of managerial behaviour thought fitting for low-discretion roles no longer secure management's purposes in the new context. In that sense, management no longer legitimizes them for the new high-discretion roles, and therefore changes them.

In describing these operations of the high-trust dynamic we are employing a concept which we have seen to be crucial for the theoretical analysis. This is the concept of legitimacy. The case has been presented of management significantly enlarging the discretionary element of a given role or set of roles and introducing other changes which enter into the high-discretion syndrome. The proposition was then advanced that provided this trend is legitimized by the role occupant or occupants, they are likely to reciprocate in ways which generate high-trust relations. But they may not legitimize it. Some may reject the opportunity to exercise greater discretion in their work, either because they are psychologically structured to need dependency and submissiveness, or because they have been so strongly shaped by their subculture and their own adaptive responses to low-discretion work that the change is seen as distasteful and threatening.

Another important possibility is that some work groups will gladly accept greater discretion in their work but yet reject some of the crucial accompanying elements in the higher-discretion pattern that is being offered them by management. They reject the invitation to behave according to the principles of shared goals and values, open communications, diffuse obligations, and mutual confidence. Why should they adopt such a stance? The reason would lie in their having internalized an ideology, too entrenched to be reversed, which enjoins them to be permanently wary of management and its policies. They may, for example, be members of a craft group with a traditional doctrine of eternal vigilance which seeks to ensure that management, however seductive and subtle its wooing, does not undermine the defences on which the long-run security and rewards of the craft depend. While the members of such a group would be very ready to have their discretion enlarged – and would certainly fight strongly any proposal to reduce it – they would be keenly suspicious of any accompanying implications, conveyed by managerial words or deeds, that they should now drop their guard, abandon their stance of divergent interests, and generally behave according to the mutual-confidence implications of a higher-trust work pattern. In other words, they would not be legitimizing management's attempt to promote a high-trust situation and would not, therefore, be reciprocating with high-trust behaviour of their own. Similar resistance to a high-trust invitation might be encountered from a non-craft group in an industry or occupation with a long and bitter history of labour relations which has left employees with a deep-rooted, institutionalized legacy of distrust towards management. Here, too, attitudes of suspicion may be so ingrained as to be, for all practicable purposes, irreversible.

These possibilities have been ignored by some of those proselytizing for greater discretion, autonomy, job control, and participation in decision-making for lower level members of organizations. They have tended to assume that changes in the high-discretion direction would invariably generate consensus on ends and means. It is clear, however, that greater rank and file control may promote conflict 'if the rank-and-file members act simply in terms of their own interests . . . or do not accept the contributions of members at higher echelons' (Smith and Ari 1964). Any management which hopes, by enlarging discretion, to build up high-trust relations, with their promise of employee commitment and identification with top management goals, faces the need to make a judgement more delicate and tricky than perhaps it realizes. It seeks to reverse the low-trust attitudes and behaviour of its low-discretion employees. But are they reversible? If the answer is no, management stands to lose more than the high-trust relations for which it had hoped, for it has now placed increased discretion in the hands of those who cannot be relied upon to exercise it in ways of which management would approve, thus rendering its own position worse than before. Perhaps the most difficult appraisal concerns those groups which are neither obvious candidates for translation to high-trust relations nor obviously committed against it. Conditioned, perhaps, by previous work experience and a particular subculture to expect and acquiesce in low-discretion, low-trust work relations, yet not ideologically structured to oppose a closer assimilation to managerial goals and values, these groups might, after some experience of higher discretion in their work, adjust their attitudes and behaviour appropriately. But how much; after how long; and in response to what degree of enlargement of discretion? Management may be discouraged by what seems a slow learning rate. This is important since other managers will be involved in administering the new work patterns besides those who designed or introduced them. Impatience on the part of the former may prompt some reversion to previous designs and modes, thereby generating a full resumption of low-trust behaviour by the subordinates concerned. This will be hailed by the sceptics as evidence of original sin which justified the low-discretion work design in the first place.

There remains to consider, in this discussion of the high-trust dynamic, only those situations where subordinates maintain or secure for themselves a degree of discretion which management would reduce if it could, i.e., if it had an appropriate technological or organizational innovation to hand, and felt that the costs of conflict would be justified by the benefits. Management may be acquiescing in this situation but is certainly not legitimizing it. This is one of those cases, therefore, where high-discretion roles are not accompanied by high-trust relations. It might be characterized in terms of that paradoxical usage noted at the outset: 'We'll just have to trust them' – where, because the discretion is extended only under constraint, the term 'trust' is a misnomer.

We conclude this exposition of the theoretical structure of the argument by considering what relevance these trust dynamics bear to the responses and attitudes people have in mind when they use such terms as 'job satisfaction'. One way into this confused and confusing field is via the distinction between substantive and procedural aspirations (Fox 1971: Chap. 1). In so far as the individual or group has procedural aspirations there is a wish to play a greater part, directly or indirectly through representatives, in the decision-making processes of the organization. These aspirations could conceivably extend to top policy-making or remain confined, at the other extreme, to the degree of discretion in the individual task. Whatever the level aspired to, there is a wish to redefine roles in a way which gives greater access, direct or indirect, to the exercise of discretion through the decision-making process. This may be sought for its own sake or in order to affect the nature of the decisions emanating from this process – or of course both. In referring to aspirations to affect the nature of decisions made we are concerned with substantive aspirations.

Men may express dissatisfaction about particular substantive outcomes of the existing decision-making processes without necessarily aspiring to change those processes. They may, for example, at any one time, feel dissatisfied with the pay, conditions, or nature of their work, yet not seek to change the methods by which these are decided. This means that, while deploring these particular decisions, they continue to legitimize the prerogative of the manager who made them, or the joint union-management regulative machinery which negotiated them. It does not follow, therefore, that dissatisfaction with particular decisions will lead to low-trust responses aimed at limiting the discretion of those who made them. To be sure, their dissatisfaction may be strong enough and recur frequently enough to push them eventually towards procedural aspirations to change the methods of decision-making. But they may hold to ideological beliefs, traditions, or simply habits which restrain them. In this sense they legitimize 'employer's rights', or a particular pattern of collective bargaining. Perhaps their dissatisfaction is about something of lesser priority for them which they fear to challenge lest it disrupt something of greater priority – as when assembly line workers dislike the work system which management has designed yet assume that the relatively high pay which is their more pressing priority is contingent upon legitimizing that work system.

While substantive dissatisfactions are not necessarily accompanied, therefore, by appropriate procedural aspirations, it also has to be said that procedural aspirations are not necessarily accompanied by *present* substantive dissatisfactions. Men may have few complaints about their current job role and the treatment they receive yet hold ideological beliefs, derived from *past* events, that certain decision-making processes should be structured differently. Steel industry employees in Britain with jobs which they saw as relatively well paid and satisfying could nevertheless be found actively supporting nationalization of the industry.

These considerations are relevant in that they help to illustrate some of the complexities which mediate in the operations of trust dynamics and which, along with differences in power relations, states of 'consciousness', and sentiments of legitimation, account for variations between industries and groups in the timing and nature of those operations. They demonstrate the absence of any simple and direct relationship between observable employee responses in the low-trust direction and expressions of satisfaction or dissatisfaction. One cannot expect to gain useful insight into past or probable future operations of trust dynamics by presenting employees with sponge questions about 'job satisfaction'.

Reference to these complicating variables draws attention to the fact that, while illustration has been given of the low- and high-discretion and trust syndromes as such, no empirical examples have yet been offered of low- and high-trust dynamics in action. This will be the task of the next chapter, which examines some well-known items from the literature and suggests how their empirical data might be interpreted in the light of the framework presented here.

3 · Trust Dynamics: Illustrations from the Literature

The purpose of this chapter is to illustrate the operation of low- and high-trust dynamics with case studies drawn from the literature. Since the authors of these studies were pursuing aims and applying emphases different from those of the present book, their material has to be selectively presented and interpreted so as to serve our current concern. On the whole it lends itself easily to that purpose. Nevertheless the facts need to be stressed that in each case the author concerned has much to say on other themes and that the account offered here is selected to illuminate the ideas of this book, not of his. In no sense, therefore, must the present treatment be seen as offering potted versions of the original works; neither must their authors be associated with the use made here of their material.

Low-Trust Dynamics: The Gypsum Plant

With these provisos, we turn first to two early works by A. W. Gouldner that have become standard items in the literature of industrial sociology – *Patterns of Industrial Bureaucracy* and *Wildcat Strike*, both published in 1954. They deal with the same situation – a gypsum plant employing some 225 people in the United States in the late 1940s. The plant consisted of two basic divisions: 'the subsurface mining and the surface factory processing operations'.

Gouldner's description of the social organization of the plant prior to certain major changes which overtook it offers an example of comparatively high-trust relations between management and lower level employees, who enjoyed what for wage earners was a high degree of discretion and freedom of movement. Supervision was open and loose. There was no social distance between management and men, relations being informal and relaxed with little emphasis on hierarchical and status differences. Rule enforcement was minimal and management showed a marked reluctance to punish. '. . . there were comparatively few rules in the plant, and fewer still that were strictly enforced' (Gouldner 1955: 51). Employees were allowed to use company materials for private purposes without charge provided their appropriations remained within decent limits. Management was flexible and tolerant about timekeeping, absence, sickness, and overtime. Provided a certain quota of work was done few questions were asked. In one sentence, especially, Gouldner identifies what we have noted to be the essence of high-trust, diffuse, social exchange as against low-trust, specific, economic exchange. '. . . the Company did not appear to strive for a return on every cost, for a gain against every outlay . . .' (1965: 22). It was this disposition by management to extend favours well beyond the call of the employment contract as narrowly defined 'that allowed workers to feel that they were being treated humanly' (1955: 54). This pattern of relations was particularly apparent in the mine, where indifference to formal authority and 'diffuseness of spheres of competence' were specially marked. 'Diffuse work obligations might be thought to derive from the physical and technical peculiarities of mining; that is, since the amount of gypsum rock available is beyond control, and not entirely predictable, this might be the basis of vague work responsibilities in the mine.' But not all task constraints below ground were so pressing, and even groups facing more predictable situations, such as track layers, 'adhered to a relatively unspecified work program' (1955: 111).

Employees strongly legitimized this pattern of organization and relations. Many of them felt the plant's wage rates to be relatively low, but had not pressed their trade union towards militant action. Gouldner's data (1965: 32–3) suggest that in their psychological contract with the company, low wages were balanced by high-trust treatment. Workers 'had *not* made an issue of this because they felt that they were being well treated'. This was one way in which they reciprocated.* Had their aspirations for rising money wages been stronger this basis for equilibrium would not, of course, have existed. Workers would not have felt able to say, as one did, that the low pay

* Similarly, in a study of a pipeline construction industry, Graves describes a pattern of diffuse loyalties not only among workers but also between workers and supervisor which the latter could mobilize for his own benefit. 'It is this loyalty ("he's around when you need him") which restrains the pipeliner in his pursuit of the most financially advantageous jobs' (1970: 77–8).

'is like a balance for the working conditions. It sort of balances things' (1965: 32). But Gouldner makes it clear that money aspirations were not yet very strong. Employees were 'not yet men of the market, perpetually "on the make" ', but very much 'men of the community and loyal to its traditional values' (1955: 38). In any case this was not the only way in which employees reciprocated management's high-trust treatment. They trusted their supervisors, reacted favourably to the plant and company, and were happy to go on working for it.

During the period leading up to the crisis which Gouldner describes, therefore, the perceptions and aspirations of management and employees were such as to create a balance of reciprocity which had been for some time in equilibrium. Employee aspirations with respect to pay and work relations balanced management aspirations with respect to employee behaviour and output. And as we have seen, this equilibrium existed at what for wage earners was a relatively high level of trust relations. It was potentially open to disturbance from either side. Disturbance could have come from the employees. Currents in the wider society might have changed local community values in respect of what constituted an acceptable standard of life, leading to dissatisfaction with pay. The employees' union might – possibly to compete with a rival union for members – have initiated a national or regional wages policy to raise pay all round which, willy-nilly, included the gypsum plant. Either way the reciprocity balance would have been disturbed. Employees would no longer have been prepared to trade relatively low wages for relatively high-trust treatment. Management would have had to consider whether, in the face of sharpening collective challenge to its pay policy, it could continue reposing the existing degree of discretion on output policy (for such it was), in the hands of those mounting such a challenge.

In the event, the disturbance came from management. A quickening of market competition in the late forties soon revealed top management at Company head office taking the view that employee goodwill was expendable in the quest for lower unit costs and the fight to retain market share. The death of the plant manager was followed by the appointment of a new broom, Peele, under instructions to tighten up, rationalize, and increase production. There followed a perfect example of a high-trust equilibrium disturbed in a low-trust direction under the initiative of management. Operating rules were enforced and freedom of movement forbidden. An efficiency expert was introduced to rationalize and speed up work processes. A system was initiated requiring daily and weekly reports from foremen and supervisors on production results, accidents, and breakdowns. These pressures were communicated by them to their subordinates; supervision became close and punitive. Failures of performance were detected and punished. Paper work multiplied. 'A college educated authority conscious, rule-oriented', personnel and safety manager 'was substituted for an informal "lenient" man who had little taste for "paper work" ' (1955: 63). Disciplinary practices and punishments were formalized. A new emphasis was placed on hierarchical and status differences; '. . . henceforth, foreman-worker relationships were to be bound by the formal regulations of the Company' (1955: 61), and social distance emerged. 'A cold, impersonal "atmosphere" was slowly settling on the plant' (1955:69).

Gouldner himself uses the language of trust in describing this situation. 'The extreme elaboration of bureaucratic rules is prompted by an abiding distrust of people and of their intentions. Quite commonly, such rules serve those whose ambitions do not generate the ready and full consent of others; they diminish reliance upon and withhold commitment to persons who are viewed as recalcitrant and untrustworthy.' Peele, the manager in question, was 'motivated to extend bureaucratic methods when he developed a specific conception of his subordinates, namely, when he lost trust in them and defined them as failing to perform their role-obligations' (1955: 137, 179). He was only partially successful in applying the new régime. The surface situation was one thing; the underground situation quite another. 'The mine supervisors had to ask themselves, would the introduction of bureaucratic discipline into the mines, and an emphasis on strict conformity to work regulations, *succeed here*?' (1955: 142, his italics). There were important features of the underground situation which led them to answer in the negative. Seeing it as 'an emergency-packed, dangerous place', they were inclined to see the miners' patterns of work behaviour as legitimate. But, more conclusively, they perceived miners as having the power and the will to frustrate the new régime. Management felt it would be 'unwise to tamper with the miners' established work customs or to subject them to close, bureaucratic control' (1955: 143). Thus although management would have liked to impose a lower-discretion work pattern on them, it considered that their ability to resist would make the task too troublesome. Here is an example, then, of role occupants asserting a degree of discretion greater than management would have freely chosen to bestow but which it feels constrained, through power considerations, to accept. The fact that it does not fully legitimize these higher-discretion role definitions means also that it does not extend to them the corresponding degree of trust.

The response of employees to management's disturbance of equilibrium in a low-trust direction was clearly to feel that their psychological contract had been violated. In Gouldner's words: 'The workers wanted to show management that "two can play at the game"; that they, too, could conduct their affairs in the impersonal, "business-like" manner that had been increasingly evident since Peele's succession' (1965: 33). Or in the language of the framework presented here: faced with a manifestation by management of low-trust attitudes towards them, employees reciprocated with low-trust attitudes in return. These took the form of countering management's increasingly rigorous prescription of their behaviour with increasingly rigorous prescription of management's. This response became bound up with a wage claim which might be seen as consequential on management's violation of the psychological contract. If low wages were regarded as being compensated by a high-trust work situation, a management-initiated movement towards a low-trust situation removed the justification for the low wages. Out of this complex situation a strike developed.

Not all the employees were happy about the trend of affairs. Some, the traditionalists, wished for a renewal of the old high-trust pattern of relations. The dominant leadership, however, was in the hands of the 'market men', who wanted formal recognition of new rights and obligations – better grievance procedures; union participation in determining production norms; 'clear-cut directives' by top management to foremen 'ordering stricter conformance to the contract' (1965: 62) – a trend, in other words, towards the economic exchange implied by the impersonal, formal, market contract. 'If the traditionalists sought a return to a relationship governed by "trust", then the market men desired a situation in which trust did not matter; they wanted their prerogatives safeguarded by legal guarantee . . . were willing to set aside the informal privileges of the indulgency pattern in exchange for new, formally acknowledged union powers' (1965: 63).

They achieved their objective. 'The agreement which ended the strike did so by way of delimiting spheres of competence and authority, centralizing the hierarchical system, extending the sway of formal rules, and reinforcing the propriety of impersonal attitudes within the plant. . . . For example, the new rules specified that union stewards must first receive the consent of their foremen before leaving their department, while another rule was to be established covering the conditions under which foremen might work. Both of these rules would serve to make explicit the discretionary limits of those involved. In short, the rules clarified rights and obligations, spelling them out and making them unambiguous' (1965: 119–20).

This case study illustrates, then, the low-trust dynamic in action. A second example of the same process can be found in another postwar classic of the literature: Allan Flanders's analysis in *The Fawley Productivity Agreements* of the first closely studied comprehensive 'productivity agreement' in Britain (1964).

Low-Trust Dynamics: The Fawley Productivity Agreements

Flanders's description of work organization and relations at Fawley, a large oil refinery near Southampton employing about 2,500 wage earners in 1957, shows certain similarities with Gouldner's gypsum plant. Before the changes which he describes, the prevailing managerial emphasis – which amounted almost to a cult – was on 'informality of inter-group standards or what one may call the principle of imperfect codification. . . '. Role definitions and role relations were much shaped by 'custom and practice' which had never been codified and which were subject to some flexibility. This informality and flexibility extended to the institutional procedures through which management and union or workgroup representatives resolved employee claims and grievances. 'The written procedural rules governing collective bargaining at Fawley could hardly be less explicit or rigorous' (*Ibid*: 41–3). There was no definition of the precise status of the employee representatives, nor of any specific and successive stages through which disputes must pass, nor of any timetable governing the speed with which they must be taken up and dealt with – all of them common features of procedure agreements elsewhere – including other oil refineries. Neither was there any up-to-date codification of the substantive rules emanating from this set of arrangements.

The whole pattern, with its reliance on informality and flexibility, was one in which management took pride, seeing it 'as a sign of good relations and the mutual confidence supporting them' (*Ibid*: 45). It was, therefore, as management saw it, a high-trust pattern. Events were to suggest that the employees and their unions were less disposed to 'trust the company' than management believed; nevertheless their acquiescence in management's preference for informal and diffuse modes of conducting joint relations certainly suggests that an element of trust was present, manifested in their readiness to conduct day-to-day operations with a certain amount of give and take, a phrase which implies a degree of diffuseness and of social as against economic exchange.

Management, for its part, certainly gave as well as took, for work role definitions included many 'job demarcation' norms which originated from the various workgroups rather than from management, though management acquiesced in them and played its part in sustaining them. Their purpose was to secure the job rights, status, and security of the groups concerned, and their effect was to regulate rights and duties as between craftsmen and non-craftsmen, between craft groups and supervisors, between different craft groups, and between different non-craft groups. They thereby limited managerial discretion in respect of deployment of labour, allocation of work and lines of supervisory authority. They led, in management's view, to 'considerable inefficiencies of working' (*Ibid:* 267), and the effect of some of them upon supervisory authority is demonstrated by the management statement that 'At present certain Craft Unions stipulate that their members may only receive instructions from a first-line Supervisor who is a member of that union; and on occasion craftsmen have declined accepting an order, instruction or request from an Area Supervisor' (*Ibid*: 280).

These were not the only aspects of job control which were in the hands of workgroups or their union representatives rather than those of management. Systematic overtime had become a legitimized expectation throughout the plant, serving a useful purpose both for wage earners, by supplementing their pay packets, and for management, by strengthening recruitment and retention of labour. So far as management was concerned it was an expensive institution, with its high administrative costs, its tendency to encourage managerial slackness in use of manpower, and its incentives to employees to spin out work in order to justify it. Moreover, its allocation had passed into the hands of the shop stewards, thereby enlarging their role, authority, and status. 'The administration of overtime had been an important foundation of the stewards' authority in the work-place' (*Ibid*: 201).

As with Gouldner's gypsum plant, therefore, management and employees reciprocated a certain degree of high-trust, diffuse relations. Management allowed control of some important aspects of labour deployment to remain in the hands of workgroups and their leaders; workgroups in turn acquiesced in a degree of informality and flexibility of arrangements which they trusted management not to exploit to their disadvantage. The resultant equilibrium was viewed by management as a high-cost system, however, and when, in the middle fifties, competitive pressures became keener and called for a closer attention to costs it was obliged to turn a more rigorous eye upon this pattern of relations. Leadership by a management group eager for reform of manpower utilization received powerful re-inforcement from bold and far-reaching consultancy recommendations. Management became convinced that elimination of the wastes produced by plantwide systematic overtime was bound up with a more flexible and efficient deployment of the available craft and non-craft skills and with a consequential reorganization of work patterns and arrangements. It came to believe that in order to resume its control, currently lost to the shop stewards, over the working and distribution of overtime, it had to enlarge its discretion over the allocation of tasks and duties, which would of course bring more general benefits besides the drastic curtailing of overtime. In these respects, management's gain would be a loss for certain groups of employees. The stewards' loss of their discretionary administration of overtime opportunities would deprive them of an important source of authority and status. The surrender by craft groups of customary job rights and practices in the interests of managerial discretion would be a significant breach in their defences and culture.

The nature of the management proposals can be more fully gauged from a passage relating specifically to the Maintenance and Construction department. '. . . we needed to do three things to make ourselves a highly efficient maintenance group. . . . Firstly we needed to reorganize the supervisory structure of the department to give more direct lines of supervision, to define more clearly the responsibilities of supervisors, and to see that these responsibilities were matched by the necessary authorities. Secondly we needed to plan and schedule our work in much greater detail. And thirdly we needed to make changes in the ways of working of our union personnel' (*Ibid*: 266). To secure these changes management would need the discretion to deploy the various craft and non-craft skills more flexibly than had been permitted by workgroup norms hitherto. For some workers the result might be that in terms of work activities their role definitions would be enlarged, in the direction of greater variety, or even enriched, in the direction of greater discretion, though no systematic evidence is available on this point. What is certain was that in terms of the allocation of duties and the pattern of supervisory authority, management sought to enlarge its own control at the expense of workgroup norms and workgroup leaders.

The response of the craft stewards to these proposals showed that they regarded them as disturbing equilibrium in a low-trust direction. The attitudes characteristic of economic exchange at once became manifest. They declared themselves ready to consider concrete proposals for relaxing demarcation custom and practice provided there were satisfactory guarantees about the effects on employment and 'something was offered in exchange for the things given up' (*Ibid*: 96). This is no place for a full account of the negotiations which followed and the agreement with which they were concluded. The points selected for emphasis here provide a sufficient basis for appreciating the nature of the low-trust dynamic initiated by this management exercise.

That management was unaware of the dynamics governing trust relations is revealed by their hope that the exercise would render labour relations 'more responsible and constructive by demonstrating the advantages to be gained from cooperation. The time being devoted on both sides to continual haggling over such matters as the distribution of overtime or the observation of various job demarcations was to be used more profitably in improving the refinery as a place of employment. The aim was to create a framework of relations that would emphasize the common interests of management and unions in better working methods and organization'

(*Ibid*: 191–2). In other words, management hoped that the effect would be to heighten the trust extended by the employees to the company. Yet their proposals were designed to deprive employee leaders, the shop stewards, of an important source of discretion – the administration of overtime – by resuming it themselves, and moreover to enlarge their own discretion over the allocation of work, hitherto a matter in which workgroup norms had played a decisive part. Management was asking the stewards and the unions 'to agree to an extension of its rights to act in ways from which it had previously been barred' (*Ibid*: 201). As the preceding analysis has shown, such changes as these would only have been accepted by employees on a high-trust basis had they perceived management goals as fully congruent with their own. Management's hopes therefore suggest that, while it had long been forced to recognize that employees, stewards, and unions defined their relations with the company to some extent in conflict terms, it saw these attitudes as reversible. Flanders himself indicates that this was in fact the prevailing view. While management felt constrained to accept the division of authority and conflict of loyalties introduced by trade unionism and collective bargaining into the plant, it appeared to believe that they could eventually be eliminated by policies which stressed 'the identification of the workers' interests with the firm' (*Ibid*: 200).

The productivity negotiations revealed the fallibility of this belief. Conflict attitudes proved to be irreversible. Employee leaders responded to management's initiatives on a low-trust rather than a high-trust basis. In other words, they perceived management's proposals to reduce their discretion as a low-trust initiative to which they countered with low-trust responses, handling the negotiations and the implementation of the resulting agreement as an exercise in economic rather than social exchange. Management's hope for the latter, as an expression of the higher trust it was aspiring to promote, was manifested in its concern that 'the spirit rather than the letter of agreements would prevail in intercraft flexibility. . . '. This was another way of saying that it hoped for a sense, on employees' part, of diffuse rather than of specific obligations. These hopes 'were almost wholly shattered. The boilermakers were the most insistent in conceding nothing to which they were not specifically committed by the agreements, but most of the other trades adopted similar attitudes. The shop stewards and union delegates honoured their stated commitments when called upon to do so, but they refused to go beyond them, and management's requests for a more liberal interpretation met with a firm refusal' (*Ibid*: 177–8). A management report lamented that 'One of the effects of working to a more detailed and specific set of agreements had been the development of a more critical attitude on the part of the unions. The wording of the agreements has become the subject of much closer scrutiny than in the past. This has meant that several arrangements which we had taken for granted as being customary practices are now being questioned and in some cases challenged' (*Ibid*: 180). Flanders offers the verdict that labour relations generally 'acquired a greater formality in that they were governed by more explicit and less flexible rules', and that this greater formality 'made for less give-and-take and ease of accommodation in daily relations'. Management had hoped to promote greater trust, but the unions 'were saying in effect "a bargain is a bargain". They adopted a measured attitude towards their obligations under the agreement and refused to give anything away they had not signed for' (*Ibid*: 199, 206). Management criticized this as 'an expression of opportunistic economic calculation on the unions' part', but our preceding analysis would suggest that it was no more than was to be expected.

In sum, then, management's initiative had drawn it 'inescapably into a paradoxical situation. To relax practices which it found restrictive, it had to compromise much of its earlier cult of informality. It could only obtain more flexibility in working practice by conceding – at least for the time being – less flexibility in the agreed rules regulating it. Understandably, the unions had insisted on limiting the extent of their concessions with a fair degree of exactitude. This had meant formulating agreed written rules, either on new subjects like temporary shift working, or on such matters as craft demarcations where previously looser understandings had allowed greater play for daily give and take. One has only to compare the size of the 1960 agreements with those they were amending to appreciate the difference' (*Ibid*: 142–3).

In this study of the Fawley productivity agreements, therefore, we see another example of how changes initiated by one side which were perceived by the other as being in a low-trust direction led to greater specificity, formality, and inflexibility of rules and relations. Management's move to strengthen its control over the workgroups was countered by workgroup moves to contain and limit that enlargement of control by precise definition and rigorous policing of the new frontiers. In applying that countering strategy, the workgroups showed that the degree of trust they felt towards the company was significantly less than management had supposed. Like many managements before them, and many no doubt to follow, it did not realize the extent to which the structure and organization of the large industrial enterprise, even in the relatively favourable circumstances of oil-refining, creates a set of wary, economic-exchange attitudes among the lower ranks which shape their perceptions of, and responses to, every management act and initiative.

Low-Trust Dynamics: Automation and the Tinplate Industry

The third illustration of the low-trust dynamic is drawn from Chadwick-Jones's study of the introduction of automation to the tinplate industry (1969). In the pre-automated technology, physical effort was 'the most obvious characteristic of the work, but there . . . were operations which required the exercise of judgement and discretion by the operative; above all, the work environment was socially complex, in its alternations and exchanges of jobs between individuals and in the procedures formulated among the workers for their coordination' (*Ibid*: 11). These exchanges and procedures lay within the discretion of the workers themselves. Each crew enjoyed considerable autonomy; external direction was minimal and supervisory checks infrequent. The trade union branch, organized as it was on a plant basis, even administered such managerial functions as filling vacancies, deciding promotions, setting work performances and applying disciplinary standards.

Heading this relatively autonomous crew was the rollerman, who made decisions on output, work pace, and even starting and finishing times. Communications from supervisors to the crew were channelled through him, thereby reducing the likelihood of direct contact between supervisors and the majority of mill grades. This freedom from close supervision was perceived as among the advantages of production line work. It made the supervisor's role akin to that of 'a technical specialist whose services are available to production staff', providing auxiliary and service functions in ways which were egalitarian in form and procedure. Men and supervisors alike saw their relationship in terms of trust; one supervisor observing explicitly that: 'Men don't like to be watched, they like to be trusted' (*Ibid*: 133, 134). Relations with higher management can be predicted. With work crews left virtually to run themselves without managerial intervention, the result was known among the men as 'the no-discipline'. Managers were, in effect, disengaged at the operational level, for given the nature of the technology 'no system of check was possible on the skills of judgement and discretion . . .' (*Ibid*: 146).

We can recognize in this sketch many elements of the high-discretion, high-trust syndrome. In the changes which overtook it as a consequence of automation we can also recognize many of the factors likely to transform high-trust into low-trust work relations. Under the new technology, 'physical intervention' was replaced by 'instrument settings to prescribed limits at the start of machine runs of operations. During long periods of the shift the job tasks entailed surface attention and monitoring of machines or control panels.' The 'work routines of most operatives involved monitoring duties to well-defined limits' laid down by prescheduled and fixed machine programmes. The senior production worker of a team 'was required to undertake search behaviour to locate the source of a fault', but for the rank and file operative 'care and attention in performing simple instrument settings, reporting faults and taking avoiding action to prevent breakdowns, were the full extent of his accountability' (*Ibid*: 57, 62, 69, 70). Since operations 'were on a much vaster and more complex scale' a breakdown at any point became 'an emergency for the whole process' and this called for a new role and new qualification requirements for supervisors. Senior supervisors were now younger and university trained; even assistant supervisors might have technical qualifications; and there was much less emphasis on shopfloor experience. The effect was that supervisors and supervised no longer shared a common background. Changes in the supervisory role itself were marked. 'The larger technical responsibility of the supervisor' involved him in closer supervision, and supervision of a more directive kind '. . . the nature of the authority vested in the role had changed and augmented.' All grades of employees became conscious of coming under more frequent checks; supervisors initiated interaction much more than before and its content was far more 'job focused'. These factors combined to produce greater social distance and formality, with decision-making no longer shared. It became management policy, in fact, to maintain social distance between supervisors and supervised in order that the control function should not be relaxed as a consequence of informal and expressive bonds, and the supervisory shift system was arranged in such a way as to ensure rotation between the work teams. Along with this increased formalization and social distance in supervisory relations went an attenuation of the support function and a keener sense among operatives of being governed by impersonal rule. 'The fact that the discretionary area which used to belong to the operative was reduced, and the authority of supervisors increased, might suggest a prediction that there would be an awareness on the part of the operatives of a stricter application of general rules . . . ' (*Ibid*: 136–41). These consequences were accentuated by the fact that higher management was now more directly involved in the conduct of, and responsibility for, plant operations. Formal procedures which could no longer be bypassed were seen by the operatives as regimentation – 'A few of the men compared the prevailing management culture with a military hierarchy of ranks.'

Employee responses to this pattern of changes were complex. The decrease in physical strain was welcomed and there was a higher degree of overall approval of the job. There were negative responses, however, which focused on boredom and lack of interest. 'The automated plant offered fewer rewards to the men which were intrinsic to the job or the work group; individuals participated less both in the production operations, and in reciprocal social behaviour.' Of most concern to the present argument, however, is that the shift in the work situation from a relatively high-discretion to a relatively low-discretion syndrome was perceived by the workers as a move in a low-trust direction to which they were already responding with low-trust attitudes. 'For the employees it was now more sharply clear that managers had sentiments and interests which were not shared with the work force' (*Ibid*: 127, 151).

This study of automation in tinplate is like the preceding two examples in lending itself to interpretation in terms of the theoretical apparatus developed in this book. There are many other documentations of technological and organizational change which suggest that similar interpretations might be made if the relevant facts were available. For example, one study of the application of electronic data processing to office work describes increased formalization of procedure; rationalization of organization; substitution of rules, regulations, and machine programmes for individual decision-making; less autonomy for individuals and groups to set their own pace; the need for more precise coordination of activities and a consequent shift towards more centralized control; increasing costs of error and therefore tighter standards of performance; and finally a keener concern with absence and lax timekeeping. Each group 'had to process a specific number of accounts every day or perform specific operations'. The programming of some areas of decision-making eliminated important functions and even certain positions; functions which 'supported a job-occupant's claim to a title and a grade of some status within the system'. The 'elimination of these status positions and the further restriction of the areas of employee decision-making fell as a severe blow on status position occupants.' All these changes were clearly in the direction of the low-discretion syndrome. For some groups there were other reorganizations in the direction of job enlargement which may or may not have offset these low-trust changes to some degree for the persons concerned, and the researchers note, too, that 'Employees and supervisors learned to work together in problem solving groups in a way which neither would have thought possible before the change started.' They conclude, however, that the 'final effect on the individual members of the organization who were caught up and embroiled in this change is still to be learned' (Mann and Williams 1960). In a non-unionized situation especially, as this was, the forms taken by whatever low-trust responses on the part of employees did materialize might well take some time to emerge and require sensitive and subtle inquiry to identify and measure.

A great deal of additional suggestive evidence could be offered, given the space, to illustrate the operation of the low-trust dynamic. Attention must now be turned, however, to illustrations of the high-trust dynamic. The first is taken from an account by Cotgrove *et al.* (1971) of changes in work organization negotiated by management and unions in a nylon spinning plant.

High-Trust Dynamics: The Nylon Spinners

The situation before the changes bore clear marks of the low-discretion syndrome. 'For nearly all of the low-skilled operatives the work was characterized by a division of labour that allowed only for the repetitive performance of a limited set of standardized tasks. Moreover, particularly for spinning and drawtwist operatives, their work was organized for them to the extent of informing them on which machine to perform their tasks, the precise time to do this, and the time limits for carrying out the tasks. . . . The operatives were in a strait-jacket of standard practice and generally fairly tight supervision: "It was all laid down as standard methods. You had a book more or less like a bible and it told you everything; how to fetch your steps, to position your steps, in order to change your cake" ("cake" – local term for cylinder of yarn)' (*Ibid*: 42–3).

Management's aim was to negotiate changes towards job enlargement and job enrichment which it hoped would 'result in more satisfying work, offering more scope for individual responsibility and initiative, and thus, for self-actualization' (*Ibid*: 43). Expressed in the theoretical terms being used here, this hope was that a movement in the direction of higher discretion would promote higher-trust relations, with all that these imply for personal involvement, identification, commitment, and a mutual sense of diffuse rather than specific obligations. The authors' own elucidation of the strategy informing the programme echoes the terms of the high-discretion syndrome. It sought to introduce a 'group participative type of management in which there is a high level of group-participation in decision making, with high levels of communication. Emphasis was on participation at the grass roots, between the supervisor and the work group.' Thus would be promoted 'willing compliance with organizational goals. Those who work in the organization become motivated from within rather than coerced from outside. Decisions are ones which they have had a share in making, and are in this sense "their" decisions.' This strategy contrasts 'with the use of sanctions, threats and punishments' (*Ibid*: 64).

A fuller statement of the changes introduced and their behavioural consequences establishes this case study as a useful illustration of the dynamics with which we are concerned – though as before the authors must not be associated with this interpretation of their material. In practical terms, 'a major objective of the agreement was to achieve a reorganization of work so that the operative was subject to less detailed control by the rule book and by supervisors. Accordingly, supervision was reduced and much responsibility which was formerly borne by supervisors was transferred to operatives. The most important change here is that operatives now plan and organize their own work . . . A system which involved close checking would be inappropriate in the new situation where the worker was to be given more responsibility' (*Ibid*: 49–50). In addition, there was some job enlargement, which took the form of adding minor maintenance tasks to the roles of production operatives, and some interchange between different roles as the situation demanded.

To a considerable extent these changes achieved the desired effects. Before the agreement, less than 17 per cent of the workers interviewed felt 'they had any chance to exercise discretion or take decisions'. Subsequently, 80 per cent or over considered that there was now more opportunity to take decisions; that there was less supervision; and that they had more responsibility. The supervisory role changed in the direction one would expect. Before the changes the assistant foreman's role, in the words of one of them, 'was mainly checking operatives on the ways and means of doing the job. They revolved around a ritual. . . . I think the factory at that time was run on a military plan, and we more or less enforced this. . . . They were given a sheet of paper and it said "at a certain time you will go to a machine and you will doff it in accordance with the methods laid down" ' (*Ibid*:105–6). This 'authority-based role in which rules were enforced and directives given' underwent a shift of emphasis towards 'a more participative approach' characterized by joint discussion, less social distance, and a supportive rather than a punitive role (*Ibid*: 106). One operative illustrated the latter with the words 'If you make a mistake your attention is drawn to it but you don't get this bullying attitude – "you shouldn't have done this or you shouldn't have done that" ' (*Ibid*: 71).

The authors are careful not to overstate these changes. The technology 'sets the parameters for organizational change' and the 'gains', though real, were limited (*Ibid*: 134, 135). Nevertheless, in the context of our present theoretical framework it is interesting and significant that 80 per cent of those interviewed saw the new arrangements 'as a sign of more trust', remarking, for example, that it is 'going to instil more trust in both sides – you sort of get to know each other that much better' (*Ibid*: 91). This shift in the direction of social exchange could hardly be more clearly conveyed than in the authors' verdict on the success of discussions in securing 'a significant modification in attitudes towards the job – away from the preoccupation with nicely calculated rewards for discrete quanta of effort and towards a greater willingness to accept responsibility for the overall execution of the job following the abolition of detailed and close supervision' (*Ibid*: 113).

High-Trust Dynamics: A Car Assembly Plant

The second illustration of the high-trust dynamic is drawn from Guest's account of a management-succession situation in a mass production car assembly plant (1962). In certain respects this presents a mirror image to Gouldner's gypsum plant, though it focuses on relations within the management system rather more than relations between management and wage-earning employees. Briefly, it describes a shift, under new plant leadership, from a punitive, low-trust pattern of relations to a participative, high-trust pattern.

The earlier pattern had been generated by the response of the then plant manager to strong external pressures from company divisional level to increase production, improve quality, shorten delivery dates and keep costs down; dimensions along which the plant was failing to show acceptable performance. These pressures took the form both of general exhortations and specific directives on particular aspects of administration. The plant manager's response had been to direct upon his managerial colleagues and subordinates a set of low-trust attitudes and behaviours which, in accordance with a tendency familiar in organizational experience, they transmitted to their own subordinates in a process which, duly repeated at successively lower levels, continued until relationships throughout the whole plant were shaped along these lines. Low-trust responses were institutionalized by becoming structured into the ways people habitually did their work and interacted with others. Departmental heads found their discretion invaded by frequent direct orders from the plant manager and their sense of security threatened by his punitive and authoritarian attitudes. Predictably, they sought to insure their position by treating their own subordinates in the same way. Guest refers to 'the tendency . . . for those at higher levels to "hold the reins" on decisions and not trust those at lower levels', and this forced middle and lower management to follow suit. In the words of one foreman: 'The plant operates in a constant atmosphere of suspicion and pressure' (*Ibid*:

22, 63). From the same source came attempts at rigorous enforcement of rules. '. . . the top boss has the idea that the rules aren't being enforced strictly. . . . Next week, for example, he has ordered that everyone has to work exactly from whistle to whistle . . . It's been a custom for years to allow some wash-up time.' In an effort to control absenteeism, which had been increasing substantially, 'upper management came to rely more and more on strict rule enforcement. Moreover, final decisions on disciplinary measures were to an increasing extent being assumed by those at levels higher than the foreman' (*Ibid*: 23, 28). On many other issues, also, fear resulted both in higher levels being anxious to protect themselves by taking decisions into their own hands and in lower levels being only too ready that they should do so. 'Supervisors at middle and lower levels reported that the overwhelming number of contacts were initiated by superiors, that most contacts involved the issuance of orders by superiors, and that these communications took place in response to immediate technical and organizational emergencies' (*Ibid*: 24). Meanwhile a technically inefficient layout and work flow remained unreformed because both in their vertical and in their lateral interactions people were too preoccupied with defensive manoeuvres, mutual recriminations, and other manifestations of interdepartmental distrust. The whole pattern of interaction, in fact, demonstrated the truth that bad communications are as likely to be an effect as a cause – that distrust is as likely to be the cause of communications distortion and blockage as their result.

As might be predicted, this pattern of relations prevailed not only between line departments but also between line and staff. The work study department, for example, was apt 'to dictate in some detail precisely how each foreman should arrange the job elements and operations in his own section'. It saw itself, and was seen by the foreman, purely as a control mechanism. The trade union reciprocated appropriately with low-trust responses of its own. '. . . when a complaint came up, the union would ask for a detailed breakdown of the elements and time from the standards department. Then the union would check these against their own observations. Sometimes it took more than three months to settle it.' Often a strike was necessary before agreement was reached. The foreman concerned had no effective role in all this. 'Whenever there was a grievance about overwork, the time standards man would come in and say "This is it" and you had to take it' (*Ibid*: 72–4). In sum, therefore, the prevailing pattern was one of distrust, expressing itself in, and being reinforced by, restriction of discretion, close supervision, attempted enforcement of prescriptive rules, emphasis on obedience to authoritarian command, and threats of punishment.

The plant's performance failed to improve under this treatment and higher authority became restive. After an unofficial stoppage the executives at divisional and company levels replaced the plant manager. The new incumbent received 'very few specific instructions . . . as to how to proceed'. From the day of his taking office there was 'an abrupt reduction of "interference from above" '. Guest considers that the divisional manager had been 'urged by superiors to allow the new plant manager considerable latitude in "running his own show" ' (*Ibid*: 42, 108). Granted this wide discretion, he could afford to extend discretion to others, and immediately made apparent his intention to introduce a relatively high-trust, supportive, and non-punitive strategy. Observing that the plant was 'operating from day to day on a kind of "emergency" basis', he initiated, with all levels of management and with the union, consultations on his proposed long-term plan for the plant. He later observed that 'as planning actually became an accomplishment, they began to trust you and build up mutual trust again'. As Guest himself notes, however, 'for a new pattern of behaviour to become established and enlarged to cover all segments of an organization, something more is necessary than a shift in the relationship between single individuals and the head of the organization. Ways must be found to "institutionalize" the basic sentiment-interaction pattern so that it is no longer random or fortuitous behaviour . . .' (*Ibid*: 44, 110). The manager therefore established various types of regularly scheduled meetings with the different management groups, making clear during the course of them his preference for open and free exchange. Gradually the new modes spread and became institutionalized in such structured forms as regular discussions and habitual practices of consultation between different line departments and between operating and service departments. Guest found no evidence that these were 'specifically ordered by the plant manager or his immediate subordinates'; he attributes them rather to the fact that 'the fear complex was disappearing and that those at lower levels felt that the "higher-ups" would support greater self-determination of action at lower levels' (*Ibid*: 46–7). The general lessening of tension released energies for systematic inquiry into, discussion about, and implementation of, improvements in layout, work flow, and materials control, and these relaxed tension further by removing what had been potent sources of conflict under the old régime.

The shift away from authoritarian, directive, low-trust management can be objectively described in one of its manifestations as a change in the pattern of interactions. Under the old régime it was 'apparent that members of the organization acted primarily in response to actions initiated by their superiors; the *direction* was predominantly downward.' There were 'approximately five superior-originated interactions for every one subordinate-originated interaction . . .' (*Ibid*: 84). Under the new régime the ratio became approximately two to one. Equally important, the content of communications changed in emphasis. There was an increase in the number of 'interactional events' involving planning and the transmission of technical and administrative information both vertically and laterally among sections and departments. This recalls, of course, that one element of the high-discretion, high-trust syndrome is a tendency for the role of superiors to be supportive and facilitative rather than directive and punitive. A shift from the latter to the former was very apparent over the period in question. It was, of course, slow and gradual. Guest's respondents 'indicated that they had to go through many experiences – *successful* experiences in solving technical problems – before fear and distrust of the intentions of their superiors could be eliminated'. But the new pattern grew along with the gradual easing of tight, prescriptive management styles towards high-discretions modes. 'Foremen believed that general foremen and superintendents were helpful in solving technical problems by concentrating on the problem rather than on fixing blame on the foreman' (*Ibid*: 59, 61–2).

The theme of high-trust relations emerges clearly and explicitly from Guest's reporting. He quotes a superintendent giving practical evidence of 'his trust in the ability of his subordinates to run departmental operations without him'. General foremen also 'often cited examples to illustrate how they had come to trust their foremen to manage their sections with a minimum of interference from above'. One of them, recalling that previously he insisted the foremen make no moves without consulting him, said 'Now I don't worry all the time about my foremen getting me into hot water. They have the kind of information which allows them to see beyond the next minute or the next hour. My job is to help them get what they need.' Just as the low-trust pattern had permeated the whole plant, so now the move towards high-trust relations filtered down the hierarchy. 'The theme of trust in subordinates was expressed by the foremen themselves as they discussed their relationship to the hourly operators.' In the words of one of them: 'Years back when someone did something wrong, the attitude was "throw him out". Now there is a different attitude. . . . We take time to do more teaching on the job now' (*Ibid*: 63–4).

Relations between line and staff reflected the new pattern. For example, after several months of discussion between the work standards department and operating supervision at all levels, a change was made in the policy of 'the old days when time standards was boss'. 'Now the foreman was made chiefly responsible for determining the work assignment of the individual worker', and the 'new role of the work standards representative was that of providing advice and information'. The change was described by foremen in such terms as: 'If the foreman wants the facts, O.K; the time standards man will come out. However, usually if there is a discrepancy, the foreman decides how to settle that discrepancy.' Again: 'Once in a blue moon they'll bring a standards man in, but for the most part they leave it right up to the foreman. They trust me. Everything used to be real tight before, and the standards people pretty much dictated what was involved in an operation. The foremen were afraid to buck it. Now it's up to the foreman' (*Ibid*: 72–4). This represented a significant shift from conditions in the earlier period when higher management, seeking 'to maintain rigid controls over the disposition and use of manpower', insisted that deployment and work loads be determined by work study experts with direct authority over production foremen. In the later period the relationship between the staff men and the foremen 'was one of collaborative effort'. The 'new role of the work standards representative was that of providing advice and information', and his department 'was regarded by foremen as a service, rather than as a control group' (*Ibid*: 74, 75).

The union representatives of the hourly paid workers reciprocated this overall relaxation of the earlier rigidly prescriptive approach with a spirit of give and take markedly absent previously. In the words of a union officer: 'Now what we do when we hear a complaint is to take a quick look at it. If a man doesn't have a gripe, we tell him. If he does, we talk to the foreman and get it settled.' Moreover, a foreman recorded that 'the union takes more interest in the jobs now, too. Since they can discuss it with the foreman, they make suggestions about how to redistribute the elements.' The foreman might or might not agree, 'but if you build up mutual trust, it makes it easier' (*Ibid*: 73–4).

High-Trust Dynamics: Military Organization

As in the case of the low-trust dynamic, there are many other studies of organizational change which, while not offering data of the particular kinds necessary for use as illustrative material here, nevertheless contain much that speaks directly to our theme, such as that of Trist, *et al.* (1963), Rice (1963), and Kuriloff (1963). In a review of these studies McGregor (1967) identifies some of the important similarities. In each case the appropriate unit of organization was taken to be an 'interdependent team' with a primary task 'complex enough to offer opportunities for learning, improvement in status, and genuine problem solving'. The task was 'a meaningful whole which individual members can comprehend and with which they can identify'. The group was allowed to exercise a high degree of self-regulation, determining its own organizational forms, work assignments, production standards, and quality control. It accepted responsibility as a group for problems arising and created a flexible organization for dealing with them. Subsequent to the introduction of this pattern, 'the supervisory role in each case shifted markedly from one of direction, surveillance, and control to one of providing technical help, support, and instruction'. Group members had 'a much greater degree of control over their own fate than under conventional strategies', and there was 'a marked reduction in bureaucratic controls' (*Ibid*: 90–2). These studies are clearly describing shifts in the direction of high-discretion, high-trust work situations. Similar innovations are referred to by Pym (1968), who himself uses the language of trust in describing them.

Also worth noting is that in military organization, too, changes in technology are being accompanied by changes in roles and relations.

Traditionally these have been highly prescribed in nature, with duties and responsibilities defined and specified with increasing precision the lower one's position in the hierarchy. In accordance with the low-discretion syndrome, along with highly prescribed roles went close supervision; a proliferation of impersonal, bureaucratic rules; imposed and standardized coordination; restricted interactions and communication; a punitive response to inadequacies of performance; and a general assumption that no confidence could be placed in the free and spontaneous commitment of the lower ranks to the values and objectives of superiors.

Janowitz has described important changes in this pattern (1959). He relates the earlier forms to their technical base by observing that 'When armies became mass organizations through the introduction of the rifle, the assumption developed that a rank distribution of a single broadly based pyramid was the appropriate hierarchical form. The greatest number of men were privates, all of whom performed a relative standardized task. . . .' New and complex weaponry has sharply raised the average level of skill and technical expertise required and the degree of specialist autonomy needed to exercise it. One result has been a proliferation of middle rank officers who hold their position not on the basis of how many subordinates they command but on the basis of their technical skills. This has required a shift in patterns of authority away from the bureaucratic, directive, vertical dominance characteristic of the low-discretion syndrome and towards the lateral coordination characteristic of the high-discretion syndrome. 'The technology of warfare is so complex that the coordination of a group of specialists cannot be guaranteed simply by authoritarian discipline.' The 'tasks of military authority now more often relate to lateral coordination and cooperation than to the exercise of responsibility of the highest echelons over the lowest echelons'. The function of the former is 'to create the conditions for the middle strata of specialists to coordinate their efforts. Consider a typical operation in the Korean conflict where an infantry combat team required air support from carrier-based planes, and it is abundantly clear that direct orders of a hierarchical variety are being supplemented by complex lateral coordination.'

Change has not been limited to these levels. 'In combat the maintenance of initiative has become a requirement of greater importance than the rigid enforcement of discipline.' Earlier the close order formations based on relatively low firepower could be dominated and controlled by direct and rigid discipline, but technology and social organization have been changing 'so as to throw the individual fighter on his own and his primary group's resources'. The modern combat fighter, 'when committed to battle, is hardly the model of Max Weber's ideal bureacrat following rigid rules and regulations'. He is 'not routinized and self-contained. . . . Rather his role is one of constant improvisation. . . .' Men must be trained 'not only to count on instructions from superiors but also to exercise their own judgement about the best response to make when confronted with given types of danger'. In place of domination marked by explicit instructions, threats, negative sanctions, and mechanical compliance, the aim is stable and purposeful involvement at every level, participation, group persuasion, and an emphasis on group goals (*Ibid*: 15–24, 28–39).

Costs and Benefits: Issues in Managerial Evaluation

Asked to justify these changes, their originators and sponsors would assert them to be desirable for greater effectiveness of performance. Similarly, many if not all the writers upon whom we have drawn for industrial illustrations of the high-trust dynamic assert the changes they describe to be necessary in the interests of efficiency, adaptability, creativity, or some other criterion of organizational wellbeing. These claims are not examined here. A concern with the nature of the social relations generated by differing degrees of discretion vested in work roles need not extend to assessing their instrumental value for organizational leaders. But although it is no part of this book's purpose to discuss nostrums for successful management, it is part of its purpose to illustrate how men's choices in their construction of social organizations have consequences whose nature they often fail to appreciate and which may confound their expectations. Frustration, disappointment, and disillusion are common managerial responses to the behaviour characteristic of employees in low-discretion roles. They explain the growing interest of a few managers in writings which extol the instrumental as well as the humanitarian value of enlarging discretion through the enrichment of jobs. But beyond the relatively sophisticated few are the unsophisticated many who see no connection between defining work roles with only minimal discretion and discovering that their occupants display only minimal identification with those roles.

The analysis developed here suggests that the tendencies towards reciprocity in human exchange have the consequence that, unless some compensating mechanism such as power or legitimizing sentiment is present to support a situation of imbalance, institutionalized distrust will evoke its like in return. Whether this reciprocation is manifested in explicit rules or in habitual working practices and behaviours, the likelihood is that the parties will draw each other into a spiral of distrust which brings their relationship ever closer to the conditions of economic exchange. Faced with employee responses characterized by precise and grudging calculation of effort and compensation, by suspicion of managerial motives, and by withholding of personal involvement, managers are apt to urge subordinates to 'trust the company' and to greet the failure usually attendant upon such appeals with an intensification of low-trust tactics and a renewed conviction of the moral weakness of most wage earners.

Whether work designers are aware of it or not, therefore, the organizational patterns they devise and the changes they introduce in them embody dynamics of trust relations. A proposal to modify job roles or to introduce some technological innovation which has organizational consequences may well have long-term or even immediate implications for the behaviour of the participants. Forces may be generated which have far-ranging effects on future patterns of rules, roles, and relations. The processes of search and the evaluation of costs and benefits rarely if ever include a review of these probable consequences. This lack of concern with trust dynamics is not confined to management. Employees, too, either as individuals or in groups may, by manifesting institutionalized low trust towards management, initiate a reciprocal sequence towards economic exchange which may or may not serve their perceived interests when all costs and benefits are taken into account.

For managers who come to perceive the connection between, on the one hand, the design of work roles and relations and, on the other, the dynamics of reciprocity which shape the development of low- and high-trust relations (subject to the analytical qualifications which will not be repeated), there may seem considerable plausibility in the recommendation to enrich work roles and thereby promote the employee commitment which appears so attractive and yet so elusive. Much of the literature urging this strategy does so with few, if any, reservations. It may well be that too uncritical an acceptance by managers of the benefits of the Scientific Management approach, with its precise programming and prescription of employee behaviour, its close supervision and authoritarian direction, its reliance on the external goals of punishment and financial reward, its crucial separation of 'planning' and 'doing' – all characteristic features of the low-discretion syndrome – has resulted in the costs of this approach being ignored or undervalued. The current self-actualization vogue has not left us in any doubt about one particular set of ideas which embody this charge. But such is the tendency to move from one extreme position to another that the benefits of the new vogue come to be accepted as uncritically as were those of the old.

The fact is that an adequate appraisal of costs and benefits from management's point of view is more complex than is usually recognized. A low-discretion pattern may serve management's purposes well provided it enjoys a large enough power advantage. Such a pattern may lose validity, however, if the power balance shifts. This can be deduced from the terms of our analysis. It was noted that an imbalance of reciprocity manifested in terms of a managerial restriction of employee discretion which is unmatched by employee restriction of managerial discretion can be supported either by legitimizing sentiments on the part of employees or by coercive power on the part of management. We will make the assumption least favourable to management and suppose that its low-discretion system is not legitimized by the participants and therefore evokes low trust. It may be that management's power is sufficient to prevent or contain some of the possible low-trust responses which might otherwise emerge, and that it has assessed and is prepared to accept the manifestation of others. Let us suppose it, for example, to recognize that its conveyor belt methods will generate only instrumental compliance and an economic-exchange approach to work which it cannot prevent. It may have costed this motivational weakness and decided that the balance of advantage still lies with conveyor belt methods. There are other possible (though far from inevitable) ways by which men may manifest low-trust responses if they get the chance – absenteeism; indifferent performance; high sickness, accident or wastage rates; sabotage; obstructionism; and collective challenge to management aims, priorities, and policies.* Management's power may be adequate to keep these costs within acceptable bounds – by fully exploiting, say, its advantage in a high-unemployment area where the position of labour is weak; its aspirations low, and unionism non-existent. Such a combination of circumstances might lead even a management fully cognizant of trust dynamics to choose a low-trust work design.

A shift in power relations, however, may require, from management's point of view, a reassessment of this calculation, though it will not necessarily receive one. A situation of labour scarcity, a rise in employee aspirations, the emergence of effective trade unionism; these may weaken management's power sufficiently to allow low-trust responses to emerge in substantial measure. Against the benefits conferred by extreme division of labour, prescribed behaviour, and rigorous external control, would then have to be set the costs of the various forms of low-trust disaffection and withdrawal of commitment in which employees were now much freer to engage. Again, however, such a review of the changed nature of costs and benefits would not necessarily point to a different managerial strategy.

In sum then: work designers seeking to maximize the return on resources would find it as misleading to assume the Scientific Management approach to be always wrong as to assume it to be always right. It is true that a management which 'justifies minute subdivision of the task into its simplest component parts, on the ground that many men prefer repetitive and relatively meaningless jobs, will not benefit from a release of creative interest in the job. Similarly, a management that emphasizes the coercive element in the moving line, on the ground that no one works effectively without externally imposed pressure, will not find the improved productivity that comes from people working hard because they want to and

* The factors which determine what kinds of low-trust response emerge in different situations would need a study in their own right. Meanwhile their complexity can be illustrated by car assembly. Few industries in Britain display relationships between management and hourly paid workers which are closer to the economic-exchange pole in certain respects than car assembly. Manifestations of the low-trust pattern abound in this textbook example, where workgroup representatives bargain keenly and militantly over small variations in piece rates, gang size, or work load. Yet 'accidents are not frequent in the car firms by comparison with other industries. Absence from work is (so far as one can judge) comparatively modest . . . and . . . labour turnover seems relatively low' (Turner, Clack, and Roberts 1967: 330).

because they participate in setting the goals which are to be reached' (Turner 1955: 47–8). But such assertions beg the question. Perhaps the productive system is designed deliberately to sacrifice the chances of securing creative interest from hourly paid workers on the grounds that, for the task in hand, an extreme subdivision of labour at one level and the fostering of creativity at a higher level is the best way of organizing production. Perhaps it is expressly designed to secure high productivity not by reposing confidence in the commitment of men's hearts and minds but by goading them with externally applied carrots and sticks along programmed and pre-planned patterns of behaviour. To be sure, such a system is marked by waste of some men's creativity and capacity for deeper commitment. The existence of waste *per se*, however, is not and never has been sufficient indication in itself that resources are being inefficiently used for the purpose in hand. Millions of plastic containers, for example, are currently wasted because in present circumstances recovery would not justify the cost. Further questions have to be asked – how *much* of a given resource is being wasted relatively to the available supply? A shift in this ratio may call for a reassessment of methods – if labour becomes scarcer then systems which waste it may seem to management to require review. But even then the outcome depends on calculations unique to each situation. Certainly the emergence of labour as a scarce and increasingly expensive resource may affect the calculation in two ways. Work designers may come to believe that they can decreasingly afford to waste any man's creativity and capacity for moral involvement. This may point towards redefining work roles and relations on a higher discretion basis in the hope of evoking the high-trust syndrome. Success depends not only on the insight, skill, and patience with which change is designed, applied, and subsequently implemented but also, as we have seen, on how far behaviours and attitudes shaped by the earlier situation are reversible. The second way in which the calculation may be affected is through the enhancement of employee power brought about by labour scarcity. By enabling employee groups in low-discretion situations to reciprocate more freely with low-trust responses of their own, this may bring management to a realization of the low-trust spiral into which it is moving and a decision to break out of it if possible.

But we cannot assume even then that management will feel rational criteria to point to such a decision. The economic advances made possible by the Scientific Management low-discretion strategy have been enormous and its potency probably remains great. The benefits it offers those concerned to maximize profits or economic growth are hardly likely, in a society where labour is a commodity, to be forgone simply because it is seen to involve some waste of human faculties. Like the ubiquitous plastic container, much human potentiality is 'surplus to requirements'. Perhaps as labour becomes increasingly expensive the waste will come to seem economically irrational, but in our kind of society the case is not established simply by pointing to the fact of waste as such. These considerations must be seen as neither commending the low-trust strategy nor belittling the high-trust strategy, but as simply indicating that the calculations bearing on management's organizational choices are more complex than enthusiasts for self-actualization sometimes allow.

Yet the appeal, for management, of high-trust relations is very strong, for obvious reasons, and one commonly finds it hoping to enjoy the best of both worlds. Even where management is not moved to reshape work organization in a high-trust direction it can sometimes be found trying to evoke high-trust behaviour from subordinates without undertaking structural changes of the sort required for the institutionalizing of high trust. Managements in this category would agree with Bendix's much quoted dictum: 'Beyond what commands can effect and supervision can control, beyond what incentives can induce and penalties prevent, there exists an exercise of discretion important even in relatively menial jobs, which managers of economic enterprises seek to enlist for the achievement of managerial ends' (1963: 251). While retaining the menial jobs they hope, by means of welfare policies, verbal appeals, ideological persuasion, and other techniques which all stop short, however, of institutionalizing high trust, to arouse the personal involvement and commitment that are its sought-for manifestations. This hope received stimulus from popularized and often vulgarized expressions of the human relations movement that enjoyed a considerable vogue during the forties and which is still percolating down through the many levels of industry, business, and commerce. Disappointment is not inevitable. Our theoretical framework provides for the possibility that under certain conditions management may be able to bend the ideological perspectives of employees to such effect that they fully legitimize the highly unequal distribution of discretion and bring to their own low-discretion roles high-trust behaviours and attitudes. It was also noted, however, that in the hierarchical business structures of Western society this is increasingly rare. Differentiations of reward, status, authority, and function tend to generate a sense of divergent goals and values, and even the mainstream culture offers ideological support for collective challenges to managerial rule, to say nothing of subcultures born of past conflicts and group self-justifications. In this context, low-discretion roles throw up low-trust responses as soon as a modicum of power enables employees to embody their attitudes in behaviour. Verbal appeals by management to subordinates with low-trust perceptions that they should demonstrate personal commitment and loyalty to the company may do its cause more harm than good. It is directing the language of high trust towards those who see management itself in low-trust terms, and by so doing may reduce their trust still further. Management might serve its own interests better, first, by satisfying itself that the low-trust attitudes are irreversible and, second, by then offering a total and open acceptance of the implications of its organizational strategy. These are that low-discretion work roles tend to promote, in the conditions of Western society, a move towards low-trust, economic-exchange relations between superiors and subordinates; and that these relations are best structured through negotiated collaboration. Whether even this offers long-term stability of the present patterns of work organization will be examined later. Even today it represents for many managers a doctrine of pessimism and despair. They may recognize that the preceding two centuries have seen a massive shift towards extreme division of labour, rationalization of work, and ever larger work organizations, with a consequent growth of hierarchy, bureaucratic regulation, supervision, and control. But, they may ask, is all this to be accepted fatalistically as a slide into low-trust relations, with the implications this carries of a deterioration in the quality of economic cooperation?

Neither the significance of the question nor the complexity of the answer can be fully grasped until the discussion is located within its wider social setting. To gain the perspective we seek, the growth in low-discretion work must be seen in the whole context of emerging industrial-commercial-urban society, with its characteristic features of markets, money, and, above all, contracts. It then becomes clear that the growth of low-trust relations in work is but one manifestation of a more general growth of low-trust relations which increasingly characterize social life as a consequence of industrialism, commercialism, and urbanism. Only in the context of this vast theme can trends in work relations ultimately be judged. But to enable ourselves to do this we need to sketch out this dominant theme not in conventional historical terms but in terms of trust, contract, power, and exchange. To this task we now turn.

4 · Work Roles and Relations in the Wider Social Setting

The preceding chapter closed on a note which may give a false impression about the themes and purposes of this book; an impression which could influence the reader's perceptions of what follows. The assertion was made that low-trust relations in work are but one manifestation of a more general growth of low-trust relations which increasingly pervade social life as a consequence of industrialism, commercialism, and urbanism. Propositions of this kind sometimes herald a diatribe mourning 'the world we have lost' and condemning modern Western society *in toto*. A reference to low-trust relations, taken by itself, may invoke such associations purely as a consequence of the words being used. The reader is asked to accept for the moment, however, that in abstracting from the whole social process one strand of human interaction, albeit one of major importance, there is no necessary implication that judgements about the one are judgements about the whole. With this as a background consideration we turn to the task of locating changes in the trust relations of work within their wider setting of emergent and developing industrialism. This we begin by selecting from that development certain features which constitute a major difference as between industrial and pre-industrial society.

The Nature of Contract

The nature of these features can be briefly indicated with the proposition that in an important sense pre-industrial society is pre-contractual society. This proposition rests upon a certain definition of contract, for as Weber observed, contract 'in the sense of a voluntary agreement constituting the legal foundations of claims and obligations, has . . . been widely diffused even in the earliest periods and stages of legal history' (Rheinstein 1954: 105). Within this general category, however, can be found different forms, the most fundamental distinction among which is seen by Weber as that between 'status' contracts and 'purposive' contracts. The status contract 'is a voluntary agreement for the creation of a continuing relationship, especially one that affects the "total legal situation" of the individual' (Selznick 1969: 54). 'By means of such a contract a person was to become somebody's child, father, wife, brother, master, slave, kin, comrade-in-arms, protector, client, follower, vassal, subject, friend, or, quite generally, comrade' (Rheinstein 1954: 106). The conditional element of the contract is attenuated because only a general reciprocity is expected. The commitments are diffuse and are not premised on explicit consent to particular obligations. 'Such a contract fits the requirement and the ethos of a status-based society...' (Selznick 1969: 54).

The purposive contract, on the other hand, is the characteristic legal institution of an exchange economy which is strongly market oriented and based on the use of money. 'It is a contract made to complete a specific transaction or to further a discrete objective. Only a tenuous and temporary association is created. The purposive contract is infused with the spirit of restraint and delimitation: open-ended obligations are alien to its nature; arms-length negotiation is the keynote' (*Ibid*: 54). The emphasis is on a transitory arrangement for limited and specific performances.

We have here a distinction similar to that between high-trust social exchange and low-trust economic exchange. The definition of pre-industrial society as pre-contractual society rests upon a definition of contract in terms of limited and specific commitments as against open-ended and diffuse commitments. Parsons refers to 'the freedom to enter into private agreements with limited content without involving the total status of the parties, but only specifically limited interests. What we think of as "freedom of contract" would not be possible in an institutional system in which, as in the Middle Ages, all the principal elements of an individual's status were treated as bound together. The granting of a fief . . . involved property interests, a status in the system of political authority, and a fundamental reciprocal relation of personal loyalty "for better or for worse" in whatever exigencies might arise between lord and vassal. . . . A feudal contract is . . . peculiar in that it involves a total status and diffuse mutual obligations of loyalty. It is thus not like a modern business contract' (1964: 64, 83). Marx noted that the feudal lord's 'family history, the history of his house etc. – all this individualizes the estate for him and . . . personifies it. Similarly those working on the estate have not the position of *day laborers*; but they are in part themselves his property, as are serfs; and in part they are bound to him by ties of respect, allegiance, and duty. . . . Finally, the feudal lord does not try to extract the utmost advantage from his land. Rather, he consumes what is there and calmly leaves the worry of producing to the serfs and the tenants.' Capitalism required, *inter alia*, 'that the rule of the proprietor appear as the undisguised rule of private property. . . . that the relationship between proprietor and worker be reduced to the economic relationship of exploiter and exploited . . .' (1964: 101).

As against the diffuse commitment which Marx describes, it is the purposive, economic-exchange relationship to which the language of contract as now used normally refers. Davis, for example, defines a contract as 'essentially an agreement between two or more individuals to behave in a certain specified way for a certain specified length of time in the future. What distinguishes a contractual relation from most other relationships is the fact that the reciprocal rights and obligations are limited to those specified in the contract. Thus the relationship between members of a family can hardly be said to be contractual, since there is no detailed listing of the number and duration of the rights and duties; there is usually the presumption that any particular member of the family will go far beyond his normal responsibilities in case of an emergency involving another member. The relationship which we call friendship is similar in nature' (1955: 470).

Pre-Contractual Society and Diffuse Relations

What was the structural basis on which this pre-industrial, pre-contractual society rested? Occupational division of labour was, of course, minimal compared with our own time. In England, more than nine-tenths of mediaeval workers were peasants. Such markets as existed were mainly local, limited, and personal. Trade, industry, the money market; 'all that we call the economic system, was not a system but a mass of individual trades and individual dealings.

Pecuniary transactions were a fringe on a world of natural economy. There was little mobility or competition. There was very little large-scale organization' (Tawney 1938: 40). With some important exceptions, the artisan was a small master employing perhaps a few journeymen and apprentices who had expectations of becoming masters themselves in due course. In the mediaeval cities, 'with their freedom, their comparative peace, and their strong corporate feeling, large enough to be prolific of associations and small enough for each man to know his neighbour, an ethic of mutual aid was not wholly impossible, and it is in the light of such conditions that the most characteristic of mediaeval industrial institutions is to be interpreted'. Tawney draws attention, certainly, to the fact that in a few large commercial centres in Europe there could sometimes be found in the latter Middle Ages 'a capitalism as inhuman as any which the world has seen, and from time to time ferocious class wars between artisans and merchants'. He notes, too, 'the gross facts' of the 'edifice of feudal society – class privilege, class oppression, exploitation, serfdom'. Yet these were more often than not accepted 'with astonishing docility', widely legitimized as they were on the basis of a 'functional theory of society' underpinned by shared religious beliefs. Helping to sustain legitimacy was undoubtedly the fact that the harsh edges of this social order were softened for its lower strata by a partial acceptance by higher strata of certain diffuse, personalized obligations. 'Within classes there must be equality; if one takes into his hand the living of two, his neighbour will go short. Between classes there must be inequality . . .', but in this relationship of inequality there was a modicum of protection as well as repression. 'Society was interpreted, in short, not as the expression of economic self-interest, but as held together by a system of mutual, though varying obligations.'

Mediaeval guilds, with all their monopolism, conservatism, exclusiveness, and indifference to the interests of those defined as outside the fraternity, nevertheless maintained an 'attempt to preserve a rough equality among "the good men of the mistery", to check economic egotism by insisting that every brother shall share his good fortune with another and stand by his neighbour in need, to resist the encroachments of a conscienceless money-power, to preserve professional standards of training and craftsmanship, and to repress by a strict corporate discipline the natural appetite of each to snatch special advantages for himself to the injury of all. . . .' Such an environment, with its personal economic relationships, was 'a not unfavourable field for a system of social ethics'. Much that subsequently became impersonal and mechanical 'was then personal, intimate and direct, and there was little room for organization on a scale too vast for the standards that are applied to individuals. . . .' Among the fundamental assumptions of mediaeval writers, assumptions that were not without some echo in reality, were 'that economic interests are subordinate to the real business of life, which is salvation, and that economic conduct is one aspect of personal conduct, upon which, as on other parts of it, the rules of morality are binding' (*Ibid*: 37, 39, 40–2, 44).

The bonds and sanctions which fostered and supported this social order derived from common religious beliefs and the personal, face-to-face relations engendered by physical propinquity, small scale organization, and local markets. Belief in God and an afterlife underpinned the use of the oath as a mechanism of social integration and order. Hill quotes Ralegh to the effect that oaths defend 'the life of man, the estates of men, the faith of subjects to kings, of servants to their masters, of vassals to their lords, of wives to their husbands, and of children to their parents . . .' (1969: 383). It was a totally personalized commitment to which were attached personalized ramifications reinforcing the religious sanction against default. 'In pre-contract society, a man's bond was his kinsman or members of his community who knew him intimately' (*Ibid*: 384). The same emphasis on personalization emerges in Davis. 'So long . . . as the only known kind of relationship among individuals is a personal (particularistic) relationship of reciprocal rights and obligations, contract in the modern sense cannot develop. A debtor-creditor relationship or any sort of promise by one individual to another was in the Middle Ages, for instance, such a personalized matter that the transfer of the obligation to a third person was inconceivable. It was a "personal promise of oath and fidelity" arising out of the mutual confidence the two parties to an agreement placed in each other' (1955: 472).

Veblen suggested the fuller implications. 'In the older days, when handicraft was the rule of the industrial system, the personal contact between the producer and his customer was somewhat close and lasting. Under these circumstances the factor of personal esteem and disesteem had a considerable play in controlling the purveyors of goods and services. This factor of personal contact counted in two divergent ways: (1) producers were careful of their reputation for workmanship, even apart from the gains which such a reputation might bring; and (2) a degree of irritation and ill-will would arise in many cases, leading to petty trade quarrels and discriminations on other grounds than the gains to be got, at the same time that the detailed character of dealings between producer and consumer admitted a degree of petty knavery and huckstering that is no longer practicable in the current large-scale business dealings. Of these two divergent effects resulting from close personal relations between producer and consumer the former seems on the whole to have been of preponderant consequence. Under the system of handicraft and neighbourhood industry, the adage that "Honesty is the best policy" seems on the whole to have been accepted and to have been true . . .' (1958: 30–1).

Even this briefest of sketches enables us to relate pre-industrial society and Weber's concept of the status contract. His definition of the latter reveals it to be highly congruent with the characteristics of the former. It was a logical feature of a society dominated by diffuse commitments and obligations. In describing these commitments and obligations as diffuse we are calling attention to the relative absence of specification, to the need for each party to define for himself in the first instance where his obligation began and ended and what form it should take. In other words, we are describing them as requiring the exercise of discretion and the readiness of men to trust each other when they exchanged commitments. In the earlier analysis it was noted that whereas the discharge of an obligation to observe prescribed terms requires only obedience (along with the necessary ability and facilities), the discharge of a discretionary trust requires choice and therefore the involvement of the person as a moral agent. Here we find an accord, therefore, with the emphasis in the forgoing sketch upon the personalized nature of relations in pre-industrial society. Because of minimal division of labour, minimal differentiation of structure and function, and maximal incidence of face-to-face dealings, the individual as a moral agent cannot, in this type of social order, be separated from his economic activities. When Tawney refers to the sentiment, 'fostered both by the teachings of the Church and the decencies of social intercourse among neighbours, which regarded keen bargaining as "sharp practice" ' (1938: 164) the reference is to a situation in which the economic impulse is tempered by diffuse social obligations deriving their support from the institutional setting within which economic transactions are carried out.

Primitive Societies and Social Exchange

Evidence from social anthropology on the nature of exchange within and between primitive societies further exemplifies the process whereby diffuseness of obligation goes along with a personal involvement of the parties to the relationship. 'The outstanding discovery of recent historical and anthropological research is that man's economy, as a rule, is submerged in his social relationships. He does not act so as to safeguard his individual interest in the possession of material goods; he acts so as to safeguard his social standing, his social claims, his social assets' (Polanyi 1945: 53). Parsons notes that in primitive society 'a very large proportion of economically significant exchange is formally treated as an exchange of gifts ' (1964: 169), and Mauss, in the first classic comparative study of gift giving (1954), showed that it 'introduces certain emotive qualities into a relationship. Status and wealth questions are immediately involved, and the recipient must decide whether, and in what form, he must reciprocate. This involves an analysis of the relationship, the purpose of the gift, and customary procedure' (Belshaw 1965: 47). The personal involvement implied by these discretionary, choice-making processes is plain to see. The gift and the timing and nature of its reciprocation are expressions of the attitudes and sentiments of the parties to the exchange. Gift giving therefore takes on strong symbolic significance (as it does in personal relations in our own societies) by creating obligations and by generating trust, goodwill, and fellowship when these obligations are reciprocally discharged.

Behaviour which moves away from this social exchange pattern towards an economic exchange pattern may come under disapproval. 'Among the Plateau Tonga, selling cattle for cash is considered quite unethical. This, after all, does not establish a continuing social relationship' (*Ibid*: 34). And Parsons observes that in primitive society 'the specific characteristic of purely economically rational exchange, namely bargaining, is not only absent but is specifically prohibited (1964: 169).

Mauss drew normative conclusions from his study. 'We live in a society where there is a marked distinction . . . between real and personal law, between things and persons. This distinction is fundamental; it is the very condition of part of our system of property, alienation and exchange.' Greek, Roman, and Semitic civilizations, too, distinguished clearly between obligatory presentations and pure gifts. But these civilizations passed through earlier phases 'in which their thought was less cold and calculating'. They practised 'customs of gift exchange in which persons and things become indistinguishable' (1954: 46). Evans-Pritchard takes up this theme in his introduction to Mauss's monograph. 'Mauss is telling us . . . how much we have lost, whatever we may have otherwise gained, by the substitution of a rational economic system for a system in which exchange of goods was not a mechanical but a moral transaction, bringing about and maintaining human, personal relationships between individuals and groups' (*Ibid*: ix). A similar note is struck by Polanyi, who describes 'a broad reciprocity relying on the long-run working of separated acts of give-and-take' and operating on a highly personalized basis (1945: 56).

Division of Labour: The Trend Towards Specificity and Economic Exchange

The structural changes which both encouraged and were encouraged by the transition towards the economic exchange of Weber's purposive contract are of course familiar. They include the enlargement of markets and an increasing 'division of labour in which the interdependence of specialized groups requires a certain precision in the coordination of efforts. . . . A series of contracts, specifying obligations and rationally negotiated, is a vital necessity for such an organization of economic activity' (Davis 1955: 473). The need for specific definition became the greater as economic relations burst the bounds of local communities, for now men dealt increasingly with strangers whom they never saw and towards whom they felt less constrained in terms of traditional bonds and sanctions. The growing use of money reacted back upon and quickened the whole process. 'Money plays an extremely important part . . . because it makes possible the estimation of the values exchanged in quantitative and fixed, rather than in subjective, terms. Economic relationships thus free themselves from the particular ties and obligations of local community structure . . .' (Giddens 1971: 163–4). Moore suggests that 'if one were to attempt a one-word summary of the institutional requirements of economic development, that word would be *mobility*. Property rights, consumer goods, and laborers must be freed from traditional bonds and restraints, from aristocratic traditions, quasi-feudal arrangements, paternalistic and other multi-bonded relations' (1965: 31–2).

As exchange relations became ever more numerous and pervasive, more geographically wide ranging, and more based on specific and structurally differentiated functions and services, the more attenuated became the relevance and indeed the practicability of diffuse long-term reciprocation. The personal relations, traditional bonds, and community ties which could underpin purely local face-to-face transactions could not bear the weight of spatially dispersed markets, the emergence of intermediaries, and the increasing rationalization of economic activities in the direction of monetary measurement and acquisition. Relations became increasingly marked by specific short-term reciprocation – by economic as against social exchange.

Even on the land Britain witnessed as early as the sixteenth century a trend towards economic exchange which some modern historians see as one contributory cause of the social disequilibrium that made possible the English Revolution. Stone, for example, refers to population growth and expansion of agricultural output. 'On the land there was a massive shift away from a feudal and paternalist relationship betweeen landlord and tenant, towards one more exclusively based on the maximization of profits in a market economy. . . . The hold of nobles over client gentry and tenantry was weakened because of the increasing absenteeism of the former, and the shift to economic rents, which severely reduced the service element in landlord-tenant relationships.' There was 'a sea-change in men's ideas of loyalty. . . '. And more generally, too, 'economic developments were dissolving old bonds of service and obligation and creating new relationships founded on the operations of the market' (1972: 68, 72, 74).

The depersonalization of economic relations as their terms became increasingly specific – i.e. decreasingly reliant on the discretion of the parties – meant that the individual's consciousness of responsibility for the discharge of even the prescribed terms became attenuated. It was suggested in the earlier analysis that as the discretion in the individual's role is reduced, his observance of the prescribed terms becomes more problematical. The weakened sense of personal identity, consequent upon loss of discretion, weakens the sense of responsibility for the specific obligations. A passage by Veblen discusses this effect. In modern circumstances, the 'head of an industrial enterprise is commonly removed from all personal contact with the body of customers . . . The mitigating effect which personal contact may have in dealings between man and man is therefore in great measure eliminated. The whole takes on something of an impersonal character. One can with an easier conscience and with less of a sense of meanness take advantage of the necessities of people whom one knows of only as an indiscriminate aggregate of consumers. . . . Equity, in excess of the formal modicum specified by law, does not so readily assert its claims where the relations between the parties are remote and impersonal as where one is dealing with one's necessitous neighbours who live on the same social plane. . . . Business management has a chance to proceed on a temperate and sagacious calculation of profit and loss, untroubled by sentimental considerations of human kindness or irritation or of honesty' (1958: 31).

Low-Trust Relations: The Separation of Economics and Ethics

The trend towards the specific reciprocation of economic exchange, with its accompanying features of bargaining, grudging concession and wary mutual inspection, provided an encouraging context for the growth of doctrines which separated economics and ethics, utility and morality. Such doctrines rationalized a species of alienation already being structurally created by the growth of highly differentiated, highly specific roles and relations which minimized the contribution of the ethical self in the reciprocating act. 'Contempt for sentimentality is the hardening of the self to *endure* isolation in order that one's market options should not be preempted' (Gouldner 1971: 387). In rationalizing this 'hardening of the self' such doctrines helped to legitimize and promote it. Thus the adage 'Trade is one thing, religion is another'; once advanced as 'an audacious novelty, the doctrine that religion and economic interests form two separate and co-ordinate kingdoms, of which neither, without presumption, can encroach on the other . . .' came to be accepted 'with an unquestioning assurance at which its earliest exponents would have felt some embarrassment' (Tawney 1938: vi). The great merchants and capitalists of the sixteenth and seventeenth centuries, moving 'in a world where loans were made, not to meet the temporary difficulty of an unfortunate neighbour, but as a profitable investment on the part of not too scrupulous business men, who looked after themselves and expected others to do the same', threw their weight 'against the traditional restrictions', and resented 'the attempts made by preachers and popular movements to apply doctrines of charity and "good conscience" to the impersonal mechanism of large-scale transactions . . .' (*Ibid*: 165).

A society marked by the symbol of the oath of loyalty was giving way to a society marked by specific contract. 'The employment of industrious labourers, not the maintenance of loyal dependants, is the way to prosper now', writes Hill (1969: 264). He quotes Adam Smith: 'A man grows rich by employing a multitude of manufacturers, he grows poor by maintaining a multitude of menial servants', and adds: 'Smith realized that he was dealing with a distinction between two historically different social orders' (*Ibid*: 264–5). Such symbols of diffuse personalized commitment as oaths could not take the strain of securing obligations in the emerging order of economic exchange, a fact recognized by Samuel Butler, who described them as 'like ribbons and knots in dressing, that seem to tie something but do not at all. For nothing but interest does really oblige' (*Ibid*: 400–1). Hill seeks to cap the point by observing that 'supernatural sanctions became less necessary in a society in which honesty was manifestly the best policy . . .' (*Ibid*: 386). But was it? For all that Commons, the legal theorist, could describe 'confidence in others' as 'the largest of all the utilities' in the complex interdependence of capitalist society (1924: 14), there remains a great deal more to say. Davis says some of it. 'Reliance for the successful formation or emergence of this "largest of all the utilities" upon a natural identity of interests, upon Adam Smith's "invisible hand", leads to food adulteration, monopoly prices, fraudulent advertising, and flimsy construction. . . .' Confidence may prove to be misplaced 'and there tends to be a closer and closer supervision of standards and performance by societal agents. One characteristic of modern economic institutions, then, is a steady growth of the role of the government, the only organization presumed to represent *all* members of a society, in controlling economic activities. The investor, the consumer, and the worker are all protected more and more explicitly by a multiplication of laws and a proliferation of government agencies' (1955: 473–4). There could hardly be a passage more germane to the proposition that, given increasing specificity in roles and contraction of the discretionary element, the participants' sense of responsibility for observing the prescribed terms becomes increasingly problematical.

This proposition is not without significance for understanding certain other characteristics of urban life, complex in causation though these obviously are. Moore refers to 'crowds without true social interaction' and to the 'segmental and even transitory interaction' which abounds in cities. In these circumstances, the maintenance of *primary* or informal social control by family and friends is 'difficult and occasionally impossible'. Formal social control by police and the law is developed to take the strain – methods taking the form of impersonal disapproval rather than moral outrage. 'The efficiency and integrity of the police are questioned, legitimately or not; but personal responsibility for maintaining order and decency is radically reduced' (1965: 91). We need not follow Moore into what he admits to be an exaggerated picture of deviant and antisocial behaviour in urban centres – exaggeration deliberately introduced for purposes of exposition. It is enough for our purpose to note that crime and delinquency are disproportionately urban and to suggest that this is connected with the high incidence of specific low-trust roles and relations.

Gouldner speaks to the same theme. 'A technologically advanced civilization reduces and standardizes the skills required for wanted performances: it simplifies and mechanizes many tasks. It is therefore not as dependent on the rhetoric of morality or the mobilization of moral sentiment to ensure desired performances. Thus, within the technologically advanced sectors of society, individuals are less likely to be required to possess moral qualities and to be treated as moral actors. . . . For men are becoming more interchangeable, more replaceable, and removable at lower costs. . . . In other words, men are less likely to experience themselves as potent and in control of their own destinies as bureaucracy, technocracy, and science become increasingly autonomous and powerful forces by which men feel entrapped. Men's capacity and need to see themselves as moral actors are threatened. Many, therefore, will be disposed either to reassert their potency *per se*, aggressively or violently and without regard to the moral character of such affirmation, or to relinquish the entire assumption that they are moral actors and capable of moral action' (1971: 277).

These trends towards economic exchange were also producing new meanings in the concept of cooperation which can still entangle us in semantic confusions. Paradox can be useful when the effort to unravel it yields fresh insight. This is exemplified by opposing the proposition that 'Present forms of organization are unable to elicit cooperation' with the proposition that 'Large enterprises exemplify cooperation developed to an unprecedented degree.' The confusion is resolved by identifying two distinct connotations of the principal term. 'Despite the romantic yearnings of efficiency experts for the warmth and comradeship of the mediaeval workshop, modern organization is unmistakably bent towards the elimination of cooperation as a moral and emotional element in work, so that cooperation as a technical coordination of resources may be enhanced. In the former case, cooperation is something which may be freely given or withheld; in the latter, it is an abstract quality of a productive system in which necessary functions are appropriately interlocked' (Caplow 1964: 27–8).

The Ideology of Bourgeois Liberalism

Accompanying the emergence of this new social and economic order was the ideology of classical bourgeois liberalism. '. . . Its fundamental system had been . . . firmly elaborated in the seventeenth and eighteenth centuries . . . Its general assumptions about the world and man were marked by a pervasive individualism . . . In brief, for classical liberalism, the human world consisted of self-contained, individual atoms with certain built-in passions and drives, each seeking above all to maximize his satisfactions and minimize his dissatisfactions, equal in this to all others, and "naturally" recognizing no limits or rights of interference with his urges . . . In the course of pursuing this self-interest, each individual in this anarchy of equal competitors found it advantageous or unavoidable to enter into certain relations with other individuals, and this complex of useful arrangements – which were often expressed in the frankly commercial terminology of "contract" – constituted society and social or political groups' (Hobsbawm 1964: 278–9). Along with celebrating freedom of contract, liberal ideology 'refused, in any profound or coherent way, to consider the state as a potential source of social good' (Laski 1947: 256). Some role for the state there had to be. '. . . it would suppress force and fraud, keep property safe, and aid men in enforcing contracts' (Hobhouse 1911: 89). For the separation of economics from ethics was making clear that the concept of contract had to include not only 'the process of bargaining for advantage, in which each party, with particular goals and interests and the particular advantages or disadvantages of his position, seeks to make the best possible bargain', but also the social provision of impersonal, impartial, and authoritative mechanisms for adjudicating whether a given disputed act by either party was consistent with his obligations under the contract, and for applying socially prescribed and sanctioned rules also to such issues as 'guarantees of interest of third parties, restrictions on fraud and coercion and the like' (Parsons and Smelser 1956: 104–5).

Indeed, the seventeenth century theorist Hobbes had placed at the centre of his political philosophy the need for an all-powerful centralized state to enforce these social prescriptions. Without it men would live in the 'state of nature'. Hobbes's state of nature 'is a statement of the behaviour to which men as they now are, men who live in civilized societies and have the desires of civilized men, would be led if all law and contract enforcement (i.e. even the present imperfect enforcement) were removed' (Macpherson 1964: 22). According to Macpherson's persuasive interpretation, Hobbes argues that men in society are driven into an endless struggle for power over others; not necessarily because they themselves seek ever more power and gratifications but because if they are to defend what they have against the power-hungry predators they cannot opt out of the contest. That Hobbes argues in this way implies an assumption on his part that social arrangements are such as to permit some men to prey upon others. Were there to be any customary protection of men's positions and life chances, any customary limitation of their competitive activities, the need for this contest would be correspondingly reduced. His assumption therefore embodies a model of society which permits and indeed requires the continual invasion of every man by every other. Since no society could permit this to take place through physical violence, Hobbes must be assuming one which provides peaceful, non-violent ways by which every man can constantly seek power over others without destroying the social fabric.

This Macpherson terms 'the possessive market society' – a society in which, by contrast with one based on custom and status, there is no authoritative allocation of work or rewards and in which, by contrast with a society of independent producers who exchange only their products in the market, there is a market in labour as well as in products. If a single criterion of the possessive market society is sought it would be that man's labour is a commodity, i.e. that a man's energy and skill are his own, yet are regarded not as integral parts of his personality but as alienable possessions, the use and disposal of which he is free to hand over to others for a price. Such a concept also includes the characteristic that where labour has become a commodity, market relations so shape or permeate all social relations that we may refer not simply to a market *economy* but to a market *society* (Macpherson 1964: 40–8).

More fully expounded, Macpherson's concept of possessive market society includes the following features. There is no authoritative allocation of work or rewards. Each individual seeks rationally to maximize his utilities, and his capacity to labour is his own property and is alienable as are such forms of private property as land and other resources. Men pursue their utilities within an authoritative definition and enforcement of contracts. Necessary for the system to work 'is a substantial inequality of command over resources. There must be a class of men with sufficient resources to employ the labour of others, and a class of men with so little resources as to offer themselves for employment' (*Ibid*: 53–4, 85).

How widely is this system legitimized? 'Is the lifelong wage-earner, living at bare subsistence level, capable of acknowledging obligation to a sovereign whose main function is to make and enforce the rules of contract and property, rules which the wage-earner may feel are what have put him and keep him in this precarious position?' He may, of course, see no alternative. But he may also be socialized and indoctrinated. In Hobbes's words: 'the Common-peoples minds, unless they be tainted with dependance on the Potent, or scribbled over with the opinions of their Doctors, are like clean paper, fit to receive whatsoever by Publique Authority shall be imprinted in them' (*Ibid*: 98–9). And if the common people could be taught the need for these rules, the enterprising men of property would certainly be capable of seeing it for themselves.

Hobbes's perspective was amended by Locke in ways which need not concern us here, but the essential picture of possessive market society remained. The normality and justice of the market in labour was as much a commonplace of seventeenth century thinking as the normality and justice of the markets in commodities and capital. To Locke a man's labour was so unquestionably his own property that he might freely sell it for wages, with the labour thus sold becoming the property of the buyer who was then entitled to appropriate the produce of that labour. And the implications went further. To insist that a man's labour is his own is not only to say that it is his to alienate in a wage contract; it is also to say that his labour and its productivity is something for which he owes no debt to civil society – a further perspective on the separation of economics and ethics. The traditional view that property and labour were social functions with social obligations was thereby undermined (*Ibid*: 215–21).

The Survival of Diffuse Relations in the West

Models always carry the danger, however, of being mistaken for descriptions, and the possessive market society model is no exception. The construct of economically rational, acquisitive behaviour in free and impersonal markets assumes that all extraneous considerations are put aside, including such sentiments, values, and relationships as might obscure, complicate, or confuse a purely economic calculation. We need to remind ourselves, therefore, that a purely contractual social order does not and could not exist. This much could be deduced from the initial elements of our theoretical framework, when it was noted that no work role was totally without discretion and that pure economic exchange marked by totally prescribed terms was not possible. But more fundamentally, our examination of work role definitions in the light of costs and benefits showed some work designers calculating that, in order to evoke a desired degree of moral involvement and commitment, certain job definitions should be cast in diffuse, high-discretion terms.

Macaulay's description of non-contractual business relations in the United States (a description easily recognizable as relevant to other countries of the West) speaks directly to the principles and propositions embodied in these arguments. He defines contract in terms of low-trust economic exchange. It comprises 'Rational planning of the transaction with careful provision for as many future contingencies as can be foreseen' and 'the existence or use of actual or potential legal sanctions to induce performance of the exchange or to compensate for non-performance' (1963: 56). The model is therefore similar to the low-trust syndrome used here to analyse low-discretion work role definitions, with their specific prescriptions for all contingencies and their tendency to resort to punitive sanctions for maintaining performance. Macaulay is concerned with, among other things, the costs and benefits to businessmen of using contract in relationships with customers and suppliers. His researches show that 'while detailed planning and legal sanctions play a significant role in some exchanges between business, in many business exchanges their role is small . . . Detailed negotiated contracts can get in the way of creating good exchange relationships between business units.' One major reason is the 'danger perceived by some businessmen . . . that one would have to perform his side of the bargain to its letter and thus lose what is called "flexibility". Businessmen may welcome a measure of vagueness in the obligations they assume so that they may negotiate matters in light of the actual circumstances.' But another factor is the objection by some businessmen 'that in such a carefully worked out relationship one gets performance only to the letter of the contract. Such planning indicates a lack of trust and blunts the demands of friendship, turning a cooperative venture into an antagonistic horse trade.' Here, of course, is the expression in a different context of the same low-trust, economic-exchange dynamic that we saw developing out of highly prescribed work rules and relations. 'Businessmen often prefer to rely on "a man's word" in a brief letter, a handshake, or "common honesty and decency" – even when the transaction involves exposure to serious risks . . . Disputes are frequently settled without reference to the contract or potential or actual legal sanctions. There is a hesitancy to speak of legal rights or to threaten to sue in these negotiations.'

Underlying such responses is a rough and ready assessment that their benefits outweigh the costs when measured by the needs of a continuing relationship. One of Macaulay's respondents expressed a common attitude in saying 'You don't read legalistic contract clauses at each other if you ever want to do business again. One doesn't run to lawyers if he wants to stay in business because one must behave decently.' And another remarked: 'You can settle any dispute if you keep the lawyers and accountants out of it. They just do not understand the give-and-take needed in business.' A give and take relationship is, of course, a high-trust relationship. But business situations vary and not all assessments come out on the side of maintaining high-trust relations. 'Exchanges are carefully planned when it is thought that planning and a potential legal sanction will have more advantages than disadvantages.' This corresponds with the assessment made by work designers when they decide that low-discretion roles and relations are economically preferable. These assessments are not necessarily valid. They may fail to take certain consequences into account, or be overtaken by change in an important variable which shifts the balance of advantages but remains unperceived.

Macaulay notes, but possibly puts too little emphasis upon, the importance of power in determining the quality of business relations. Our analysis of work roles stressed that weakness may constrain a subjugated group to submit to an employment relationship dictated in its nature by the more powerful party, which itself remains free of regulation and control. In his own context, Macaulay notes that 'Even if the controller of a small supplier creates a contractual system of dealing, there will be no contract if the firm's large customer prefers not to be bound to anything.'

In order to demonstrate the importance of diffuse orientations among such high-discretion professionals as scientists we may turn to Hagstrom's study (1965) of gift giving as an organizing principle within their community; a study which brings together many of the related notions deployed in this and preceding chapters. The gift in question is the unpaid contribution to a scientific periodical. By analogy the analysis covers contributions to learned journals over the whole range of academic disciplines. The return on this gift is highly diffuse in nature. The donor's status as a scientist is established and he hopes for prestige and recognition. As in all gift giving, the expectation of a return cannot be publicly acknowledged as the motive. Were it to be so the danger would arise of the exchange of gifts ceasing, 'perhaps to be succeeded by contractual exchange' (1965: 106). In other words, even to articulate the expectation of some defined return is to risk stepping on a slippery slope towards ever more specific reciprocation. Hagstrom then notes, however, that gift giving, precisely because of its particularist and diffuse nature, 'usually reduces the rationality of economic action'. Rationality is maximized when the costs of alternative courses of action can be assessed, and such costs are usually established in free markets or in the plans of central directing agencies. In other words, the rationality of economic action is maximized by economic exchange, whereas gift giving is, of course, social exchange. Why, then, should the gift persist in these and other areas of professional activity 'when it is essentially obsolete as a form of exchange in most other areas of modern life . . . ?' Hagstrom's reply begins by noting that the rationality of professional services is different from the rationality of the market. 'In contractual exchanges, when services are rewarded on a direct financial or barter basis, the client abdicates, to a considerable degree, his *moral control* over the producer. In return, the client is freed from personal ties with the producer, and is able to choose rationally between alternative sources of supply' (his italics). Hagstrom is here referring to the way in which economic exchange tends to reduce, even exclude, ethical and expressive relations. In the professions, however, 'the abdication of moral control would disrupt the system'. The producer of professional services must be strongly committed to higher values, for the client's dependence is heightened by his inability to evaluate the service and his consequent vulnerability to exploitation. The professional 'must be responsible for his products, and it is fitting that he be not alienated from them'. The diffuse exchange of gifts for recognition helps to maintain such orientations. The recipient finds it difficult to refuse them, while the donor is held responsible for adhering to central norms and values. The principle of *caveat emptor* does not apply. 'Furthermore, the donor is not alienated from his gift, but retains a lasting interest in it. It is, in a sense, his property.' Hagstrom generalizes from this the proposition that '*whenever strong commitments to values are expected, the rational calculation of punishment and rewards is regarded as an improper basis for making decisions*' (his italics). Self-discipline is regarded as of equal or greater importance. Thus 'the gift exchange (or the norm of service), as opposed to barter or contractual exchange, is particularly well suited to social systems in which great reliance is placed on the ability of well-socialized persons to operate independently of formal controls' (*Ibid*: 114–17).

As the preceding analysis has suggested, the same approach can be turned upon all high-discretion roles. High level managers and administrators whose decisions cannot be easily or quickly monitored are treated as members of a high-trust fraternity sharing certain goals and values and receiving diffuse (as well as specific) rewards. Thus can their superiors hope to retain moral control over them. Should either party to these arrangements seek to increase the specificity of the service or the reward, reciprocation in like vein will follow unless prevented by power or legitimizing sentiments.

Contract and Diffuse Relations in Japan

We now need to carry over, into this sketch of the wider setting of work, our recognition of the importance of cultural or subcultural values which may or may not legitimize emergent trends in the organization and conduct of economic activities, thereby encouraging or discouraging them and shaping the responses of those caught up in them. Acknowledgement of this factor drew our attention earlier to the possibility that occupants of low-discretion roles in a complex hierarchy might fully legitimize their situation, thereby inhibiting the low-trust dynamic from coming into operation and ensuring high-trust relations.

This consideration can be applied to the emergence of contract. Some Western European cultures are thought to have lent themselves more readily than cultures elsewhere to the accommodation and legitimation of the values of economic exchange. Japan offers an interesting contrast by carrying much further than Macaulay shows to be the case in Western societies the continued infusion of economic activities with diffuse orientations. Traditional values 'were given a new meaning in the context of modern industrial Japanese society'. Along with the familial system, 'the collectivity values and various forms of the traditional particularistic obligatory relationships between individuals were also emphasized . . . The élite persistently inculcated the masses with a view that individualism and individual freedom were contrary to the virtues and traditions of Japan.' As a consequence, 'Various forms of particularistic, hierarchically-oriented obligations in interpersonal relationships are still very much evident in almost every sphere of Japanese life, including the large bureaucratic organizations. Indeed, the traditional reciprocal obligations have been given a new meaning. . . .' Under the Japanese philosophy of managerial organization, 'a precise definition of individual functions and responsibilities is deemed unnecessary, and it is believed that it may even disrupt the harmonious cooperative relationships between various groups' (Yoshino 1971: 25, 42–3, 204).

Kawashima argues that the 'contractual relationship in Japan is by nature quite precarious and cannot be sustained by legal sanctions' (1964: 188). He relates this to two major characteristics of Japanese society. 'Not only the village community and the family, but even contractual relationships have customarily been hierarchical. From the construction contract arises a relationship in which the contractor defers to the owner as his patron; from the contract of lease a relationship in which the lessee defers to the lessor; from the contract of employment a relationship in which the servant or employee defers to the master or employer; . . . from the contract of sale a relationship in which the seller defers to the buyer (the former being expected, in each case, to yield to the direction or desire of the latter). At the same time, however, the status of the master or employer is patriarchal and not despotic; in other words, he is supposed, not only to dominate, but also to patronize, and therefore partially to consent to the requests of his servant or employee. Consequently, even though their social roles are defined in one way or other, the role definition is precarious and each man's role is contingent on that of the other.' What are being described here are diffuse high-trust relations. 'Second, in traditional social groups relationships between people of equal status have also been to a great extent "particularistic" and at the same time "functionally diffuse" . . . their social roles are defined in general and very flexible terms so that they can be modified whenever circumstances dictate.' Within this harmony definition of social roles, there 'is a strong expectation that a dispute should not and will not arise; even when one does occur it is to be solved by mutual understanding'. Similarly, parties to a contractual agreement are not expected to become involved in serious differences 'and rather hesitate to ask for any kind of written agreement, fearing that such a request might impair the amicable inclination of the other party'. Both social and business custom 'forbids one to terminate a harmonious social tie by selfishly insisting on one's own interests' (*Ibid*: 185–8).

Contract observance and enforcement of the economic-exchange type, relatively common in the West even allowing for Macaulay's qualifications, still therefore meets some cultural resistance in Japan, where its divisive effects in rupturing diffuse social relations (and thereby initiating what is called here the low-trust dynamic) meet with a certain disapproval. This diffuseness of relations has to some extent marked the labour policy of Japanese employers, for whom it proved a useful calculated strategy to adopt when, in the early years of this century, they sought ways of creating a stable and amenable industrial labour force (Taira 1964: 217–18). 'Management began to extol the virtues of the traditional family ideology and to emphasize that the problems of employer-employee relations could be approached much more effectively through the application of the familial concepts of benevolence and reciprocity, rather than through labour legislation or organized labour movements' (Yoshino 1971: 75). This strategy has been summarized by Rosovsky. '. . . membership in a particular group is usually permanent and irrevocable; recruitment into the group is based on personal qualities; status in the group is a continuation and extension of status held in the society at the time of entry into the group; reward in the productive group is only partly in the form of money and is based on broad social criteria; the formal organization of the factory is elaborated in a wide range and considerable number of formal positions; and finally the penetration of the company into the life activities of the workers and the responsibility taken by the company for the worker are extensive' (1961: 102–4). Thus the predominant nexus between management and worker 'is not a contractual relationship in which each party agrees to an employer-employee relationship, bearing certain conditions and terms, which can be terminated at the option of the parties involved. The Japanese employment relationship is an unconditional one, requiring *total* commitment on the part of employer and employee' (Yoshino 1971: 229). Whereas in most countries industrialization broke down traditional diffuse relationships beyond recall, Japanese employers found it possible to reconstruct a traditional organization in the factory. 'No other society has been innovational in a precisely parallel way' (Hagen 1965: 345).

But while a strategy based on long-term mutual commitment and diffuse obligations offers benefits in terms of the stability and attachment of the labour force, it also involves costs in terms of rigidity and inflexibility which are coming to be seen as increasingly heavy in the face of economic fluctuations, labour shortages, and needs for rapid structural adaptation and change (Yoshino 1971: Chapter 8). 'As time passed, the ideology of managerial paternalism became burdensome for the Japanese employers' (Taira 1964: 218). Even within the management system itself there are moves towards detailed job classifications, more precise allocation of responsibility and decision-making, tighter controls, and rewards for individual merit (Yoshino 1971: 223, 238, 263, 269). The rank and file labour force is certainly no less affected. Increasingly now, it is said, the emphasis is on labour as a commodity, subject to the forces of demand and supply. 'Management is increasingly taking the offensive in getting rid of the rigidity of "lifetime commitment" . . . Inter-firm competition for labour is increasing . . .' (Taira 1964: 225). This trend towards the more specific obligations of market contract and economic exchange in the employment relationship is rationalized by the ideology of progress and economic growth.

We would expect this movement by management in a low-trust direction to evoke low-trust responses on the part of employees and unions. Many Japanese unions have been confined to an individual enterprise, and only loosely federated in national associations. Within these enterprise unions, employees have been closely and sympathetically identified with the interests of company and management, and union bargaining aspirations and strategy have shaped themselves accordingly. If management increasingly narrows the nexus between itself and its employees by sharpening it towards calculative economic exchange, employees could be predicted to turn outwards in seeking high-trust alliances with those similarly placed elsewhere. This is indeed envisaged by current Japanese commentators. 'It is becoming more and more evident that the structure and bargaining strategy of the enterprise unions can no longer command the loyalty of the workers . . . To meet the challenge of the management offensive, workers will now have to break through the psychological and operational barriers of enterprise-consciousness to form larger and stronger defence alliances with as many fellow-workers as possible' (*Ibid*: 226). Another observer agrees that 'Under the impact of technological and managerial innovations and rationalization, which management will strive to introduce . . . , enterprise unions will . . . have to seek more assistance from "outside" when they confront management . . .' (Shirai 1965: 206).

It would be a mistake, however, to assume that the impulses

towards low-trust relations were imparted only from the management side. A quickening competition between employers for mobile labour – one of the symptoms of the move towards a perception of labour in more specifically contract terms as a commodity – could not have developed unless some workers, too, were prepared to accept such a definition of the employment relationship. '. . . as the post-war excess supplies of labour were absorbed after fifteen years of recovery and growth, workers began to look around for better employment opportunities . . .' (Taira 1964: 227). Another relevant force at work is the strong drive within Japan, as in many countries, to gain the full recognized status of 'modernity', where 'modernization' is defined as the creation 'of relationships more closely resembling Western models' (Nakayama 1965: 226). Sometimes it is argued, as for example by the (then) President of Japan's Institute of Labor, that in accord with the predictions of 'convergence' theory (Kerr *et al.* 1962: Chaps. 2, 9, 10), 'labour-management relations in the industrialized countries appear to be moving towards the creation of a common pattern' (Nakayama 1965: 225–6). The combination of an aspiration to appear modern, i.e. Western, and a conviction that in any case underlying forces point in that direction, may influence leadership choices towards a Western low-trust pattern of relations marked by perceptions of divergent interests, a conflict stance, and other characteristics of economic exchange. It is difficult not to sense a note of hope in the President's statement that 'even under what are called typically Japanese conditions the modern pattern of industrial relations has steadily been and is emerging' (*Ibid*: 235).

The Employment Relationship: The Growth of Specificity

The Japanese employers' strategy of using traditional, diffuse cultural dispositions as a resource for labour control would have been impossible in Britain, where the modern pattern of contractual employment relations was established by the latter part of the sixteenth century, long before industrialization and the factory system. 'There is plenty of evidence that England approximated closely to a possessive market society in the seventeenth century. Very nearly half the men were fulltime wage earners; if the cottagers are counted as part time wage earners, the proportion is over two-thirds. And while the wage relationship was not as completely impersonal as it was to become in the following century, it was already, as Hobbes knew, essentially a market relationship' (Macpherson 1964: 61). As we shall see later, a few employers in the early decades of the present century tried to reconstruct a more diffuse relationship with their employees, hoping thereby to evoke a corresponding commitment and identification. Here and there enough of a return emerged to make the policy worth while. But it could never offer a general basis for Britain's industrial order, for by this time such cultural traditions of the wider social setting as might have given it the necessary support had, in the urban industrial centres at least, been severely eroded by mobility, class hostilities, and other consequences of the employment market relationship which treated labour as a commodity.

This brings us to the point where we need to examine this employment relationship more closely in the context of the contractual society that had emerged. What is meant by the 'employment contract'? Is this the significant feature at which to look when we explore the wage relationship? The answers to these questions will lead us into an analysis of the changes wrought in that relationship by shifts of power, the emergence of new ideologies, and the operation of the low-trust dynamic.

It has already emerged that while work roles and relations can never be so tightly prescribed as to manifest economic exchange in its pure form, some may be sufficiently so as to incline us to categorize them in those terms. Others may be so far removed from this model, as a consequence of being infused with non-specific expectations and obligations, that we characterize them as diffuse. It was found necessary, in constructing our theoretical framework, to distinguish between situations where the pattern of roles and relations is legitimized by both parties, and situations where it is actively imposed by one party against very different preferences held by the other – differences which can result in a variety of responses ranging from forced passive compliance to periodic collective revolt. While there is a direct use of power in the latter situations, power is also likely to play an indirect part in the promotion of the former, by enabling those with command over resources to socialize and indoctrinate others into convenient beliefs and values through which they then legitimize the *status quo*. Given legitimation by both parties, any pattern takes on a high-trust quality for its participants in the sense that the situation embodies no dynamic making for change in a low-trust direction. Should either party withdraw legitimation, aspiring towards change in a direction not desired by the other, any pattern is likely to be pushed by the non-legitimizing party in a low-trust direction when the requisite power comes to hand. But the probabilities with respect to the granting or withholding of legitimation are such that, provided this variable is kept in mind, we can develop subsequent analysis on the assumption that low-discretion work roles in the context of Western industrial societies tend to generate low-trust relations.

Gauging the quality of work relations is difficult enough even in the contemporary situation; it becomes far more so when we look back to pre-contractual times. There is, however, some usefulness in turning to anthropological analyses of non-industrial tribal societies of today and the more recent past. Udy's data drawn from a wide range of sources bring out clearly the distinction between social and economic exchange in work arrangements. Among traditional peoples, contractual work seems initially to make its appearance as something of a last ditch response to a shortage of labour and only then if they see no alternative. The response to a work load too heavy for the familial group to handle is at least as likely to be an extension of the familial principle to reciprocity among families as to be an effort to recruit workers by contractual means. If help is received from another family in non-routine tasks like, for example, house construction, 'reciprocation is definitely expected' in 'roughly equivalent amounts of time and effort' but the 'time and occasion for reciprocation are indefinite' (Udy 1970: 67) – an instance of social exchange. Routine tasks like planting and harvesting may lend themselves to a more clearcut rotational reciprocity under which all obligations are discharged within a relatively short-term cycle. Such a pattern is somewhat nearer the economic-exchange end of the continuum by virtue of being less diffuse. It remains true, however, of this as of other familial work that performance itself is a direct means for fulfilling some social obligation and avoiding the sanctions attached to non-fulfilment.

The further along the continuum the nearer we approach pure economic exchange, characterized as contractual work in which general social obligations to participate are minimal. Contractual labour depends upon the presence of a reward system that can replace them as an effective means of motivating work. 'A *reward*, in this context, is any object or state of affairs beyond the discharge of a social obligation deemed desirable by a worker and accruing to him as a result of participating in a work organization' (*Ibid*: 74). It is usually and necessarily different from the product. While it may be money, food is the most common reward in traditional contractual arrangements.

In the transition from full social to full economic exchange intermediate stages can be identified. A work contract is *employer-specific* if a worker or group of workers agrees to perform diffuse services for some party in return for some reward. In a *job-specific* arrangement the worker supplies explicitly specified services as well as having a specific employer. 'By specifically defining and delimiting the worker's job, this type of arrangement greatly narrows the extent of his diffuse obligations to his employer.' An occupationally based contract is similar to a job-specific contract except that workers are recruited at least in part by virtue of their identification with recognized occupations embodying the specific tasks to which they are to be assigned. 'Each successive stage represents a progressive disengagement from the social setting . . .' (*Ibid*: 76, 79).

Returning now to Western societies in their early phases of industrialization, we can trace the process of continuing refinement of specificity in Smelser's analysis (1959) of the cotton industry in Britain, the pacemaker of the Industrial Revolution. Defining 'advanced' or 'developed' society as possessing a complex organization of differentiated social and cultural components, he demonstrates how older and more diffuse roles and structures become differentiated out, under economic pressures, into new and more specific ones. Care is needed in relating Smelser's analysis to the concepts and categories used here, for he is not concerned with changes in discretionary content. Since it cannot be assumed that the increased specificity in terms of narrower task range which he describes is necessarily accompanied by increased specificity in the sense of lower discretion, attention will be confined to the situations where this was demonstrably the case.

Before the 'putting-out' system of production began to develop in the late seventeenth century, role differentiation was limited. Most of the production was carried on domestically by weavers and their families, with a fusion of master's and workman's labour, sporadic marketing, and only a 'fuzzy differentiation' between decisions about technical processes, decisions to produce, and decisions on capital spending (Smelser 1959: 52–3). The 'semi-independent weaver' who owned his own goods could gauge his output freely and was under no obligation, beyond the pressure of the market, to meet definite schedules.

Under the putting-out system, merchants asserted greater control over the productive process, giving out raw materials to the weavers who worked them up at home and returned them to the merchant for payment. Since the merchants did not relinquish ownership of the materials their control became both more definite and supported by a legal right of ownership. The weaver was now losing discretion over decisions to produce and over control of working capital even though it remained physically in his hands. The independent weaver-producer who sold for profit to merchants gave way to the weaver who earned wages for working up raw material. Later the employer came to supply looms on the worker's own premises; sometimes he supplied both looms and premises. Relations sharpened increasingly into those between a relatively powerful superior exercising far-reaching discretionary control over relatively weak subordinates. Smelser offers abundant evidence that these shifts towards low-discretion roles generated a gathering withdrawal of legitimacy on the part of those subjected to them. The resulting low-trust patterns manifested themselves in a variety of ways. There was a marked decline in the observance of the prescribed elements of the employment relationship. 'Theft and embezzlement of raw materials probably concerned the employers most' (*Ibid*: 65). The low-trust dynamic was now under way. Acts of Parliament in 1702, 1710, 1740, and 1749 sought to stamp out such practices but were difficult to enforce. Manufacturers' dissatisfaction mounted, too, with other characteristics of the putting-out system – failure of coordination in production and delivery; difficulties of enforcing work schedules and quality standards; problems of punctuality and work discipline generally. The answer was seen in terms of bringing the workers into factories in order the better to control them. 'Workers who had been their own masters . . . were now subjected to penalties which reflected . . . the employer's anxious endeavour to control their every move' (Bendix 1963: 39). The emergence of the factory system owed as much to the drive for closer coordination, discipline, and control of the labour force as to the pressures of technology. It was not long, however, before the latter were contributing their own powerful influence to the low-trust dynamic. The introduction of steam power differentiated still more sharply between 'roles involved in the control of capital' and 'those involved in the processes of production'. By the same token, it differentiated more completely between those responsible for the decisions to produce and those engaged in production. 'Workmen became more subordinated to a work discipline, because the power-source lay in steam, not in their own muscles; they could no longer pace their industry in the cottage or even work sixteen hours a day during the last days of the week in a hand-mule shed to make up for a leisurely Monday and Tuesday. The introduction of steam, therefore, did not create new roles, but pushed the old to a new level of specificity' (Smelser 1959: 118).

A decline in the disposition to observe the prescribed elements of the employment relation was but one aspect, however, of the gathering low-trust pattern. Another was a reactionary nostalgia for the older, more diffuse division of labour for which William Cobbett was one of the better-known spokesmen. 'The social ideology of Cobbettism idealized the division of family labour of the recent past. Cobbett visualized an independent yeoman or craftsman at the head of the family and a wife who rose early, worked hard, reared her children, baked and brewed. What prevented this Utopia was the whole commercial and industrial system – interest, paper money, money lenders, Jews, rich and crude factory-owners, and sinecures' (*Ibid*: 250).

Reactions of this kind gave way, however, to accommodative responses by which employees accepted the essential features of the system but sought marginal modifications for their own advantage. Collective organizations of employees reciprocated low-trust regulation of their work behaviour by employers with attempts to restrict the discretion of the employers on issues which they considered important. Sometimes these attempts were indirect, as when political campaigns sought to induce Parliament to enact legislation controlling working hours. Sometimes there were direct efforts by certain occupational groups to impose specific work rules upon employers. What eventually emerged as the method destined to predominate was collective bargaining, through which trade unions sought to negotiate, on a compromise basis, marginal improvements for their members in wage rates and other terms and conditions of employment.

The Employment Contract: Was it a Contract?

Before we pursue more fully the implications of collective bargaining for our analysis, other questions must be answered if we are to assimilate into that analysis what has been noted so far about the employment relation under industrialization. One of the master symbols of the emergent social order has been seen to be contract. Voluntary agreement forged through bargaining over specific terms, the essence of economic exchange, was seen as the mechanism which articulated atomistic, self-regarding individuals into the collaborative aggregates and linked processes necessary for civil society. How did the employment relation fit into this contractual society and into the ideologies prevalent within it? Can the contract of employment be seen as simply another manifestation of this increasingly pervasive form of exchange?

Certainly one would expect to find a strong ideological drive asserting it to be so. If mediaeval ideology, nourished and sustained by powerful interests, idealized the personalized bonds and commitments of feudal social structure as an equal balance of reciprocal diffuseness, the dominant ideology of newly emergent industrial society might be expected to idealize the employment contract, like all other contracts, in terms of an equal balance of reciprocal specificity. And evidence does indeed suggest a strain in this direction. Laski points to 'a growing sense, both in parliament and in the courts of law, that the nexus between master and man is purely economic, a relation, not a partnership implying reciprocal social duties' (1947: 155). And did not the evolving law of employment come increasingly during the nineteenth century to emphasize 'the personal and voluntary exchange of freely-bargained promises between two parties equally protected by the civil law alone'? (Wedderburn 1971: 77). Capitalism indeed 'provides a legitimation of domination which is no longer called down from the lofty heights of cultural tradition but instead summoned up from the base of social labor. The institution of the market, in which private property owners exchange commodities – including the market in which propertyless private individuals exchange their labor power as their only commodity – promises that exchange relations will be and are just owing to equivalence' (Habermas 1971: 359).

But the impersonal, calculating, low-trust attitudes of economic exchange were never universally accepted by employers, either in practice or in theory. Undoubtedly the general trend throughout the century was towards an' impersonal management of labor which depended upon the formulation of the conditions of employment and upon elaborate controls which verified the workers' compliance with these conditions' (Bendix 1963: 57). But persistently in some industries 'management depended upon a personal relationship between an employer and his workers, and hence upon the accidents of personal knowledge as well as upon the well-understood but unformulated relationship of trust which existed traditionally between a master and his men' (*Ibid*). This persistence might have its roots not only in cultural isolation or inertia but also in a social philosophy which stressed the coincidence of business success with high moral practice and with the principle of the master conducting himself as trustee of his men's 'true best interests'. This philosophy recommending *social* exchange in master–man relations, so far from becoming extinct, was to enjoy a minor revival in circumstances to be examined later.

We must also note the coexistence of ideology celebrating the employment contract as 'the personal and voluntary exchange of freely-bargained promises' with practical attitudes expressing a clear determination that it should be nothing of the kind. Such was the inequality of power between the employer and the individual employee that to describe 'agreements' between them as 'freely-bargained promises' obscured the high probability that for much of the time the latter felt virtually coerced by the former into settling for whatever he could get – a picture hardly consonant with the glories of contract as celebrated by, for example, Spencer (1969: 174–8, 317). Few of those who lauded the new industrial order were prepared explicitly to emphasize, as did Adam Smith a century before Spencer was writing, that 'It is not . . . difficult to foresee which of the two parties must, upon all ordinary occasions, have the advantage in the dispute, and force the other into a compliance with their terms . . . In all such disputes the masters can hold out much longer. A landlord, a farmer, a master manufacturer, or merchant, though they did not employ a single workman, could generally live a year or two upon the stocks which they have already acquired. Many workmen could not subsist a week, few could subsist a month, and scarce any a year without employment. In the long-run the workman may be as necessary to his master as his master is to him; but the necessity is not so immediate' (1904: 68).

But it was not only that the brute facts of power made the employment contract something a good deal less than contract. Had this been the case we should simply be confronting the commonplace situation of a definition diverging from reality. There was, however, a further ambivalence relating to *definition*. The legal construction which was put upon the contract of employment left it virtually unrecognizable as contract. To appreciate the reason for this the starting point must be that, for employers and their sympathizers, the application of pure contract doctrine to the employment relation, had this ever happened, would have borne a damaging double edge. Certainly there seemed to be a strong legitimizing principle available to hand in the idea, betrayed in practice though it might usually be, of free and equal agents negotiating contractual arrangements on the basis of each seeking to maximize his utilities in competitive markets. The legitimizing strength of this idea could surely be brought to include within its persuasiveness those who contracted to participate as employees in collaborative associations for the production of goods and service, and thereby help to integrate and stabilize the productive system?

But application of the contract system proper to the employment relation would have suggested implications alarming to property owners. Since no employment contract could anticipate all relevant contingencies arising in work relations, many issues had to be settled during the everyday conduct of business. How hard was the employee to work? Under what material, social, and psychological conditions? With what tools, machines, and materials? Within what framework of rules, discipline, and sanctions? With what rights to demur against specific instructions, managerial policies, and proposals for change? These constituted the reality of life under an employment contract. But who was to settle them? How were the empty boxes of the contract clauses to be given the necessary content? The damaging implication of pure contract doctrine for the employer would have been that it could not allow him to be the sole judge of whether his rules were arbitrary or exceeded the scope of his authority.

Certainly even under contract doctrine he might be granted – by the contract – the right to make rules, but he would not have the unrestricted right to decide whether the rules he had made or proposed to make were consistent with the contract (Selznick 1969: 135). For, as noted earlier, contract theory included the notion of appeal by either party to some outside adjudicating body in the event of behaviour claimed to be inconsistent with the contract. This incipient threat to so integral a part of everyday control as their wide discretionary powers over the labour force would have been intolerable. It followed that contract as the pure doctrine defined it could not be seen by the property-owning classes as an adequate foundation for governing the employment relation. Their needs were met by infusing the employment contract with the traditional law of master and servant, thereby granting them a legal basis for the prerogative they demanded. What resulted was a form of contract almost as far removed from the pure doctrinal form as the status relationship which had preceded it.

Master-Servant Relations

From the fourteenth century the law of employment, such as it was, had relied on the legal imagery of 'master and servant'. The law of master and servant 'was rooted in a society in which everyone was presumed to belong somewhere, and the great parameters of belonging were kinship, locality, religion, occupation, and social class. In all spheres of life, including spiritual communion, *subordination to legitimate authority* was thought to be a natural, inevitable, and even welcome accompaniment of moral grace and practical virtue' (Selznick 1969: 123, his italics).

Master and servant law looked to the household as a model and saw in it the foundations of orderly society. Hill, noting that the government of a family was likened 'to that of a ship, a corporate town, or a state', quotes a seventeenth century writer to the effect that 'In a family, the master or *paterfamilias*, who is a kind of petty monarch there, hath authority to prescribe to his children and servants . . .' (1969: 446). Servants included wage earners; all those who worked for an employer for a wage. The reason for this usage was that the household model was appropriate not only to the – overwhelmingly predominant – agricultural family unit in which hired labour supplemented the work of family members, but also to the pattern of work and training among skilled artisans. Within this setting, the relation of master and servant was diffuse and paternalistic. Work was carried out in the master's house or in a small shop near by, with the workman living as a member of the household. The positions of the master and servant were conceived in status terms. This was perfectly compatible with the notion that some terms of their association, such as its duration and the wages to be paid, could be contractual and therefore subject to bargaining and mutual assent. But beyond this it was never contemplated that the parties would design their own relationship. By far the greater part of the framework of mutual rights and obligations within which they connected themselves was to be taken as given. Its sources were custom, ideology, and the law, which between them defined the expectations and obligations accepted by all who entered into the master-servant relation. The servant was seen as contributing personal service, conceived not as specific labour duties but as a general contribution to the needs of the enterprise, be it household, farm, or workshop. 'In some vague but important sense, it was assumed that the whole person was committed to the relation' (Selznick 1969: 124). This is a conception closely akin to that which the earlier analysis saw as embodied in high-discretion roles and relations. These, it will be recalled, were analysed in such terms as diffuse, social exchange, and commitment of the whole person as against the segmental attachment of the alienated. In the pre-industrial situation the diffuseness of the servant's obligations derived not only from the fact that the division of labour was minimal, but also from his being expected to offer a 'general contribution to the needs of the enterprise'. This diffuseness was matched by reciprocal obligations bearing upon his employer. 'So far as the law was concerned, the status of master carried with it a responsibility for the general welfare of the servant' (*Ibid*: 128). Selznick quotes sources which indicate that this reciprocity was not wholly mythical, but even when it palpably failed the employee was ill equipped to enforce it. In the courts, which made themselves freely available for the supervision of the master-servant relation, using both criminal and civil sanctions, the 'magistrate was mainly at the service of the master, and the employee was at considerable disadvantage when he asserted a claim or grievance' (*Ibid*: 129). For while the authorities might well feel that some masters needed restraining occasionally when they stretched the social fabric too clumsily, there could be no questioning the overriding importance of passive obedience on the part of employees however badly their masters behaved: 'a king might be called to account by his subjects, but not a master by his servants' (Hill 1969: 460). The Webbs made the same point. 'The enactments rendering the workman liable to imprisonment for simple breach of a contract of service are historically to be traced to the period when the law denied to the labourer the right to withhold his service or to baragain as to his wages. Any neglect or abandonment of his work was, therefore, like a simple refusal to work at all, a breach, not so much of contract, as of a duty arising out of status and enforced by statute' (1920: 250, fn.).

The Employment Contract, Power, and Exploitation

So long as the family farm and the small family business predominated, this patriarchal paternalistic concept corresponded to economic realities in the sense that the division of labour and the social setting of work provided a context in which the participants could readily act out the concept if they chose to. And provided reality could be shown to approximate for at least part of the time to a genuinely reciprocal exchange, the concept could offer a legitimizing service by appearing to provide something of a justification for class domination.

Given the growth of industrialism, however, with its increasing division of labour, impersonal markets, and the segmental and specific relations thereby created, the old traditional diffuse relationship was not only structurally undermined in the practical sense that changing forms made it increasingly difficult to operate, it was also challenged in principle. Some employers, to be sure, might cling, in practice as well as precept, to the old assumptions, and their employees might support them. In our presentation of the theoretical framework we noted that an initial response of some when subjected to a movement in the low-trust direction is to yearn for a return to the old diffuseness. This response can be seen not only at the level of the work organization itself, as in the contemporary example of Gouldner's gypsum plant, but also in inchoate social movements such as that symbolized by the figure of William Cobbett. 'The social ideology of Cobbettism idealized the division of family labour of the recent past

. . . In terms of the social division of labour, Cobbettism represented a *de*-differentiation of roles . . . it was an idealization of a *less differentiated* form of society. Such idealization appears frequently when social roles are under pressure to differentiate' (Smelser 1959: 250–1, his italics). The same impulse emerged in the Romantic movement in literature; in the mediaevalist nostalgia of, for example, the Pre-Raphaelites, William Morris, and later A. J. Penty; and in certain forms of political expression such as rural Toryism and its links with some brands of Chartism and other working-class movements (Hill 1929).

But along with Political Economy, 'Progress, Reform, and the March of Intellect' went the doctrinal assertion of contract as economic exchange, purged of all traditional particularistic bonds and ties which might obscure economic calculation and impede the mobility of resources (including labour) in their ever vigilant search for the highest return. Many employers were ready to embrace a doctrine which divested their authority of any diffuse sense of duty, obligation, and responsibility towards those they employed. From this point of view the old master-servant law needed streamlining down towards the concept of contract. To define the employment relation as contract was to emphasize (a) the limited nature of the commitment made by the parties to each other and (b) the high value placed on the freedom of individuals, whatever their station, to enter contractual relations and define for themselves the terms of the bargain (Selznick 1969: 131).

The first of these propositions was acceptable enough to employers with respect to many of the work roles they had in mind, though as will emerge later its appeal was to lose some of its bloom. The second, however, as we have noted, could only be seen as explosive if ever it were to be applied in its full literalness to the employment contract. The pure milk of the contract gospel had to be diluted if the entrepreneur was to enjoy practical and moral support in his unfettered command over labour resources. The law did not, therefore, treat the conditions of employment as the outcome of free bargaining and mutual assent. The concept of contract had to be adapted to maintain, in Selznick's phrase, 'the organizational strength of the business enterprise' (*Ibid*: 136). This was done by marrying contractualism to the traditional master-servant notions. Although contract theory ostensibly gave full discretion to the parties in defining the nature and scope of authority, in fact the law imported into the employment contract a set of implied terms reserving full authority of direction and control to the employer.

Thus once the contract was defined as an employment contract the master-servant model was brought into play – though of course not all the original aspects of it. The notion of the employer's diffuse obligations was distinctly in decline. What was most important for the propertied classes was that element which legitimized the employer's prerogative. But along with this there was also carried over into contract an expectation that the personal status relations characteristic of the master-servant model would remain. 'The capitalist is very fond of declaring', wrote the Webbs, 'that labor is a commodity, and the wage contract a bargain of purchase and sale like any other. But he instinctively expects his wage-earners to render him, not only obedience, but also personal deference. If the wage contract is a bargain of purchase and sale like any other, why is the workman expected to touch his hat to his employer, and to say "sir" to him without reciprocity, when the employer meets on terms of equality the persons (often actually of higher social rank than himself) from whom he buys his raw material or makes the other bargains incidental to his trade?' (1902: 842, fn.).

When, into this picture of attitudes towards the employment relation, we introduce yet another strand – the ethic of work as a redemptive activity – complexity and ambivalence become compounded. Labour emerges as a highly peculiar entity – at once a commodity, an obligation to social superiors, and a source of spiritual or secular enhancement for the self. We must content ourselves here, however, with noting that by 'the end of the nineteenth century the employment contract had become a very special sort of contract – in large part a legal device for guaranteeing to management the unilateral power to make rules and exercise discretion' (Selznick 1969: 135). In the very heyday of contract, the evolving modern law of employment was drawing heavily on the old master-servant law by incorporating the traditional subordination of the workman. To be sure, this was not the only legal prop available to sustain managerial authority, which was also taken to be 'an incident of ownership, a matter of property right' not dependent on contractual agreement. But although this view probably had wide acceptance, 'legally it was not clear that the employer's property right gave him the authority to govern employees as he saw fit' (*Ibid*: 137). Young, in fact, expressly denies that it did (1963). 'In the end', argues Selznick, 'most stress was laid on the theory that ownership carried with it the right to freedom of contract . . .' (*Ibid*: 137).

But this, as we have seen, was no ordinary contract when applied to the employment relation, as is evidenced by some of its social and legal consequences. The nineteenth century saw the continuation of a practice, dating from the Statute of Labourers (1351) of passing enactments which 'subjected workmen who failed to fulfil their duties to the master employing them to criminal penalties, including imprisonment. Similar penalties did not attach to employers who broke their contracts . . .' (Wedderburn 1971: 75). In 1854, for example, over 3,000 workers were imprisoned for 'leaving or neglecting their work', and in 1872 there were 17,100 prosecutions and 10,400 convictions under the Master and Servant Act of 1867. Three years later all these enactments were swept away under mounting pressure from the organized labour movement, since when criminal liability for breach of contract of service has been rare. The essential asymmetry of employment law remained, however, in its emphasis on 'the personal and voluntary exchange of freely-bargained promises between two parties equally protected by the civil law alone'; a model 'suffused with an individualism which necessarily ignores the economic reality behind the bargain' (Wedderburn 1971: 77). Later we shall inquire into what meaning can be given to the notion of free and equal bargaining even when employees are collectively organized.

Meanwhile we take up again the other major sense in which the employment contract diverges from the pure contract model. 'The written labor contract in large part does not determine the specific obligations of the seller over a fixed period of time. To do so would require the parties to resolve what each employee were to do over the life of the agreement, which is hardly practical' (Young 1963: 246). Nearly half a century ago Commons argued in his classic work that the labour contract 'is not a contract, it is a continuing implied *renewal* of contracts at every minute and hour, based on the continuance of what is deemed, on the employer's side, to be satisfactory service, and, on the laborer's side, what is deemed to be satisfactory conditions and compensation' (1924: 285).

Commons's point can be developed to bring out its significance for our propositions about trust dynamics. When the employer initiated an employment relationship he was not concluding a contract; he was hiring an asset from which he expected to get a return that was not, however, specified. Over the course of the relationship it was open to him to seek to enlarge the return by increasing the work load or by contriving more fruitful combinations of the human resource with other factors of production. Normally he sought to maintain as large a difference as possible between its yield and its terms of hire. The legal and social context of industrialization favoured him. The law supported his demand for prerogative in deploying and conducting his resources as he saw fit, and supported, too, a structure of highly unequal property ownership which left the labour resource weak in arranging its own terms of hire. It was from this situation, of course, that Marx derived his theory of exploitation and social class. The propertyless worker was forced, in his search for subsistence, to live by the alienation of the only commodity he possessed – his power to produce wealth by labouring upon machines and materials he did not own. Dependent for his living upon the sale of his labour power, he was unable to secure an income except by resigning all claim to the product of his own labour. The employer's interest lay in maximizing the product derived from this labour power and minimizing the cost of its hire. His greatly superior position served him in both endeavours.

There is more than one aspect of asymmetry to this relationship. Already noted is the fact that the worker has to sell his labour power in order to live whereas the employer is not similarly constrained to buy labour. But in addition the worker receives a defined and visible rate for the job whereas the employer receives an impalpable potentiality whose ultimate development and fruits it is largely for him to determine. 'The worker's wage is thus negotiated and bargained for in a manner quite distinct from the manner in which dividends and capital gains arise in the production process. From the employer's side the labour contract is open-ended. In principle the nature of the exact tasks the worker has undertaken to perform becomes the province of management' (Blackburn 1967: 39).

Increasing Specificity and Scientific Management

It remains now to extract from these arguments the points of special significance for trust relations. We began by tracing the rise of contract as the master symbol and touchstone of legitimacy within the new industrial order; the relevant model of contract being that characterized as economic exchange. In studying the employment relation within this social setting, however, it has become clear that the nature of the exchange relationship in work cannot be gauged by reference to the so-called *contract* of employment. The realities of the exchange have to be sought through a study of each particular work situation and such changes as were overtaking it.

We had occasion in the first chapter to glance at broad-brush generalizations about the impact of industrialization on the division of labour and discretion in work roles. Their deficiencies as historical judgements derive from their failure to recognize that in all phases of the Industrial Revolution many new skills and occupational groups have been created as well as old ones destroyed. The engine builder and the engine driver, the railway signalman and the mule spinner, the managerial specialist and the technician, the accountants, actuaries and quantity surveyors, and the gas, water and mechanical engineers; these along with bankers, doctors, teachers, and company promoters are as much parts of the picture as all the groups whose roles were destroyed or simplified.

Only exploration along these lines would yield the kind of data necessary for an historical testing of the propositions advanced here about trust relations. What would be necessary for such testing is documentation not only of the changes towards the low-discretion syndrome which overtook the old roles but also of similar changes which overtook the new ones. For the evidence suggests that not until the last decades of the nineteenth century did there begin to emerge on any scale that quickening pace of rationalization, mechanization, measurement, and 'speed-up' which is particularly significant for the concept of the low-trust syndrome. There is not the space here to locate this trend in its historical context of capitalist development; a task performed, albeit briefly, by Friedmann (1964). It was certainly this period, however, which began the development of those forms of mass production, programming, and control which fragmented and mechanized many types of work previously done by skilled craftsmen into operations calling for no more than a relatively simple kind of easily acquired dexterity. Although the craftsmen who survived often needed higher skills, and new roles emerged for draughtsmen, rate fixers, and minor administrators, the proportion of skilled craftsmen in manufacturing industry began to fall (Cole 1955: 35). It was this period, too, that saw the rise, particularly in America, of Scientific Management and the 'systemizers'. The systemizers were 'a diverse group of accountants, engineers, and works managers who rose to some prominence in the last decades of the nineteenth century, along with the growing size of American factories and business enterprises' (Haber 1964: 19). The literature of system leaned heavily upon analogies to the human body, the machine, and the military. The body and the machine usually illustrated the need for close integration within the factory while military organization exemplified hierarchy and discipline. It was Frederick W. Taylor, however, who gave strong leadership towards a coherent body of Scientific Management methods and doctrine. This made explicit a powerful impulse developing throughout the industrializing world which is highly germane to our theme and which had great influence on the theory and practice of work organization and job design (not invariably in line with Taylor's own doctrine). It is with us still in the form of an orientation which seeks to apply its spirit and methods to the functions of management and technical specialists as well as to humbler tasks. Taking as its basic assumption that greater efficiency was derivable from a minute subdivision of labour and the accompanying characteristics of tight coordination, hierarchy, and discipline, Scientific Management applied these methods in an extreme version of the low-discretion syndrome. The central principles were the withdrawal of discretion from the performers of lower level tasks; the vesting of much decision-making in the hands of a small élite group, and the rigorous control of rank and file by means of close supervision and discipline supported by sanctions. The role of the élite was to study scientifically by careful and precise measurement the best ways of performing tasks and the performance actually achieved, and to arrange for the rank and file to be inculcated with the correct methods. The role of the rank and file lay in obedience and response to external incentives. 'Incentives were important because man was naturally lazy' and likely to find factory work 'tiresome and uninteresting' (Haber 1964: 23). In Taylor's own words, the workers must 'do what they are told promptly and without asking questions or making suggestions . . . it is absolutely necessary for every man in an organization to become one of a train of gear wheels' (quoted, *Ibid*: 24).

It was difficult to find a place for trade unions in Taylor's scheme of things. Under Scientific Management, wages, hours, and working conditions were subjects for scientific determination rather than for collective bargaining. Yet whatever the attitudes of their masters, who used those elements of Scientific Management which served their purposes and dismissed the rest, the practitioners themselves were rarely implacably hostile to unions and wage earners as such, viewing many of their weaknesses as due to bad management rather than to orginal sin. Scientific Management as Taylor, for example, saw it would not so much crush unionism as eliminate its causes. It was to achieve a 'mental revolution' which set the employer and worker pulling together rather than apart. For 'both sides take their eyes off the division of the surplus as the all-important matter, and together turn their attention toward increasing the size of the surplus until this surplus becomes so large that it is unnecessary to quarrel over how it shall be divided' (Taylor, quoted in Tillett *et al.* 1970: 88).

Taylor and his followers were looking to the emergence of a pattern, described in our earlier theoretical exposition, within which occupants of low-discretion roles would come to legitimize them and thus move from low- to high-trust relations. Taylor articulated this hope in the clearest possible way. 'It is along this line of complete change in the mental attitude of both sides; of the substitution of peace for war; the substitution of hearty brotherly cooperation for contention and strife; of both pulling hard in the same direction instead of pulling apart; of replacing suspicious watchfulness with mutual confidence; of becoming friends instead of enemies: it is along this line, I say, that scientific management must be developed' (*Ibid*: 88–9).

The analysis offered in this book suggests reasons why this did not prove possible. In a complex hierarchical structure marked by great inequalities of role discretion and located in a highly competitive, economic-exchange, acquisitive society, those at the base of the structure are likely to perceive their superiors as exercising discretion over them in the interests of goals that are not shared. Symptoms of low trust on their part make their appearance. Aware of these divergent perspectives, superiors counter with further restrictions on employee discretion and the low-trust dynamic is under way. If such structures are to escape low-trust symptoms of one sort or another, superiors must enjoy exceptional facilities for inducing employees to retain a high-trust frame of reference in the face of strong structural pressures in the opposite direction. A deeply rooted paternalist tradition; a stable, long-service labour force; cultural or geographical isolation; a charismatic figure at the top – these may afford facilities of the sort required. The disciples of Scientific Management were neither the first nor the last to hope that, even without such exceptional facilities, employees in low-trust situations could be persuaded to adopt high-trust perspectives without there being any modification of roles and relations in the direction of greater discretion. They seem to have been the only group who hoped to achieve this while at the same time continuing to restrict employee discretion still further.

It is an inadequate perspective, however, which sees the Scientific Management movement as simply a manifestation by tame technicist hacks with no thought beyond heeding their masters' voices. In its broader expression it embodied a social philosophy which saw past and present social ills as the outcome of inefficiency, muddle, confused thinking, and an inability to grasp the full implications of the scientific and technological revolution. Reform in whatever field was seen as less a process of good prevailing over evil than of intelligent management, control, and regulation prevailing over ignorance, stupidity, and error. Describing the process as 'scientific' strengthened its appeal further by suggesting disinterestedness, rigour, and the application of laws both of legislatures and of nature which made appeals to conscience unnecessary. The appeal of this doctrine extended far beyond industry and the businessmen who realized they could make use of some of it. It reached some members of the rising young technical and professional groups produced by broadening education in response to the needs of an increasingly complex industrial society. Haber (1964) describes this approach in its American manifestation, referring to such exponents as Brandeis, Croly, and Lippman, with their distaste for commercialism and acquisitiveness and their admiration for professional commitment and specialist expertise. In Britain, utilitarianism was re-emerging through the Webbs and other Fabians who saw the cool professional collection of facts, application of intelligence and scientific method, and acceptance of 'enlightened leadership' as the answer to muddle, inefficiency, and social conflict.* For reformers of this persuasion the only fault to be found with that rationalizing spirit which played down expressive and particularistic bonds, sentiments and loyalties in favour of the instrumental and universalistic approach was that there had not been enough of it. They did not go unresisted by those who considered that there had been a great deal too much. Besides individual protests there were two groups which brought opposition to bear – certain of the protagonists of 'industrial welfare', and the forces of organized labour.

Resistance to Scientific Management: The Industrial Welfare Movement

Industrial welfare, sometimes known as industrial 'betterment', was an uneven and varying mixture of philanthropy, humanitarianism, and commercial shrewdness. Along with men of religion seeking redemptive agencies, philanthropists identifying suitable recipients for benevolence, and men of letters engaging in mediaevalist nostalgia, were businessmen of whom some were trying to reconcile profit making with a nagging conscience and others were simply sniffing what they took to be the way of the wind. Among them were a few who, having experienced in their business capacity the employment relation defined in terms of cash nexus and impersonal contract, had begun to suspect that it had costs as well as benefits. It might be all very well for the employer to define his obligations to the employee in precise specific terms, but what must happen to loyalty, commitment, and moral involvement when the employee reciprocated? Some employers, from habit or conviction, had tried to maintain the traditional diffuse relationship (Briggs 1961: Chap. IV; Child 1964; Williams 1931); but many others had allowed themselves to be pushed by structural and market pressures in the direction to which contract ideology pointed; that of purging the employment relation of all personal and particularistic bonds, considerations,

* Few British writers reveal more artlessly than H. G. Wells the essential naïveté of some who held this perspective, with their élitist assumption that the gifted few, using the spirit and methods of science, could quickly rationalize human life and be rewarded by the wondering docile gratitude of the masses.

and sentiments. Circumstances were now prompting a few of them towards a keener awareness of the costs. Those circumstances included the quickening economic competition between the industrializing countries, which led some employers to rue the absence of a corporate team spirit which might have enabled them to meet the challenge with a quicker adaptive response; the spread of effective trade unionism and collective bargaining; the clear manifestation in some quarters of the class war; stirrings of social conscience towards the poor and oppressed; and some unease about the abundant symptoms of social conflict – then usually described as 'unrest'.

What some of the diverse adherents of welfare hoped for was a reversal of that trend towards impersonality, mutual indifference, and lack of trust in employment relations which idealists saw as destructive of the social bond and a few progressive businessmen saw also in terms of the effect on their profit and loss account. The logic seemed clear enough. If the current trend, legitimized by a popularized political economy, towards specificity in the relations between master and men was now producing costs in excess of benefits, the trend must be marginally reversed by reintroducing a measure of diffuseness. On the assumption of reciprocity, this could be achieved by the master demonstrating a degree of concern with the welfare of his employees both within and, equally important, beyond the immediate work situation. As employees responded, the mutual bonds of personal loyalty and commitment would be reknit.

Elizabeth Cadbury was among those who made explicit the principles of this approach. In many public lectures and addresses given during the early years of the twentieth century she urged that it required not only the payment of a 'just and living wage' but also good healthy conditions of employment; educational and recreational facilities; canteens supplying nourishing food; foremen 'chosen for their character and gifts of leadership'; and joint management-worker committees to discuss 'common problems affecting the life of the factory and its output. . . .' Beyond these it called for a style of personal relations cultivated by management, characterized by respect, consideration, and fair dealing, on the basis of which 'the good employer can establish a feeling of sympathy and cooperation between himself and his people akin to the old family feeling that existed between the master and his apprentices in the days before machinery and huge industrial centres.' Nor must this diffuse concern stop at the factory gates. '. . . the domestic background of their lives, the conditions of their homes and their families, were all part of a complex of related facts, affecting the attitude of the workers at the bench, their energy, their capacity for concentration . . .' (Scott 1955: 88–91). Many applications of welfare stopped far short of aspirations like these, being directed simply to a view of the employee as a passive, machine-like instrument which could be made more efficient by proper feeding, housing, and medical care. Some of Robert Owen's writings carry this flavour (1927: 9–10, for example). Welfare inspired by this approach was itself a branch of Scientific Management. But the view of welfare as re-creating diffuse bonds between employer and employed often frowned on the more extreme applications of Scientific Management principles.

Beginning in the first decade of the twentieth century as a programme of amelioration in the employee's lot which might not only render him physiologically more efficient but also evoke loyalty, trust, and goodwill, the betterment approach became briefly stimulated by the idealistic wartime fervours of 'reconstruction' and 'national unity' into something even grander in theory if not in practice. One of the leading theorists on business organization and management in Britain, John Lee, had no hesitation in taking up the mediaevalist imagery of writers like A. J. Penty, an inspirational light of Guild Socialism, whose book *Towards a Christian Sociology* in 1923 mourned the growing instability of industrial civilization. Penty was 'an extreme and consistent mediaevalist, with an uncompromising hatred of inventions and machinery and division of labour, and with a burning desire to make everyone a skilled craftsman, such as we encounter in the 38th chapter of Ecclesiasticus or in the best historical romances' (Gray 1946: 441). Penty quoted the twelfth century John of Salisbury – '. . . a well-ordered constitution consists in the proper apportionment of functions to members and in the apt condition, strength and composition of each and every member; that all members must in their functions supplement and support each other, never losing sight of the weal of the others, and feeling pain in the harm that is done to another' (Lee 1924: 50). This description of a set of high-trust relations pointed, in Lee's view, to the condition sought, often unconsciously, by the welfare movement. 'Welfare work, even in its crudest form, is some sort of reversion to the underlying spirit of such an organization of society' (*Ibid*: 45). It represented a search for 'features of human relationship which bound men together more loyally than they are bound together in industrial aggregations' (*Ibid*: 47–8). The 'old school' of employers, 'to whom it seems beyond question that an employer has a right to purchase labour in the cheapest market and to employ it under conditions as favourable to himself as possible, in so far as he obeys the law' (*Ibid*: 4), would have to understand that 'to cultivate industrial welfare is to cultivate efficiency' (*Ibid*: 22). Only thus could be secured again the corporate spirit and overriding sense of common purpose characteristic of mediaeval social organization; only thus could be constructed 'a more permanent and abiding relation' than was common under the present mobilities of the 'free' labour market.

This approach to management-worker relations was taken up in the thirties and given a slightly more sophisticated dress by Elton Mayo and his associates, who are often presented as its pioneers. Their nostrums will be examined later; meanwhile we can note Lee anticipating central Mayo themes in his observation that 'we live as an aggregation of unrelated individuals rather than as an organism, mutually bound together' (*Ibid*: 84) and his reporting of the benefits derived in one factory from allowing employees to associate themselves in 'voluntary groups' for work purposes (*Ibid*: 57). There is even a faint adumbration of the still later notion of self-actualization in his assertion that 'true welfare is based upon a desire to enable each worker to rise to his full stature, and thereby to produce the best result and at the same time to ensure the best personal development' (*Ibid*: 26–7). In all this he saw the beginnings of a movement which might discover 'within the bounds of private ownership, the direction in which we shall find a solution for the central problem of our time' (*Ibid*: viii), thereby avoiding a 'gigantic overthrow' (*Ibid*: 52).

After this it comes as something of an anticlimax to note the practical expressions to which the welfare approach commonly remained limited. They included a concern with ventilation, lighting, rest pauses, and other issues related to fatigue such as monotony and boredom; with the provision of canteens,* libraries, sports facilities,

* As late as 1949 it was possible for an enthusiast for industrial canteens to see them as one element in the creation of welfare and community centres based on factories or groups of factories. These would draw 'not only indi-

social clubs, and housing; with the establishment of works councils, and profit-sharing schemes; and with 'welfare supervision' which offered personal counsel and support (Phelps Brown 1959: 75–81; Child 1969: Chaps. 2 and 3).

There was nothing here of the repudiation of low-discretion work urged by such as Penty. The application of welfare was to be judged by long run criteria which served, rather than clashed with, economic rationality. That there was a genuine humanitarian drive behind the movement, especially from leading Quaker employers, there can be no doubt. Nevertheless, what looked like being bad for business somehow managed to become defined as not being in the employees' best interests. The general secretary of the Institute of Welfare Workers (formed in 1913 under the name of the Welfare Workers' Association) expounded its rationale in a lecture in 1919. The older work patterns which 'allowed for the existence of strong personal ties between masters and men' had been replaced by impersonal, dehumanizing operations and by 'hatred, bitterness, and distrust' on the part of workers towards employers. Industry must therefore be personalized and humanized again. The 'quantity and quality of a man's labour' being 'very largely governed by the state of his mind', that state must be transformed by ensuring 'the full development of each worker as an individual'. The preamble to the Institute's constitution declared its aims as 'assisting the individual to fulfil his functions both as a citizen and producer in the interest of the community, as well as of the particular enterprise with which he is concerned', and promoting 'a better understanding between employer and employed, based on just dealing and mutual cooperation'. Hereby, declared the secretary, would be lessened 'that unnatural gulf . . . which is so detrimental to the best interests of both' (Voysey 1919: 114, 115, 118, 120).

That welfare was expected, indeed designed, to yield a commercial return just as surely as was Scientific Management made it likely that some employers would practise both. For Seebohm Rowntree, the leading figure in Britain's industrial welfare movement, welfare was a necessary contribution, hitherto badly neglected, to business

viduals but whole families back into the community circle as they used to be in mediaeval times', and would foster a joint spirit of harmony, cooperation and service between capital and labour. 'Industrial welfare is – or should be – capitalism's answer to industrial unrest' (Curtis-Bennett 1949: 289–94).

efficiency. From his writings and his behaviour the inference can be drawn that, like any other resource, welfare policies should be applied up to, but not beyond, the point when they cease to serve that overriding aim. '. . . our objective has been', he wrote, 'to raise the status of the workers of all ranks from that of servants to that of co-operators', so far as that was possible 'without lowering efficiency' (Rowntree 1921: 1). 'The ideal at which we should aim is that every one should work with as much enjoyment, energy, and intelligence as if he were working on his own account' (*Ibid*: 98). The Scientific Management approach must be applied in the same spirit. Rowntree declared a company object of eliminating 'all useless or ineffective expenditure of energy and all other kinds of waste', but disavowed any intention of introducing American-type 'speeding-up' and 'heartless drive' which would not 'in the long run, produce good results' (Briggs 1961: 184). In pursuing this combination of policies Rowntree, like others, was applying an approach of which Robert Owen had been a well known but far from unique exponent. Owen had combined a traditionally diffuse conception of the master-servant relationship, in which the master thought for the servant and protected him from the hazards of life as well as from his own weaknesses, with aspirations towards a highly efficient organization of production and a system of performance controls very much in the spirit of Scientific Management (Bendix 1963: 50).*

As might be expected, industrial betterment evoked the customary terrors among the comfortable classes lest it spoon-feed the poor (Lee 1924: 3). Well-to-do commentators, writing in the servant-tended comfort of their studies, searched their consciences lest welfare innovations rot the moral fibre of the working classes. In the words of one employer, deeply uneasy about this 'benevolent interference': 'There is a God who is guiding us. We must not hasten the work' (*Ibid*: 80).

In any case the hastening did not, as we have seen, extend to proposals for reversing the division of labour. Leaders of the betterment movement certainly 'accused scientific management of exaggerating the division of labor and of making man into a machine'

* Pollard describes the notion of Owen's 'great ability as a businessman' as a myth, and attributes his competitive advantage to, *inter alia*, 'his ability to win the cooperation of his workers while paying them no more than competitive wages . . .' (1968: 286, 293).

(Haber 1964: 64), but practical men were derisive of attempts to reverse the trend and movements in this direction were minimal. In practice, therefore, such efforts as were made to increase the diffuseness of the employment relation on the employer's initiative were directed mainly to the physical, the social, and to some extent the psychological *context* of the job. The task behaviours of the job itself, and the authority, supervisory, and other control structures in which it was embedded, were largely left untouched. The attempt at enlarging diffuseness therefore stopped short of what this book argues to be at the heart of the relationship. Employee behaviour in their actual task roles remained relatively highly specified and prescribed, and low-trust relations remained likewise. This is not to deny that welfare could bring returns, at least for a while, in terms of a firmer attachment of employee to company. But a firmer attachment was not equivalent to a moral involvement. It was fully compatible with a purely contractual, cash-nexus relationship with the enterprise.

Resistance to Scientific Management: Organized Labour

If exponents of betterment had reasons for questioning the further advance of Scientific Management, organized labour had them no less. Whatever the theoretical disclaimers, it seemed to many workers that Scientific Management made for a quickening in the intensity and pace of work and that all union and workgroup practices susceptible of being labelled restrictionist constituted its *bête noire*. On a more fundamental level of analysis the diametrically opposed interests of the two forces become even clearer. Scientific Management represents the impulse to minimize the discretionary content of work roles at lower levels. We earlier noted the significance of this as a technique of control. The union or workgroup interest can therefore be summarized in Crozier's words: 'Subordinates try to increase their amount of discretion and utilize it to oblige higher-ups to pay more for their cooperation' (1964: 160). And if the amount of discretion cannot be increased then at least it can be prevented from becoming even smaller.

The resistance of organized labour to inroads made or threatened by Scientific Management did not, however, make it the ally of all expressions of betterment. Certainly some employers like Rowntree came to combine a keen concern with immediate efficiency and a long-term faith in welfare with a readiness to grapple with the middle-range problems thrown up – as well as resolved – by collective bargaining. But others made it clear that their interest in welfare was inspired by a hope that in binding the employee more closely to the firm it would weaken both the attractiveness and the cohesion of the trade union. At its deepest level, betterment in the full sense of a search for corporate unity and transcendent purpose was as logically incompatible with union functions as were the more extreme impulses of Scientific Management. The latter could yield no legitimate place for collective bargaining since methods, organizations, and rewards were all deemed susceptible to scientific measurement and rational selection of the best decision. The former, being a unitary conception of common purpose, could not legitimize organizations predicated on the proposition that since group purposes within the firm might diverge there could properly be organized challenges to managerial authority.*

Fortunately for the development of trade unionism and collective bargaining, neither of these orientations in its extreme form was acceptable to the men of power; the owners and controllers of resources. Scientific Management was for them a useful tool when kept in its place. There had been signs that given its head it might try to step out of its place. 'The Taylor system placed restrictions upon the . . . manager in the factory as well as the worker . . . The discovery of a science of work meant a transfer of skill from the worker to management and with it some transfer of power. Yet this power was fixed not directly at the top but in the new center of the factory, the planning department' (Haber 1964: 24–5). In Taylor's own words: 'The shop (indeed the whole works) should be managed, not by the manager, superintendent, or foreman, but by the planning department. The daily routine of running the entire works should be carried on by the various functional elements of this department, so that, in theory at least, the works could run smoothly even if the manager, superintendent, and their assistants outside the planning room were all to be away for a month at a time' (*Ibid*: 25). This was no way to win friends. Too many managers resented this attempted

* It is not irrelevant that after the failure of Guild Socialism Penty later emerged, still searching, presumably, for a unifying corporatism, as a disciple of Oswald Mosley's British Union of Fascists (Coates and Topham 1970: 38.)

substitution of specialist techniques for their own discretion and rejected it as an interference with prerogatives (Bendix 1963: 280).

Neither were the new 'scientific professionals' of work planning likely to enjoy reliable support against this recalcitrant line management from owners and entrepreneurs. Some of the Taylorites were not only apt to be free with their disdain for 'mere money making' but also, more fundamentally, revealed in their approach that there might occasionally be a dissonance between mechanical efficiency in terms of input-output ratio and commercial efficiency in terms of profit. When it became clear that their choice of the latter was not invariably unerring, their place in the scheme of things swiftly became defined as that of just another specialist who must be on tap but not on top. In other words, the collective power of property owners and controllers did not support the concept of the business organization as a completely systematized structure of scientific management.

Nor did it find any more acceptable, save as an ideological instrument to be used when appropriate, the concept of the organization as a corporate unity dedicated to an overriding purpose. To be sure, such a concept had useful functions to serve in the ever necessary campaign to win legitimacy in the eyes of employees, consumers, and the public. But when profit interests clashed with the manifest preferences of any of these groups, this concept had to be put aside in favour of others which, though lacking in popular appeal, were firm in the support they enjoyed from the law and the State – concepts such as property rights, private enterprise, the long-run coincidence between business viability and the public good. This meant that the use of mediaevalist imagery could never be more than a temporary expedient, for the need might arise at any time to strike such dissonant notes as the glories of free and equal contract; or the manufacturer's right, since he was 'not in business for his health', to 'do what he liked with his own'; or the bracing moral qualities of Social Darwinism by which the strong thrived and the weak perished. The powerful thrust of these principles of contractual industrial society meant that, however exalted the vision with which a few might support it, betterment could never be more than a policy of labour management marginally modifying the employment relationship.

Legitimation of the Labour Contract through Collective Bargaining?

The inability of either betterment in its corporate unity sense or Scientific Management in its total control sense to provide the master pattern for industrial organization left the way clear, given vital preconditions, for the most important marginal modification of all – collective bargaining. If property owners and controllers were precluded, by their own interests, from fully operating a concept of the enterprise either as a corporate unity accepting diffuse obligations within and beyond its boundaries, or as a scientifically determined system to whose impersonal 'needs' they as well as all other participants must submit, only certain possibilities remained. They could continue attempting to assert their prerogative in pursuit of ends and means defined solely by themselves, where necessary against the interests of other groups in the enterprise, and with or without the support of government and the State. Or they could concede a marginal role in rule-making to the groups of organized labour which, increasingly as the nineteenth century progressed, were pressing for recognition of this claim. The issue was decided in favour of the latter, partly by the manifest ability of organized labour to make non-recognition costly; partly by the disinclination of governments and influential opinion groups to give property owners the support needed to suppress labour's claims; but even more fundamentally by the readiness of organized labour, given rising standards and therefore something to lose, to accept the master principles, values, and conventions most important to property owners, and to work constitutionally within them not for radical change but simply for marginal improvements in their lot. Given this readiness, some groups of employers found, albeit reluctantly, that trade unionism and collective bargaining could have positive advantages for them, and this strengthened these institutions to the point where, provided they continued to accept society's master principles, values, and conventions, they had realistically to be seen as permanent features. As will be seen in more detail later, this employer acquiescence in the intrusion of organized labour into the decision-making process accorded ill with traditional conceptions. Under the unitary master-servant ideology, the employer alone defined both the ends and the means of business activities and the duty of employees was to legitimize his definitions from a posture of unqualified loyalty and obedience. Under collective bargaining their representatives introduced, into certain limited aspects of decision-making, perceptions of their own interests which led them to challenge his authority.

There have always been many employers who saw in this development a threat which must be contained by asserting ever more actively, by means coercive or manipulative, the sanctity of employer prerogative. For them the unitary ideology, expressed perhaps in somewhat smoother terms of 'leadership' and 'team spirit' to suit the democratic ethos of the age, was a necessary instrument. Those, however, for whom the potential usefulness of collective bargaining was more apparent were ready, implicitly if not explicitly, to acknowledge a modification of the traditional conception towards a somewhat more pluralist perspective which conceded, within strict limits, the right of subordinates collectively to define their own interests and assert them against the employer's preferences.

Such a perspective made sympathetic resonance with other developments. The wider society itself was becoming characterized by political forms which theorists were increasingly to designate as pluralist in nature. But more immediately relevant for our purpose is that collective bargaining could be presented as restoring legitimacy to the operation of contract in labour markets. Such a legitimation could serve a useful ideological purpose for those concerned to justify and rationalize the industrial order which was emerging. Scepticism about 'free and equal' contract in labour markets went back at least as far as Adam Smith, and here and there within the Victorian middle classes were consciences tender on the subject (Webb, S. and B. 1902: xxvi). In so far as trade unionism appeared to offer redress of that inequality between master and man which some were now prepared to acknowledge, collective bargaining could be held as providing legitimation for a system characterized by extreme division of function, mobility of resources, and free contract. Labour might be a commodity, but given collective bargaining it sold its services under fair regulative procedures which removed what had admittedly been a genuine grievance.

The search for legitimizing ideologies was understandable and we have already noted, for example, Roll's opinion that the marginal utility school of modern economic theory was, in its origins, 'strongly influenced by a desire to strengthen the potentially apologetic character of economics' (1945: 376). It was understandable because the new order was by no means going uncriticized even by members of the more comfortable classes. Some of the doubts and forms of unease have emerged during the preceding argument. In some cases they were popularized versions of more systematic critiques developed by social theorists whose work reached only a tiny minority. Nisbet, among others, has traced the ways in which these questionings about the new order helped to shape the characteristic themes of the sociological tradition (1967). Since some of them bear especially upon the theme of trust relations the next chapter will examine selected pieces of theorizing that are particularly relevant. They are no more than fragments chosen to illustrate the ubiquity and relevance of the trust theme; some seeking to validate the new order and others to appraise it more critically or even condemn it. Fragmentary though they are, they go some way towards sketching in a theoretical background for the chapter which follows it. This will explore, alongside the unitary ideology of master-servant relations, the implications of the pluralist frame of reference which challenges it, and the nature of the radical perspective which challenges both.

5 · Industrialization; Contract; and the Division of Labour: Some Relevant Theorizing

The purpose of this chapter is to select from the writings of certain nineteenth century theorists, reacting as they were to the shocks of gathering industrialism, interpretations (and sometimes prescriptions) bearing upon the themes with which this book is specially concerned. As before, there is need to stress the selectivity of the approach. This may ignore certain central preoccupations or emphases of a given theorist simply because they are not relevant to our present interest.

Selectivity was, of course, as it had to be, a characteristic of the theorists themselves. Each focused on certain aspects and drew out his theorizing from his own emphases. The object here will be, first, to identify these differing emphases in the light of the present analysis and, second, to examine their relevance for understanding social development as industrial societies have since experienced it. The interest, therefore, is not in the theorists *per se*, but in certain of their ideas. In some cases there is a direct reference to the work situation and the relevance to it of the particular theorist's approach. In others the concern is with the wider society alone, and in all cases this is the concern which predominates. But, as emerged in the discussion of contract, the essential nature of changes wrought by industrialization and commercialization in the work situation can sometimes be illuminated by an examination of what was happening outside. If, as is being argued here, dynamics of trust relations were operative in both, the interpretations by contemporary observers of broad social changes should help in confirming and casting additional light on the changing nature of relations in work.

Ambiguities in the Division of Labour Concept

In seeking to assimilate the discussion of work, power, and trust relations to these nineteenth century responses we must recall the ambiguity in the concept of the division of labour. Unless this ambiguity and its clarification are borne in mind, the interpretations of our selected theorists may appear more at odds than in fact they are. As we have seen, the concept is sometimes used to refer simply to a narrowing of the task range covered by a work role; the role being differentiated out into a number of separate tasks each allocated to a person who then proceeds to specialize in it. This usage carries no necessary implications for the effect of differentiation upon the amount of discretion vested in each of the differentiated roles. Perhaps all the tasks covered by the old role were of low discretion, in which case the separate new roles will be of low discretion likewise. Some tasks may have been of low and some of high discretion; with the result that differentiation results in the creation of new low-discretion roles. If, on the other hand, all the tasks of the old role were of high discretion, differentiation would of itself do nothing to create low-discretion roles.

It is differentiation of this last kind which produces, or indirectly encourages the emergence of, the specialist in Friedmann's sense, such as the physician or surgeon who specializes in applying great skill and knowledge to one particular part of the body (Friedmann 1961: 88). Differentiation and specialization of this sort is often followed by a heightening of skill and knowledge as the result of a concentration of energy and thought upon a limited range of problems. It would therefore be easy for an observer with this aspect uppermost in mind to characterize the division of labour as enriching the common life of men by creating the conditions for a mutually beneficial enhancement of ability, insight, and expertise.

Division of labour may, however, result in the creation of roles embodying very little discretion which give scope for increasing dexterity but none for increasing skill. Observers with this aspect uppermost in mind have characterized division of labour in terms of fragmentation and dehumanization. It is this distinction we need to bear in mind when reviewing nineteenth century responses. The same considerations apply when we turn to roles and relations outside work. One emphasis is upon the mutual enrichment derived from the enormous diversity created by modern specialization of function; the other upon the impoverishment of relationships as economics squeeze out ethics and men define each other in increasingly segmental and instrumental terms.

Spencer, Maine, and Contract

Among those who developed the former emphasis, few hymned the glories of contract between free and equal specialists with more conviction than Herbert Spencer. Spencer, like many other social theorists, worked with a model which contrasted traditional with modern society, and in his hands it was the former which emerged from the contrast as inferior. Freedom was the touchstone. 'Some kind of organization labour must have; and if it is not that which arises by agreement under free competition, it must be that which is imposed by authority' (1969: 320). The two forms of social organization which Spencer was postulating had been designated by Maine twenty-three years earlier as contract and status (Maine: 1931). Contract was a system of voluntary cooperation 'in which the individual is left to do the best he can by his spontaneous efforts and get success or failure according to his efficiency' (Spencer 1969: 317), freely bargaining in the open market and drawing the reward appropriate to the skill and diligence he has to offer. The typical structure of this system could be seen in 'a body of producers or distributors, who severally agree to specified payments in return for specified services, and may at will, after due notice, leave the organization if they do not like it' (*Ibid*: 63). The massive and complex systems of interdependence which had developed on this basis between 'entire classes of producers and distributors' rested on the degree to which 'contracts are unhindered and the performance of them certain' (*Ibid*: 175). Status, on the other hand, was a system of compulsory cooperation in which the individual 'has his appointed place, works under coercive rule, and has his apportioned share of food, clothing, and shelter' (*Ibid*: 317). This pattern was typified in military organization, 'in which the units in their several grades have to fulfil commands under pain of death, and receive food and clothing and pay, arbitrarily apportioned . . .' (*Ibid*: 63). Status in this sense needs to be related to our usage of the term in Chapter 1 as a statement of the individual's 'rights, privileges, immunities, duties, and obligations . . . and, obversely, by a statement of the restrictions, limitations, and prohibitions governing his behaviour . . .' – a statement to which is attached a corresponding allocation of positional prestige or esteem. Status as Spencer (and of course many others before and since) used it carried the implication that the individual had no control over either his station or its duties. These were determined by forces in which he had no effective hand; they were to be accepted as given. This contrasts with a contract society in which the individual, liberated from these traditional shackles and their fixed unchanging duties, is given the freedom to shape his own destiny and choose his own obligations through the bargaining processes of the market. In sum: contract society could be socially and politically characterized as urban, modern, and Liberal; status society as rural, traditional, and Tory. The transition had been described by Maine in the much quoted proposition that 'the movement of the progressive societies has hitherto been a movement *from Status to Contract*' (1931: 141, his italics); Maine seeing status reciprocity as having its origin in those diffuse family and group ties from which the self-determining individual was now emancipating himself as a contracting agent.

Although Spencer believed in the existence of altruistic sentiments, 'it might be rationally held' that a free contract system 'under the negatively regulated control of a central power' (by which he meant suppression of violence and a 'quick and costless remedy for breach of contract'), and operated under the motivation of enlightened self-interest, 'would work out, in proper order, the appliances for satisfying all needs, and carrying on healthfully all the essential social functions' (1969: 301). Not that Spencer imagined this felicitous condition to have been achieved. Present society was marked by such major evils as great divisions of social rank; 'immense inequalities of means'; and disproportion in the shares of the social product received by managers and the managed. These would only be remedied, not by retrogression to the tyranny of socialism, but through the universal promotion and adoption of self-disciplines by which each man would acknowledge the contractual freedoms of others and observe the scruples required by contract society (*Ibid*: 314–35).

That Spencer defined the essential nature of contract society in terms of high-trust relations is undoubted. Maine had earlier seen in the history of contract a gradual emergence of 'good faith and trust in our fellows' (1931: 254), and Spencer concurred. Their reasoning is easy enough to trace. In status society, men's behaviour was externally determined by the groups and social ranks in which they found themselves. In contract society, it was self-determined by the contractual commitments to which they freely pledged themselves. Transition to the latter therefore implied an increasing readiness among men to trust each other in honouring these pledges.

This trust is not, however, the kind we are principally concerned with here – the trust which becomes institutionalized in social-exchange relations when the parties define their mutual obligations diffusely and trust each other to maintain an understood reciprocity. We do not grant the manufacturer discretion as to whether he supplies his product in good working order or not; our customers discretion as to how much they pay for our goods; or the builder discretion as to whether he meets our architect's specifications. These aspects of their behaviour we prescribe for them in certain specific terms, explicit or implied, in the contract. The trust hailed by Maine is of the kind, referred to in Chapter 1, extended by each contracting party towards the other's observance of these prescribed terms. Maine and Spencer argue that, simply by enlarging their readiness to contract, men manifest increasing trust in each other to observe the specified terms on which they have agreed. But it was argued earlier that as the diffuse discretionary elements in a relationship are reduced the risk increases that observance of the prescribed terms will suffer. In work relations, a reduction of discretion is accompanied by increasing supervision, inspection, checking, monitoring, and other forms of policing the prescribed elements. This was explained in terms of the decline in personal involvement by the self as discretionary obligations give way to prescribed obligations for which only obedience is required. In business and commercial contracts, indeed, the exclusion of moral sentiment and diffuse involvement was, as we saw in Tawney's lament, celebrated as a necessary and beneficial feature of the new economic calculus. As our argument would predict, the growth of contract has been accompanied by a parallel growth of legislation and policing mechanisms designed to cope with contractual evasion and default. In relations between producer and customer, impersonality and specificity have led to problems of substandard service which have had to be countered by ever more specific protective regulation – each new protective fence being outflanked by the less scrupulous and requiring extension. It seems, then, that the more we seek to impose upon our fellows behaviour that is highly specific and prescribed the less we trust them in punctilious observance, for we find ourselves setting up an ever mounting battery of controls which have to serve as substitutes for personal responsibility, weakened as it is by the specificity and depersonalization of the transaction or relationship. Spencer himself enumerates a long list of recent enactments, vastly extended since his day, designed to this end and, after referring to adulteration, cheap imitations, short weights, false measures, bribery, deception, and fraud, concludes that 'The system under which we at present live fosters dishonesty and lying' (1969: 71–5, 315). These features of commercial and business practice help to illuminate the similar developments in work relations, for the dynamics underlying both are the same.

Another feature of the Spencerian perspective was the 'assumption that contract – whether between two entrepreneurs or between entrepreneur and worker – is the simple and unmediated consequence of reason and free will, not the by-product of tradition or social code' (Nisbet 1965: 10–11). It was noted in the last chapter, however, that in fact the employment contract embodied a social code of the utmost significance for the work situation – the traditional code of master-servant relations. Maine had traced the origins of status to the authoritarian paternalist structure of the family, but failed to point out that this had been conveniently carried over into systems of employment relations which extended far beyond the house servants or the farm labourer or apprentice who 'lived in'. This was one of many ways in which status remained a powerful determinant of social relations in a society loudly proclaimed as contractual. Through the imposition of this code the coercive forces of the State were used to support and supplement the power advantage enjoyed by the employer by virtue of his command over resources, thereby helping to uphold the imbalance of exchange reciprocity under which the employer was far more able to impose highly specific, highly prescribed behaviours and obligations upon his employees than they upon him. This enforcement of a traditional relationship of subordination went unacknowledged in the nineteenth century ideology of contract, which served a legitimizing function by presenting the employment relation as a bargain between equals. This did not escape the heavy irony of Veblen. 'Under the current *de facto* standardization of economic life enforced by the machine industry, it may frequently happen that an individual or a group, e.g. of workmen, has not a *de facto* power of free contract. A given workman's livelihood can perhaps, practically, be found only on acceptance of one specific contract offered, perhaps not at all. But the coercion which in this way bears upon his choice through the standardization of industrial procedure is neither assault and battery nor breach of contract and it is, therefore, not repugnant to the principles of natural liberty . . . the case is therefore outside the scope of the law' (Veblen 1958: 132).

Spencer expressed no such unease. His criticisms of nineteenth century society were not of competitive contractual society as such, but of the ways in which institutions and values were failing to adapt to, or live up to, the logic and disciplines required if the full benefits of contract society were to be obtained. A contemporary theorist, Tönnies, working with a two-model framework similar in many respects to Spencer's, offered an analysis of social transition which cast a more appraising eye upon the nature of contract relations. Here we take up the celebrated contrast between the two constructs of *gemeinschaft* and *gesellschaft*.

Gemeinschaft and Gesellschaft

It is soon apparent that Tönnies's categories and interpretations contain much that accords with elements of the present analysis. Tönnies saw social relations as being created by either 'rational' will or 'natural' will. A 'group or a relationship can be willed because those involved wish to attain through it a definite end and are willing to join hands for this purpose, even though indifference or even antipathy may exist on other levels' (Loomis, in Tönnies 1955: xv). By contrast, men might associate 'because they think the relation valuable as an end in and of itself . . . Natural will is the conditioning and originating element in any process of willing which is derived from the temperament, character, and intellectual attitude of the individual, whether it has its origin in liking, inclination, habit, or memory' (*Ibid*). Examples of natural will were groups based on friendship, neighbourliness, or blood relations.

This is the same distinction as that embodied in the dichotomy of instrumental versus expressive relations. Parsons also points to the link with specificity and diffuseness. Actions and relationships based on rational will tend to be informed by motives which are specific and limited; those based on natural will by motives that are more diffuse (1949: 686–94). Tönnies characterizes the two models as *gesellschaft* and *gemeinschaft*. The three principal pillars of *gemeinschaft* society were kinship, neighbourhood, and friendship, the prototype being the family, but there were also *gemeinschaft* unions 'of spirit and mind based on common work or calling and thus common beliefs', such as the corporations or fellowships of the arts and crafts, the communities, churches, and holy orders (Tönnies 1955: 223). Common to all these was that 'reciprocal binding sentiment . . . we shall call understanding (*consensus*)'; the 'special social force and sympathy which keeps human beings together as members of a totality' (*Ibid*: 53). Relationships within this kind of social pattern "blanket in" many obligations. . . . The burden of proof is on him who would evade such an obligation . . .' (Loomis, in Tönnies 1955: xx–xxi, fn).

Gesellschaft differs at every point. 'Here everybody is by himself and isolated, and there exists a condition of tension against all others. . . . Nobody wants to grant and produce anything for another individual nor will he be inclined to give ungrudgingly to another individual, if it be not in exchange for a gift or labor equivalent that he considers at least equal to what he has given' (Tönnies 1955: 74). Thus in *gesellschaft*, 'where contractual relations prevail the obligations are specific and positively defined. The burden of proof is on him who would require the performance of an obligation not explicitly and obviously assumed' (Parsons 1949: 690). The more extensive the area and scope of trading, 'the more probable it is that the pure laws of exchange trade prevail and that those other non-commercial qualities which relate men and things may be ignored' (Tönnies 1955: 90).

This contrast accords closely with that between diffuse social exchange and specific economic exchange. Tönnies then turns to the question of how far the latter is informed by trust. 'Seemingly, contracts, in so far as they are not executed concurrently, are based on confidence and faith, as the term credit indicates. This . . . can, in an undeveloped stage, be and remain really effective. . . .' But with continued development towards *gesellschaft* comes 'more and more calculation'. Compliance with the contract rests increasingly on the fear of sanctions, 'i.e. it is to the self-interest of the contracting party because he has given a valued security or because possible future business depends on proven solvency' (*Ibid*: 224). The correspondence between Tönnies's approach and that presented here is strengthened by his observation that 'confidence has become highly impersonalised through modern trade. Personality has come to be of little or no importance. . . . It is assumed, and usually on valid grounds, that self-interest will induce even the personally less reliable businessman to pay his debts as long as he is able to do so. Personal reliability fades as it is transferred into reliability as a debtor' (*Ibid*: 7). What emerges from this is the increasing importance in *gesellschaft* of obedience to prescribed terms and a diminishing reliance upon the individual's personalized interpretation of what he ought to do to discharge certain diffuse obligations. Veblen concurs with Tönnies that in this situation the observance of prescribed terms becomes increasingly problematical. However, the growth of distrust, chicanery, and fraud is met by 'the increased astuteness and vigilance exercised in men's dealings with one another, whereby an appreciable portion of energy goes to defeat these artifices of disingenuous worldly wisdom' (1964: 173).

As with the discussion of trust relations, the terms used in expounding the *gemeinschaft* and *gesellschaft* models can easily give the impression that value preferences are being expressed. Tönnies, accused by critics of recommending the former as good and condemning the latter as bad, disclaimed any such intention (Loomis, in Tönnies 1955: xii), and Nisbet gives reasons for accepting the disclaimer, 'Bear in mind that examples of genuine *Gemeinschaft* include the ethnic ghetto as well as the village community, the totalitarian nation as well as the family, extreme social caste (as in India) as well as the guild or religious parish' (1970: 106). In the same spirit, one could draw attention to the enormous alleviations in the human lot that have been achieved through low-trust organization and relations.

Simmel and Exchange

Another theorist whose interpretations are relevant to our interests is Simmel, who draws out the distinction between economic and social exchange and relates it to commercialization and urban life. After noting that all 'contacts among men rest on the scheme of giving and returning the equivalence', he observes that in many cases the equivalence can be enforced. 'In all economic exchanges in legal form, in all fixed agreements concerning a given service, in all obligations of legalized relations, the legal constitution enforces and guarantees the reciprocity of service and return service . . .' (1964: 387). But there are many other exchange relations in which 'enforcement of equivalence is out of the question'. Here reliance is placed on gratitude to maintain 'the reciprocity of service and return service even where they are not guaranteed by external coercion' (*Ibid*).

With the growth of commercialization and contract, however, exchange relations become drained of personal sentiment. Exchange is the objectification of human interaction. 'If an individual gives a thing, and another returns one of the same value, the purely spontaneous character . . . of their relation has become projected into objects'. This objectification, 'this growth of the relationship into self-contained, movable things', becomes so complete that 'in the fully-developed economy, personal interaction recedes altogether into the background, while goods gain a life of their own. Relations and value balances between them occur automatically, by mere computation: men act only as the executors of the tendencies towards shifts and equilibriums that are inherent in the goods themselves. The objectively equal is given for the objectively equal, and man himself is really irrelevant, although it goes without saying that he engages in the process for his own interests' (*Ibid*: 388).

The process of depersonalization which accompanies precisely measured exchanges of objects therefore reaches its peak in modern money economy. 'Because money expresses the general element contained in all exchangeable objects, that is, their exchange value, it is incapable of expressing the individual element in them.' In so far as objects figure as salable things the individual element is 'leveled down to the general which is shared by everything salable, particularly by money itself' (*Ibid*: 390–1). Thus is derived the 'increasing objectification of our culture, whose phenomena consist more and more of impersonal elements and less and less absorb the subjective totality of the individual (most simply shown by the contrast between handicraft and factory work) . . . ' (*Ibid*: 318). With this reference Simmel demonstrates that he, too, sees the same dynamic at work in the increasingly specific definition of some work roles as in the increasingly specific nature of commercialized money relations in general.

Simmel characterizes city life accordingly, for the 'metropolis has always been the seat of the money economy'. He refers to 'a matter-of-fact attitude in dealing with men and with things; and, in this attitude, a formal justice is often coupled with an inconsiderate hardness. . . . Money is concerned only with what is common to all: it . . . reduces all quality and individuality to the question: How much? . . .' In small primitive groups 'production serves the customer who orders the good, so that the producer and the consumer are acquainted. The modern metropolis, however, is supplied almost entirely by production for the market, that is, for entirely unknown purchasers who never personally enter the producer's actual field of vision. Through this anonymity the interests of each party acquire an unmerciful matter-of-factness; and the intellectually calculating egoisms of both parties need not fear any deflection because of the imponderables of personal relationships. . . . Only money economy has filled the days of so many people with weighing, calculating, with numerical determinations, with a reduction of qualitative values to quantitative ones. Through the calculative nature of money a new precision, a certainty in the definition of identities and differences, an unambiguousness in agreements and arrangements has been brought about in the relations of life-elements . . . ' (*Ibid*: 411–12).

How far the use of money is correctly represented in these extracts need not concern the present argument. A balanced appraisal might put more stress on the fact of its being an effect as well as a cause. What matters for us, however, is that, like all the other references quoted in this chapter, they identify in contractual society certain mechanisms and dynamics which have produced certain types of relations. The argument of this book is that the same mechanisms and dynamics have operated within the work situation to produce essentially similar relational patterns.

In demonstrating the points at which this argument bears upon the preoccupations and propositions of some nineteenth century theorists we have so far touched upon the work of Spencer, Maine, Tönnies, Veblen, and Simmel. No set of ideas lends itself so fully, however, to discussion in this context as that of Marx and Engels.

Many of the familiar themes of this tradition – the rise of bourgeois society on the basis of power and exploitation; the impact of economic exchange upon social relations; the nature of alienation in its various forms – can readily be related to the concepts and dynamics expounded here.

Marx, Engels, and Exploitation

Engels presents a picture of how 'the capitalistic mode of production thrust its way into a society of commodity producers, of individual producers whose social bond was the exchange of their products.' Previous to this, in mediaeval times, production had 'satisfied, in the main, only the wants of the producers and his family', along with those of the feudal lord in places where relations of personal dependence existed. As a surplus emerged over and above these needs there developed a limited degree of commodity exchange. But the market was small and local; the methods of production were stable; and exclusiveness and local group unity prevailed (Engels 1967: 210–12). Such exchange as there was involved 'fairly direct bargaining between individuals or groups who were generally aware of each other's needs, and who produced for those needs' (Giddens 1971: 54). Compared with what was to come, market and work relations were diffuse. Economic relations were not based on the model of economic exchange, but were fused with personal relations between individuals – not necessarily, as has been stressed already, wholly benign, but not devoid, either, of a certain sense of mutual obligation which Engels identified as their social bond. In Marx's words, the more closely the means of exchange remain 'connected with the nature of the direct product of labour and the immediate needs of those exchanging, the greater must be the power of the community to bind the individuals together: the patriarchal relationship, the ancient communities, feudalism and the guild system' (McLellan 1971: 67). Moreover, at this stage the individual producer owned his product. The 'owner of the instruments of labour . . . himself appropriated the product, because, as a rule, it was his own product and the assistance of others was the exception'. Where external help was used it was 'compensated by something other than wages'. In accordance with our notion of the diffuse employment relationship, the 'apprentices and journeymen of the guilds worked less for board and wages than for education, in order that they might become master craftsmen themselves' (*Ibid*: 209).

With the growth of capitalist production this particular pattern of reciprocity balance becomes eroded and finally destroyed. Division of labour, mechanization, and the factory system bring about concentrations of economic resources owned by a minority of private individuals and supported in their ownership by the coercive forces of the State. Forced off the land, and unable to acquire the concentrations of property needed to initiate production for themselves, the many are compelled to put their labour power at the disposal of the few in exchange for the means of subsistence and on the condition that they surrender all claim to the product of their exertions. It then becomes the interest of the property owner, exploiting the superior power with which this situation endows him, to maximize the worker's product relative to the wage he receives; a process made technically specific in Marx's concept of surplus value. This he does by imposing upon the workers division of labour, mechanization, and disciplinary rules, and supporting these measures, where necessary, by means of his ability to apply – or cause to be applied – coercive power, sanctioned and legitimized by master-servant law. In many cases it is not necessary, for as Marx, like Hobbes before him, notes: 'The class which has the means of *material* production at its disposal, has control at the same time over the means of *intellectual* production, so that thereby, generally speaking, the ideas of those who lack the means of intellectual production are subject to it' (quoted in Giddens 1971: 41). In other words, since the dissemination of ideas and values requires resources, the property-owning class enjoys a great advantage in disseminating those which provide legitimation of their own interests and dominance. In so far as workers subjected to influence in this way can be brought to legitimize the system they do not need to be directly coerced. 'In the course of capitalist production, there comes into existence a working class which, by education, tradition, and custom, is induced to regard the demands of this method of production as self-evident laws of nature. . . . The direct use of force, apart from economic conditions, goes on, of course, from time to time but has now become exceptional' (Marx 1930: 817). The power relationship, of course, remains, to be ever confirmed by the tendency of labour saving devices to create recruits for the 'reserve army' of unemployed who drag down wages in their bid for employment. This power relationship is all-pervasive – '. . . the worker, though he can exchange one individual capitalist for another, cannot escape from the Capitalist' (Renner 1949: 38). The workers' participation in this division of labour is therefore an enforced collaboration 'entirely brought about', in Marx's words, 'by the capital that employs them. Their union into one single productive body and the establishment of a connexion between their individual functions are matters foreign and external to them, are not their own act, but the act of the capital that brings and keeps them together', the act 'of the powerful will of another, who subjects their activity to his aims' (quoted, *Ibid*: 34).

At the centre of this employer-worker relationship lies the massive asymmetry of reciprocity which spells exploitation. The employer imposes upon the worker a role of increasing specificity which reduces his discretion to minimal levels, while the employer himself appropriates the maximum discretion in making decisions about the goals and methods of the productive process, the disposal of the product, and the behaviour and rewards of the participants. Wielding great control over their behaviour, he comes under none from them. The extreme case of this type of relationship would, of course, be slavery, where the owner has full rights of disposal over the slave, who can claim no rights in return against the owner. Hence the notion, by analogy, of wage-slavery. In line with our preceding analysis, we see that this asymmetry is maintained by power, exercised over the worker either directly through the employment relationship or indirectly by supporting socialization agencies which lead him to legitimize the system and his place in it.

This legitimation comes under strain as workers in a common situation develop an increasing consciousness of grievance about specific aspects of employers' decision-making, such as wage rates, working hours, work methods, or other features of the explicit or implied terms of contract. However, a readiness by the State to limit employer discretion through legislation, or by employers themselves to accept some degree of limitation through a process of joint rule-making with trade unions, or even through self-regulation by employee groups themselves has, historically, tended to renew the legitimation. In the extreme situation workers may develop a consciousness of the system as fundamentally exploitive. Totally withdrawing their legitimation of it, they become, in Marx's phrase, a 'class-for-itself' and seek basic changes in economic relations by which resources would be removed from the ownership of the exploiting minority who appropriate the fruits of their labour. But more commonly the system has provided enough satisfactions, and been supported by sufficiently strong ideological underpinning, to maintain at least the necessary minimum of legitimation by its low-discretion members provided they were able, by one means or another, to limit employer discretion on certain issues which they perceived as immediately touching their welfare.

The asymmetry is therefore potentially a source of major social change. It is, however, those relatively minor changes in the distribution of discretion and patterns of decision-making which asymmetry has generated in Western countries with which our present analysis is concerned. This is one major direction in which the low-trust dynamic has operated – a direction to be explored more fully in the next chapter. But it has also been apparent in our analysis that low-discretion roles, in generating a low-trust dynamic towards a counter-proliferation of rules designed to limit employer or managerial discretion, thereby reveal a lack of personal commitment to, identification with, and moral involvement in, the work situation. Marx's theory of alienation is of major relevance to this aspect of the argument.

Marx and Alienation

The literature on Marx's concept of alienation is vast and ever-growing.* No more can be offered here than the barest indications of how the present analysis has relevance for his usage and thereby for the whole alienation debate.

Marx's concept has four main aspects: '(a) man is alienated from *nature*; (b) he is alienated from *himself* (from his own *activity*); (c) from his *species-being* (from his being as a member of the human species); (d) man is alienated from *man* (from other men)' (Mészáros 1970: 14, his italics). At this juncture we are concerned mainly with aspects of (b) and (d).† The aspect of man's essential nature on which

* Three recent references offering different perspectives, all with full bibliographies, are Mészáros 1970, Ollman 1971, and Schacht 1971.

† Until recently there has been a tendency to contrast the 'young' Marx with the 'mature' Marx, on the argument that the latter abandoned, as a key concept, the notion of alienation as developed by the former (see, for example,

Marx placed greatest emphasis expressed itself through labour; through productive life. For Marx, 'productive activity corresponds to the dimension of individuality or personality, and is that through which the individual personality expresses and thereby realizes itself (Schacht 1971: 74). By acting upon the external world and changing it, through the labour process, man 'at the same time changes his own nature. He develops the potentialities that slumber within him, and subjects these inner forces to his own control' (Marx 1930: 169). Labour is properly, therefore, an activity through which man 'fulfils himself' and can 'develop freely his spiritual and physical energies' – the 'satisfaction of a need' rather than simply a means to satisfy other needs. Above all, work should be 'voluntary' and 'free'; it should be a man's 'own work', his own 'spontaneous activity' (Marx, quoted in Schacht 1971: 79). A man's labour is truly his own labour only when it is spontaneous, free and self-directed activity. 'Marx's conception of "freedom" is . . . close to the notion of autonomous self-control. . . . To be free is to be autonomous, and thus not impelled by either external or internal forces beyond rational control . . . '(Giddens 1971: 227).

One can select from these phrases and interpretations many which speak directly to the value set upon high-discretion work in our society. Jaques, indeed, though rarely concerned to relate his own analysis to any wider dialogue, sometimes uses exactly the same words. 'When required to use your own discretion, . . . it feels like doing your own work' (1967: 88). The significance of 'doing your own work' in the context of the alienation debate lies in its contribution to the individual's growth. Here we find ourselves using a theory of human personality which stresses the importance of men being open to experiences through which they meet challenges and overcome obstacles, develop their aptitudes and abilities, and enjoy the satisfactions of achievement. In the course of these experiences men undergo psychological growth, realize themselves, and reach due stature as full, mature and autonomous moral agents. The central notion can be expresssed in language which we have found ourselves using throughout this study; the language of decision-making, choice, and responsibility. Men make themselves through their own

Bell 1961). His *Grundrisse*, however, written in his middle period and only recently more widely known, shows this approach to be mistaken (McLellan 1971; Mészáros 1970).

choices – by taking decisions and accepting responsibility for what they choose.* This is the process of self-determination and growth. A work situation of low discretion which offers no – or only the most trivial – opportunities for choice, decision, and the acceptance of responsibility is therefore one which offers no opportunities for growth. Conversely, the greater the discretion vested in the work role, the greater the degree to which the occupant has literally to express himself when making the choices and decisions demanded of him. In the words of Wright Mills, when describing the 'craft ethic' of high-discretion work: 'As he gives it the quality of his own mind and skill, he is also further developing his own nature; in this simple sense, he lives in and through his work, which confesses and reveals him to the world' (1956: 222). Hence the tendency in discussing high-discretion work to emphasize the 'contribution of the individual'.

Hence, too, the tendency, when referring to low-discretion work, to grope for terms such as anonymity and dehumanization. Here the individual is not being asked for *his* contribution; merely for conformity and obedience to someone else's. In terms of Schacht's interpretation of Marx: '. . . the product ceases to be the objective embodiment of the individual's own personality and the distinctive expression of his creative powers and interests. On the contrary, it is not at all distinctive, and has no relation to his personality and interests. He does not choose to make it, but rather is directed to do so. He does not even choose *how* to make it; he is compelled to suppress all individuality in the course of its production' (1971: 85). Marx therefore terms labour 'alienated' when it ceases to reflect the individual's own personality and interests and instead comes under the direction of an 'alien will', i.e. another man. In Jaques's words: conforming to prescribed rules 'feels like doing work which someone else has already decided about . . .' (1967: 88). In these circumstances, seen by Marx, of course, as created by the capitalist system of production, work becomes perverted from its essential function of expressing the worker's individuality and, since it is no longer 'the

* We may also note the accord here with some expressions of the existentialist standpoint. For Heidegger, ' "Authentic" existence is self-determined existence, shaped and given direction by decisions and choices which are truly one's own . . ., and are made in full awareness of the fundamental conditions of human life (e.g. . . . being responsible for what one is and does).' The alienated state is one in which the individual does not exist in this authentic manner (Schacht 1971 : 201).

satisfaction of a need', becomes merely 'a *means* to satisfy needs external to it'. These and related propositions, quoted with perhaps wearisome frequency, can still bear repeating here for their relevance. Alienation lies in the fact that 'labor is *external* to the worker, i.e., it does not belong to his essential being; that in his work, therefore, he does not affirm himself . . . does not develop freely his physical and mental energy. . . . His labor is therefore not voluntary, but coerced; it is *forced labor* . . . it is not his own, but someone else's . . . he belongs, not to himself, but to another' (Marx 1964: 110–11). Less frequently quoted is a passage from *Capital* in which Marx writes of capitalism that 'all the means for developing production are transformed into means of domination over and exploitation of the producer; that they mutilate the worker into a fragment of a human being, degrade him to become a mere appurtenance of the machine, make his work such a torment that its essential meaning is destroyed; estrange from him the intellectual potentialities of the labour process in very proportion to the extent to which science is incorporated into it as an independent power . . .' (1930: 713).

This emphasis on alienation as 'self-estrangement' converges with that which sees alienated work as 'work which is not intrinsically satisfying'; a key feature being lack of control over one's work life (Seeman: 1967). That this analysis needs to distinguish between alienation and conscious articulated dissatisfaction has been demonstrated by Goldthorpe *et al.* (1969), who explore the attitudes and behaviour of relatively affluent workers who see their work as offering mainly extrinsic rewards but who have adapted to this pattern of expectations (see also Argyris 1972). In so far as their acceptance of the situation expresses, in some sense, repudiation or neglect of that essential part of their self which can only be developed through choice and decision-making (self-determination), they can be said, in the language of this tradition, to be self-estranged.

The contrast between this pattern of work orientations and that of the occupants of high-discretion roles requires us to revise Marx's proposition that alienation is an inevitable outcome of all employment relationships involving some degree of direction by another. Wherever labour is regarded as something to be exchanged for pay and directed by another it becomes, for Marx, a surrender to an alien will and thereby loses its human significance and worth. But differences of degree in direction, control and surrender among employed persons create widely differing patterns of work experience. The employment contract *per se* does not create the alienated state. This gives further substance to the distinction drawn by Lockwood between market situation and work situation in his refinement of Marx's concept of class. The former consists of 'source and size of income, degree of job security, and opportunity for upward occupational mobility'; the latter 'the set of social relationships in which the individual is involved at work by virtue of his position in the division of labour' (1958: 15). Included among the differences of work situation are the contrasting syndromes of characteristics displayed by low-discretion and high-discretion roles. Propertyless employees bound by a pay contract differ profoundly, therefore, in how far their role and its attendant syndrome of characteristics generates a community of sympathies, values, and objectives with their employers or top management. For, as was noted earlier, the contrast extends to such issues as high and low status, rewards and privileges; the existence or otherwise of a community of values with superiors or leaders, and the generating of relationships bearing some approximation to mutual confidence based on common objectives. When all the necessary qualifications have been made concerning the individualistic competitiveness, rivalry, and gamesmanship which can enter into relationships among occupants of high-discretion roles, it remains to be said that these are normally contained within a framework of institutionalized cooperation and confidence markedly different from relations between superiors and their low-discretion subordinates.

On this subject we can refer again to Marx. Bearing in mind that his characterization of the alienated state is only valid for what are being described here as low-discretion roles, his depiction of alienation *between* men can be shown to relate, in one of its manifestations, to the same social context. It will be recalled that the low-discretion model implies a lack of confidence on the part of top management in subordinates' disposition to obey rules and comply willingly with its leadership, a tendency to diagnose their failures of performance as due to careless indifference; and an assumption that underlying these responses lies a more general refusal to accept a commitment to top management goals and interests. These low-trust attitudes are, as we saw, usually reciprocated by the subordinates. Marx speaks to this situation in his treatment of alienation between men. This 'is to be understood as involving a complete absence of fellow-feeling, an estimation of others as of no more positive significance than that of means to personal ends, and an antagonism based on . . . the anticipation of attempted counter-exploitation' (Schacht 1971: 96). Or in the words of Marx himself: '. . . within the relationship of estranged labor each man views the other in accordance with the standard and the relationship in which he finds himself as a worker' (1964: 115). The capitalist, too, suffers the alienated state. 'Because workers cannot have human relations with him, he cannot have human relations with them . . .' (Ollman 1971: 155).

Marx sees these characteristics as appearing in many other types of relationship throughout the wider bourgeois society. Money exchange, competition, commercialism – these produced relational consequences which Marx described in terms readily assimilable to the low-trust dynamic. 'The necessity of exchange' – by which he meant economic exchange as Blau uses the term – 'and the transformation of the product into a pure exhange value progress to the same extent as the division of labour. . . .' The act of exchange 'splits into two acts that are independent of one another: exchange of commodities for money, exchange of money for commodities – buying and selling. There is no longer any immediate identity, since they have been separated in time and space, each one having acquired a form of existence which is indifferent to the other.' The commercializing of all goods and services into money exchange values 'presupposes both the disintegration of all rigid, personal (historical) relationships of dependence in production, and a universal interdependence of the producers. . . . The mutual and universal dependence of individuals who remain indifferent to one another constitutes the social network that binds them together.' Exchange value is, then, 'a general factor in which all individuality and particularity is denied and suppressed' (reproduced in McLellan 1971: 60–6).

The central role of money makes it, for Marx, 'the epitome of human self-alienation under capitalism, since it reduces all human qualities to quantitative values of exchange. Capitalism thus has a "universalising" character, which breaks down the particularities of traditional cultures . . .' (Giddens 1971: 214). With the growth of capitalism there 'was ended', wrote Engels, 'the old, peaceful, stable condition of things'. It produced, *inter alia*, 'the loosening of all traditional moral bonds, of patriarchal subordination . . .' (1967:

194, 212). Their joint product, *Manifesto of the Communist Party* of 1848, portrayed the bourgeoisie as having 'put an end to all feudal, patriarchal, idyllic relations. It has pitilessly torn asunder the motley feudal ties that bound man to his "natural superiors" and has left remaining no other nexus between man and man than naked self-interest, than callous "cash payment"' (Marx and Engels 1967: 82). Elsewhere Engels traces the spiral of distrust that develops in such a society dedicated to competitive acquisitiveness and economic exchange purged of all diffuse ties and non-pecuniary considerations. 'Everyone must try to sell as dear as possible and to buy as cheaply as possible. So wherever buying and selling occurs, two men with diametrically opposed interests confront each other. . . . Each knows that the interests of the other fellow are opposed to his own interests. Hence there is mutual distrust. And this mistrust is justified. . . . The first maxim of trade is the concealment of everything that might reduce the value of the article in question. In commerce one is allowed to take the utmost advantage of the ignorance and the trust of the opposing party. . . . In other words trade is legalized fraud' (1967: 153).

That this is a travesty of much trading is as evident as that many of the other generalizations and models produced by nineteenth century theorists leaned excessively on an awareness of the novelties of the age. All were responding to the first shock waves of industrialization, and all supposed that its impulses were in process of overwhelming the older patterns. In fact, as we have seen, trade and commerce are never conducted on a wholly economic-exchange basis; status mechanisms powerfully resist the encroachments of contract; mechanization and the division of labour leave intact, or create, many high-discretion work roles marked by reciprocally diffuse, high-trust relations; and similar personalized bonds and ties abound likewise outside as well as within work situations.

But when these necessary qualifications have been made it remains apparent that important changes were overtaking some types of social relations; changes which different theorists were interpreting and conceptualizing in different ways. They have been conceptualized here in terms of institutionalized trust; a notion which seems to have relevance not only for work situations but also for other kinds of relations. This approach has been seen to have particularly sympathetic resonance with the writings of Marx, providing as these do a synoptic view in which the concept of alienation plays either an explicit or an implicit role. But a divergence appears when we note that Marx's analysis of the various forms of alienation is predicated on a postulated connection between the increasing division of labour and the emergence of a polarized class structure based on ownership of the means of production. It has become apparent that class structure as Marx defined it is not a necessary condition of a progressive differentiation in the division of labour and all the structural features associated with it. The power to initiate, structure, uphold, and enforce such a progressive differentiation can certainly lie with the private ownership of resources, but that power is ultimately upheld by the political forces of the State and these can just as easily provide the underpinning directly without the intervening term of private ownership' (Dahrendor 1959). Controllers of communally owned resources have shown themselves no less able and willing than private owners to pursue the division of labour to its fullest low-discretion syndrome. The dynamic of profit-seeking which for Marx was the essential impulse behind capitalistic organization, mechanization, and the division of labour has been shown to be only one of a number of drives which can take the same direction. However convincing a case can be made, managerial apologetics notwithstanding, that profit maximization remains the most powerful drive within the private sector, the behaviour of management within the public sector indicates that a change of ownership within a society which otherwise remains acquisitive, sets great store by economic growth, and is bent on using labour as a commodity, brings no necessary modification to the hierarchical bureaucratic structures of organized inequality with which industrial societies are familiar.

From this point of view, Weber's divergence from Marx is one we have to note. This points to rational calculation as 'the primary element in modern capitalistic enterprise', and to 'the rationalisation of social life generally' as 'the most distinctive attribute of modern western culture' (Giddens 1971: 241). Weber's description of the bureaucratic patterns which result from the application of rationalization, calculation, and measurement to formal organizations is almost identical to Marx's account of alienation under capitalism. But whereas for Marx these alienative characteristics stem from society's class character based on property and would be eliminated by a basic restructuring, for Weber they derive from a bureaucratic rationality which is integral to modern industrial society whether capitalist or socialist. For all that they represent a denial of some of the most distinctive values of Western culture – freedom, individuality, spontaneity, creativity – they are seen by Weber as part of the price we pay for material abundance.

Durkheim and the Division of Labour

No more for Durkheim than for Weber is class structure the essential feature of industrial society on which to focus; neither is class conflict for him a constructive dynamic making for a new social order. He emphasizes instead the 'organic' solidarity which develops out of the progressive differentiation of labour and which he compares with the 'mechanical' solidarity of traditional society. Traditional society, which Durkheim presents in terms similar to those of Tönnies's *gemeinschaft*, is characterized by very limited and rudimentary division of labour. There is little occupational differentiation. This is matched by an equally minimal differentiation among men in terms of individuality and personality. Within their small local communities their behaviour is closely regulated by highly prescriptive uniform rules, rigorously and repressively enforced, which cover every aspect of their life. '. . . individuality is nil . . . personality vanishes . . .' (Durkheim 1964: 130). Then comes the transition towards the increasing division of labour of modern society and, with it, mobility, uprootedness and change. 'As we advance in the evolutionary scale, the ties which bind the individual to his family, to his native soil, to traditions which the past has given to him, to collective group usages, become loose. More mobile, he changes his environment more easily, leaves his people to go elsewhere to live a more autonomous existence, to a greater extent forms his own ideas and sentiments' (*Ibid*: 400).

From this kind of sketch other theorists had drawn pessimistic conclusions, but Durkheim sought to show that there is nothing intrinsic to the division of labour as such which necessarily promotes 'a systematic debasement of morality' as a consequence of mobility and uprooting. Certainly there develops a crucial change in the nature of the social bond, but bondedness remains, and indeed it is of a superior order to that of traditional society. The new organic solidarity grows out of the increasingly complex occupational differentiation and the individual differentiation accompanying it. Freed from the prescriptive rules punitively imposed by the older, repressive, tradition-bound community, men are able to develop and express their individual personalities while yet acknowledging the complex mutual indebtedness which binds them together in their increasingly differentiated society. There has to be greater tolerance of social and moral heterogeneity, but this is contained within an overarching common moral consciousness among men that they are one with another in their growing interdependence. 'Implicit throughout *The Division of Labour* is the notion that the performance of complex differentiated functions in a society with an advanced division of labour both requires and creates individual variation, initiative, and innovation, whereas undifferentiated segmental societies do not' (Bellah 1959: 165). But this implies no necessary loosening of the social bond. In place of the autocratic discipline found in traditional societies there develop quite different forms of authority which draw their strength from this moral consciousness of interdependence and from men's awareness of their place in the total scheme. Thus with 'the rise of technology and the general emergence of individuality from the restraints of the past, it becomes possible – for the first time in human history – for social order to rest, not on mechanical uniformity and collective repression, but on the organic articulation of free individuals pursuing different functions but united by their complementary roles. . . . Justice will be restitutive, rather than penal; law will lose its repressive character, and there will be a diminishing need for punishment' (Nisbet 1965: 35).

Before pursuing Durkheim's analysis further we can note that his description of organic solidarity accords more closely with a high-discretion than with a low-discretion pattern. The picture of men pursuing specialized roles, becoming more individual and autonomous, yet bound by a moral authority born of their consciousness of interdependence, bears a distinct resemblance to what was characterized earlier as the high-trust fraternity. By contrast, structures of low-discretion roles and relations, with their prescriptive rules enforced by disciplinary sanctions and their lack of individuality and personality development for the participants, seem closer to Durkheim's mechanical solidarity. Modern industrial society must therefore be said to include both: a fact which Burns and Stalker (1961) had in mind when they contrasted two different patterns of managerial structure to which they applied the terms 'mechanistic' and 'organic' for the purpose of bringing out the same distinctions. If we recall Friedmann's contrast between the specialist exercising a high-discretion skill upon what, judged by the standards of pre-industrial societies, is a narrow range task, and the specialized worker, exercising only low discretion in a narrow range task, we seem to see in Durkheim's analysis evidence that he had the former rather than the latter in mind when he extolled the social strengths of differentiated division of labour. This impression is strengthened by what he has to say about the division of labour as exchange. 'The social relations to which the division of labour gives birth have often been considered only in terms of exchange, but this misinterprets what such exchange implies and what results from it.' The actual process of exchange is 'only the superficial expression of an internal and very deep state' (Durkheim 1964: 31). The terms in which Durkheim elaborates this approach suggest the social-exchange relations of high-discretion situations, not the economic-exchange relations of low-discretion situations. Yet he obviously had to explain, besides other forms of social disorganization, both the class conflict and the 'debasement of human nature' which he admitted were the consequences of extreme fragmentation of functions 'in exceptional and abnormal circumstances' (*Ibid*: 317–72).

The explanations did not lie, in his view, in the division of labour *per se*, which does 'not produce these consequences because of a necessity of its own nature' (*Ibid*: 371). They lay in the inadequacy of normative regulation and in the maladaptation of social forms and institutions to the requirements of this extreme functional differentiation. These gave rise to abnormalities which he refers to as the 'anomic' and the 'forced' division of labour. Anomie, the state of inadequate regulation, revealed itself in many spheres of economic life – for example in the anarchic instability of nationwide or even worldwide markets which periodically erupted in commercial and industrial crises and business failures. With the increasing differentiation, specialization, and complexity of functions, markets, and organizations, there came a corresponding need for elaborate regulation of a wide variety of kinds for purposes of integration and coordination, but this was often lacking. Of special concern here were the anomic forms of work behaviour which Durkheim saw as manifested by men who, in pursuing narrowly specialized functions, had been furnished with no understanding of their place in the complex interdependent scheme of things. They had not come to relate their contribution to the larger end which it served and with which they needed to identify. Consequently their work had no meaning for them. Feeling no moral involvement in it, they were unable to regulate their own behaviour along those lines of willing cooperation towards a common end which the division of labour implied if it was to be a source of organic solidarity. Instead they fell into mechanical and uninterested routine, becoming passive, inert, and unresponsive to the changing needs and circumstances of the organization. Thus developed a 'debasement of human nature', the 'ruin of the individual', and a drain upon 'the very source of social life' (*Ibid*: 371).

The remedy was to supply the individual with insight and understanding of the social purpose to which he was contributing. He would not then be 'a machine who repeats his movements without knowing their meaning', but would know 'that they tend, in some way, towards an end that he conceives more or less distinctly. He feels that he is serving something' (*Ibid*: 372). He thus needed to be provided with a 'clear conception of a unity of purpose which binds his work actively together with the collective productive endeavour of society'; a 'moral awareness of the social importance of his particular role in the division of labour' (Giddens 1971: 230). In terms of trust analysis this moral awareness can be seen as the basis on which the individual is brought to legitimize his part in the whole, thereby ensuring that he manifests high-trust responses even though occupying, perhaps, the humblest of low-discretion roles. Thus is brought about a moral consolidation of the division of labour.

It is clear that the work behaviours referred to by Durkheim as anomic are those seen by Marx as alienated. For Marx they were an outcome of class relations for which the appropriate treatment was elimination of the power basis underpinning those relations – namely the concentration of property ownership in the hands of the few. With the abolition of these exploitive relations would go dissolution of the division of labour as an organizing principle of human intercourse. For Durkheim, too, a transformation in power relations was a precondition of the sort of moral regulation he considered necessary for organic solidarity. Attempts to impose upon men, by means of coercive power, work roles and relations which they saw as unjust could only compound the evil. Two aspects receive emphasis in Durkheim's treatment; equality of opportunity and equality in contractual relations. Under the forced division of labour a privileged class monopolized the higher occupational positions, thereby denying others the opportunities for self-development and self-expression. The resulting situation in which men were forced to do work ill fitting to their preferences or capacities could constitute no basis for moral consolidation of the division of labour. In developing this argument Durkheim reveals his own social ideal as that of a meritocracy; 'a society with multiple occupational positions, in which access to the leading strata will depend, not upon transmitted privilege, but upon competitive selection of the talented through the medium of the educational system' (Giddens 1971: 232). To evoke organic solidarity the division of labour must be spontaneous in the sense that each man occupies the role for which at the given moment his aptitudes, abilities, skills, and stage of development equip him. If the class or caste structure 'sometimes gives rise to anxiety and pain instead of producing solidarity, this is because the distribution of social functions on which it rests does not respond, or rather no longer responds, to the distribution of natural talents' (Durkheim 1964: 375). Solidarity requires that there be 'absolute equality in the external conditions' of the social competition for position and place (*Ibid*: 377). But this equality involved more than simply removing obstacles from the path of able men. It involved providing all men with the chance to *become* able, i.e. removing 'everything that can even indirectly shackle the free unfolding of the social force that each carries in himself' (*Ibid*: 377).

But even more than this was required if men were to legitimize the division of labour and their place in it. As men related themselves to others in the complex interdependencies characteristic of organic society they must do so increasingly through contract. Durkheim's treatment of contract cannot be elaborated here, though we may note his insistence on a point made earlier in our analysis that it can only be sustained within a framework of social regulation, obligation, and enforcement which is not embodied in the contract itself. 'What shows better than anything else that contracts give rise to obligations which have not been contracted for is that they "make obligatory not only what is expressed in them, but also all consequences which equity usage, or the law imputes from the nature of the obligation", (*Ibid*: 212). Unlike Spencer's treatment, this leaves full room for the notion presented in the preceding chapter of traditional master-servant status regulation being read into the contract of employment as industrialization developed.

But of more immediate concern for us is Durkheim's argument that it is not enough to rely on *enforcement* of contracts; solidarity requires that the great majority be *spontaneously* kept. 'If contracts were observed only by force, contractual solidarity would be very precarious.' But what was the condition of spontaneous adhesion to contract? Expressed assent by itself offered no guarantee, for this may be extorted by superior power – which can come from indirect as well as direct sources. 'If the engagement which I have extorted by threatening someone with death is morally and legally void, why should it be valid if, to obtain it, I profited from some situation which I did not cause but which put someone else under the necessity of yielding to me or dying?' For the 'obligatory force of a contract to be complete, it is not sufficient that it be the object of an expressed assent. It is still necessary for it to be just, and it is not just by virtue of mere verbal consent. . . . It is necessary that the contracting parties be placed in conditions externally equal.' Durkheim's vision here was one which liberal apologists were apt to write about as if it already existed – a society of free and equal contracting parties. Durkheim suggests the corrective. 'If one class of society is obliged, in order to live, to take any price for its services, while another can abstain from such action thanks to resources at its disposal which, however, are not necessarily due to any social superiority, the second has an unjust advantage over the first at law. In other words, there cannot be rich and poor at birth without there being unjust contracts' (*Ibid*: 384).

There now becomes apparent the sense in which 'equality of external conditions' both in occupational selection and in the making of contracts had to be seen by Durkheim as crucial not only in its own right but also as a condition for the remedying of anomie. Durkheim did not visualize the individual developing a moral awareness of his occupational place in a social unity of productive purpose (and thereby promoting organic solidarity) if both his place and the contract which regulated it were imposed upon him against his will by superior power. This was not to say that mitigation of the forced division of labour would itself cope with the problem of anomie, but rather to assert it as a precondition. Power relations could be changed without eliminating anomie, but anomie could not be dispelled except by policies resting firmly on a foundation of equality and justice. Within this context of reasoning, the explanation becomes apparent for the failure or at best very limited success of policies noted in the preceding chapter by which employers hope to generate moral involvement among employees by promoting their physiological, social or psychological welfare. These were policies which, it could be argued, were directed at anomie while leaving intact the power-enforced structures of bureaucracy, subordination, and reward which gave rise to it.

In acknowledging that the external equalities necessary for organic solidarity do not exist, Durkheim concedes that it might seem as if 'we have not the right to consider as normal a character which the division of labour never purely presents'. However, as society evolves towards ever higher forms the inequalities tend to level out, thereby enabling the division of labour to approximate its intrinsic characteristic of organic solidarity. In the first place, Durkheim sees a progressive decline in inequality of opportunity as a definite historical tendency accompanying the division of labour, which by its individualizing effects creates a pressure for individual self-fulfilment. And second: contract law 'tends more and more to detract all value from conventions where the contracting parties are found in situations that are too unequal' (*Ibid*: 385). For Durkheim, therefore, the existing social and economic order contains the seeds of evolutionary redemption which it does not have for Marx, who sees the revolutionary destruction of bourgeois power as a precondition for emancipating men from alienation in all its forms. Moreover, whereas for Marx division of labour was alienative *per se*, for Durkheim there was a trend towards a situation in which each individual, located occupationally according to his talents and merits, and receiving rewards determined under the rules of free and equal contract, could be brought to legitimize, by the appropriate moral education, his place in relation to the whole, thus removing the abnormality presented by the anomic division of labour. The vision is one of social integration based on moral norms of individual obligation serving a corporate solidarity. It is essentially a unitary conception of social structure.

Our earlier trust analysis diverges from both these conceptions. On the one hand it recognizes that occupants of low-discretion roles may be so ideologically oriented as to legitimize the division of labour and their place in it, thus manifesting no alienated or anomic behaviour. On the other hand, it points to the apparently declining disposition of such occupants to offer this legitimation, and stresses the difficulties faced by managers of large organizations in trying to promote it. These difficulties are relevant to Durkheim's proposal for a corporate structure in each branch of industry. He suggests corporate associations which, as legally constituted and public institutions, would establish an occupational ethic; promote moral integration between the various groups and strata; and foster organic solidarity within their respective fields. The trade union could not meet these social needs, since it was organized for a permanent power struggle with employers. Such agreements as were made between the two groups could express no moral authority and integration but 'only the respective state of their military forces'. There existed 'no common organization . . . where they can develop a common authority, fixing their mutual relations and commanding obedience . . .' (*Ibid*: 6). The strain towards unity and social integration expressed in these ideas is apparent. In Coser's words: 'To Durkheim a divided society can be neither normal nor good. The "good" society is cohesive' (1964: 218–19). Such a perspective was, as we have seen, bound to haunt the imagination of many employers and managers. Never absent from the industrial scene, it received fresh stimulus in the 1930s and 1940s from the writings of the Mayo school.

Mayo and Human Relations

It was to be expected that from among those committed to the *status quo* – to those structural features described by Durkheim as resulting in the forced division of labour – there would nevertheless come hopeful attempts to remedy the disadvantages for employers and managers resulting from anomie. We saw in the preceding chapter how, during the closing years of the nineteenth century and the early decades of the twentieth, a few theorists and practical men of business were beginning to see the limitations of the Scientific Management logic. Extreme division of labour, close supervision, bureaucratic rules, and tight discipline could produce remarkable economic benefits, but they could also produce economic costs in the form of indifference and lack of commitment if not worse, and shrewd men had begun to speculate about ways of swallowing the sugar and spitting out the pill. Early ideas recommended management to manifest a diffuse concern for the individual employee in terms of his immediate physical work environment and the welfare services and amenities available to him. This, it was hoped, would evoke a reciprocal diffuse orientation on the part of the employee towards management in place of the grudging narrowness produced by the stark cash nexus of a purely economic exchange. Practical disappointments, together with the grandiose interpretations placed upon the findings of the Hawthorne experiments conducted in a Western Electric Company plant in Chicago between 1927 and 1932 (Roethlisberger and Dickson 1939; Roethlisberger 1942; Baritz 1965) prompted Elton Mayo to offer a somewhat less crude conception of the way forward. Focusing on the isolated individual and his welfare was not enough; concern must be directed to the social bonds which bound the individual within his solidary work group, for here lay the springs of obligation, loyalty, and commitment which could be harnessed for managerial ends.

In this context, certain of the themes emphasized if not necessarily originated by Durkheim have proved to have considerable appeal in their popularized – and often bowdlerized – form for leaders, administrators, and their advisers and mentors. Attention must be confined here to the world of industrial management, where Durkheim's conception of unitary occupational structures to which even the humblest members contribute a willing moral involvement as a consequence of grasping its meaning and their place in it, has had its vogue, in vulgarized forms, among managers struggling with problems of motivation in large organizations. Recent decades have seen a variety of attempts, often associated with the fashionable fetish of communications, to arouse rank and file enthusiasm by, as the phrase has it, 'putting them in the picture'. Devices used have included works councils, consultative committees, graphic displays, and house magazines.

But these ventures have constituted only one aspect of a broader movement – usually characterized as Human Relations – which saw the work organization ideally as a unitary integrated structure and sought managerial methods and devices for realizing the ideal in practice. The more recent researchers working in the Human Relations tradition have broadened and diversified their approach to the point where the label loses precise meaning, but the early exponents conducted their search within narrower limits. They were preoccupied solely with the anomic division of labour to the exclusion of the forced division of labour. In other words, they sought ways of inducing the rank and file to legitimize higher management control and leadership without in any way modifying the structure of power and decision-making. The discretionary content of jobs at all levels was to remain the same, but lower participants were to be manipulated by a mixture of ideological indoctrination and 'supportive', 'permissive', 'participative', and non-punitive supervision (as against the autocratic, punitive, and openly coercive variety) to identify with the organization and its goals as defined by top management. Later the search for legitimation extended, in a few cases, to granting the work group a limited degree of discretion over certain of its processes. This was based on the assumption, of course, that the group would take the 'right' decisions, and where the experiment failed to serve management purposes it was discontinued. Later still such ventures became bolder to the point of making significant changes in the discretionary content of work roles, and these have brought, as was noted earlier, some changes in attitudes and motivation. But there is no doubt that much of the application of human relations techniques has sought to evoke the personal commitment characteristic of organic solidarity from work situations that are predominantly mechanistic – or, in other words, to evoke the high-trust pattern characteristic of high-discretion situations from structures that are predominantly of a low-discretion nature. It has been an attempt to enjoy the best of both worlds – on one hand, the benefits of extreme rationalization and Scientific Management of work, and on the other, the identification and commitment of men seized by a felt obligation to serve a common goal. Attempts to apply these methods have not been directed only at lower ranks. Where size, bureaucracy, and routinization have threatened to sap the moral involvement of white-collar staffs, including perhaps lower and even middle management, the response by high authority has been to seek its renewal through these psychological techniques rather than fall back on alienative authoritarianism.

The whole approach has been criticized on two different levels. On the moral level it has been seen as manipulative in the pejorative sense in that, within a structure marked by profound inequalities, it seeks to evoke from the relatively deprived a spirit of commitment akin to that manifested by the relatively privileged, and to evoke it not through significant changes in the inequalities deemed by management to be so beneficial for its purposes but through persuasive ideologies, psychological devices, and personal styles of supervision. 'The formal aim, implemented by the latest psychological equipment, is to have men internalize what the managerial cadres would have them do, without their knowing their own motives, but nevertheless having them. Many whips are inside men, who do not know how they got there, or indeed that they are there. . . . The engineering of consent to authority has moved into the realm of manipulation where the powerful are anonymous' (Mills 1956: 110). Raymond Williams has characterized other aspects of this management approach. '. . . of course you have to command, but since a leader has to be followed he must be diligently attentive to the state of mind of those he is leading: must try to understand them, talk to them about their problems (not about his own, by the way), get a picture of their state of mind. Then, having taken these soundings, having really got the feel of his people, he will point the way forward.' This is 'the stance of the leader who is merely listening to the discussion to discover the terms in which he can get his own way' (1961: 306–7).

On the practical level, one criticism is directly suggested by the argument of this book; that given the present division of labour, authority and control, and the highly unequal distribution of rewarding experiences, the tendencies making for low-trust responses among the rank and file are powerful enough to render the human relations approach a source not of greater managerial legitimacy but if anything of intensified suspicion of managerial good faith.

As one of the prophets of this approach, Mayo asserted that industrialism was undermining traditional social bonds and that modern society could hardly expect to survive unless it re-established the capacity for spontaneous willing collaboration and teamwork, which he found notably lacking in industry (1949). He renewed the Durkheimian theme in arguing that the conditions necessary for a healthy social organism are present only when every individual has a sense of social function and social responsibility; when cooperation is assured because the purposes of each are the purposes of all; when the individual feels, as he works, that he can see beyond his group to the wider society and know his labours to be necessary to it. The reknitting of the damaged social fabric required for a renewal of these conditions could not be left to chance, but must be consciously organized through appropriate styles of leadership which regenerated among men the lost feelings of belonging and meaningful membership of group and community. Class antagonism and pressure group activities – including those of trade unions – were socially destructive in that, by promoting conflict, they obstructed this creative process of organizing cooperation and mutual commitment.

It was a process which, in Mayo's view, could proceed most fruitfully at the level of the work organization. The basic social unit into which the individual needs to be integrated is his work group, and the responsibility for achieving this lies with management, which must also create the social conditions and team leadership for bending the activities of all groups towards the common goal. The primary need was for management to capture the allegiance of the group by means of supportive, non-authoritarian styles of supervision. The greater social satisfactions thus generated could then be capitalized to create among employees a keen sensitivity to, and sympathy for, organizational purposes as defined by management. Given the necessary social skills, factory groups could be rendered 'so stable in their attitudes of group cooperation that men in the groups explicitly recognized that the factory had become for them the stabilizing force around which they developed satisfying lives' (Donham, W. B., Introduction to Mayo 1949: viii).

Statements asserting the present moral bankruptcy of the large work organization have not only come, however, from those in accord with the human relations position. Contemporaneously with Mayo, Tannenbaum offered an analysis which, after sympathetically locating trade unionism and collective bargaining within a sociological analysis, went on to assert that the business corporation has 'never achieved the moral adhesion of those whose lives it ruled. . . '. It 'failed to secure that devotion because it did not represent a moral purpose to which men could be loyal. . . . The corporation rested upon economic power and bought its servants' attachment for cash, and that was insufficient.' Racked by internal divisions, it needs for its survival 'to be endowed with a moral role in the world, not merely an economic one . . . In some way the corporation and its labor force must become one corporate group and cease to be a house divided. . . .' Tannenbaum's prescriptions need not concern us; it must be enough to say that they pay no attention to the division of labour.

The writings of Tannenbaum and Mayo illustrate the persistence of this vision of a unitary corporate solidarity for the business enterprise, for they strike a sympathetic chord with the perspective of nineteenth century critics noted in the previous chapter who held out an idealized version of mediaeval society as their model. But Mayo and Tannenbaum reveal no nostalgia for a static world of handicrafts and small scale units; Mayo's message was that the skills and arts of promoting conflict-free cooperation and commitment were crucial for the survival of constantly changing dynamic societies. What appealed to him in the mediaeval scene were the supposed community of purpose among its members and the individual's sense of social function which, through its rights and duties, 'established a meaningful relationship between the individual and his society' (Bendix and Fisher 1949: 123).

Legitimation of Division of Labour through Collective Bargaining?

Experience was to suggest, however, that if the power structure and its associated patterns of discretion and decision-making remained unchanged, the Holy Grail of employee involvement would be as elusive when sought along Mayo's route as during earlier searches. These were attempts to overcome anomie and alienation while leaving untouched Durkheim's other major abnormal form of the division of labour: that ensuing from inequities and deprivations enforced through a structure of highly unequal power, command, and decision. The arguments of this book point to the difficulties facing such attempts.

But what if the grosser inequalities of power were, as Durkheim suggested, being reduced by the growth of democratic values and institutions, both in the wider political order and in industry itself? A *prima facie* case could be made to this effect. To the extent that political parties representing working-class interests gained an effective foothold in democratic political systems they could hope for access to the levers of control. And within industry could it not be argued that through trade unionism, which redressed the balance of power, collective bargaining offered a means of eliminating unjust contracts? To be sure, it might have difficulty in dealing with other Durkheimian discontents which prevented the discontented from legitimizing the system; the frustration of individual talents, for example, and the failure in most cases to promote individual self-development. But these problems might be susceptible to solution by the promotion of a meritocracy through the wider political system. At the very least, collective bargaining appeared to redeem the contract doctrine which, in its practical working on an *individual* basis, made most labour an exploited commodity. And it could be argued that industrial democracy was no less important than political democracy. Indeed, leading theorists of the late nineteenth century asserted that autocratic power in the workplace had greater alienative effects on its victims than did the more distant dominance of the State political system. 'To them, the uncontrolled power wielded by the owners of the means of production, able to withhold from the manual worker all chances of subsistence unless he accepted their terms, meant a far more genuine loss of liberty, and a far keener sense of personal subjection, than the official jurisdiction of the magistrate, or the far-off, impalpable rule of the king' (Webb, S. and B. 1902: 841).

Redress of this inequality, along with moral education and a movement towards meritocracy, would strengthen the legitimacy of the system in the eyes of lower participants. No longer powerless, their ability to participate in the rule-making which shaped their work and rewards would invest the rules with a moral authority otherwise lacking. Admittedly the picture appeared to fall short of Durkheim's vision of unitary corporate solidarity. Rather was this a pluralist scenario which presupposed divergent perceptions, compromise and the gamesmanship of negotiation as the separately organized groups bargained about the terms of their collaboration. Yet in so far as this mode of decision-making gave subordinate groups a stake in the system it promoted their commitment to it. Pluralistic pressure group activity would be pursued within an agreed framework of basic values and institutions. Thus would collective bargaining contribute something, at any rate, towards that moral consolidation of the division of labour which Durkheim saw as its normal state.

Here was a view which took as its starting point the assumption that 'In every type of social structure there are occasions for conflict, since individuals and subgroups are likely to make from time to time rival claims to scarce resources, prestige or power positions.' Provided these conflicts are about 'goals, values or interests that do not contradict the basic assumptions upon which the relationship is founded', their open acceptance, toleration, and institutionalization tend 'to be positively functional for the social structure'. By resolving tensions over competing claims, such institutionalization 'is likely to have stabilizing and integrative functions for the relationship' (Coser 1956: 151–4). Thus while, on the face of it, this approach might seem by Durkheim's lights to encourage social dissension through these processes of toleration and institutionalization, supporters could argue that in being 'realistic' about the facts of human association it promoted a stronger and more resilient stability in the social order. As will be seen, collective bargaining could be presented as having just these characteristics and consequences.

The Webbs, Tannenbaum, and the Trend back to Status

Such a perspective underlay the vision of Sidney and Beatrice Webb in their pioneering analysis, *Industrial Democracy*, first published in 1897. Operating with a pluralistic interpretation of modern society, they saw 'genuine "freedom of contract" ' as being achieved by collective bargaining with 'conditions of employment adjusted between equally expert negotiators, acting for corporations reasonably comparable in strategic strength. . . '. There was more than a suggestion that, on the basis of this joint regulation by equal partners, workers could be brought by their leaders to take a 'responsible' and 'committed' view of their work (and non work) roles which was far removed from the alienated and anomic modes analysed by Marx and Durkheim. Public opinion would expect the trade union 'to use its strategic position to secure the conditions necessary for the fulfilment of its particular social function in the best possible way – to obtain, that is to say, not what will be immediately most enjoyed by the "average sensual man", but what, in the long run, will most conduce to his efficiency as a professional, a parent, and a citizen' (1902: 816, 818–25, 842). Tawney was later to develop the theme. The necessary condition for the display by workers of professional motivation and responsible commitment was the 'drastic limitation, or the transference to the public, of the proprietary rights of the existing owners of industrial capital' (1961: 129). This would involve no reversal of the division of labour or revolutionary change in the organization of the enterprise. 'It is easy to prove that a hierarchy of authority, with gradations of responsibility, is as indispensable to modern industry as to a modern army' (1931: 254–5). Tawney assumed that abolition of the functionless property owner and the full provision of opportunities for all employees to concern themselves with the conduct and policies of the organization would render it possible to evoke from them a spirit of professional service and moral involvement. G. D. H. Cole, too, sympathetic as he was to William Morris's plea for the craft ethic, and tolerant of A. J. Penty's unqualified mediaevalism, hoped to reconcile responsible 'workers' self-government' in industry, with all the moral involvement and commitment by the individual that this implied, with a retention of large scale production and mechanization. His *Self-Government in Industry* (1917) is marked by profound ambivalences towards industrialism. There is stress upon such values as individual self-expression, participation in decision-making, and spontaneous creativity. But large scale production was not 'necessarily inimical to freedom', and to run 'counter to the stream of modern tendencies' by restoring earlier productive methods rested on 'a confusion of thought'. Freedom was not 'simply the absence of restraint'; man was 'most free where he co-operates best with his equals in the making of laws' (*Ibid*: 227–8, 245–6).

Cole and Tawney, like the Webbs, were envisaging a society in which extreme division of labour and its required organizational patterns were legitimized by all, either on the basis of collective bargaining or as a consequence of transference to public ownership – these serving to eliminate or at least counter the evils of irresponsible profit-seeking power. Given this legitimation the occupants of even the humblest roles could be brought to give freely of their personal commitment and involvement. The assumption was made, too, that the decisions and choices made by unions or employee groups within this framework of greater involvement would be such as to serve the kind of society sought by the theorists. The Webbs, for example, saw the future development of collective bargaining not in open-ended terms as leading wherever the emergent aspirations of employees took it, but as serving the presumed functional 'needs' of a liberal-meritocratic industrial society. Wise, far-seeing and responsible union leadership, guided by 'public opinion' and, where necessary, the law, would take the unions away from restrictionism, disorderly behaviour, and obstructionism towards a professionalized, regulative, pressure-group role which, in securing the members' enlightened long term interests, would also help to maintain order; keep management alert to the imperatives of economic growth; and enhance the quality of the national labour stock in a way conducive to 'industrial and civic efficiency'. Given that these were the conditions on which they would receive support and approval by 'the community', unions would become fully integrated and enjoy 'complete recognition . . . as an essential organ of the democratic state'. This would ensue upon the passing of industry 'more and more into public control'. The unions, 'thus taken directly into the employment of the citizen-consumers', would 'more and more assume the character of professional associations . . ., concerned with raising the standard of competency;' 'improving the professional equipment of . . . members; . . . and endeavoring by every means to increase their status in public estimation'. The growing emergence of the trade union as 'a definitely recognised institution of public utility' indicated that 'the very conception of democracy' would 'have to be widened, so as to include economic as well as political relations. . . . The agitation for freedom of combination and factory legislation has been, in reality, a demand for a "constitution" in the industrial realm.' The picture thus emerged of a pluralistic constitutional democracy composed of citizens practising extreme division of labour to provide each other with goods and services, and delegating to professional experts in trade unions 'the settlement of the conditions on which the citizen will agree to cooperate in the national service' (1902: Part III, Chapter IV). T. H. Marshall was to develop, half a century later, the kindred notion of collective bargaining as enlarging the status of the worker and ensuring his fuller integration into society. Defining citizenship as 'a status bestowed on those who are full members of a community', he described trade unionism as having 'created a secondary system of industrial citizenship parallel with and supplementary to the system of political citizenship'. Social progress was being sought 'through the use of contract in the open market' (1950: 28, 42–3, 44).

The theorist who developed most fully, however, the notion of collective bargaining as restoring to the worker a measure of dignity, status, social identity and integration was Tannenbaum (1964). His argument is weakened by a presentation of eighteenth and nineteenth century employment relations as based wholly on individual contract, which means that his analysis of early industrial society is in terms of its dominant ideas and legitimizing symbols rather than of its actual practice. With this as his starting point he portrays the unions as engineering a counter-revolution embodied in the shift back from contract to status. Trade unionism is seen as repudiating the competitive individualism of the French Revolution and English liberalism; those 'political and economic ideas that have nourished Western Europe and the United States during the last two centuries' (*Ibid*: 3). These produced the impersonal, atomistic, and unstable labour markets which reduced men to commodities that were bought and sold according to the unpredictable and, to their victims, meaningless fluctuations of competitive business. Insecure, deprived of their human dignity, feeling a loss of social identity, men turned to collective action in order to assert their essential humanity and fellowship; to reconstruct for themselves a social order which assured them certain rights and securities; and to deliver themselves from the role of pawns in a game devoid of human values.

Through trade unionism and collective bargaining, status is restored to this unpredictable, capricious, and non human world of contract. The occupational group or category secures for itself a bundle of rights and protections, and a worker taking up membership in the group automatically becomes entitled to claim them. They are 'givens' which transform his employment situation from an individually negotiated contract to an established status to which is already attached an array of rights and obligations. From this he derives security, social identity, and a sense of meaning, while from membership of the collective itself he gains fellowship and support in place of competitive individualism.

Modern lawyers agree that this is one of many manifestations of a movement back from contract to new forms of status (Friedmann 1972: 492–500). Tannenbaum pursues his analysis to argue that 'Without intent or plan, the trade-union movement is integrating the workers into what in effect amounts to a series of separate social orders' (1964: 140). The sense that this makes it possible for them to legitimize the basic framework of the existing industrial order is conveyed by Tannenbaum's reference to labour disputes as family quarrels. The 'quarrel between the labor union and management has always been a family quarrel. They developed together, were interdependent, and expressed different aspects of the same institution. . . . In spite of the constant bickering and seeming civil war, the thing fought over was a common possession of the workers and the employers' (*Ibid*: 83). Industrial conflict was therefore healthy. 'Discord and strife between unions and management' was 'indicative of a natural movement for remedial adjustment, and therefore a healthy thing . . .' (*Ibid*: 83).

For Tannenbaum, however, the scene darkens; the union becomes Leviathan and his argument takes paths we shall not follow here. It is clear, though, that we have arrived back full circle, after taking stock of some relevant ideas on the way, to the point at which we concluded the last chapter, with collective bargaining beginning to emerge as the symbol of what was increasingly interpreted as a legitimized pluralistic industrial order based on negotiated consent. Yet the idea of emergence could not be seen in terms of a linear progression towards a condition identified as 'maturity'. For not only was the institution of collective bargaining subject to change in ways which ruled out any notion of linear development; it was also to continue to come under challenges of fluctuating intensity from two sources both of which, from their very different standpoints, denied its legitimacy. One challenge came from those committed to a unitary perspective who, while possibly submitting to collective bargaining out of expediency, either looked back nostalgically to authoritarian master-servant relations or, more fashionably, forward to manipulative human relations techniques to promote harmony and willing cooperation under management 'leadership'. The other challenge came from those for whom a Marxist perspective was still the most powerful explanatory tool for understanding capitalist society, and who saw the pluralist scenario as an ideological mystification which masked persistent inequalities of power so great as to leave the system totally without legitimacy, collective bargaining or no. So great is the importance of these three perspectives in serving as private and public ideologies; as frames of reference which shape perceptions; and as standards of reference for behaviour, that they call for fuller analysis and comparison.

6 · Industrial Relations and Frames of Reference

It was one thing to hope that employee representation in some areas of decision-making would induce the rank and file to legitimize the organizational and social order; quite another to assume that such modifications would be legitimized by the employers. Encroachments of this kind on employer prerogative were hardly congruent with the assumptions of master-servant authority which had been asserted so emphatically down the centuries. To be sure, some masters in the older crafts of the larger urban centres had long deemed it judicious to concede their journeymen workgroups a measure of unilateral self-regulation provided this did not intolerably prejudice commercial viability. Should it come to do so they might be able to crush the journeymen's pretensions without much difficulty, but were the journeymen strong enough to make this tactic excessively costly the masters might be only too glad to resort to collective bargaining if the journeymen were prepared to negotiate changes in the craft rules. Even beyond these small privileged groups there were sections of wage earners who, as early as the mid-nineteenth century, found their employers ready to see positive advantages for themselves in modest forms of collective employee representation, joint wage fixing and arbitration (Phelps Brown 1959: Chapter III; Amulree 1929: Chaps. VII–XI). But beyond these again were the very large numbers of employers for whom trade unionism, even when confined to so minimal an encroachment on prerogative as a voice in the fixing of a market wage rate, was an intolerable intrusion into a set of private contractual relationships which contained at their heart the concept of the master's authority over his servants. The essence of the intrusion, as seen by employers, was that the union systematically promotes distrust. It introduces distrust into employer-worker relations by encouraging its members to take, in some measure, a 'false' conflict view of the work situation. Expressed in the language of our earlier analysis, this view of themselves as having their own separate interests leads them to see their position *vis-à-vis* the employer in terms of low-trust relations, causing them to challenge his discretionary decision-making about issues important to them. This reading of the trade union role still enjoys considerable support.

A Unitary Frame of Reference

The charge that trade unionism introduces distrust into the work situation implies that none was there before. This means that the charge has to be supported by an ideology which presents the 'true' picture of the work situation as characterized by harmony and trust. Thus comes to be propagated a view of the organization as a unitary structure. Emphasis is placed on the common objectives and values said to unite all participants (Fox 1966b). Arising logically from this firm foundation is said to be the need for a unified structure of authority, leadership, and loyalty, with full managerial prerogative legitimized by all members of the organization. From this view, the failure of some groups of lower, and sometimes even of middle, rank participants fully to acknowledge management's prerogative and its call for obedience, loyalty and trust is seen as springing from responses of doubtful validity and legitimacy. Employees should stop defining their situation in conflict terms of divergent goals, repose trust in their superordinates, accept their leadership, and legitimize their discretionary role. It follows from all this that conflict generated by organized – or even unorganized – oppositional behaviour on the part of employees tends likewise to be seen as lacking full legitimacy, as do the trade unions or unionized workgroups which organize it. In a recent case documented by a government-appointed court of inquiry, the managing director referred to a company policy 'to have a family spirit in the works . . . to try to have one side in industry and not two. . . . Our view is that to get two sides in industry, what you might term the masters on the one side and the men on the other, to get them up like two armies, is really a mistake' (Forster 1952: para. 70).

Along with a liberal use of team or family metaphors inspired by this presumed unity is apt to go a strong belief that in a properly ordered world managerial prerogative could always be enforced against the few malcontents by means of coercive power if necessary. The greater the tendency to see the true nature of industrial enterprise as unitary, and to see any challenge to managerial rule as of doubtful legitimacy, the greater the disposition to view the enforcement of prerogative by coercive power as desirable and justified. At this point the continuity of the unitary perspective with master-servant conceptions becomes clear. We are dealing with an ideology which, as noted in Chapter 4, has its origins far back in the historical texture of class, status, and power; in the constantly asserted and enforced 'right' of the master to demand unquestioning obedience from his servants. With the common-law development of contract this ideology passed into the assumptions of the employment contract. Even its terminology long persisted. Not until 1875 did Master and Servant legislation become the Employers and Workmen Act. Change of terminology could not, however, change centuries-old assumptions and expectations deeply ingrained in social attitudes, institutions and culture, and despite much lip-service to democracy in this field there is still evident in behaviour a strong attachment to master-servant relations.

Employers and managements may still succeed in inducing employees to share this frame of reference. Small establishments; old family firms; paternalist concerns with many long-service employees and a charismatic figure at the top; firms in relatively isolated areas where alternative jobs are few and the writ of traditional authority still runs; cultures or subcultures which still fully legitimize the rule of the 'boss'; these are among the situations where a unitary frame of reference may still inform the attitudes and behaviour of the rank and file. Within such a deference pattern there may be little or no challenge to management's discretionary rule. Even if there exists an apparently independent collective organization among employees it may in practice be highly receptive to management leadership in such a way as to make it little more than an auxiliary arm of control. Lane and Roberts offer an interpretation of one situation which, before certain changes overtook it, bore an approximation to this pattern (1971).

The Union as a Partner in Control?

The unanimity, however, with which employers and managers have asserted the unitary frame of reference in its unqualified form has long been impaired in Britain as elsewhere by a certain lack of conviction among some of their number which has blunted the edge of ideological – and practical – resistance to the unions. This has stemmed from the consciousness that the unions might have something useful to offer provided they were prepared to accept the essential framework of the social order and did not develop ambitious aspirations to encroach too seriously upon managerial discretion. In Britain, as we have seen, such a consciousness was in evidence well over a century ago. In certain types of industrial situation, for example, the employer found himself supplying product markets so keenly competitive that he was prepared to yield the union some voice in wage regulation provided it was strong enough to impose uniform terms on his rivals, thereby mitigating the rigours of competition. Sometimes, too, the employer was subject to such a succession of minor disputes and stoppages that he was ready to recognize a union if in return it was willing and able to control his employees and process their grievances in an orderly manner with the minimum of disruption (Clegg, Fox, and Thompson 1964: 24, 29, 198–204).

As a steady counterpoint, therefore, to the recurrent loud cries and alarums of employers who denounced unions for their mischievous interference and wilful obstructionism, there has persisted this sober theme of their potential value as a possible partner in the growing problem of labour regulation and control. Any one employer or group of employers might manifest extremes of both these reactions at different times according to variations in their circumstances. Employer attitudes have rarely, however, displayed complete synchronization. At any one period there have been important groups among them who considered that they could derive positive benefits from trying to work with the unions.

But the preconditions remained crucial. Unions could be useful partners in regulation and control only if their aspirations to share in rule-making remained 'responsibly' confined within whatever limits management currently found appropriate. Understandably, therefore, from the point of view of management and those sympathetic towards its problems, one of the major strands of thought and action in this field has been concerned with maintaining trade union aspirations and behaviour between lower and upper limits of ambitiousness and effectiveness. A picture emerged of 'moderate' and 'responsible' trade unionism which served its members well enough to retain control over them but not so well as to inconvenience the comfortable classes and the values they espoused. A similar approach was brought to bear upon the role of unions in the wider society. At their responsible best they were seen as a force for stability and order. The political economist, Professor J. S. Nicholson, looking back in 1896 at changes in 'public opinion' over recent decades, commented not only that 'Many masters . . . were found to admit that dealings with the Unions were more satisfactory than with individuals', but also that 'The oldest and strongest Unions became so orderly that continental statesmen regarded them with envy as bulwarks against Socialism and Anarchy.' Viewing them at their irresponsible worst, however, he saw 'violent speeches' and 'wild proposals' as intensifying 'class hatred and distrust' (1896: 21, 27, 29). E. A. Pratt, in a book based on a series of articles in *The Times*, declaimed in 1904 against 'the more militant and unreasonable phases of trade union rules or practices' which were 'eating the very heart out of British industry', but was at pains to point out that he had nothing against unions of the 'legitimate' type, whose 'chief function' was simply to regulate wages and administer friendly benefits. Unions of the other type, however, with 'their coercive policy, their restriction of output, and their systematic interference with the . . . rights . . . of masters', must be denounced. The distinction which Pratt was drawing, largely an imaginary creation designed to serve a polemical purpose, was between unions which confined themselves to influencing the terms on which labour was hired, leaving the employer a free hand as to how he utilized and deployed his labour in day-to-day operations, and unions which encroached more seriously upon employer prerogatives by attempting to control these processes of utilization and deployment. It was a popular distinction among many with no direct personal axe to grind, for while helping to appease middle-class consciences nagged by awareness of low wages and 'sweatshops' it preserved the right to condemn any alleged union threat to Britain's productivity and progress in an increasingly competitive world.

Both prongs of this approach were separately represented in

responses from the two ancient universities to the long and bitter stoppage of 1897–8, when the Employers' Federation of Engineering Associations sought to destroy aspirations by craftsmen of the Amalgamated Society of Engineers to resist the introduction of new skill-reducing – and wage-reducing – machinery. From Cambridge the economist Professor Alfred Marshall wrote to Edward Caird, the Master of Balliol: 'I want these people [the craftsmen] to be beaten at all costs.' But when the Federation showed clear signs of seeking to break the union altogether as a regulatory force, Caird joined with fourteen other prominent Oxford dons in a public protest against this attack on 'the principle of collective bargaining' (Clegg, Fox, and Thompson 1964: 166).

Sidney and Beatrice Webb, in a passage quoted earlier in a different context, combined the two perspectives in an approach similar in some respects to Pratt's. 'Democratic public opinion' would expect unionism in 'each trade to use its strategic position to secure the conditions necessary for the fulfilment of its particular social function in the best possible way – to obtain, that is to say, not what will be immediately most enjoyed by the "average sensual man", but what, in the long run, will most conduce to his efficiency as a professional, a parent, and a citizen'. There must be no 'resistance to inventions'; nor 'any obstruction of improvements in industrial processes'; nor restrictions on entry to a trade; nor assertion of 'any exclusive right to a particular occupation or service'. There must, on the other hand, be an extension of joint regulation of terms and conditions of employment, interpreted in the broadest sense to cover not only wages and working hours but also education, sanitation, health, recreation, and leisure; with enforcement of national minima through legislation. This would serve the efficiency of industry and also the nation by promoting health, intelligence, and character, and by eliminating 'sweating' and those 'parasitic' employers and industries using 'subsidised or deteriorating labor'. Thus could 'British Trade Unionism . . . best fulfil its legitimate function in the modern democratic state'. Trade union pressure for higher wages would also keep management alert in seeking more efficient techniques and locations, new markets and new materials (Webb, S. and B. 1902: Part III, Chapter III, and 809–10, 816–22). Thus the Webbs, too, worked to a conception of trade unionism and collective bargaining which saw them as having a valuable practical contribution to make to economic progress provided they were kept by 'public opinion' and the law within certain functional limits and aspirations.

Such views helped to create a body of opinion likely to support the counsels of those employers who, at recurrent moments of class confrontation in industry, have demonstrated uneasiness at the thought of extinguishing totally the regulatory role exercised by the unions. However modestly they assessed its net usefulness to them, they have appeared to give it enough value to render unattractive the alternative strategy of destroying it, with all the bitter conflict and lasting illwill which would certainly have resulted (Clegg, Fox, and Thompson 1964: 362–3). Thus for over a century in the history of Britain's industrial relations, prominent leaders can be identified who spoke for a body of opinion among employers that urged 'the possibility and desirability of an industrial system which met the needs of the unions while leaving the traditional structure of industry in essentials unchanged' (Charles 1973: 273). It was men of this persuasion who, usually at times of considerable class tension, were ready to join union leaders in publicly staged conciliatory councils and conferences designed to relax the mood and reknit the over-stretched social fabric by defining the terms of their relationship and stressing whatever could be found in the way of consensus – even if it were no more than agreement on the importance of conciliation and negotiation in which each party respected the survival needs of the other. Such occasions took place in 1895 and 1900 (Clegg, Fox, and Thompson 1964: 175–6), and in 1911, 1919, and 1928 (Charles 1973.)

The growth of this accommodative perspective helps to explain why, despite the wide diversity of attitudes towards trade unions manifested over the whole period, recent historians feel able to say that at the close of the nineteenth century 'it was increasingly argued that they were making a positive contribution to social welfare by joining with the employers in regulating industry so that order should prevail' (Clegg, Fox, and Thompson 1964: 485). This change had been recognized by the Royal Commission on Labour of 1891–1894. In their *Final Report* (C–7421, 1894), the Commissioners noted that 'Powerful Trades Unions on the one side, and powerful associations of employers on the other, have been the means of bringing together in conference the representatives of both classes; enabling each to appreciate the position of the other, and to understand the conditions subject to which their joint undertaking must be conducted. The mutual education hence arising has been carried so far that, as we have seen, it has been found possible to devise articles of agreement regulating wages, which have been loyally and peacefully maintained for long periods. We see reason to believe that . . . in such industries there will be, if not a greater identification of interest, at least a clearer perception of the principles which must regulate the division of the proceeds of each industry, consistently with its permanence and prosperity, between those who supply labour and those who supply managing ability and capital . . . When organizations on either side are so strong as fairly to balance each other, the result of the situation is a disposition . . . to form a mixed board, meeting regularly to discuss and settle questions affecting their relations. . . .' The evidence submitted to them pointed, in their opinion, to 'the conclusion that, on the whole and not withstanding occasional conflicts on a very large scale, the increased strength of organizations may tend towards the maintenance of harmonious relations between employers and employed in a manner suitable to the modern conditions of industry. The belief was expressed both by employers and workmen that where a skilled trade is well organized, good relations tend to prevail, and countless minor quarrels are obviated or nipped in the bud.' Rather more sophisticated theories of conflict management were to be adduced later as functionalist justifications of collective bargaining, but meanwhile there can be no doubt that its potential contribution to managerial control in securing consent, regulating the labour market, and handling conflict was among the factors making the unions 'more closely integrated into the fabric of society' (Clegg, Fox, and Thompson 1964: 485).

This approach to trade unions was never, it need hardly be emphasized, universal among employers, and there were periods when conviction wavered even among its strongest adherents. Yet it is safe to say that even then there were influential figures who remained convinced that unionism was not simply an inescapable social fact, but a fact that could be turned to managerial advantage provided certain conditions were met.

Emergence of a Pluralist Perspective

By the thirties the increasing size of many enterprises was making the case seem even stronger. 'The larger firm with the more complex organization required greater sophistication in its labour relations as in all other aspects of its operation. It was easier for it to see the advantage of having labour as partner rather than as rival. . . . A cooperative workforce was preferable to one that was not cooperative and the way to treat the workforce in order that it might cooperate was to be prepared to respect its rights as it saw them and negotiate with its legitimate independent representatives' (Charles 1973: 263, 272).

If unions were to be seen, however, as legitimate organizations for these purposes, consistency appeared to require modification in the traditional model of the enterprise as a unitary structure of authority, leadership, and loyalty which contained no independent source of power that could effectively challenge management and induce it to accept unpalatable modifications in its policies. Admittedly it was possible to argue that bureaucratic rule-making and control could be served by collective representation of employees which stopped short of *independent* organization among them. Certainly there have been situations where management has found itself able to manipulate collective organization among employees largely as an auxiliary arm of control, and delay for long periods the development of any independent aspirations. But in many industries it has been a prerequisite of the union's usefulness to management that the union be seen by its members to be independent and not simply an auxiliary arm. This apparent paradox is easily explained. The employees looked to the union because they distrusted management; if the union appeared to be management's mouthpiece the trust which was the primary source of the union's control over the employees would be destroyed. But if the union was to be accepted, then, as an independent source of authority, leadership, and loyalty, logic seemed to point to a theory of managerial governance which rested, not on the traditional notion of the master's total command over his servants, but on the notion of a prerogative limited and qualified in certain respects by its employees collectively and independently organized.

Such a notion informed the work of the Webbs in their *Industrial Democracy* (first published 1897) and *History of Trade Unionism* (first published 1894), but managerial acceptance has proved slow and hesitant. The reason is plain to see. If the right of a certain degree of encroachment upon managerial prerogative by employee collectives were to be formally enshrined in the theory of the enterprise, was there not a danger of theory being used to legitimize – indeed even incite – a progressive encroachment far beyond the point which management found convenient? In the face of this possibility it was often consistency that had to go; employers recognized and negotiated with unions but clung to unitary notions and behaviour by which they hoped to protect the main body of their prerogative and rally whatever loyalty could be salvaged (for a current case study: Hawkins 1972: 122–6). In Dubin's words: 'The tactic of protecting management prerogatives is essentially to fight a delaying action at all points where unions seek a voice in management decision' (1958: 47).

Yet even though many managers might have difficulty in internalizing and acting by it, a theory of the social structure of work organizations which made sense of, and fully legitimized, trade unionism and collective bargaining had, as we have seen, long been evolving and needed only a coherent formulation and explicit statement. The influences in this direction were several. Business was increasingly under examination by academic inquirers who might also be called upon to advise managements and governments, conduct research, and take part in settling disputes. Whether they were conscious or not of the need for an explicit theoretical framework, they could not operate without revealing in their utterances and writings certain assumptions and attitudes which bore theoretical and ideological implications even though they might be unaware of them. But some were certainly interested in developing an explicit body of theory, as were also a few employers and executives in the accommodative tradition who were concerned both to clarify their own thoughts and to legitimize their social role on the basis of some systematic ideas. Government departments, too, were becoming drawn into an interventionalist role in industrial relations and had to feel their way towards an acceptable set of notions about the union role in both enterprise and society. Implicit in these were views about managerial prerogative, employee rights, and a suitable working definition of 'good industrial relations'.

The involvement of all these three groups in what practical men currently saw as 'problems' led, in its major emphasis, to a convergence upon a pluralist perspective which legitimized intergroup conflict in industry and sought its institutionalization through collective bargaining. Charles has traced, in the British context, the existence of a 'positive philosophy of industrial relations' through certain selected practical manifestations between 1911 and 1939. 'In summary that philosophy . . . can be stated as follows. The unions and the employers agreed that they can co-exist within the system and on the basis of strong organization negotiate their respective needs cooperatively out of self interest, accepting the moral obligation to observe agreements.' The norms which result 'meet the needs of efficiency by leading on to productivity bargaining . . . and so are beneficial to the employer and the nation as well as the wage earner' (1973: 302–3).*

While sometimes receiving explicit expression, this perspective more often remained implicit as a set of unspoken assumptions, beliefs, and attitudes. Where explicitly stated, it might be accompanied by a rejection of the unitary perspective as being inappropriate, not only to the spirit and 'needs' of 'democratic' society, but also as a basis for management in the taxing task of promoting consent, cooperation, and adaptation in the large bureaucratic work structures now emerging (Bakke 1946; Kerr, Dunlop, Myers *et al.* 1953). The increasing size and social complexity of work organizations; shifts in power relations within industry; changes in social values; rising aspirations; the weakening of traditional deference towards officially constituted governance – these were among the factors increasingly said to require managers to develop a new ideology and new sources of legitimation if they were to maintain effective control.

The Pluralist Standpoint – Management and Union Statements

There are, however, as might be expected, many varieties of emphasis within the broad mainstream of this perspective. An illustration of one important orientation on the management side can be found in a recent statement by Martin Jukes, Director-General of the Engineering Employers Federation, largest of the employers' associations in the Confederation of British Industry. Jukes offers a pluralist picture which legitimizes the role of trade unions in protecting their members

* We are here examining a set of ideas implicit in the policies and behaviour of *some* sections of British employers. They were far from universal, and they were scarcely integrated at all with the very different set of unitary ideas known as Human Relations which was becoming increasingly popular among management theorizers (Child 1969), though some companies tried to combine both.

vis-à-vis the employers and adds that 'Today there is a recognition of mutual interests. . . . Both sides recognize the paramount need to keep industry prosperous and the need to cooperate on many issues.' Among employers 'there is now acceptance of responsibility to shareholders, to the enterprise itself, to the employees, to the customers of the enterprise and to the public and the State.' Within this complex of responsibilities and constraints it 'is the duty and responsibility of the employer to manage'. In managing his employees he must remember that 'important though a man's right to a job may be, it is perhaps of even greater importance that he should work as a reasonably contented member of a team. . . . High on the list of those things which are essential to the smooth running and efficiency of an enterprise is good communication with workers on the shop floor.' Besides promoting team consciousness, good communication is necessary in securing employee acceptance of change. 'Employees, particularly those on the shop floor, are generally conservative and resistant to change.' Communication and consultation can remove suspicions. There are now substantial areas of management decision where failure to consult 'would be not only unwise but also fatal to normal working'. In some cases there may be a need not only 'to explain what is going to be done but also to get agreement about it. . . the willingness of their work force to co-operate is a condition of the achievement of efficiency.' All these purposes require dealings 'with the representatives of the men initially. Shop stewards are such representatives, and without them consultation and communication would be very difficult, if not impossible' (1970: 67–71).

A representative statement from the trade union side overlaps this at all the crucial points. The Trades Union Congress, in its written evidence to the Royal Commission on Trade Unions and Employers' Associations (1965–8), made the point, obviously central to its whole perspective, that 'Recognition of the fact that the interests and preferences of individuals and groups are different, according to the perspective of each of them, is embodied in the structure of individual trade unions and in the trade union movement as a whole.' And it went on to say that 'Recognition of the legitimacy of distinct and often diverging interests is also the basis of bargaining between trade unions and employers. Bargaining depends on each side recognizing the legitimacy and representative capacity of the other.' There is involved 'both recognition by the trade union of the legitimacy of the functions of the employer and recognition by the employer or employers' organization of the legitimacy of the function of the trade union.' The statement legitimized the management role with the proposition that 'The function of management is to run an enterprise in such a way as to achieve whatever objectives it sets itself, in terms of growth of sales or whatever other yardstick. . . . It is management's job to give a lead in these matters.' But management could help itself by exercising its leadership and authority in a certain kind of way. '. . . all the various considerations which are relevant should be brought into the picture at the earliest possible stage. What is required is not a diminution in managerial authority but a new conception of how this authority should be exercised. Many decisions, if presented in the right way, with the right emphasis, possibly with modifications of substance, might well be acceptable which at present are unacceptable and therefore the subject of conflict. Accordingly, management has an interest in involving employees in day-to-day decisions as the means of removing this factor of unacceptability' (Trades Union Congress 1966: 30, 47–8, 101).

Such statements as these are understandably fragmentary in presenting the pluralist ideology since this is not their purpose. Their limited nature draws attention, therefore, to the need for a fuller delineation of the assumptions, beliefs, and attitudes embodied in, or implied by, the pluralist position in industrial relations. The next section draws upon but also supplements certain earlier writings in an attempt to supply this need (Ross 1958; Fox 1966b; Fox 1973).

The Pluralist Ideology*

From this perspective the enterprise is seen not as a unitary structure but as a coalition of individuals and groups with their own aspirations and perceptions which they naturally see as valid and which they seek to express in action if such is required (Ross 1958; Ross 1969). The term coalition is used by, among others, Cyert and March (1959). It includes the notion that individuals and groups with widely

* In describing an ideology there is always the difficulty presented by the existence of many individual variants. Some adherents accept while others may reject each given item of the syndrome. Only a generalized picture can therefore be offered. This means that a person subscribing to any one pluralist belief presented here cannot be regarded as necessarily identifying with, or even being aware of, the others.

varying priorities agree to collaborate in social structures which enable all participants to get something of what they want; the terms of collaboration being settled by bargaining. Management is seen as making its decisions within a set of constraints which include employees, consumers, suppliers, government, the law, the local community, and sources of finance. It is in response to the pressures of these constraints that management forges its compromises or rises above them with some new synthesis, and in their absence pluralists would be doubtful if even the roughest of distributive justice, as they define it, would be likely to emerge. One of the best-known earlier sources where a statement approximating to this pluralist position can be found is the Webbs's *Industrial Democracy* (1902: 818–25). After discussing the interests of consumers, employers, workers, and 'the permanent interests' of the community as a whole in such matters as health, efficiency, and environmental pollution, they conclude that 'industrial administration is, in the democratic state, a more complicated matter than is naïvely imagined by the old-fashioned capitalist, demanding the "right to manage his own business in his own way" ' (*Ibid*: 822).

This perspective on the structure of the business organization and its place in society is widespread throughout the West and has been particularly well developed in America. Davis and Blomstrom present a fully elaborated analysis of pluralistic business in a pluralistic society, with the manager seen as trustee. 'The president's suite in today's business is less a place for autocratic decisions than a place for reconciliation of the multitude of competing interests impinging on business' (1971: 21). Thus the enterprise is seen as a complex of tensions and competing claims which have to be 'managed' so as to maintain a viable collaborative structure within which all the stakeholders can, with varying degrees of success, pursue their aspirations. Some degree of conflict between the interests is expected. The (Donovan) Report of Britain's Royal Commission on Trade Unions and Employers' Associations (1965–8) opens with a statement about the nature of the business enterprise. 'The running of large businesses is in the hands of professional managers. . . . While in the long term shareholders, employees and customers all stand to benefit if a concern flourishes, the immediate interests of these groups often conflict. Directors and managers have to balance these conflicting interests, and in practice they generally seek to strike whatever balance will best promote the welfare of the enterprise as such' (Donovan 1968: para. 18). The *Industrial Relations Code of Practice*, introduced by the Conservative Government in 1972, describes management and employees as having 'a common interest in the undertaking's success because without it their aims cannot be achieved. But some conflicts are bound to arise. With good industrial relations they can be resolved in a responsible and constructive way.' There are felt, by pluralists, to be no clear-cut criteria which can measure how well management is performing this task of balancing the conflicting interests with respect to its employees. A certain amount of overt conflict and disputation is welcomed as evidence that not all aspirations are being either sapped by hopelessness or suppressed by power. On the other hand, conflict above a certain level is felt to be evidence that the ground rules need changing; that marginal adjustments in rewards or work rules are required; that management is failing in some way to find the appropriate compromises or syntheses.

The pluralistic view assumes, therefore, that given the divergent pressures and claims to which managers are subject they may be tempted to govern their human resources in ways which one or more subordinate groups experience as arbitrary, summary, or contrary to their own interests, and which they are likely to challenge through independent collective organization. It sees trade unionism, not as a regrettable historical carryover, but as just another manifestation of one of the basic values of competitive, pressure-group, democratic societies of the Western model – that 'interests' have rights of free association and, within legal limits, of asserting their claims and aspirations. It also sees trade unions or organized workgroups as possibly being able to readjust the power balance within the enterprise to such effect as to enable subordinates to impose *their* preferences in ways which *management* may find arbitrary and summary. Trade unions are nevertheless accepted by pluralists as legitimate expressions of legitimate challenges to managerial rule. Indeed they may be positively welcomed as giving expression to a mode of joint rule-making by managers and managed which is valued in its own right, simply 'as a method of regulating relationships between people in industry', whether or not it succeeds in 'pushing wages as high as possible' (Clegg, n.d.).

The pluralist seeks to persuade employers and managements to accept this perspective in fully legitimizing the role and functions of trade unions and organized workgroups. 'To the champion of pluralism as an instrument of democracy, tolerance is the live-and-let-live moderation of the marketplace. Economic competition is a form of human struggle . . . in which each combatant simultaneously acknowledges the legitimacy of his opponent's demands and yet gives no quarter in the battle. . . . Tolerance in a society of competing interest groups is precisely the ungrudging acknowledgement of the right of opposed interests to exist and be pursued' (Wolff 1965: 29).

Where such a perspective is combined with an awareness that collective organization enables subordinates to assert their claims and grievances with some vigour, it suggests that the whole question of managerial governance must be regarded as problematical, and that management may not be able to enforce without serious loss to itself a total assertion of prerogative in areas of policy where it is challenged by a determined union or workgroup. The pluralist urges upon managers the full acceptance of what he sees as the implications of this frame of reference – that the legitimacy of their rule in the eyes of subordinates is not automatic but must be actively pursued and maintained; that the interest-group structure of the enterprise calls for coalition-type bargaining based on frank recognition of divergent group perceptions; that management's power superiority is no longer sufficient to permit the luxury of imposed solutions; that 'leadership' in a coalition structure has to be defined quite differently from that in a unitary structure; that ideologies and rallying-cries based on unitary assumptions may prove counterproductive in a pluralistic situation and, finally, that in current circumstances their best chance of being able to control events lies in their being ready to share that control with the groups they are seeking to govern.

Such an approach would hardly make sense without an accompanying assumption that the divergencies between the parties are not so fundamental or so wide as to be unbridgeable by compromises or new syntheses which enable collaboration to continue. Clark Kerr has observed that 'a pluralistic industrial system . . . can only operate well if the ideology impelling its important groups is consistent with pluralism, i.e. a philosophy of mutual survival' (1955: 12). Bakke had earlier defined the desirable situation as one in which, 'although pursuing each his own interest, the parties recognize their mutual dependence upon each other, agree to respect the survival needs of the other, and to adjust their differences by methods which will not destroy but rather improve the opportunities of the other' (1946: 81). Shepard relates this situation to the nature of trust relations. 'The amount of trust needed to handle conflict at various points on the continuum differs drastically. At the suppression and war end of the continuum, there is complete absence of trust. There is a minimum amount of trust needed in order to engage in limited war. Bargaining presupposes more trust and a definite belief in coexistence. Each party can count on the fact that the other party needs him' (Kahn and Boulding 1964: 134).

Pluralists would argue that the situation in most advanced Western industrial societies does in fact bear an approximation to this picture of a basic procedural consensus. They make, therefore, the working assumption that, given 'goodwill' and such external stimulus, help, and structural support as may prove necessary, managements and unions will always and everywhere be able ultimately to negotiate comprehensive, codified systems of regulation which provide a fully adequate and orderly context making for the promotion and maintenance of orderly behaviour. The Donovan Report, 'seeking to identify the underlying causes of unofficial strikes', considered 'the root of the evil' to be the 'present methods of collective bargaining and especially our methods of workshop bargaining', and 'the absence of speedy, clear and effective disputes procedures' (Donovan 1968: para. 475). Reform of these methods and procedures was expected to reduce very considerably the problem of 'disorder'. Clearly the assumption was being made of a widespread basic consensus which needed only the 'right' institutional forms in which to emerge.

What are the fuller implications of these attitudes? The first is that every industrial conflict situation can, in sufficiently skilled and patient hands, be made to yield some compromise or synthetic solution which all the interests involved will find acceptable and workable – that no group, for example, retains a continuing concern with maintaining what other groups define as disorder. This in turn requires that each party limits its claims and aspirations to a level which the other finds sufficiently tolerable to enable collaboration to continue. It would obviously be possible for one party to make claims which the other found totally unacceptable and on which compromise or synthesis proved impossible. The pluralist presumption would be that in such a case the consensual ethic governing joint regulation would be ruptured, and a forced collaboration would emerge when one party succeeded in coercing the other. The operation of a pluralistic system requires that such situations be the exception rather than the rule, and that in the main the claims of each party fall within the range found bearable by the other. On the basis of a shared confidence that they both subscribe to this philosophy of mutual survival, the parties are able to operate procedures of negotiation and dispute settlement characterized by a consensual code of ethics and conduct. This includes the principle that, provided certain jointly agreed processes of consultation and participation in decision-making are followed, culminating in freely, equitably, and honourably negotiated agreements, the participant groups must regard themselves as morally committed to observing the terms of the resulting decisions (Charles 1973: 30).

The concept of honour is important in bringing out a crucial element of the pluralistic perspective – the working assumption that there exists between the parties something approximating to a balance of power. 'Collective bargaining', writes a modern lawyer in what has become a standard and influential study of the relationship between law and society, 'has substantially restored equality of bargaining power between employers and employees . . .' (Friedmann 1972: 130). Such an assumption is central because of its bearing on the degree of moral obligation which each party feels towards observing the agreement – and equally importantly, the degree of obligation which independent observers consider *ought* to be manifested by the parties. We noted in the preceding chapter Durkheim's point that 'for the obligatory force of a contract to be complete . . . it is necessary that the contracting parties be placed in conditions externally equal' (1964: 383). A sense of having been pressured by superior power into accepting certain terms is not conducive to a feeling of being in honour bound to observe them. Of course men observe agreements from motives other than moral obligation. There may be, and normally are, reasons of expediency. Men may fear punishment, calculate that their long-term interests call for punctilious observance, consider that to default would provide the other party with an easy excuse for doing the same. Yet those interested in the observance of rules of whatever kind usually consider expediency to be an unstable basis for order. In a world of constant flux, expediency may point in a given direction one day and in a very different direction the next as circumstances and mood change. 'There is nothing less constant than interest. Today, it unites me to you; tomorrow, it will make me your enemy' (*Ibid*: 204). Observance based solely on expediency lasts only so long as expediency appears to require it. If by good luck or skilful leadership an employee group finds itself in a specially advantageous position, permanent or temporary, its reading of expediency may lead it to flout an agreement which it considers to have been imposed without its full participation and consent, or which it had earlier felt constrained to accept out of relative weakness.

Our rulers therefore usually combine expediency arguments with ethical arguments. We are not only threatened with punishment if we rob banks; we are also taught that it is morally wrong to rob banks. The more we accept the latter the less the strain on the law-enforcing processes required by the former. Similarly, if men can be induced to respect agreements not only from expediency but also from ethical considerations, there is less risk of their violating agreements should expediency appear to them to point in that direction. Employers, governments, and many other observers have therefore urged the paramountcy of moral obligation in this context. Trade union leaders, too, have found themselves using the language of ethics to reinforce what they may see as predominantly an argument of expediency. In the words of the Trades Union Congress evidence to the Donovan Commission: 'The General Council acknowledged, as would every responsible trade union leader, that procedure agreements embody promises and therefore should not be broken by any union representatives' (1966: 111). This ethical principle becomes the more difficult to assert with conviction, however, and the less likely to be received as persuasive, the greater the extent to which the promises are experienced or perceived as having been extorted by *force majeure*. There can be no doubt that moral exhortation of this kind carries a more convincing ring if the parties are believed to negotiate as equals or near equals with full knowledge of facts and probable consequences.

Pluralists would acknowledge that this condition is not always met. They would agree that, more commonly in the past than the present, agreements might be concluded that are so manifestly and blatantly imposed coercively by greatly superior power that they must be seen as accepted only 'under duress' and therefore not morally binding. Half-starved workers of the past who were admitted back to work after an employers' lockout on condition that they renounced union membership for ever have not been morally criticized by historians as behaving dishonourably when they resumed union activities on regaining enough strength.* But this is not seen as the characteristic pattern of modern industrial society. The normal pluralist stress on the moral obligation to observe agreements therefore implies a belief that power is not so unevenly matched as to introduce the extenuating concept of duress. (This aspect is more fully explored in Fox 1971: 34–9, 159–60.) Specially interesting is the modern pluralist's attitude to recent situations in which a unitary-minded management compels every employee to sign an individual contract of employment in which he declares 'on his honour' that he will not retain union membership while in the company's employment. Such a case was documented by a government-appointed court of inquiry in 1952 (Forster 1952). Among the facts considered by the court was the dishonouring of this pledge by a small number of employees who kept their union membership secret. The court appears to have found itself in some difficulty. It was apparently not prepared to accept that even in the relationship between employer and *indivdual* employee was there an imbalance of power sufficient to justify the employee in defaulting on the contract. Yet it was obliged to recognize that, for the trade union movement, 'To demand of a workman in fear of possible unemployment an undertaking that he will not join a union is regarded . . . as a form of duress which drives the trade unionist underground and can justify . . . his signing the undertaking even though he has no intention of honouring it' (*Ibid*: para. 122). In a report which dealt tenderly with management susceptibilities it declared that 'While we do not seek to condone the action of employees who break their signed contract by joining a union, we view with misgiving a requirement by an employer which

* This behaviour by engineering craftsmen after the great three-months' lockout of 1852 was described by a judge at the time as 'inexcusable', but the Webbs made short shrift of this opinion. 'A promise extorted under "duress" carries with it little legal and still less moral obligation.' They quoted with approval a union Executive Circular which declared 'every man who unwillingly puts his hand to that detestable document which is forced upon us to be as much destitute of that power of choice which should precede a contract as if a pistol were at his head and he had to choose between death and degradation' (1920: 216).

can lead to such action on the part of men whose honourableness is not otherwise in question' (*Ibid*: para. 137).

On the trade union side, official statements sometimes manifest an anxiety to sustain rank and file commitment to collective bargaining by stressing the degree of equality between the two organized forces rather than the degree of inequality. The Trades Union Congress evidence contains a passage which offers clear echoes of a belief in a rough balance of forces as they are brought to bear in the negotiating process. 'In the vast majority of cases collective bargaining proceeds smoothly on the basis of mutual recognition, each side recognising the strength and legitimacy of the other. However, in a minority of cases it does not. In such situations both sides use their strength overtly to force the other side to make concessions which it would not otherwise make' (1966: 48). This belief that effective combination could enable workers to redress their market weakness as against the employer sufficiently to ensure tolerable equity goes back at least as far as John Stuart Mill and, by the time the Webbs were writing, was accompanied by a conviction that the union might hold an undesirable whip hand. '*Wherever the economic conditions of the parties concerned are unequal, legal freedom of contract merely enables the superior in strategic strength to dictate the terms*' (italics in original). If there was to be 'genuine freedom of contract' the conditions of employment must be 'adjusted between equally expert negotiators, acting for corporations reasonably comparable in strategic strength. . . '. When 'workmen combine the balance is redressed, and may even incline, as against the isolated employer, in favor of the wage-earner', resulting 'in a strong union relentlessly enforcing its will on the capitalists, without deigning to consult with them beforehand' (Webb, S. and B. 1902: 217, 842). Nervousness lest the balance of power should tilt too far in this direction has not abated over the years. Tannenbaum in 1951 asserted the union to have become so powerful as to reduce 'both the worker (member) and the employer to a subordinate position' (1964: 130), and the recent American literature of industrial relations has been apt to strike the same note. 'Even among intellectuals basically sympathetic toward the institution of unionism there was a tendency to stress the growing power of trade unions. Slichter argued that their power now exceeded that of the business community' (Miernyk 1962: 66). Davies and Blomstrom report widespread feelings in the postwar period that the dice were now loaded 'too heavily in favor of labor', and describe legislative attempts 'to reverse the pendulum of power and bring the power relations of business and labor nearer to equality' (1971: 249). A similar mood has emerged in Britain and elsewhere.

For all these recurrent alarms, however, the overall picture which emerges bears a resemblance to the structural-functionalist's consensus as modified by Coser (1956). The assumption is being made that while, to be sure, conflicts arise over the terms of economic cooperation, values and norms are not so divergent that workable compromises cannot be achieved. Underlying the cut and thrust of market-place and organizational encounters, in other words, lies the firm foundation of a stable and agreed social system. Men may disagree about the distribution of the social product and other terms of their collaboration – and it is healthy and desirable that they should – but their disagreements are not so great and lasting that they seek to destroy the system or even put it under serious hazard. In order to maintain that system they submit to compromise and find themselves able, for this purpose, to share moral beliefs which teach the importance of observing agreements freely and honourably undertaken.

It is clear that the beliefs and assumptions of pluralism as applied to industrial relations begin to broaden out here to beliefs and assumptions about society as a whole. In this wider sense, pluralism is a philosophy, widely held in Western societies, which rejects both the classical liberal tradition, in which the legalisms of 'free and equal contract' between atomistic individuals facilitated exploitation by masking gross disparities of power, and the engineered 'social integration' of totalitarian (unitary) societies in which an imposed ideology and set of values are used to mask manipulation and coercion by a dominant ruling group. Independent combination among the weak which enables them to enhance their strength, and a judicious curbing of the power of the strong, together with the mechanisms of party political democracy and a free market in ideas, are seen as the best ways of avoiding these two rejected images of society. '. . . pluralism's goal is a rough parity among competing groups . . .' (Wolff 1965: 58). In the words of another American theorist, pluralists 'see society as fractured into a congeries of hundreds of small special interest groups with incompletely overlapping memberships, widely differing power bases, and a multitude of techniques for exercising influence on decisions salient to them . . .' (Polsby 1963: 118). 'Freedom' plays an important part in the argument. 'As a theory of the social foundations of freedom, pluralism rests its hopes on civil antagonism. It sees in group conflict a benign disorder . . .' (Selznick 1969: 41). This approach sometimes leads to what Pen describes as 'an extremely innocent view of society'. The 'criss-crossing of small conflicts has stabilizing functions; this fits into the picture of a pluralistic society. One step further and we arrive at a balance of forces . . .' (1966: 278–9).

We find once more, then, the central assumption of pluralism that a rough balance of power exists as between the principal interest groups of society. In Miliband's words, most Western students of politics 'tend to start, judging from their work, with the assumption that power, in Western societies, is competitive, fragmented and diffused: everybody, directly or through organised groups, has some power and nobody has or can have too much of it' (1969: 2). This view has, 'in one form or another, come to dominate political science and political sociology, and for that matter political life itself, in all . . . advanced capitalist countries' (*Ibid*: 3). Wrong offers a similar picture. 'The various conceptions of "pluralism" in contemporary sociology and political science are models of systems of intercursive power relations' (Wrong 1968: 47). *Intercursive* refers to 'relations characterized by a balance of power . . . where the power of each party . . . is countervailed by that of the other, with procedures for bargaining or joint decision making governing their relations when matters affecting the goals and interests of both are involved' (*Ibid*).

Industrial relations pluralists have articulated such views with respect to their special interest. Clark Kerr echoes Galbraith's principle of countervailing power in arguing that 'The state at least should seek to effect a balance of power among the private groups . . .' (1955: 10), while Selekman asserts that shifting alliances and coalitions, temporary or long term, already operate to effect balances of power – 'The equality of strength brought about by these alliances prevents the establishment of any single dominant overriding power for any length of time' (1956: 162). 'We end up with a pluralistic system of power, the parts checking and counter-checking each other . . .' (*Ibid*: 181).

Frames of Reference and Trust Perceptions

The choice men make as between a unitary or a pluralistic perspective towards the work organization has a crucial bearing upon their judgement on the longstanding and widespread charge, with which this chapter began, that trade unions must bear the responsibility for introducing distrust into management-worker relations. Those holding the unitary view argue that union or workgroup action is originated and sustained by men who play an essentially mischievous role by inducing their gullible fellows to take up a conflict stance towards the management function. As a consequence of defining management-worker relations in terms of divergent interests and values, employees perceive what are simply functional necessities in terms of low-trust relations and respond accordingly. Those holding the pluralistic perspective, on to other hand, are committed to the view that a certain amount of conflict is structured into the situation by virtue of the coalition nature of the organization. The interests both of the participant stakeholder groups, and of the 'organization' itself as a going concern serving necessary social purposes, require that this conflict, instead of being regarded as something to be suppressed or susceptible of being eliminated by the right kind of leadership, be provided with institutionalized forms of resolution. In this way the needs of the participant interests receive expression, and workable compromises or new syntheses are forged through agreements and understandings which preserve the coalition as a mechanism of collaboration. Pluralists differ in respect of whether they emphasize the first or the second of these purposes. Some may be specially concerned with ensuring the democratic rights of employees; others with the contribution which institutionalized forms of conflict resolution can make to the effective conduct of the enterprise – 'effective' being defined in terms of profits or economic performance – while yet others may be concerned with both. All will agree, however, on the need for 'orderly' procedures perceived by all parties as expeditious, 'fair', and appropriately designed for their location.

Both the unitary and the pluralistic perspectives are frames of reference through which men perceive and define social phenomena, and their perceptions and definitions determine their behaviour. Only when subordinates come to perceive management's shaping of their work situation as revealing that it defines its own goals and values differently from theirs do they reciprocate with low trust. History and current observation show that management may succeed, with a judicious blend of authoritarianism and propagation of the unitary ideology, in moulding subordinates' perceptions very differently, particularly if it can draw support from the cultural values of the local community or wider society. In Western societies, however, management's ability to maintain this strategy has been in steady decline over a long period, and the trend is for subordinate groups to adopt a stance based on perceptions of divergent goals. But this must alert us to explore the reasons for this probability – sharply rising aspirations within competitive pressure-group society; weakening respect for officially constituted governance; growing perceptions of injustice and the double standard; the weakening legitimation by many of what they once accepted as traditional expectations for themselves and their children; and that withering of community consciousness endemic to low-trust industrial society which was bound to stand revealed as soon as subordinate groups could mobilize enough power to break out of the quiescence to which weakness had previously confined so many of them.

The analysis so far reveals the unitary conception, which seeks to legitimize the traditional assertion of an employer prerogative and leadership unqualified by any organized employee challenge, coming under practical and ideological check by the pluralist notion of a prerogative limited in certain respects by the organized expression of such interests of the employees as they feel diverge from those of management. Such actual or potential rents in the social fabric as are created by these divergent interests are mended or prevented by collective agreements which reconcile the disagreements or eliminate them with a new synthesis. By working to the assumption of an approximate balance of power, pluralists are able to argue that since only rarely can either side plead exemption from moral obligation by virtue of coming under coercive duress, both are in honour bound to observe the agreements to which they commit themselves. On this basis pluralists can agree with the coercion of defaulters. To be sure, it may be said, there will sometimes be situations where justice is distinctly rough, with one side or the other being favoured by circumstances and enjoying a bargaining advantage, but in a market society this is unavoidable and, provided measures are taken to mitigate glaring disparities and cushion the misfortunes of the ill-favoured, can be tolerated for the sake of the benefits derived from the system as a whole.

Here, then, is a doctrine which offers ideological legitimation of the concept of contract in labour markets. It enables one to think in terms, not of isolated individuals forced by weakness to accept whatever terms the employer thrusts at them, but of strong collectives able to negotiate freely and equally the conditions of their collaboration. Its significance could be argued as going even further. For if the institution of collective bargaining on those issues seen as being of legitimate employee concern justifies a demand that they observe the resulting agreements, does it not also justify the expectation that they will loyally endorse the whole industrial system of which collective bargaining is such a crucial and integral part? It is, after all, it might be said, usual to argue that pluralism in the wider political sense, with its democratic party apparatus, its pressure groups, its diffused and fragmented power, its voting and its compromises, places upon citizens a burden of obligation to respect majority decisions, obey the law, and respect the integrity of the system even when their own interests or opinions are currently not favoured. With some straining of analogies it might seem plausible to argue that industrial pluralism places upon employees obligations of a comparable kind. Those holding a pluralist view of modern society tend to argue that this is indeed so and that such obligations are usually accepted. Collective bargaining 'helps to "humanize" the operation of an essentially impersonal price system by making it more generally palatable to workers as a group. . . . The worker probably feels . . . a little more happy about living under the private-enterprise system. . . . The emphasis which collective bargaining places on human values, therefore, provides him with a rationale for believing in the existing enterprise system' (Harbison 1954: 276–7).

We now have to take account, however, of the fact that the pluralist perspective itself comes under radical challenge from those who do not accept it as a valid picture of how Western industrial society operates. We shall apply this radical critique to the pluralist interpretation of industrial relations and show how that interpretation emerges as a doctrine which, whatever the personal motives of its adherents, simply serves, in a somewhat more sophisticated manner appropriate to a society of complex organizations, rising aspirations, and restiveness against authority, the same kind of integrative function as was served by unitary notions in more respectful epochs. Criticism will be offered here not of pluralism as a political *ideal* (many radicals would presumably approve the fragmentation of power), but of the kind of analysis which presents *existing* Western industrial society as pluralist in nature.

The Radical Challenge

Of the various types of radical ideology, 'by far the most important alternative to the pluralist-democratic view of power remains the Marxist one' (Miliband 1969: 5). Central to this alternative is the belief that industrial society, while manifestly on one level a congeries of small special interest groups vying for scarce goods, status, or influence, is more fundamentally characterized in terms of the overarching exploitation of one class by another, of the propertyless by the propertied, of the less by the more powerful. From this view, any talk of 'checks and balances', however apt for describing certain subsidiary phenomena, simply confuses our understanding of the primary dynamics which shape and move society – a useful confusion indeed for the major power-holders since it obscures the domination of society by its ruling strata through institutions and assumptions which operate to exclude anything approaching a genuine power balance.

It follows that any strategy by a class-conscious proletariat to take up the class war against the bourgeoisie could hardly be reconciled with the pluralist notion of mutual survival. The drive behind such a strategy would not be to live and let live, but to test class relations to destruction. From this perspective the interests of the bourgeoisie are not seen as legitimate, and an ideology which formally recognizes them as such strengthens the exploiters against the exploited, whether it is aware of doing so or not. Instead of drawing the attention of the propertyless to the facts of their subjection, pluralist ideology presents them with a view of the owners and controllers of property as simply one group of claimants among many. It thereby becomes another of the conditioning influences which indoctrinate the victims of an exploitive set of economic and social relations into accepting the system.

This type of critique asserts there to be, then, a vast disparity of power as between, on the one hand, the owners and controllers of economic resources and, on the other, those dependent upon them for access to those resources as a means of livelihood. This power is exercised not only directly in industry, business, commerce, and financial institutions, but also indirectly in a multitude of ways (Miliband 1969). Gouldner enumerates some of them. 'The rich exercise power, including political power, . . . through their control of great foundations, with their policy-shaping studies and conferences and their support for universities; through a variety of interlocking national associations, councils and committees that act as legislative lobbies and as influences upon public opinion; through their membership among the trustees of great universities; through their influence on important newspapers, magazines, and television networks, by virtue of their advertising in them or their outright ownership of them, which, as Morris Janowitz once observed, sets "the limits within which public debate on controversial issues takes place"; through their extensive and disproportionate membership in the executive branch of the government, their financial contributions to political parties, . . . and through their control of the most important legal, public relations, and advertising firms' (1971: 300). This view of the American scene differs only in detail from other Western societies. An exhaustive account would have to include many other ways in which the influence of the rich and powerful pervades and permeates the texture of our everyday life, usually so impalpably that, like the air we breathe, we do not register it. Anderson offers a more structured version of what is essentially the same argument. 'There is no parity of power between "Management" and "Labour" in a capitalist society, because labour is an untransformable element which can only be withdrawn (or at best used for, say, occupation of factories), whereas capital is *money* – a universally transformable medium of power which can be "cashed" in any number of different forms. Thus capital can be switched into control of information media, resources for a lockout, support for a propaganda campaign, finance for private education, funds for a political party, budgets for weaponry in a social crisis. . . . The unions' *basic* sanction is their control of labour power and this is a singularly rigid and limited weapon' (1967: 267–8).

From this starting point an argument can be fashioned which is highly damaging to the pluralist position. It begins by stressing the contrast between this conception and the one which figures, explicitly or implicitly, in so many pluralist statements, of a rough balance of power among 'the congeries of hundreds of small special interest groups' in society.* Certainly a convincing case can be marshalled for arguing that, in respect of capital-labour relations, the disparity of power can be, and has been, mitigated. The propertyless are indeed dependent upon the propertied for access to resources, but the latter are also dependent upon the former for getting work done, and combination enables employees to offset somewhat the power of their masters. Yet to enjoy control of resources – a control upheld by the law and in the last resort by the armed forces of the State – seems such a decisive advantage that the fact of a widespread belief in the existence of a power balance presents us with a puzzle. In Gouldner's words: 'Anyone with an ounce of empirical curiosity could not help but wonder how it could be possible for the man with a million dollars to be content to have no more of a vote than the man living on public welfare, particularly since the latter could vote to tax his fortune' (1971: 299). By no means all of those who believe in a power balance are property-owners whose selective perceptions can easily be understood – there are even many in the wage-earning class who now consider organized labour to have a power superiority which they consider it misuses.

How is this puzzle to be explained? If property-owners and controllers enjoy great superiority of power, how are we to account for this impression that organized labour, far from suffering a severe disadvantage, has now managed to level up the score and even, in many instances, to overshoot the mark? One important fact supporting such an impression is that the owners and controllers of resources very rarely need to exert publicly and visibly in open conflict more than a small part of the power that lies at their disposal. This is important because unless power is being actively and visibly exercised in terms of sanctions its effect on behaviour often passes unnoticed. In fact, of course, it is in precisely those power relationships where the power disparity is greatest that its active exercise is least necessary. Consciousness even of the implicit threat that remains unspoken bends our minds towards whatever pattern of behaviour is required to prevent the threat being made manifest. The behaviour of those

* Some appropriate references are Miliband 1969; Mills 1959; Wolff 1965; Gitlin 1965; and Castles *et al.* 1971, where the ideologies both of pluralism and of the radical critique can be studied.

dependent in any way on the powerful is 'continually influenced by the *awareness* . . . that superiors can give or withhold at will things that men greatly want . . .' (Gouldner 1971: 294). The impact of power on behaviour is therefore pervasive despite the absence of obvious evidence. It is the absence of obvious evidence, however, which is likely to shape popular impressions on the subject.

The major reason, however, why the powerful rarely need to make their power visible and obvious is that all the social institutions, mechanisms, and principles which it is crucially important for them to have accepted and legitimized are accepted and legitimized already and come under no serious threat. These range far beyond such basics as the institutions of private enterprise and profit making. They cover such matters as the influence of wealth and resource-control over economic, social, and political decision-making; over the content of the mass media and communications; and over the major objectives of the economic system. Crucial for them, too, is the virtually universal acceptance of class and status stratification, and of the hierarchical organization of work with its massive inequalities of authority, reward, status, and job autonomy. Essential, in turn, for the acceptance of these inequalities are such cultural beliefs as, for example, that those in authority ought to enjoy higher rewards than those they command, and that the alleged (and probably engineered) scarcity of a particular skill, talent or ability justifies its holder in demanding a larger allocation of life chances than those of more common or modest attainments.

If we ask how it comes about that this widespread legitimation and acceptance exists of institutions, mechanisms, principles and beliefs so necessary and convenient for the owners and controllers of resources, the answer is, of course, that, as was noted earlier, their very power affords them the facilities for creating and maintaining social attitudes and values favourable to that acceptance. The greater the extent to which power can be used indirectly to shape perceptions and preferences, the less the need for it to be used directly in ways which make it visible. We also need to recall that power often creates its own legitimation in a sense described by Gouldner. 'Those who obey because they are afraid do not like to think themselves unmanly or cowardly; in an effort to maintain a decent regard for themselves, the fearful frequently find ingenious ways in which they can define almost any demand made upon them as legitimate' (1971:

293). Provided these essential strategic institutions, principles and beliefs remain major built-in features of the social structure, the owners and controllers of resources enjoy a highly protective environment. Society is already in the shape which serves their essential interests and purposes, thanks to the power and influence exerted to this end by past as well as present generations of property-owners and their many agents and sympathizers.

But however widespread the acceptance of the master institutions of society there remains, from the power-holders' point of view, a never-ending need for what might be called 'fine tuning'. Flanks have to be protected, fences mended, new doors to power opened as old ones close, new and subtler techniques developed of exercising it. In the field of work, as elsewhere, many marginal issues have to be resolved – exactly how much authority for a given level of management; exactly how much more financial reward for this workgroup as against that; exactly what pattern of work organization in this particular factory. Meanwhile pressures develop from below for some voice in these decisions. But the essential protections for wealth, privilege and power are still largely accepted by those mounting these pressures. Their aspirations are for marginal improvements in their lot, not for eliminating private property, hierarchy, extreme division of labour, and the principles and conventions which support great inequalities of wealth, income, and opportunities for personal fulfilment. This is partly because they have been sufficiently socialized by power-holders to continue legitimizing this basic framework; partly because they see the power arrayed against them as so overwhelming as to make that basic framework appear inevitable, or challengeable only at disproportionate cost to themselves and things they value.

These perceptions and acceptances make it possible for power-holders to concede subordinate groups or representatives a voice in certain limited kinds of decision-making, since they can be confident that their more fundamental prerogatives will not be attacked. If this expectation were not fulfilled they would seek to withdraw the concession, at whatever cost in social conflict. Meanwhile their present readiness to maintain it strengthens as early, primitive, unitary resentment at any challenge to their prerogative, however modest, gives way to more sophisticated pluralistic concepts and techniques of conflict management. They increasingly see a limited concession of prerogative as only judicious in that, by meeting modest and marginal aspirations, it avoids the risk of these becoming inflamed by frustration into more fundamental and dangerous demands. More positively, the satisfaction of these marginal aspirations strengthens the legitimacy of the system in the eyes of those subordinated to it, thereby enhancing rather than weakening managerial effectiveness. Dubin, under the heading 'Assimilation – The Victory of Management', argues that 'If it is appropriate to talk about "collectivization" of business management through collective bargaining . . . then we should add that this takes place largely on management's terms, within a framework of managerial ideology. Management has gone a long way in assimilating some of the broader social goals championed by labor unions. . . . But we have also seen a counter move of union assimilation of the procedures of management and its ultimate goals. This has more firmly entrenched the managerial functions and their ideological bases' (1958: 187). This strengthening of legitimacy is likely to extend to the wider economic and social systems. 'Collective bargaining', wrote Harbison in a sustained panegyric which echoed the envious 'continental statesmen' of a much earlier day, 'provides one of the more important bulwarks for the preservation of the private-enterprise system' (1954: 274), a view supported in essence by Dubin, who refers to 'its stabilizing influence upon the whole society' (see under Harbison 1954).

These arguments suggest that the sufferance which owners and controllers of resources extend to organized interest groups among the propertyless, and which some theorists elevate into 'ungrudging acknowledgement of the right of opposed interests to exist and be pursued', is far removed from any balanced reciprocation of mutual rights as between groups of equal power, status, and respect. It is heavily conditional upon the interest groups concerned being prepared to accept as given those major structural features which are crucial for the power, status, and rewards of the owners and controllers. It is because this condition is usually fulfilled that owners and controllers are rarely driven to call upon their reserves of power in any overt and public exercise. Only the margins of power are needed to cope with marginal adjustments. This, then, is what accounts for the illusion of a power balance. Labour often has to marshal all its resources to fight on these marginal adjustments; capital can, as it were, fight with one hand behind its back and still achieve in most situations a verdict that it finds tolerable. What many see as major conflicts in which labour seems often now to have the advantage are conflicts only on such issues as labour deems it realistic to contest, and these never touch the real roots of ownership, inequality, hierarchy, and privilege. Only if labour were to challenge an essential prop of the structure would capital need to bring into play anything approaching its full strength, thus destroying at once the illusion of a power balance. For example, a demand backed by strike action that wage earners receive equal rewards with top management would soon demonstrate which side could, and would feel impelled to, last out longer. The 'power balance' illusion thus rests on the continuing acceptance by the less favoured of social institutions and principles which support wealth and privilege, and which the wealthy and privileged would exert their great power to defend if that acceptance were to pass into attempts at repudiation. But the illusion itself contributes towards acceptance, for by concealing gross disparities of power it fosters the belief that all the principal interests, at least, of society compete fairly for its rewards, thereby helping to legitimize the system.

The critique of pluralist ideology cannot, however, end there. The point has been made that for management to concede collective bargaining and other means by which employees or their representatives can participate in the making of some kinds of decision may well strengthen rather than weaken their control. This argument now needs elaboration.

Despite the continued rejection by many employers and managers of pluralist notions and values, it is not difficult to argue that the propagation of such an ideology represents, in the context of modern business, a high point in sophisticated 'managerialism', in the sense that it serves managerial interests and goals whether pluralists themselves identify with those interests and goals or not. Admittedly it urges the full acceptance by managers of rival focuses of authority, leadership, and claims to subordinate loyalty. It recommends the limited sharing of some rule-making and decision-taking, It deprives managers of all theoretical justification for asserting total prerogative. Yet the outcome of these concessions is visualized, not as the weakening of managerial rule as we now understand it, but as its strengthening and consolidation. Pluralism would certainly be defended by at least some of its exponents on the grounds that it is more likely than the unitary view to promote rational, efficient, and effective management.* Certainly support for pluralism can spring from other values as well, such as those underlying the notion of self-determination by self-defining interest groups. Nevertheless the pluralist position remains open to the interpretation of being no more, or no less, than sophisticated managerialism, for where the objectives of efficient and effective management conflict with the objectives of would-be self-determining workgroups, pluralist concern tends to be directed towards finding ways by which the latter can be contained within a regulative framework that promotes and maintains the former. The postwar trend in Britain towards workplace bargaining characterized as 'largely informal, largely fragmented and largely autonomous' (Flanders 1967: 28), was described by the Donovan Report as conferring the 'important benefits' of 'a very high degree of self-government in industry' (1968: paras. 129–30). The Report condemned it, nevertheless, and proposed reversing the trend by means of comprehensive company and factory agreements, on the ground that 'the benefits are outweighed by the shortcomings: the tendency of extreme decentralisation and self-government to degenerate into indecision and anarchy; the propensity to breed inefficiency; and the reluctance to change – all of them characteristics which become more damaging as they develop, as the rate of technical progress increases, and as the need for economic growth becomes more urgent' (*Ibid*: para. 130).

Such propositions as these suggest that pluralists do not envisage as the outcome of joint regulation by management and labour any major change in the organization of industry, in the fundamental distribution of power and control, or in the broad objectives towards which the industrial effort is directed. Rather is it assumed that there

* The present writer has made this point himself in the past. 'The pluralistic frame of reference, which openly concedes the severe limitations on management power, constitutes thereby a source of potential strength rather than weakness' (Fox 1966b: 14). See also Flanders: 'The paradox, whose truth managements have found it so difficult to accept, is that they can only regain control by sharing it' (1970: 172), and Chamberlain: 'Thus it is only good management to seek to secure consent of the governed who could otherwise make it impossible for management to achieve the very objective which it has set for itself' (1963: 190). Finally, the Donovan Report itself argued that a whole-hearted acceptance by management of comprehensive, speedy and equitable negotiation and grievance procedures would promote pay structures which were, *inter alia*, 'conducive to efficiency' (1968: para. 183).

is basic agreement on these issues and that pluralistic mechanisms must be valued, not only as ends in themselves, but also as means for articulating, institutionalizing, and resolving marginal discontents and disagreements which, though of considerable significance for the immediate parties, leave the essential structure of control basically intact. Pluralism could be presented, in fact, as the far-seeing manager's ideology for a future in which those in positions of rule come increasingly under challenge, have to seek new legitimations, and must turn intelligence and patience towards the growing task of winning consent. It becomes the recommended frame of reference most likely to enable managers to pursue their purposes successfully amid the multiple values, the diverse and rising group aspirations, and the shifting power relations of a complex society undergoing an accelerating rate of economic and social change. From this view, either management learns these new modes of governance or it will suffer, at worst, the destruction of its present form or, at best, obstruction so severe as to render it incapable of pursuing adaptation and growth.

Seen in this light, the pluralist ideology would be the choice of a structural-functionalist seeking to identify the appropriate integrative mechanisms for industrial relations systems in Western societies – functionally appropriate, that is, whatever its professed intentions, in maintaining the *status quo* of highly unequal power, wealth, and privilege.* The very concept of the industrial relations *system* would then take on a theoretical significance familiar in the United States but going well beyond what has usually been given it by most academic industrial relations specialists in Britain. For the latter, 'system' has borne only its weak sense of a set of related behaviours, norms, and values which can usefully be studied together for their significance and meaning with respect to a selected field of interest. Located, however, within a body of assumptions about basic consensus, the concept might appear to bear a much stronger sense. The norms and

* The Webbs's *Industrial Democracy* has a marked functionalist as well as pluralist orientation. Working to a criterion of national economic efficiency, they define trade unionism as having a responsible and legitimate future in so far as, by raising regulative standards governing the reward, education, and general treatment of employees, it enhanced the quality of labour as an economic resource, but predicted failure and downfall if it violated the canons of progress by promoting restrictionism, disruption of production, resistance to change, and doctrines of vested interest (1902: 809–17).

values of joint regulation would be viewed by some theorists as an integrative subsystem which acts as one of the self-equilibrating mechanisms ensuring the survival and adaptation of the total system. These notions that an institutionalizing of conflict and an open coming-to-terms with dissident groups under one's command may, given certain conditions, be positively functional for the manager are, as was noted in the preceding chapter, familiar in sociological theory (Coser 1956).* The idea that the functionalist approach could not deal with conflict had to be laid to rest as it became increasingly clear that institutionalized mechanisms for identifying and regulating conflict could, given consensus on the basic framework of the relationship, be defined not as a threat to, but as a prerequisite of, social stability and integration in its deepest sense.† American exponents of pluralism have, as we saw, been insistent on the value of such mechanisms in providing 'very substantial support for our system of democratic capitalism' (Harbison 1954: 276).

So far we have applied the radical critique to the pluralistic perspective only on the most general level. We now need to argue the case with specific reference to the work organization as such.

A Radical Perspective on the Work Organization

Were it possible to see the organization as a voluntary and spontaneous coming together of independent and autonomous participants

* Such notions are receiving practical application. In an article in the *Harvard Business Review*, 'Make Conflict Work for You', J. Kelly argues that 'old concepts of human relations, including the notion that conflict *per se* is harmful and should be avoided at all cost, do not square with the facts any longer. Indeed, the new approach is that conflict, if properly handled, can lead to more effective and appropriate arrangements. . . . The way conflict is managed – rather than suppressed, ignored, or avoided – contributes significantly to a company's effectiveness' (July-August 1970:103).

† The same applies to pluralism in the wider political system. In Britain the Labour Party, once seen by many, as were the trade unions, as a threat to the established order, is now defined as a functional necessity for full stability. The country 'needs' an effective (though of course 'responsible') opposition. The definition depends upon the Party, like the unions, accepting assimilation within the basic framework of values and institutions. 'And in every case, of course', notes Raymond Williams, 'to accept the proposed limitation of aims may lead to important short-term gains in practical efficiency . . . But . . . each of these institutions is discovering that the place in existing society proposed for it, if it agrees to limit its aims, is essentially subordinate: the wide challenge has been drained out, and what is left can be absorbed within existing terms' (1961: 302–3).

with equal knowledge and power, on the lines of the Spontaneous Consensus model discussed in Chapter 2, it could certainly be claimed as offering pluralistic arrangements of a superior order which serve both economic and human values. Comparison with the world of reality, however, reveals the claim to stand in need of severe qualification. People do not come together freely and spontaneously to set up work organizations; the propertyless many are forced by their need for a livelihood to seek access to resources owned or controlled by the few, who derive therefrom very great power. The few can use this power to determine the behaviour of the many, not only directly, but also indirectly through the many agencies of socialization, communication, and attitude forming. Thus is promoted the high degree of acceptance of the *status quo* which is such a marked feature of our society. Thus is promoted acceptance of the social institutions, principles, and assumptions which embody and generate inequality of rewards, privileges, and other life chances.

It is a tendency of socialization and social conditioning, moreover, for the conditioned – and indeed the conditioners – to be unaware that the beliefs, assumptions, and institutions which they accept are conventional and artificial in the sense of being open to conscious collective choice and change, and are in no way inevitable or the consequence of natural laws inherent in the cosmos. It is probable that for much of the time most men do not perceive the conventional and arbitrary nature of many of the social arrangements under which they live, and suppose them to be the only possible ones given 'the nature of things' – a notion which usually includes belief in an unchangeable 'human nature'. This unawareness itself helps to make possible the continuance of the existing order. And in this context we must always bear in mind that the conditioners are themselves conditioned.

What all this means is that when union or workgroup representatives take their place with managers at the negotiating table, they do so not as free and equal citizens, but as men who have already been socialized, indoctrinated, and trained by a multiplicity of influences to accept and legitimize most aspects of their work situation; a situation designed in the light of the values and purposes of the major power-holders. '. . . The goals for which interests struggle are not merely given: they reflect the current state of expectation and acceptance. Accordingly, to say that various interests are "balanced" is generally to evaluate the *status quo* as satisfactory or even good; the hopeful ideal of balance often masquerades as a description of fact' (Mills 1959: 246. See also Westergaard 1965: 99). Those aspects of their situation and of the economic and social order which the union bargainers do not legitimize they nevertheless acquiesce in because to challenge such fundamentals seems futile. Perhaps in any case they appear inevitable. Thus the 'harmony' that is engineered by the pluralist's 'accommodation – the mutual adjustment of groups that preserve their distinctive identities and interests' (Selznick 1969: 119), is only possible because the representatives of labour leave unchallenged those institutions, principles, and assumptions which ensure to the owners and controllers by far the greater part of their privileges and power. The two sides cannot be seen, then, as moving off from the same start line to settle jointly the nature and terms of their collaboration. Overwhelmingly the greater part of the collaborative structure and its mode of operation is settled already; settled on terms and principles which discriminate in every important respect in favour of its owners and controllers, and which the rank and file do not contest.

Conditioning and power combine, then, to produce acceptance and submission; a process in which pluralist ideology plays its part. If inequalities are being imposed upon people by forces which they shrink from challenging, one way by which they can avoid psychological discomfort is to be receptive to all those influences, direct and indirect, explicit and implicit, crude and subtle, which assure them that the inequalities are necessary and legitimate, are accepted as natural by other groups in society, and are inevitable in some form or another the world over. It is in this context that the activities, writings and utterances of industrial-relations pluralists cannot help but take on an ideological significance, however unintended. They focus their interest on the substance and methods of rule-making and conflict regulation within the existing institutions and objectives of work. Their 'problem areas' they tend to share with individuals, groups, and agencies who are concerned to promote forms of economically rational, efficient, and humane management which, directed though they may be to profit making, are seen as producing such incidental benefits as lower cost operations, better terms and conditions of employment, and 'mutually satisfactory' procedures of joint regulation and conflict regulation. These individuals, groups, and agencies include 'progressive' managers, some employers' associations, certain voluntary organizations concerned with managerial problems and techniques, government departments, and public agencies with the relevant terms of reference. The interest is in 'order' – not an imposed order but one negotiated with representatives of participant interests.

It is being argued here, however, that this negotiation of order within the enterprise takes place only at the margins. Management and the interests do not jointly build their collaborative structure from the ground floor up. Power and social conditioning cause the employee interests to accept management's shaping of the main structure long before they reach the negotiating table. Thus the discussion may be about marginal adjustments in hierarchical rewards, but not the principle of hierarchical rewards; about certain practical issues connected with the prevailing extreme subdivision of labour, but not the principle of extreme subdivision of labour; about financial (extrinsic) rewards for greater efficiency, but not about the possibility of other types of (intrinsic) reward with some sacrifice of efficiency; about measures which may achieve company expansion and growth but not about the principle of company expansion and growth; about how the participant interests can protect and advance themselves within the structure operated by management to pursue its basic objectives, but not about the nature of those basic objectives.

Frames of Reference and Behavioural Implications

Those who hold the radical ideology just outlined may or may not choose to make it the inspiration for such industrial or political action as they may undertake. They may decide that reasons of personal or political expediency require them to behave *as if* the pluralist analysis were valid and should govern their actions (see Fox 1973 for an examination of this aspect). It would be reasonable to suppose, however, that some shopfloor leaders and workgroups in industry conduct their relations with management in the light of the radical perspective. The responses to their behaviour which come from power-holders and other observers are more likely to be shaped by either the unitary or the pluralistic ideology. The nature of the unitary response may easily be guessed; it is likely to be one which turns quickly to tactics of authoritarian repression. More interesting is that the pluralist, too, may feel driven, in the last resort, in similar directions. If the belief is, first, that economic and political groups compete on not too grossly unequal terms for political power (through which is decided the basic structure and institutions of society) and second, that within the work organization, management and labour, again on roughly equal terms, negotiate their particular sector of order, there is likely to be little patience with the few who refuse to cooperate within this apparently admirable system. It will seem that they wilfully reject the principle of majority decisions; prefer anarchy and disorder; are maliciously disposed against their society on personal grounds. And indeed it may well be true that they include some whose behaviour owes more to their own psychological quirks than to any rational preferences of social and economic organization. But it is a further demonstration of the ideological content of pluralism that it leads logically towards categorizing *all* nonconformers in these terms. The categories offered by the Donovan Report to describe these situations are those 'in which strike-proneness is due to irresponsibility or to agitation by eccentrics or by subversives' (1968: para. 508). Against activities of these kinds 'it would be neither unjust nor futile to apply legal sanctions' (para. 509). The same view prevails in the United States. Clark Kerr, after stressing the importance of the pluralistic consensus in the stability and effectiveness of the industrial relations system, declares that 'No significant group can be allowed to sabotage it because of a conflicting exclusive ideological orientation' (such as a philosophy of class war). 'The effective response to such tactics does raise real questions about the role of compulsion in a democracy in the handling of such groups and individuals' (1955: 12). And indeed, what reasonable person is likely to question the use of sanctions where sabotage, 'irresponsibility or ill-will is the root cause of the evil' (Donovan 1968: para. 509)?

Those acting in accordance with the radical analysis will of course have very different perceptions. They see what pluralists define as 'free and equal joint regulation' as no more than 'bargaining under duress'. If they aspire to demands which represent a repudiation of all or some of the conventionally received notions and principles which are the condition of their negotiating activities being tolerated by the major power-holders, but are conscious of being contained within the conventional bargaining limits by those power-holders, they are likely to see such negotiating as they are permitted as being under duress. Despite management complaints of being helpless before union or workgroup demands, employees who reject conventional beliefs and assumptions about the rewards, organization, and general conduct of industry may be well aware that the widespread acceptance of these conventions is due, in part to a sense of overwhelming odds which it would be futile to challenge, in part to deep doubts about the legitimacy of such a challenge. Seeing both these responses as the outcome of greatly unequal power, the nonconformers view the whole apparatus of joint regulation as just another mystification which confuses industry's rank and file about the nature of the system.

Given a consciousness of bargaining under duress, what happens to the moral obligation to observe agreements 'freely and honourably negotiated'? Those who feel coerced feel no obligation. Appeals from persons of high status and power to behave 'responsibly' by keeping agreements may be regarded by nonconformers as the culminating frustration, especially when accompanied by threats of legal coercion. The whole structure may appear as no more than a confidence trick; the praise bestowed on 'responsible' behaviour as no more than a variant on the technique of 'cooling the mark out';* and the 'dignity' and 'self-respect' displayed by employees and their leaders within this pattern of joint regulation as no more than the much praised behaviour of Uncle Tom, dignified and uncomplaining under exploitation. The challenge presented by the radical perspective to the beliefs and assumptions which underpin the existing industrial relations order is therefore apparent. It generates more alarm among higher status groups but less among lower status groups than does the challenge presented by the unitary perspective, which can nevertheless lead to considerable 'disorder' when employee expectations of pluralistic accommodation are denied by an employer who refuses to recognize and negotiate with a trade union.

One major aspect of the challenge presented to ruling groups by the radical analysis can be easily stated. Such positive value for its own purposes as management sees in trade unionism and collective

* A process examined by Goffman (1952: 482–505). The 'mark' is the conman's victim, cooling the mark out is an exercise in the prudent art of consolation – 'An attempt is made to define the situation for the mark in a way that makes it easy for him to accept the inevitable and quietly go home.'

bargaining can be expressed in one word: control. But this rests on the observance of negotiated agreements, particularly those regulating employee, shop steward, and union behaviour with respect to the processing of claims and grievances. The more capital intensive, closely integrated, and interdependent become the activities of modern industry, the more important for management becomes the avoidance of stoppages by employee groups whose actions produce dislocations far beyond their own boundaries. So important is it, indeed, that the discussion and sometimes the practice of direct legal coercion is never far away. But for management purposes direct coercion is a technique with serious disadvantages, since it is bound to prejudice the whole future of what must be a continuing relationship. Preferable by far is the acceptance by employees and their leaders of a moral obligation to honour agreements. But it has been argued here that the strength of their sense of obligation must vary inversely with the degree to which they are conscious of being pressured by superior power. To the extent that they are conscious of being constrained to accept certain terms of employment or certain modes of disputes procedure by superior power, they will observe the relevant rules only from a sense of expediency and prudent calculation. As was argued earlier, observance offered from these motives constitutes a reliable basis of order only as long as the given power relationship is maintained. Any marginal increment of power accruing to those who feel subjected is liable to be used by them to pursue what they perceive as legitimate aspirations, regardless of existing rules and procedures to which they do not feel in honour bound. Only a sense of equal participation can be expected to induce an observance based on moral obligation as against calculative expediency. Equally significant are the implications for third-party observers, be they members of the government, publicists, or others with a personal or professional interest in industrial order. Should they seek to promote a stable order by emphasizing the moral imperative to observe agreements, their success with those who see themselves as pressured or coerced is likely to be limited.

The strong appeal of pluralist doctrine for these groups is therefore apparent. The assertion that employees, by organizing themselves in strong unions, may succeed not only in redressing the old inequality but even in tilting the balance in their own favour, serves as an ideological instrument which it is hoped will induce them to accept a moral obligation to honour the agreements covering their work behaviour. We do not know how many rank and file employees accept this picture of power relations in industry, but we may safely surmise that they are far fewer than management would like. That many managers themselves assert such a picture implies no conscious deception on their part; their very conviction of its truth strengthens the confidence with which they exhort employees to recognize the claims of honour. Indeed, one might almost describe this perspective on power relations as a functional necessity for the modern sophisticated manager unless he is capable of a Machiavellianism rare among human beings, who normally prefer to protect themselves against the self-abrasive edges of such cynicism with appropriate rationalizations. The detached observer under no such pressures may be prepared to consider less conventional propositions. When rank and file workgroups who find themselves in a strong bargaining position appear unwilling to submit to the restraints of constitutional procedures the cause may be, not that they are incapable of recognizing moral obligation, but that they do not acknowledge its relevance in a situation which they feel is determined in its fundamentals by a power, status, and privilege greatly superior to their own.

The continuing assertion by power-holders and their supporters of the pluralist position and its ethical imperatives in the face of what seems flat repudiation represents more than forlorn persistence. For if the attempt is to be made to coerce men to observe agreements there must be a mobilization of support among other groups and sections of society and a set of justifications produced which explain and legitimize the action proposed. Those responsible for these measures will act with all the greater self-confidence and sense of rightness if they are convinced of the validity of the pluralist interpretation of modern society.

Radical Perspectives and the Role of the Union

In examining the significance of these points for institutionalized trust relations we may begin with the aspect of prescriptive trust – with the question of how far men covered by prescriptive rules are trusted to discharge their obligations without being policed and threatened with punitive sanctions. The collective contract or agreement prescribes certain specific terms which the parties expect each other to observe. As we have noted, disparity of power between contracting parties may be sufficiently great as to introduce the extenuating concept of duress which relieves the weaker party of its obligation to honour the agreement. But a belief that power relations bear sufficient approximation to a balance to exclude such extenuation means that both parties are held to come fully under the obligation to observe the terms. Failure in this respect may then be held to justify punitive sanctions against the defaulting party, in accordance with accepted principles of contract enforcement. Thus the beliefs characteristic of the pluralist perspective can play an important part in promoting and legitimizing certain social attitudes and public policy in this field. They appear to give moral validity and force to the institution of contract in labour markets by seeing it as brought under collective regulation by approximately equal representative powers. The radical perspective, however, challenges this view of power relations and with it the moral validity of most collective bargaining in capitalist society.

This creates the potentiality for tension between the radical perspective and that informing the role of the trade union in Western industrial society. Trade unionism in the West has for the most part acted according to the implied assumptions that its survival and wellbeing depended upon severely limiting its aspirations and scrupulously observing negotiated agreements. Being an expression of men's needs as they were aware of them in the here-and-now of the daily work situation, it focused upon the issues that were immediately pressing and, even if conscious of a wider social vision, considered that to attempt to effect a transformation by industrial action would achieve no more than the destruction of such limited foothold in rule-making as it had managed to achieve for bread-and-butter purposes. This approach has brought it disparagement from those who entertain the larger hope (Anderson 1967: 263–80), and vigorous defence from its supporters (Flanders 1970: 38–47). Certainly the very nature of collective bargaining as generally conducted implies a firm foundation of consensus, and the features which the unions are prepared to accept as given constitute the very social and economic framework which radical critics seek to challenge. Hence the condemnation of trade unionism as opportunism, class collaboration, or mini-reformism. In place of a 'struggle of the working class not only to achieve profitable terms for the sale of labour, but also to achieve the annihilation of the social order which forces the have-nots to sell themselves to the rich', the structure has been stabilized by institutions of joint regulation and conflict settlement through which 'the sellers of labour learned to sell this "commodity" on better terms and to fight the buyer in the manner of a purely commercial transaction' (Lenin 1970: 104). Although this is hardly an adequate account of the trade union role in Western society, that role can certainly be seen as one of pursuing reforms which, however valued by the recipients, leave the master institutions and conventions of capitalist society in recognizable shape. A debate developed, therefore, as to whether 'the working class, solely by its own forces, is able to work out merely trade-union consciousness, i.e. the conviction of the need for combining in unions, for fighting against the employers, and for trying to prevail upon the government to pass laws necessary for the workers, etc.' (*Ibid*: 80). As against this 'series of primitive demands designed merely to improve their position *vis-à-vis* their employers', could there develop spontaneously among the workers 'the Socialist theory which is aimed at abolishing this position – the position of being hired labour'? (Utechin, in *Ibid*: 29).

An examination of this debate by Hyman concludes that 'no *general* theory is available to relate the struggle for material reforms to the development of (revolutionary) consciousness.' The 'limits of trade-union consciousness can vary markedly between different historical contexts and can shift radically with only a brief passage of time. Under specific objective conditions the educative potential of collective industrial action may be immense; in other, perhaps more typical, circumstances the spontaneous development of workers' consciousness may fail absolutely to transcend the confines of bourgeois ideology' (1971: 52–3).

The principal factors which secure these typical circumstances have already emerged at different stages in the preceding analysis. Bourgeois ideology does indeed influence men's aspirations in such directions as material wellbeing and acquisition which resource-controllers are in business to serve. Men come to accept as natural laws what are no more than cultural values and social conventions which could be changed given a collective will. Consciousness of superior power may induce in them a resigned acquiescence in, and even assimilation of, the power-holder's values. To this array of factors must now be added the role of the trade union itself. In

Western societies it is through their functions of collective bargaining and political action within the bounds of pluralistic assumptions and philosophy that unions organize a mass membership; become stable and deeply rooted institutions; provide career and status opportunities for leaders; and establish a pervasive network of participative activities touching upon almost every public aspect of social and economic life. Given such a range and depth of vested interests, it would require a motivation of very great magnitude indeed to induce trade unions to break the bounds of respectability on which their social acceptance, fluctuating and chequered though it is, essentially rests. Such considerations affect, wittingly or otherwise, the kind of leadership and socialization which they bring to bear upon members. Trade union leaders, asked about internal democracy, rightly point to the many mechanisms, both formal and informal, through which they are responsive to the needs and aspirations of their members. They would be unlikely, even in the event of their being aware of them, to point to the ways in which they help to determine what those needs and aspirations are. The new recruit who asks of his shop steward 'What is the union for?' will be told that its proper and rightful purpose lies in protecting his job interests, defined in such terms as wages, working hours, overtime, holidays, redundancy, and defence against arbitrary authority. If, in a search for emancipation from alienation and for intrinsic meaning in work, he were to ask about the division of labour, bureaucracy, and hierarchy; or if, in a search for equality of another kind, he was to press for information about managerial rewards, he would probably be told that the union had enough problems on its plate already without venturing into such fanciful realms as these. Thus do unions help to socialize their members in what it is sensible for them to expect from their work and their life. Thus do unions help to socialize members in their *status*. For the argument has brought us back to the question of what men accept as given and what they aspire to change. One implication of much that has gone before is that employees as individuals and through their unions continue to accept the fundamental features of the social and economic order as given. No more than in the case of individual bargaining can collective bargaining be seen as defining (explicitly in what it includes; implicitly in what it assumes) the full terms of economic collaboration. The area which the bargaining process accepts for the most part as given remains uncontested not because lower ranks, after a process of informed inspection and comparison with conceivable alternatives, consciously decide to extend their positive approval, but because they are either socialized to see it as legitimate, inevitable, and natural, or resigned to submit to it as an expression of power which they cannot challenge except at disproportionate cost to themselves.

In so far as their acquiescence has rested upon the former, it has owed much to an acceptance of status considerations which show continuity with the master-servant tradition so assiduously promoted and enforced over many centuries by earlier generations of power-holders. As we saw earlier, even in its heyday contract as applied to the employment relation was never seen as a means by which the parties jointly constructed their relationship from the ground floor up. The foundations and basic shape of that structure were deemed as being constructed already, and if not willingly accepted by lower participants were enforced upon them. The keystone was the concept of the subordination of the employee to the decision-making rights of his master. To be sure, status might bring useful rights to the subordinate as well. The status of journeyman in a recognized, longstanding craft might provide its occupant with membership of a partially selfgoverning group which could protect useful privileges by means of restrictive rules. Even in non-craft employments, custom and practice might be strong enough to assure the entrant into a given occupation the terms and conditions habitual to the locality. Some aspects of what the employee accepted as given, in other words, could be, in certain circumstances, a source of protection. Custom was a resource which could help employees, for example, to resist an attack on wage rates by an individual employer. And when collective organization developed among them it could sometimes be for the purpose of upholding status in one or other of these forms. But status of these kinds often failed in its protective function. The technological, organizational, or market pressures of gathering industrialization could often drive employers individually or collectively to smash their way through craft status or local custom, though sometimes this tactic might prove or threaten to be sufficiently troublesome to prompt a search for other ways out of their difficulties. And in any case, of course, by far the predominant generalized implication of employee status was subordination to the existing basic pattern of work organization as determined by the employer.

Such, then, have been the limits within which trade unionism has hitherto chosen to operate. This role has meant that, while its survival at the hands of members has rested upon the readiness of employers to negotiate agreements, its survival at the hands of the employers has rested not only upon its acceptance of all the conventions, institutions, and values which the chosen role implied, but also upon an ability to ensure that members observed the terms of agreements and procedures – in other words, upon demonstrating its effectiveness as an instrument of regulation and control. To achieve this end and to convince employers that it was a reliable and 'responsible' negotiating partner, the union was often constrained to project a message not so much of expediency (with the dangerous implication that defining the expedient was a matter of opinion in which one man's view was as good as another's), but rather of moral obligation which permitted of no self-regarding calculation. But once the union accepted this role it was trapped, not necessarily against the inclinations of its leaders, within the logic of the pluralist syndrome. It could not, without placing itself in a hopelessly ambiguous position, fire its members with a radical analysis of employer-worker power relations based on the concept of exploitation, and at the same time preach the moral validity of 'agreements honourably negotiated' between the two. The very role constraints under which trade union leaders had to operate meant that, whatever their private beliefs, they were usually to be found behaving according to the pluralist perspective. The difficulties of manifesting in action both 'trade union consciousness' in Lenin's sense and 'revolutionary' consciousness were apparent. 'Even . . . Communist-oriented union leaders are forced to become expert practitioners of the art of collective bargaining in order to acquire and hold the reins of power in their organizations' (Harbison 1954: 277), thereby demonstrating the possibility of holding a radical interpretation of society and yet choosing to act in accordance with the pluralistic model. A few Communist trade union leaders in Britain have been praised by employers for consistently displaying 'integrity' and 'responsibility' in their behaviour within the procedures and conventions of joint regulation. 'Not a few communists have good trade union records which they maintain by sacrificing, on occasions, the party line to their union loyalty' (Flanders 1968: 162). Certainly if the union were to act according to policy implications suggested by the radical analysis, it would have to accept that it was inviting an industrial – and possibly, in the form of legislation, a political – power clash that might threaten its existence. Provided it observed the conditions of mutual survival implied by the pluralist doctrine there was a much better chance of its institutional interests being served and its members' most immediate and pressing grievances receiving attention. Meanwhile the union's acceptance of this role and its efforts towards socializing members in the appropriate behaviours increased the likelihood that they, too, would adopt a similar perspective.

Yet there were other factors at work which complicated this whole picture, both on the employers' side and that of the employees. Mutual accommodation on the pluralist model might be a sophisticated managerial stance, but not all managements were sophisticated and some found that they could not always afford to be sophisticated in this sense even if they wished. Moreover, in some work organizations both management and employees were divided among themselves as to the pattern of relationships they preferred; the former looking to both unitary and pluralistic models, and the latter perhaps not only to these but also to the radical model. Given three possible frames of reference, two parties, and the possibility that either or both may be divided in standpoint, there are many conceivable patterns of management-employee relations which can emerge. Before we go any further we need to examine some of the more likely ones.

7 · Patterns of Management-Employee Relations

Attention will be directed to six possible patterns of management-employee relations, to which will be given the names of Traditional, Classical Conflict, Sophisticated Modern, Standard Modern, Sophisticated Paternalist and Continuous Challenge. There is space here only for the briefest of delineations. Anything approaching a full treatment would further lengthen a book already long enough and the objective is therefore limited to indicating the directions in which the analysis leads.

Traditional Pattern

The Traditional pattern is characterized by unitary perspectives on the part of both management and employees (for a recent example see Hawkins 1972: 115–17). The latter have been induced to accept the ideology of the former which decrees that interests are shared and that any assertion to the contrary is not legitimate. Since management's prerogative is not even ideologically, still less practically, contested, its definition of roles and rewards is fully legitimized and occupants of low-discretion and high-discretion roles alike perceive these definitions in high-trust terms in the institutionalized sense with which we are concerned here. The nature of relationships between management and rank and file may lie anywhere between the extremes of benevolent paternalist and crudely exploitive. History shows that acceptance by employees of the unitary perspective is fully compatible with their being grossly illtreated even by the standards of the times. Indeed, among the most deprived groups could sometimes be found the most cowed and deferential who accepted their lot with passive fatalism and who could contemplate only with awe the idea of collective challenge to their masters. Such an organized challenge required certain preconditions, among them a consciousness of rights which could legitimately be asserted in a systematic manner against the traditional authority of the masters; an authority affirmed and emphasized with religious force by the great majority of socializing agencies which surrounded them. In no industrial society has effective and sustained trade unionism (as against the revolt born of desperation) made its first appearance among the most oppressed and deprived strata. It requires among its members convictions of their worth which are independent of the judgements of their masters as to what they are entitled to, and such convictions commonly arise first some distance above the lowest levels of the social hierarchy.

Classical Conflict Pattern

As employees acquired this consciousness they confronted unitary-thinking employers with pluralistic type demands to be allowed a voice in the making of certain decisions bearing on terms and conditions of employment. Thus the Traditional pattern passed into the Classical Conflict pattern. In terms of the analysis developed here, trade unionism and collective bargaining appear as low-trust responses by employees to what they perceive as low-trust work situations created by management. The nature of this union perspective became clear in earlier chapters. It sees management as imposing low-discretion roles upon rank and file and, by hedging them about with restrictive rules, authority, discipline, sanctions, and punitive attitudes, indicating that it has objectives and values which it does not expect them to share. While asserting its own freedom to fix rewards and other employment conditions; decide on work objectives, techniques, materials, and other arrangements; and administer unchallenged the authority and disciplinary structure; it seeks to bind rank and file employees with specific prescriptions as to their pace, methods, and quality of work, to supervise, check, and inspect their behaviour; and to limit their discretion in other ways also with precise and restrictive rules and sanctions. These behaviours are likely to be seen by the rank and file as evidence that management does not, whatever it may say, regard those whom it subjects to such work patterns as partners in a common enterprise. Rather are these behaviours taken to imply a management belief that men who are allocated low-discretion roles in an enterprise over whose purposes and conduct they have no control cannot be *expected* to offer spontaneous commitment. This means that management cannot rely on their goodwill. It dare not trust them. Hence the specific rules, programmes, and controls backed by punitive sanctions. This does not prevent managers from appealing nevertheless for commitment and 'a sense of responsibility' and from reacting with resentment and hostility when these are not forthcoming.

A radical analysis would, of course, use stronger terms. It would assert that a minority of power-holders and their agents, in exploiting the propertyless majority, cannot risk trusting those they exploit. Successful exploitation involves power-holders in treating the subjected groups in ways which are likely – in the absence of total ideological indoctrination – to lead to conflict perceptions on their part. This requires that their work behaviour be further prescribed, inspected, and controlled, lest such discretion as they do have be used in their own interests rather than those of the power-holders. This distrust seen as manifested by management evokes a reciprocal response from employees. They seek a voice in decisions which they regard both as being important for them and as being realistically within their range of influence. No more than they perceive management as trusting them do they feel able to trust management. Their interest now lies in limiting managerial discretion as far as seems practicable and desirable. This often means collective bargaining, but in some situations management may feel constrained to allow a workgroup some degree of unilateral self-determination.

Should management not legitimize these developments it will not be reconciled to them even though for motives of calculative prudence it may feel obliged to submit so long as it is at a disadvantage in the labour market. The pattern of relations which characteristically follows is a familiar one in labour history. 'If management regards collective bargaining negatively as a cancerous growth in the organizational body, a variety of crucial management decisions will be made in one way rather than another. . . . Almost inevitably, there will be a strong defensive flavour in management's actions, secrecy, antagonism, reliance on legal technicalities in negotiation, a readiness to perceive a threat in any union demand or action, and in consequence a failure to acquire the understanding of human behaviour which is a prime essential for good relations. The observer learns to expect to find many symptoms of conflict and unhealthy relations in a firm whenever he detects within management evidence of an underlying antagonism to collective bargaining (no matter how disguised or rationalised)' (Kerr, Dunlop, Myers *et al.* 1953: 73–4). 'Given such a perspective, the presence of the union in the workplace is seen, not as the natural and inevitable outcome of sectional interests, but as an intrusion into what should be a private, unified structure. It competes illegitimately for control over, and the loyalty of, the employees. Especially resented is the horizontal link with employees of other establishments, for this is deemed as introducing considerations which are foreign and alien into the private affairs of the company. For managers with this view of the scene there may be a constant temptation to adopt measures designed to weaken the union's appeal and strengthen the company's. Further resentment is induced when the union reacts with suspicion and mistrust. While this resentment may lie dormant for long periods, one would expect it to erupt as righteous indignation in moments of stress or special difficulty. It is not difficult to identify such incidents in industrial relations. Seemingly inexplicable failures of communication when unions are left ignorant of management policy vitally affecting them; abrupt refusals to negotiate; sudden assertions of managerial prerogative; outbursts of resentment against union or workgroup claims; heated moralizing denunciations of employee behaviour that is rationally designed to defend legitimate sectional interests – much of all this probably has its origin in ideological assumptions, perhaps scarcely conscious, still less examined, that there is only one legitimate source of authority and focus of loyalty in the enterprise; that rival bids are presumptuous and lacking in decent loyalty; that men are ungrateful and therefore undeserving of consideration' (Fox 1966b: 11). An extreme case in recent times of a unitary-minded management confronting union attempts at organization was documented in Forster 1952.

What we see here is, of course, the low-trust dynamic in operation. Employees who perceive management's work structures and behaviour as manifestations of low-trust counter with responses which management does not legitimize and which it in turn, therefore, sees as low-trust behaviour. It responds in like vein with tactics and reactions of the sort just described. Characteristically they take such forms as increased limitation of employee discretion, closer supervision, greater social distance, or sharpened determination not to make to individual employees any concession beyond what is defined by the prevailing agreement. The employment relationship thus moves increasingly towards a purely contractual exchange.

To use the term contract in this context is to draw upon a connotation different from that implied when it was contrasted with status. In a status situation, the person who takes up a role finds already attached to it a set of rights and duties which he is expected to accept, while contract in this context implies a process of bargaining which establishes what those rights and duties are to be. Under the usage with which we are concerned here, contract implies a wholly economic exchange of goods or services. Quantities are specifically and rationally calculated and all expressive and diffuse sentiments, ties, and obligations are excluded from the transaction. These two meanings of contract are not necessarily associated. A man may bargain for himself a highly diffuse employment relationship, as many senior managers and professional men do; or he may take up an employment status, highly specific in its terms, which has been determined by custom, authoritative fiat, or negotiation from which he has been totally excluded in every way.

It is apparent that institutionalized low-trust dynamics draw the parties increasingly towards a narrowly contractual relationship in its economic exchange sense. A marked feature of Western industrial society is the way in which the parties to the employment relation in low-discretion situations seek to spin webs of discretion-reducing rules around each other. Trapped within the dynamics of their mutual distrust, each watches the other with wary vigilance. It is hardly a formula for flexibility of operations and quick adaptations to changing circumstances and needs. But we need look no further than the low-trust dynamic to understand the attenuation of the social bond in industry mourned by so many observers who often go on to lament the mercenary stance of the twentieth century employee.

This spiral of low trust will be halted only when power considerations prompt one party to desist out of prudent calculation, or when a change occurs in the legitimacy perceptions of either side or both. The first occurs when either management or union (or workgroup) decides that to press its low-trust responses further would, in the present circumstances, produce more difficulties than benefit. The second occurs when, as a consequence of a shift in perceptions, either side (or both) comes to see the behaviour of the other as legitimate. This likewise introduces equilibrium by halting the low-trust spiral at a particular point in the trust continuum. Either side may trigger off the sequence again given further change in power relations or in legitimacy sentiments. A shift from boom to slump conditions may prompt a unitary-minded management to return to the attack; the reverse trend may enable a union or workgroup to stiffen its own low-trust responses.

Sophisticated Modern Pattern

A change in legitimacy sentiments by which employees come to see in high-trust terms what they previously saw in low-trust terms is rare; it is less so among managements. As we have seen, it is not uncommon for management to come to perceive positive benefits in collective bargaining, as did some of the early entrepreneurs when they discovered its potential usefulness for market regulation or the maintenance of industrial peace. This possibility brings us to the Mutual Accommodation or Sophisticated Modern pattern, where both management and employees share the pluralistic ideology. In these situations management legitimizes the union role in certain areas of joint decision-making because it sees this role as conducive to its own interests as measured by stability, promotion of consent, bureaucratic regulation, effective communication, or the handling of change. In the same way that occupants of low-discretion roles who legitimize those roles do not manifest low-trust responses towards management, so a management which legitimizes trade unionism and collective bargaining will not manifest the behaviours typical of unitary-minded management under the Classical Conflict pattern. It recognizes that its discretion is being limited in certain areas of decision-making, but it legitimizes these limitations and therefore does not counter with low-trust behaviours and attitudes. 'When a company accepts the union and acts accordingly, the union leaders may have confidence that management will not try to destroy the organization or undermine the workers' loyalty to it. . . . Union leaders in healthy union-management relationships . . . do not fear arbitrary action by management, or management indifference to worker welfare, or management antagonism to collective bargaining.' The authors of these comments (Kerr, Dunlop, Myers, *et al.* 1953:

80–1) write from a pluralist perspective. They confirm important aspects of our analysis of that perspective when they add that 'Acceptance of collective bargaining involves far more than mere "recognition" of the union. In all of the cases studied, the employers saw positive advantages in bargaining with a strong and well-disciplined union, and were convinced that they should take steps, directly or indirectly to encourage workers to join and support the organization which represented them. . . . If an employer accepts the union as a potentially positive force in industrial relations, he is necessarily concerned with the problems which union leaders face in developing a responsible and well-disciplined union. Consequently he is usually convinced that some measures must be taken to build worker loyalties to the union as well as to the company' (*Ibid*: 74).

This conviction extends, by definition, only in so far as management sees the union as 'a potentially positive force'. It defines the union's acceptability as lying within lower and upper limits of militancy and aspiration towards encroachment on management prerogative. As we saw in the analysis of pluralism, for management and union (or workgroup) to share the pluralist ideology requires more than agreement about joint decision-making as such. It requires also that neither side enforces claims or imposes policies which are found excessively burdensome by its counterpart. When this happens mutual accommodation has broken down and one side has coerced the other.

It follows from this analysis that management will be the readier to accept pluralistic forms of decision-making the greater its confidence that it will always be able, in the last resort, to bend employee claims towards acceptable compromises. It may even be convinced of its ability to charm them away altogether or at least much reduce them by 'rational' argument and persuasion designed to bring out the 'true' common interests. In this sense a formal acceptance of pluralistic patterns may mask unitary convictions on management's part about the nature of the enterprise. It may regard joint decision-making and a fully institutionalized handling of claims and grievances not as mechanisms for compromising genuine conflicts of interest but as devices which facilitate the 'working-through' of mistaken conceptions, psychological blockages, and organizational confusions by a process of 'rational 'clarification. An example of this variety of the Sophisticated Modern pattern can be found in the well-documented Glacier Metal Company. A study of its philosophy and organization by the chairman, Wilfred (now Lord) Brown, describes representative and legislative systems which appear fully to acknowledge a pluralistic perspective on the enterprise. Yet this is contradicted by lamentations over 'the split at the bottom of the executive system' which reveal the conventional unitary bafflement at the fact that manual workers seem to 'dissociate themselves psychologically from their daily work, and to become identified with goals which are not centred on work . . .' (Brown 1965: 292–3). These behaviours are discussed not in terms of the pluralist's 'structural conflict' but in terms which attribute 'a big part in the general problem' of industry here to 'lack of insight into organization, manning, selection and equitable methods of deciding the level of pay . . .' (*Ibid*: 293). The implication is that clarification of roles and organization methods can by themselves secure the integration of low-discretion groups into the same unified structure as that constituted by the managers, specialists, and other white-collar staffs.* This is only a marginally more sophisticated version of the unitary human relations approach which has at its core the assumption that cooperative harmony based on common interests can always be constructed on the present division of labour given the right leadership, psychological insight, and organizational methods. Understandably, one union officer involved in Glacier affairs has observed, despite its reputation for an advanced and progressive handling of industrial relations, that 'Mr. Brown's theorising overlooks the role of the Trade Union. In the pure theory of his thinking there is no need for trade union organization in his factories. . . . The theory behind the company's ideas reminds me somewhat of the theory of management-trade union relations in Communist countries; i.e. we are all working together for the common good and thus there can be no differences between us . . .' (Kelly 1968: 126–7). The Glacier case could therefore have been offered as an example of a fundamentally unitary approach. It has been noted here in a different context simply to demonstrate that unitary convictions can appear in different guises

* Brown concedes that the representative system has 'very important functions from the point of view of those who elect representatives: "Unity in Strength"; protection of interests, and so on'. But he makes this concession in a brief footnote (*Ibid*: 227) and gives it no further attention.

and that pluralistic forms carry no guarantee of pluralistic attitudes.

Even in situations where management's acceptance of pluralistic forms rests not only upon (a) the belief that the institutionalized handling of grievances can serve management's purposes but also upon (b) the belief that these grievances derive from genuine (perceived) conflicts of interest and not simply from organizational or communicational confusions, historical hangovers, or psychological blockages, its legitimation of the union presence is limited by the extent to which that presence appears useful. Should management come to see the union as 'a negative force' – in consequence of it becoming 'irresponsibly' militant or going beyond the role cast for it by encroaching on prerogative deemed to be sacred – management's whole perspective changes. The union is now seen as promoting instability, undermining the basis of negotiated consent, making regulation more difficult, distorting communications, impeding change. Management sees its discretionary powers as suffering attack on a scale and of a nature which it cannot legitimize, and therefore counters with low-trust policies, behaviours, and attitudes. The pattern of relations reverts to that of Classical Conflict. Conversely, it may be management policy towards its employees or the union which initiates disequilibrium. Attempts to reduce the union role in decision-making may obviously trigger off the low-trust dynamic, but so also may moves to reduce the discretion exercised by union members in their work. Unless compromised and legitimized within the limits of mutual accommodation, such policies will be seen as a reversion to unitary-type assertion and reciprocated accordingly with low-trust responses.

The history of industrial relations in Britain's mass production footwear industry exemplifies this sequence. At first strongly resistant to trade unionism, many employers in this highly competitive trade came to see its possible usefulness for market regulation and industrial peace. A honeymoon period in the 1880s culminated in a panegyric from the editor of the foremost employers' trade journal in 1889. 'Never in the history of the trade has [trade unionism] been so powerful, and never, on the whole has it exerted so much influence for good. . . . It is to the advantage of all concerned that chaos should be reduced to order, and that, as far as possible, uniformity of wage and practice should be attained. . . . Every manufacturer today feels that he has an interest in the settlement of the wages paid by his competitors, and although the workmen were the first to point this out, yet now that the principle has been acceded, employers are eager to carry it to its logical conclusion whenever a dispute arises. . . . The irritation which formerly existed between unionists and employers is rapidly dying out . . . ' (Fox 1958: 129).

But the employers were soon feeling constrained by market pressures both at home and abroad to seek cost reductions through technical and organizational change. These had the effect of simplifying substantial portions of the work and reducing its discretionary content. Earnings and job security for some established workers became threatened. They responded to this heightened division of labour by using the employer-fostered strength of their union to resist the changes. By 1891 the same employers' spokesman was describing the union as 'becoming dangerously strong' and satirizing the insolence of the workers in going beyond their station and challenging the prerogatives of the employers. Conflict on this issue reached a peak in 1895, when the federated employers imposed a six-weeks lockout which effectively destroyed the union's wider aspirations and confined it to a modest role in the regulation of terms and conditions of employment and the processing of individual grievances (*Ibid*: 142, and Chapter 22).

In examining the pluralistic Mutual Accommodation or Sophisticated Modern pattern, therefore, it is important to recall that for the union to respect the institutional and survival needs of management it must be confident of receiving the same respect for its own (and those of its members). Different managements in their different situations define their needs differently, but at the minimal level the union which participates in this pattern legitimizes the management role and its objectives in seeking to run the enterprise efficiently by economic criteria. But the very fact that labour is treated as a commodity and an instrumental resource in this whole process means that labour's legitimation of management's role can never, in the absence of ideological control unusual in the West, be more than provisional and conditional. For management may, at any time, come under pressures from rivals, customers, or profit-receivers, or from its own quest for power, status, or financial success, which prompt it to assert discretionary power over employees for the pursuit of ends which they do not share. In a context so fluid, so dynamic, and so subject to change as modern industrial society, no management can guarantee to maintain indefinitely a posture of treating employee interests as a major priority, though good luck may enable it to project a plausible case for periods at a time. No more, conversely, can employees and their unions, in a society marked by competitive striving and rising aspirations, guarantee that their claims on management will be contained within the limits reciprocally defined as mutual accommodation.

The Sophisticated Modern pattern tends, therefore, to be highly unstable. It represents an equilibrium situation, and in a constantly changing world any equilibrium is uncertain and precarious. We have noted how, in the extreme case of major crisis, this pattern may revert to Classical Conflict. The more common condition, however, is for the Sophisticated Modern pattern to slide off into the Standard Modern pattern. This is possibly the largest single category, for many organizations move into it direct from either the Traditional or the Classical Conflict forms.

Standard Modern Pattern

The Standard Modern pattern, in one of its versions, is characterized by ambivalence within management towards the pluralist ideology (for an example see Hawkins 1972: 117–21). The ambivalence takes either or both of two forms. First, some members of management may be convinced unitarians while others are convinced pluralists. Second, individual managers themselves may be ambivalent in the sense of fluctuating between the two according to circumstances or even mood. A common phenomenon in industrial history has been the employer who, at times of high labour bargaining strength or a fashionable mood of sympathy towards the less favoured, manifests signs of a shift to a pluralistic strategy, but who reverts to unitary attitudes and behaviour when a slack labour market returns or when the fashionable mood passes.

Certain behavioural characteristics of the Standard Modern pattern can be tentatively hypothesized. First, at times of emergency and crisis the likelihood is that unitary attitudes and policies will predominate within the management system. This is not to suggest that attempts will necessarily be made to overthrow trade unionism and collective bargaining, though this may happen. It is rather that management's freedom of manoeuvre and ability to accommodate the union are contracting, and that it feels more tightly constrained to 'insist' upon its policies and proposals being accepted. Those within the management system who speak the language of 'no-nonsense' attitudes, 'standing firm', and 'sticking to principles' are likely to emerge as the most persuasive, and it is but a short step to an assertion of management's 'right to do what is necessary'. Second, in the many situations short of this extreme which nevertheless require behavioural adaptation by one or more participating parties, many confusions and uncertainties may be caused by a management mixture of unitary and pluralistic perspectives. The presence of the former confounds the expectations of those who practise the latter, and *vice versa*. This is relevant at every level from the bottom to the top of the management structure. A foreman who practises an autocratic style based on unitary convictions may prejudice the operation of a grievance procedure which embodies pluralist principles. A departmental manager bent on a reorganization scheme may drag his reluctant senior colleagues willy-nilly into a bitter dispute with shop stewards as a consequence of his neglect of the expected communication, consultation, and negotiation processes. A plant or divisional executive may stumble into conflict with the union hierarchy from which he has to be rescued by embarrassed seniors or, more probably, by the hapless personnel department. 'Line and staff' complications between production management with unitary convictions and personnel departments operating with pluralistic assumptions are hardly rare. Finally, boards of directors may have their 'doves' and 'hawks', with either group carrying the day according to weight of personality, verbal fluency, current fashion, or the prevailing mood of colleagues.

The pattern just described might appropriately be labelled: Standard Modern (Management-Divided). Along with this division must be considered another: the Employee-Divided. Even at the rank and file level, workgroups of different occupations may divide along unitary and pluralistic lines. There may be, for example, semi-skilled women production workers, passively receptive of management prerogative, employed alongside male craftsmen on maintenance and ancillary tasks who work to a vigilant conflict stance. A top management with a unitary bias may meet sympathy from the former groups and systematic suspicion from the latter, thereby creating lateral distrust among the workgroups themselves. A pluralistic management, conversely, may receive positive responses from some groups but a mixture of disparagement and envy from others who do not themselves aspire to such treatment from top management and react sourly to seeing it offered to others. Such cross-currents are not confined to rank and file level. There may be technical, supervisory, and perhaps, in large organizations, even some middle management groups who hold unitary attitudes themselves yet feel neglected by top management and jealous of the studied care with which the representatives of lower rank groups are consulted.

Sophisticated Paternalist Pattern

The combination of a wholly or partly pluralistic management and a predominantly unitary-minded labour force may seem improbable, but is in fact capable, when undergoing change, of throwing up some of the most spectacular *causes célèbres* of industrial relations. Although infrequent they afford such puzzlement for the observer that they deserve their own category as the Sophisticated Paternalist pattern. The organization in this category has usually graduated form the Traditional Paternalist position. While the attitudes and behaviour of its employees, who tend to include many devoted long-service retainers, remain predominantly unitary in nature, the prevailing influences within top management deem it prudent to confrom to received expectations by dealing with independent organizations representing their workers. This may involve management in some active soliciting of a 'suitable' union to come in and organize the plant. Perhaps, alternatively, their employees become caught up in a popular mass fashion for union membership; enthusiasm subsides but the union remains. Either way, management finds itself with a passive and largely inert unionized labour force which throws up little or no assertive leadership of its own. Convenience appears to suggest that matters can usefully be settled with full time union officers from outside the works: an arrangement very acceptable, perhaps, to both sides. Management comes under no challenge from within the plant in its day-to-day control; the union hierarchy can play its part in regulating terms and conditions of employment without being subject to complicating pressures and cross-currents from the regulated. Interests on both sides become vested in this convenient *status quo*. It is characteristic, however, for leaders in such a position to allow the convenience of the arrangement to blunt their alertness to growing grievances. Pressure mounts but goes unheeded. Eventually a dispute of perhaps no particular significance strikes the spark which ignites the whole structure.

At this point the disposition of forces becomes highly complex. The labour force itself is likely to be divided; some will have made the leap to a low-trust conflict stance and be demanding the active pursuit of measures to pin management down to more specific protections or guarantees on disputed issues; others will blame not the paternalist top management but unworthy lieutenants who should be taught the wisdom and humanity of the old ways so that all may return to the give and take diffuseness of the *ancien régime*. Management itself may well be divided; some arguing that a new pluralist order that includes the workgroups as active participants must now be forged, others hoping that firmness can restore the convenient accommodative relationship with the union hierarchy. If the union joins hands with this faction in an attempt to reimpose the old order then confusion is complete. An approximation to this pattern can be found in the interpretation by Lane and Roberts (1971) of the 1970 strike at Pilkingtons.

Continuous Challenge Pattern

The final pattern selected for delineation here is the Continuous Challenge or Non-Accommodative pattern. This resembles the Classical Conflict situation but with the positions reversed. There we saw management refusing to legitimize the employees' claim to define for themselves, and actively pursue, interests and purposes divergent from those of management. No pattern of mutual accommodation could therefore develop. Management power might continue to hold the employees in subjection, in which case they would manifest low-trust responses in some form or another, even if only through covert non-cooperativeness. If employees were able to make management's stance costly enough they would secure certain changes in the formal institutions of decision-making on some issues, but would continue to meet distrust and the consequent hostility and antagonism from the management side.

Reversal of these positions conveys the nature of the Continuous Challenge pattern. Here we find the workgroup refusing to legitimize management's claim to assert and pursue objectives which are seen as overriding certain interests, practices, or values of the group. The group may, of course, be forced to submit but it continues to withhold legitimacy; fighting guerrilla skirmishes wherever possible, seeking always to undermine management's position and aspiring to mobilize enough power for an effective challenge. Thus, again, no systematic and stable pattern of mutual accommodation can emerge, for the will towards mutual survival is not present. As in the Classical Conflict pattern, perpetual mutual distrust prevails. No equilibrium relationship develops; only periods of uneasy armed truce as each side licks its wounds and watches the enemy for signs of a weak spot in its defences.*

These very images of war suggest that we are in the presence of the radical perspective, with its perceptions of the management role as the coercive assertion of power over men who are used as a commodity resource for purposes in whose design they have had no share. If they are to oppose this exploitation they must not only combine but must direct their collective power towards a continuous hostile vigilance and indeed active aggression. Expediency may require periods with no active hostilities, but stabilized mutual accommodation is seen as dangerous, not only because it betrays the ideology but also because to give formalized recognition to basic management interests might on some future occasion prejudice defence of crucial work rules, practices, or values.

This repudiation of the legitimacy of the managerial role can, however, stem from either of two sharply contrasting orientations which may be called the universalistic and the particularistic. Under the universalistic orientation, the challenge to existing forms of managerial control is part of a social philosophy which rejects the economic and social system as a whole; which inspires action on behalf of all employees as victims of oppressive hierarchical power; and which invokes the language of universal equality, fellowship

* For one of several documented examples in recent years, see Cameron 1957. Here the company's case was that it faced 'one of the most highly organized shop steward movements in the country, a powerful and financially strong group whose objective was destructive conflict and whose persistent activities made impossible the normal give and take of factory life' (Cameron 1957: para. 38). This report of a government-appointed court of inquiry provides a good example of the Continuous Challenge type of situation as seen from a pluralist frame of reference.

and brotherhood. Under the particularistic orientation, the challenge to managerial control derives from the self-regarding impulses of a specific group only. There is no concern among its members with the interests of other groups; indeed the strategy may be one of squeezing privileges out of the system in ways which depend upon other groups being excluded from certain jobs by means of a vigilance as hostile as that directed against the employers. Use is made of universalistic appeals for justice and equality but these cease as soon as the group's own interests are assured.

The convergence by these two orientations upon the strategy and tactics of workgroup self-determination has created some bizarre alliances. One such developed in Britain during the First World War between militant left-wing shop stewards in the munitions industries and skilled craftsmen who saw their workshop power and privileges threatened by wartime 'dilution' – the breakdown of skilled jobs into simpler low-discretion tasks performed by semi-skilled workers (Pribićević 1959). The former sought the emancipation of all workers by revolutionary action; the latter were motivated by a particularistic anxiety about their own status and rewards in the factories and shipyards where they worked. Both groups gained by making common cause against managerial and government authority under the banner of 'Workers Control'. The craftsmen gained by securing the services of a fierce and committed leadership; the militants by securing popular support which they could harness for their revolutionary campaign. The same convergence can sometimes be seen today. One of its minor manifestations on the plane of ideas is the intense interest shown by some socialists in the exclusive, highly particularistic forms of workshop craft control developed by nineteenth century groups of labour aristocrats whose social philosophy was as far removed from universal brotherhood as was that of the entrepreneurs for whom they toiled.

When disputes develop with groups which have a radical orientation, management may find in extreme cases that a pluralistic stance is a disadvantage to them. A workgroup which concedes no legitimacy to management's interests and purposes will press a bargaining advantage just as far as management is prepared to yield ground. A management working to the doctrine of mutual accommodation will expect any concessions it offers to be met halfway, but instead it finds that concessions merely prompt the group to raise the stakes of the contest by enlarging its claims. Managements in this position may therefore feel constrained to move towards a unitary stance and provoke a total confrontation.

We conclude this sketch of management-employee relations with one last observation. It is apparent from the description of the various patterns that they are in no way to be regarded as fixed states which necessarily persist for long periods of time, neither is there a sequence of linear progress through which management-employee relations move towards a state of stabilized 'maturity'. The equilibrium condition designated as the Sophisticated Modern or Mutual Accommodation model was expressly characterized, in fact, as unstable, for in a highly volatile society characterized by rapid change any mutually acceptable pattern of aspirations, legitimations, and power relations as between management and employees is likely to be precarious. Shifting economic and social pressures induce both sides to enlarge the claims they make on each other, adjust their perceptions of each other, and modify the power they bring to bear upon each other. As we noted earlier, however, neither employers and managements as a whole nor employees and unions as a whole have, historically speaking, undergone these shifting pressures and changes in synchronization. As some companies and enterprises – even industries – have moved at one stage or another during the past century, from, say, the Traditional to the Classical Conflict and then to the Standard Modern, or even to the Sophisticated Modern pattern, others have experienced, perhaps, a Sophisticated Modern phase and then moved to Classical Conflict. The overall picture suggested here then, is one of varied possibilities and mixed patterns rather than of a logically unfolding trend towards a common variety as suggested by, for example, Kerr *et al.*, 1962, or Lester 1958. All that can be said with confidence is that the days of the Traditional and the Sophisticated Paternalist patterns are numbered. None of this precludes us, however, from trying to identify what seem noteworthy current developments, and from demonstrating their significance by suggesting the likely consequences should they become widespread. The next chapter will therefore move towards a discussion of possibilities along these lines.

8 · Present and Future Problems of Low-Trust Society

Contradictions within Western Industrial Society

The purpose of this chapter is to argue that the forgoing trust analysis can be used both to illuminate what are currently seen as major social and economic problems of advanced industrial societies and to predict future possibilities if present forces continue to operate unchanged. This purpose requires a brief recapitulation of certain relevant threads of the argument.

Its starting point was that the increasing division of labour imposed by owners and controllers of resources has created large numbers of low-discretion work roles and relations. Efforts by employers, managers, and their sympathizers to induce the occupants of these roles to perceive their situation in high-trust terms enjoy diminishing success. Ideological exhortation seeks to persuade the rank and file participant to 'trust the company'; to see those in positions of authority and important decision-making as simply making their own necessary functional contribution to the common cause of producing goods or services for society; and to offer the ungrudging involvement, responsibility and acceptance of managerial 'leadership' which such a picture of economic organization might seem to imply. In earlier times the ideology was more likely to appeal to the sanctity of master-servant and property relations; where this failed power was usually available in sufficient quantity to support the employer's purposes. But the contradictions latent within the system have been increasingly manifest. Against the combination of, on the one hand, pyramidal hierarchies incorporating great inequalities of decision-making about rewards, status, and function and, on the other, social values which stress the competitive pursuit of rising material standards and individual self-development, the managerial ideology of common purpose and high-trust relations struggles increasingly in vain so far as low-discretion rank and file members are concerned. More and more they have tended to see management's structural organization and conduct of the work process as embodying a distinction between those who are, and those who are not, trusted, and to see themselves as among the latter. Low-trust reciprocation has followed. The mobilization of rank and file power which is its organized expression has proved one of the factors inclining some employers away from master-servant ideology and towards the more manipulative attempts to secure legitimation. In the event, however, legitimation has been offered by the rank and file not in response to these Human Relations leadership bids, but in return for a system of collective bargaining which, while preserving the basic economic and social framework intact, permits compromise on a number of limited issues and aspirations.

The preceding century has seen these contradictions being worked out, both through the organized bargaining process and through unorganized individual response. Men in low-trust situations have, as individuals, reciprocated with minimum commitment, grudging calculation, and a measured contribution – thereby reinforcing management's preference for low-trust strategies. Collectively they have mobilized what power they could muster and, within the limits which they have felt constrained, or been ideologically induced, to accept, have sought, with widely varying degrees of success, to spin webs of restrictive rules binding the actions and policies of management. By the very fact of being forced to mobilize and exercise power overtly to influence management's decision-making they have brought out clearly the low-trust nature of management's governance over them. For in high-trust relations the parties resolve their disagreements not by overt power tactics but by a process of problem solving or 'working through' made possible by a joint assumption of shared goals and values. The fact that the occupants of low-discretion roles have not found this possible demonstrated that goals and values are not seen as shared, and that the consequent low-trust relations have prompted subordinates to pursue their purposes through the exercise or threat of power. Managements have tended, nevertheless, to exhort such groups to join with them in conducting disagreements on a problem solving basis, i.e. by trusting management in the sense of assuming its facts, interpretations, and communication techniques to be open, unscreened, and in no way shaped by ulterior motives which it conceals because the employees are not expected to share them. This is another expression of a managerial tendency noted already: to try to induce occupants of perceived low-trust situations to extend high-trust behaviour towards management. The effort is understandable but there is no cause for surprise that it usually fails.

Given this failure, then, power manoeuvres become the preferred tactics of the employee groups concerned. Threats are often sufficient, but sometimes not. Strikes, overtime bans, working to rule, going slow; these are the continuations of bargaining by other means which mark pressure-group activity born of low-trust work relations. The fact that it is usually the employees' collective which first makes visible such power as it has been able to mobilize results in the consequent struggle being conventionally seen in terms of employees initiating this power contest to the detriment of the 'public's' interest in orderly production. In reality, of course, employees only feel the need to challenge management-determined work structures and policies through power because management asserts them through power. In the absence of a challenge, management's use of power is covert and goes unremarked. When a challenge *is* made it creates the appearance to the conventional eye of management 'defending' its position against 'attack' – hence the ideological semantics whereby employees always 'demand' and managements always 'offer'. The nature of the power relationship makes rather more convincing a view of management as attacking and employees as defending; to see management as 'demanding' that employees work under such-and-such conditions of employment and employees as 'offering' their services on somewhat better terms.

Given, then, that productive hierarchies have, from their own nature as designed by resource-controllers, and from the nature of the society and culture within which they operate, generated counter forces, counter ideologies, and counter values, the question arises as to the net effect of these low-trust responses upon the economic purposes of power-holders. Some, including employers and managers themselves, have stressed the limitations they impose on economic efficiency, flexibility, and capacity for adaptation; others (including the Webbs) have argued that the union challenge forces management into adaptative innovations from which even rank and file benefit. There is, however, another major aspect – the social stability of the productive system in question. Hitherto the low-trust consequences of the social organization of work in Western society have, in most countries, for most of the time, not been so acute as to throw that stability seriously into question. With what degree of confidence can we predict that this will remain so in the future? Evaluations of this sort are more than self-indulgent crystal-gazing. How we extrapolate existing trends helps to determine whether we contemplate the future complacently or feel a need to try to change those trends and in what direction. Despite the inevitable looseness and imprecision of our present methods there is no escaping the compulsion to make the evaluative effort, however limited the nature of our tools.

Conditions of Stability

The emergence of collective action among wage and salary earners to influence managerial decision-making about rewards and other aspects of the work situation is, of course, only one expression of the pressure group activity which is so conspicuous a feature of Western society. All such activity is low-trust behaviour in that it represents an institutionalized withholding of trust from those making certain decisions. The forces sketched out in Chapter 4 which have fostered a pervasive infiltration into every aspect of life of economic exchange, impersonal markets, contract, commercialization, and the separation of economics and ethics have, *ipso facto*, fostered the proliferation of low-trust relations, and pressure groups of many varied kinds constitute one category of them. The negative nature of low-trust relations is familiar enough. We experience them in many different forms – suspicion; jealousy; the misreading of men's motives which, when acted upon, becomes a self-fulfilling prophecy; the inhibitions to co-operation; the blockages created in the handling of differences and disagreements; the blight on fellowship and compassion; the withering of community. These are frequently remarked on when they emerge, as they often do in widely varying degree, at the level of the organization. We must note, too, the way in which low-trust behaviour by one subordinate group within the organization tends to evoke or reinforce low-trust behaviour by other subordinate groups fearful that if they trust the decision-makers they will not receive their due. This is a characteristic of trust relations which becomes specially relevant to the next phase of the argument. Our analysis has already shown that, in low-trust situations, actions and policies on the part of either side from which the other side dissents are handled not by problem solving procedures but by win-lose bargaining with its accompanying gamesmanship, manoeuvre and bluff. Moreover, once the low-trust framework exists it tends to shape the perceptions of both sides so as to maintain or enlarge rather than minimize the area of conflict. The characteristic which, while always implicit in the analysis, has not yet been made explicit is that distrust can become a galloping contagion. Low-trust behaviour by our fellows, designed to secure their interests in a situation where they feel unable to trust the decision-makers, is apt to convince us that we too must follow suit, if we can, lest our own deserts be pre-empted. Thus develop, in quickening tempo, the institutionalized forms through which individuals and groups pursue their competitive striving for limited resources and status.

This same analysis can also be directed to the level of the wider society. Organized groups and collectives, fighting for their own hand in a world which they perceive in terms of low-trust relations, communicate their distrust to others whose perceptions take on, in self-defence, the same characteristics. Thus does distrust not merely perpetuate itself but generate a creeping extension of itself. And given that low-trust relations display characteristics which are, in some degree or other, prejudicial to the social bond, the question can be asked: what is the condition on which low-trust modes of structuring human collaboration can continue to maintain social arrangements, both at organizational and societal level, which men find sufficiently stable to be tolerable? Obviously this question can only be answered here in the most general and abstract terms, but these need not be wholly vacuous in their implication. For the fact is plain enough that low-trust pressures upon managerial and administrative decision-makers by individuals and groups could become so numerous and severe as to cripple or even destroy ordered collaboration. Both organizations and societies can be so rent by responses, pressures, and conflicts generated or aggravated by low-trust relations that the minimum degree of consent and legitimation necessary for the desired level of collaboration on the existing basis is not forthcoming. The essential implication is therefore that organizational and societal stability depends upon there being limits to the incidence of low-trust relations.

What, then, are the social forces which set limits to low-trust behaviours? These have already emerged from the analysis in the form of power and legitimation. Power in sufficient quantity can prevent the manifestation of most forms of low-trust *behaviour* (though not, of course, the arousal of low-trust *sentiments* – which indeed its use normally aggravates). Legitimation of the prevailing social arrangements can lead the occupants of the humblest low-discretion roles to extend high-trust responses towards superiors. We have noted the part played by the former in promoting the latter, and that an enhancement of the power of a group can so heighten or change its aspiration that it ceases to legitimize prevailing arrangements. These considerations would lead us to expect, in a world of flux, both short and long term disturbances to social stability as a consequence of changes in power relations and in aspirations, values and other forces relevant to legitimation.

It is long term forces which are of particular interest here. Is it plausible to identify any such which may come to present a threat to the stability of Western industrial societies? To explore this question we may begin by setting up a simple model which can serve as a reference point by incorporating the minimum conditions of stability in a pressure-group society. We will assume a concentration of power in the upper reaches so extreme as to leave the lower strata largely incapable, except perhaps for a few small privileged groups, of all but brief gestures of discontent or revolt which leave structural conditions untouched even by marginal change. For most of the time this concentration of power induces a pragmatic acceptance by those subject to it and facilitates the propagation of legitimizing ideologies supportive of the privileges of power-holders. Under these condition the values and dynamics of pressure-group society present no destabilizing threat, for two reasons. First, the relevant behaviours are confined to a relatively small number of groups. Second, these groups are sufficiently conscious of being privileged to feel a commitment to the existing social framework which they therefore would not wish to put at risk through excessively disruptive methods even were they able to do so. The central features of our model thus relate to two dimensions of institutionalized low-trust behaviour which can be described in terms of *extensiveness* – the incidence of such behaviour – and *intensiveness* – the severity of the behaviour as measured by its disruptive impact upon economic operations. Given a low score along both these dimensions a society can easily contain the dislocations produced by allowing 'freedom' within a complex, low-trust economic structure. The economic price paid for these dislocations caused by shifts in power relations and legitimations within a system of divergent goals is felt to be small.

Let us now, however, postulate change along both these dimensions. First, pressure-group behaviour becomes increasingly extensive and gives signs of becoming universalized as it spreads down through the social hierarchy. Many forces contribute to this trend. Various factors combine, for example, to quicken aspirations among the lower strata. Technical revolutions affecting communications and physical mobility help to liberate men from traditional expectations concerning their life destinies and those of their children. Relevant values in the mainstream culture such as equality and individual development percolate down. Awareness that some modicum of power lies to hand through collective action awakens men's minds to new possibilities. Under these influences more and more employee groups and collectives cease to legitimize the existing pattern of decision-making to which they are subject; perceive it as a low-trust system which uses them for purposes they do not share; and counter with low-trust responses which take a variety of forms. The low-trust dynamic proceeds through mutual reinforcement, and spreads to other groups as they perceive the need for self-defence.

Second, low-trust behaviour becomes increasingly intensive also in terms of the severity and significance of the accompanying power manoeuvres. Here we are concerned not with the duration of dislocations but with the methods used to enforce, support, and extend them. We shall postulate that, whereas under the earlier standard model the groups engaging in power struggles observe certain Queensberry rules of self-restraint, the methods now coming to be used increasingly display a disregard for them. We will suppose this disregard to be the outcome of three related factors: the urgency of rising aspirations (themselves the result of certain 'official' values gaining currency among lower social strata); declining legitimation of existing procedures which are seen as favouring management's interests rather than those of employees; and increasing consciousness (fostered by the communications revolution) that many highly privileged groups secure their interests by methods which are fully self-seeking but which are officially legitimized through such accepted institutions and principles as impersonal competitive markets, the profit motive, 'labour as commodity', 'professional self-determination', or economic rationality. This combination of perceptions in a highly unequal society produces disrespect for those rules and precepts urged upon the less-favoured groups admonishing them to honour 'properly-negotiated' procedures, behave responsibly, practise self-restraint in the national interest, and confine their power tactics within bounds which inevitably limit their effectiveness. Such admonitions come to seem no more than manipulative ideological devices designed to contain rank and file pressures which might otherwise threaten the stability of privilege. Among the rank and file there are a few who universalize and conceptualize these perceptions into a systematic principled rejection of the existing social structure and its values, but the majority take a particularistic view in focusing only upon their own deprivations and demanding only changes in the immediate situation which will improve their own position within it. Nevertheless they are prepared to accept the tactical leadership of the ideologically motivated few, and this ensures that Queensberry restraints on methods come under a sceptical eye.

This picture of a competitive low-trust society need not imply that the less favoured groups taken together can succeed in improving their relative position by means of such struggles except for short periods while others are catching up.* To ensure that the process keeps going we need assume only that some groups in society are seeking to improve their position and that the others have to fight hard in order to stay in the same relative place. This accords with Macpherson's interpretation of Hobbesian society. The possessive market model 'permits individuals who want more delights than they have, to seek to convert the natural powers of other men to their use. They do so through the market, in which everyone is necessarily involved. Since the market is continually competitive, those who would be content with the level of satisfactions they have are compelled to fresh exertions by every attempt of the others to increase theirs. Those

* The view taken by many labour economists has been that any trade union aim of securing a larger share for pay at the expense of profits is, for the most part, 'merely delusive', though unions may be able to 'raise the incomes of particular groups of workers at the expense of all the rest' . . . (Phelps Brown 1962: 184–93). Glyn and Sutcliffe, however, argue that profits can be, and in recent years have been, squeezed by industrial action (1972).

who would be content with the level they have cannot keep it without seeking more power, that is, without seeking to transfer more powers of others to themselves, to compensate for the increasing amount that the competitive efforts of others are transferring from them' (1964: 58–9). Thus no assumption of universal greed is required, though to be sure rising aspirations are likely to quicken the tempo. As the tempo quickens, all those groups capable of mobilizing enough power to handle their own destinies becoming increasingly loth to repose trust in the hands of others. Within trade union hierarchies, shopfloor groups pull down decision-making about aims and methods. Intensified appeals for restraint are ignored, for no group trusts the others to heed them and thus none dares to heed them itself.

Although the competitive and defensive struggle is for real income, it has necessarily to be pursued through the medium of money, What suffers, therefore, is the value of the currency. In other words, the ultimate condition of the division of labour in advanced Western industrial states has come to be, not Durkheim's high-trust 'organic solidarity', but inflation, the supreme symbolic expression of low-trust society. By having to fight to defend what they already have in a society where they trust no institution or mechanism to do this for them, men force others to do likewise and thus the process reinforces itself. The galloping contagion of distrust is well represented in the concept of galloping inflation. Since total distrust (never reached in practice) would mean total fragmentation of all organized relations among men, any movement in this direction brings the government into the struggle to stabilize the position.

Instability and Inflation – the British Situation

Britain's experience can serve as the exemplar. During the Second World War 'the government wanted to avoid the rapid increases in prices and wages which had caused so much discontent on the home front' during the First (Clegg 1971: 1). The measures it took constituted the first and perhaps 'the most successful of all the attempts at an incomes policy in Britain. . . '. What accounted for the success? The measures themselves, which sought to peg the price level through subsidies, combined sense and guile. But also important was the high-trust temper created by the common purpose of winning the war and by visible signs of a 'sharp shift towards economic equality'. This gave effectiveness to governmental appeals for restraint. 'Success owed something to ingenuity and more to the concern of the British and American people to win the war' (*Ibid*: 1). It was the outcome, in other words, partly of (specific) economic exchange, whereby the government undertook to peg the cost of living in return for union restraint on wage claims, and partly of (diffuse) social exchange, whereby the unions reposed trust in a government which they were convinced had, as its first priority, goals which they shared.

The end of the war brought no end to governmental emphasis on the need for restraint, but it removed some of the 'spiritual and material supports of stabilization' (*Ibid*: 2). Prices were allowed to rise again and the Labour government leaned heavily on appeals that were almost totally diffuse in nature. They promised only that unspecific benefits ('recovery', 'stability', 'prosperity') would follow from union restraint. The rising cost of living was evidence that the economic-exchange element in the deal was going by default. Yet the diffuse high-trust response persisted for a time on one level. In a carryover of wartime unity into the emergency conditions of postwar rehabilitation, the unions and employers' associations responded with an effort at restraint. But at the workplace level, national unity was already dissolving into the competitive strivings and jealousies of low-trust market society. Employers became engaged in competitive bidding for labour, and employee workgroups seized their chances. Those without chances or complaisant employers grew increasingly envious of the others. In the absence of a shared purpose, diffuse verbal appeals could do little to stem these growing sources of instability. Soon the policy was tottering towards collapse.

By the time Conservative governments introduced the first of their three attempts at a stabilization policy all remnants of the war-induced mood of social unity had vanished. This meant that no basis for the success of diffuse appeals now existed at any level and the government offered no new one. Yet it reiterated such appeals while at the same time urging employers to resist union claims and adopting such policies itself in the public sector. This approach bore strong similarities to the unitary philosophy examined in Chapter 6, which combines appeals to a presumed common interest, often in practice lacking, with reliance on a coercive use of power when the appeals fail.

The return of a Labour government in 1964 brought a modified approach. Diffuse appeals continued. But there were dawnings of a recognition that, to a minimal degree at least, specific commitments might have to be made if the parties were to be rendered capable of playing their part. In effect, these were adumbrations of a pluralistic stance which sees the solution in terms of a negotiated deal between the interested parties, viewed as responsible and equal representative agencies acting on behalf of the major sections of society. Implicit here is the idea that, in the absence of any possibility of a high-trust deal, where the parties exchange diffuse promises and trust each other to discharge them in ways which give mutual satisfaction, the way forward lies through a low-trust deal, where the parties exchange specific commitments and guarantee each other highly prescribed courses of action which allay the fears, jealousies, and suspicions endemic to low-trust market society. Such an approach, while possibly continuing to be decked in the trappings of diffuse appeals to 'the national interest', relies principally on low-trust assurances that others will not be allowed to exploit the restraint of those who cooperate.

To be sure the extent to which the new approach embodied these notions was minimal indeed. The *Declaration of Intent* agreed by government, the Trades Union Congress, and the Confederation of British Industry in 1965 was a statement of general principles, not a set of specific negotiated commitments. But 'incomes policy' was at least recognized as being bound up with economic growth, prices, and profits. The behaviour asked of employers and employees with respect to wages and salaries was related to government expectations about growth and prices. 'There was some discussion of government controls over other incomes, and it was suggested that effective price control could deal with excess profits' (Clegg 1971: 11). The deal was at a very low level of specificity, but there was nevertheless some adumbration of mutual obligations. It has been seen as containing some of the elements of 'a fair bargain. The only snag was that the government did nothing, or next to nothing, to provide conditions in which the bargain could be fulfilled' (*Ibid*: 17). When a stage was reached at which, with prices rising, the government sought, in effect, to discriminate between groups which must accept a cut in their living standards and groups which were to be allowed to maintain and even raise them, there followed a mass refusal to trust government discretion on these decisions. Symptoms of distrust multiplied, such as rumours of political chicanery said to be influencing the government in giving its blessing to certain claims. 'More and more managers, trade union officials and workers believed that the policy was being applied to them while everyone else was getting away with unjustifiable pay increases' (*Ibid*: 53). In the rush that followed, the boundaries of the policy were trampled down and destroyed.

The logic of the argument might appear to suggest, then, that the concept of a low-trust deal be pressed home to its full rigorous conclusion. Government, unions, and employers' associations must commit themselves to an interrelated set of highly prescribed courses of action which guarantee each party full safety in binding itself and thereby enable it to offer the conditions required for the commitment of the other two. At the time of writing, however, it is not clear that such commitments can honestly be offered by governments and representative agencies in Western countries. For example 'the promise of stable prices enforced by price controls is highly dangerous. Governments should not pretend that they can maintain stable prices when they cannot fulfil their promises.' Similarly, employers' associations 'cannot give the policy-makers control over earnings, for they themselves have not got it to give' (*Ibid*: 45, 48–9). Trade unions, likewise, cannot dictate what decisions and agreements shop stewards and members make at their place of work. Given the existing structures of Western society, therefore, any move towards a totally low-trust stabilization policy could prove to be a move into a blind alley in that the parties cannot fulfil the basic requirement – the ability to deliver their assigned contribution to the pact. The type of low-trust regulation that is at least within reach at company and plant level, where management and workgroup leaders can realistically hope, given the will, to cultivate the observance of highly specific sets of rules, would not be a practicable proposition if attempts were made to apply it from a remote level and over a wide area.

For a more fundamental critique of the low-trust deal we must confront the pluralist perspective on which it is based with the radical analysis. The low-trust deal sees capital and labour as balanced powers between whom some approximation to 'equality of sacrifice' is being negotiated, with the government playing its necessary part.

The fact that powers are not balanced is bound, however, to disrupt the 'bargain'. The problems of making price control effective are notorious, and profits control must inevitably be frustrated sooner rather than later not only by practical difficulties but also by profit's role as motivator and fund for investment and competitive growth. The deal must founder on the facts of the productive system even if unions accept that there is equality of sacrifice. Radical perceptions on their part would ensure, of course, that no such deal was made in the first place.

Given that Western industrial society cannot solve its endemic problem of inflation either by a totally high-trust or by a totally low-trust policy, what remains? Logically enough, the leading specialist in the subject (Clegg 1971) urges an approach which, as it will be argued here, combines in effect the basic elements of the wartime policy which he considers to have been perhaps the most successful so far. It was suggested earlier that this combined a high-trust element and a low-trust element: a shared moral purpose supported by measures which went some way to allay men's suspicions that predators and chancers would be allowed to exploit the field. Clegg now proposes a tripartite administration of an agreed policy which, *inter alia*, would move towards a more equal distribution of incomes. Such a purpose could command, he believes, considerable support among trade unionists and other sections of society. 'The only effective discipline in a democratic trade union movement is self-discipline, and the source of discipline lies in a cause, a principle, or a belief. . . .' There are 'good reasons for believing that a moral purpose deeply and generally shared within the movement can overcome its structural weaknesses'. Such a purpose 'might be inspired by a programme of collective action to face and conquer our mounting economic and social problems; and such a programme would have to include an incomes policy' (1971: 82, 88). This high-trust involvement would, to use the terms of the present analysis, need to be fortified by low-trust assurances. 'The government should take powers to control prices . . . where there are reasonable grounds to believe that the public is being exploited', though this would make sense only in the exceptional cases of gross abuse.

Inflation, Organizational Stability, and the Low-Trust Dynamic

Before we can appraise this or any other stabilization policy we have to form an opinion as to the essential nature of 'our mounting economic and social problems' – or such of them as are relevant to the present analysis. To help us it will be useful to take up again the model presented in the earlier part of this chapter and try to estimate how far the changes postulated as overtaking it can be identified as being actually at work today in, for example, Britain (and other Western countries). In the process of applying the model we shall find implications emerging which are relevant, not only to the issue of inflation, but also to the stability and viability of the work organization itself in pursuing the objectives defined for it by power-holders. The cautions necessary when seeking to identify present trends and extrapolate them into the future are well known. Tendencies visible now may not be those which shape the future; they may prove to be temporary or overshadowed by others which, because of our selective perceptions, we are not yet registering. Tendencies seen as salient by one observer seem secondary to another. All that is being offered here, then, are estimates of likely developments given the continuation of certain tendencies identified as salient within the context of the present analysis.

Evidence is not lacking that the low-trust dynamic is powerfully active throughout the West, certainly not least in Britain. Its growth can be examined along both the relevant dimensions of extensiveness and intensiveness. With respect to the former, the trend seems unmistakable. While in all countries the growth of trade unionism and collective bargaining (and other forms of job regulation) has been fluctuating and subject to temporary reversals and periods of stagnation, there are good reasons for believing that the long-term trend must be upward. There are substantial numbers even of manual wage earners who are still unorganized and whose low-trust responses take inchoate forms. As they become unionized and covered by collective agreements their work situations will become increasingly prescribed in the direction of institutionalized low-trust relations. But the largest gaps in union organization exist among white-collar employees. These gaps are unlikely to survive indefinitely. 'Experience . . . leaves little doubt that many, if not most white-collar groups can be effectively organized. Even the high skill professional groups are no exception to this statement' (Sturmthal 1966: 397). Kleingartner, while personally cautious about prediction, notes 'forces at work which could make large-scale unionization inevitable'. Organizational change 'has altered in significant ways the hows, wheres, and conditions under which these employees do their work. We are well beyond the time when white-collar workers performed essentially the same tasks as the owner or manager. Today, in large organizations white-collar workers are subject to the "reign of rules" in the same way and for most of the same reasons as manual workers. In this situation there develops an inevitable separation between the rank-and-file white-collar workers and those who determine the basic working conditions. This . . . reduces . . . the impact of the mechanisms of reciprocal influences between those who make the decisions and those who are affected by them. Intermediate supervision develops. . . . The authority structure becomes hierarchical and the areas of responsibility and discretion become formalized' (1967). Kleingartner is describing, of course, moves in a low-trust direction.

Moreover, collective action may reach further up in the management ranks than was earlier expected. A number of factors now discernible may promote among middle managers a growing consciousness that individual action is no longer enough to ensure their own welfare – growth in company size; increasing application to themselves of bureaucratic rules; the spread of performance-measurement techniques and appraisal methods which sow the seeds of a feeling that they are being watched and no longer fully trusted; the threats to their security presented by takeovers, rationalization, or office automation. Out of this consciousness seems likely to develop the pursuit of some degree of collective security by imposing discretion-reducing rules or understandings upon top management. Neither, as Sturmthal suggests, will professionalism escape such possibilities. Scientists, engineers, architects, even lawyers and physicians increasingly work in complex organizations. In Wilensky's words: 'The culture of bureaucracy invades the professions . . .' (1964: 150). Complex organizations are not necessarily bureaucratic, but those which are may find that rule-governance over professionals evokes from them a corresponding degree of specificity in their attitudes and performance.

Among women employees the tendency is towards collective

action. In Britain during the sixties, women and girls supplied 70 per cent of the total increase in trade union membership, and in certain sectors the rate of increase of women's membership has been very striking. Movements towards wider female emancipation may in the future not only quicken aspirations directly, but also exert an indirect effect by enlarging women's freedom to move into those organizations and occupations which structurally facilitate combination. The popular assumption that 'women make bad trade unionists' has long ignored the fact that restrictions on choice have forced many of them into job situations which oppose structural obstacles to unionization whether by women or men.

We seem to glimpse, then, the likelihood of a universalization of those forms of the low-trust dynamic by which employee groups react to low-discretion situations or changes in that direction by seeking to limit the discretion of management on issues important to them. The social consequences of this tendency seem likely to be heightened by further discernible dispositions. There can be detected a weakening in the reference-group limits imposed on men's aspirations for themselves and their children by traditional class cultures or group subcultures. This is not the place for an analysis of all the solvents at work on these customary expectations. Reference must be limited here to the relative consumer abundance and the need of its producers to use such universal means of communication as television and other mass media to induce all classes constantly to raise their material aspirations.

Movements along the dimension of intensiveness are no less apparent then along that of extensiveness. Not only do institutionalized low-trust relations seem likely to spread ever wider throughout the world of employment relations; they show signs of intensifying. Cuts in material standards, e.g. by inflation, are resisted by means of large money wage claims, and there are signs that expectations of continuing inflation are now being built into the claims in attempts at a partial discounting of future price rises. Where, as in Britain, incitement to acquire and consume is contradicted by a stagnant economy and, allegedly, by efforts to counter the encroachment of wages on profits (Glyn and Sutcliffe 1972), keener aspirations may express their energy more through defensive struggles to retain standards than through offensive struggles to enlarge them.

Over the longer term some observers see a likelihood that men in low-discretion work will become increasingly conscious of intrinsic deprivations and less disposed to accept them as unquestioningly as in the past. This does not necessarily mean that they will seriously challenge the existing division of labour. They may accept that this is the condition, for them, of high and rising living standards, but accompany this with a demand for a larger share of the total product as compensation for frustrating and impoverishing work experience (Argyris 1972). Some observers of the American scene, however, claim to detect signs that the existing division of labour *is* being challenged. 'In the U.S., questioning of the relationship between work and satisfaction of material needs is widespread through the ranks of university students, industrial workers and minority unemployed. The viability of the belief . . . that individuals may be used to satisfy the economic goals of organizations is being seriously questioned. It appears that people may no longer let themselves be used. . . . No longer will workers patiently endure dehumanized work roles in order to achieve increased material rewards' (Davis 1971: 418). There is a link here with one of the major themes of 'futurology'. It is argued that 'Past trends of increasing affluence, increasing level of education, and changing child-rearing patterns combine to indicate that an increasing fraction of the population will be, in Maslow's terms, "growth-motivated" rather than "deficiency-motivated". This is showing itself in signs of changing values in the direction of higher valuation of the feeling and subjective side of life, of self realization, of meaning and significance in work. There is more questioning of traditional work values . . . '(Harman 1969: 47).

Whatever it is they seek, an increasing number of employees seem disinclined to leave its pursuit in the hands of distant union officials. In some industries in Britain shopfloor cohesion and strength have enabled certain of the more favoured employee groups to manifest distrust of their union's negotiating role as well as of management by pulling down effective participation into their own hands. The long term trend up until the fifties had been in the reverse direction. The pattern seemed set for the eventual consolidation in most industries of top level negotiation between the national officers of the relevant trade unions and their counterparts of the employers' association. Thus would be established terms and conditions of employment which covered the whole industry. The impact on this system of a long continuous period of price inflation, relative labour scarcity, and rising aspirations has proved explosive. The assumptions, institutions, and regulative force of industry-wide settlement became undermined as favourably placed workgroups on the shop floor used their enhanced power to press their own claims, assert their own preferred work practices, or prevent changes in established custom. Thus for substantial numbers of industrial workers the status regulation implied by top level settlements, which shaped the destinies of the individual but in which he had little voice or control, became fragmented down into something much nearer contract regulation in which he had a more direct and active involvement.

This trend is not confined to Britain. 'Throughout western capitalism, workers now feel needs which their union machinery cannot hope to satisfy, least of all machinery increasingly mortgaged to official economic policy. Appeals to traditional loyalties can have little lasting effect – they are too confident, and their confidence too solidly based on skill, scarcity and the achieved results of their own widely dispersed actions. Yet if they are not involved in the aims of their unions and their twilight committees not integrated into the union machinery there can be no hope for the consensus on which wage and labour policies ultimately rest. And without such policies there can be little life in the fragile stability achieved since the war' (Kidron 1970: 145).

The extreme forms of workgroup self-assertion have been described as 'instrumental collectivism', which can be seen as based on rational and continuing calculation of highly particularistic group interest. (The term itself is from Goldthorpe *et al.* 1968.) It is often apt to show scant respect for established procedures of settlement and for those restraints on methods which in the past were tacitly regarded as an industrial version of the Queensberry Rules but which were probably due more to weakness and lack of confidence. Kidron's summary of the situation in Western capitalist societies assesses these attitudes as prevailing, as yet, 'only in isolated pockets in any national labour movement, clearest in the fast-growing white-collar unions, the most uninhibited and demanding of them all. But . . . they are spreading. . . . If they grow, as they seem bound to, traditional working-class parties will need to work hard to stay their current supporters' slipping loyalties' (1970: 122).

Company managements, too, are being urged to work hard to stay their own slipping control (Donovan 1968). For these workgroup pressures, described by Flanders as 'largely informal, largely fragmented and largely autonomous' (1967: 28), are seen as aggravating inflation and undermining wider aspects of managerial control unless contained within an overall regulative framework negotiated with the unions to cover the whole plant or company. Unions and management are being urged by friendly and hostile critics alike, always of course within the framework of pluralist interpretations and assumptions, to articulate, codify, formalize and record their agreements and understandings. Other factors favour the same trend. What became known in the sixties as 'productivity bargaining' will wax and wane according to the prevailing mood, but over the long term will probably further the process by nudging collective agreements towards greater comprehensiveness of substantive coverage and greater precision of expression. Thus the formality of collective agreements, for long a marked feature of the American scene, is gradually increasing in Britain and it seems unlikely that this movement will be reversed. What we have here, then, is a process by which the mutual expectations of the parties become increasingly specified – in other words an intensification of the low-trust trend. Here is the low-trust dynamic at work which impels both parties to seek to bind each other ever more tightly within prescriptive rules, thereby raising the costs of organizational adaptation to a changing environment by requiring increased managerial input of analytical planning, and negotiating skill, energy, and time – resources which may or may not be in sufficient supply.

The final aspect of the tendency towards greater intensiveness to be noted here likewise became apparent in the theoretical exposition. A heightening tempo of aggressiveness in low-trust exchanges can prompt either party or both to cut corners, resort to sharp practice, default on established rules and procedures, or break down standard conventions. In the general field of business, commercial, and financial transactions, this tendency has constantly to be countered by an increasing battery of legislative protections and safeguards. In the field of collective bargaining and dispute settlement it takes the form, where it manifests itself, of diminishing respect for established procedures and Queensberry restraints, increasingly seen by some workgroups not as rules and conventions fairly agreed between equals but as restrictions with a built-in bias which favours management and privilege. Among the symptoms are the disregard of formal procedures in favour of direct coercive action; the extension of mass picketing to linked industries or businesses outside the source of the original dispute; and an impression of planned determination born of deep frustration. Attempts by the governmental and State apparatus of Western countries to control these or similar manifestations by legislative means have far less success than with commercial sharp practice. They run up against the contradictions created by their own liberal-democratic ideology which precludes the degree of visible coercive violence necessary for enforcing law against large numbers who repudiate its legitimacy.

Contradictions also become evident when we consider the numerous solvents of traditional and conventional values and constraints that are released by industrialization, with its mobilities, secular irreverencies, liberating stimuli, and facilities which encourage men to compare their lot and apply to themselves concepts such as happiness and fulfilment. We have already noted their effect on aspirations. They show other signs of heightening the difficulties of operating the complex systems of collaboration characteristic of industrialization. It has become one of the more plausible commonplaces of social comment to postulate a decline in deference towards authority as manifested within, for example, the family, the churches, the schools, and the universities. The questioning of class or functional differences in aspirations is matched by a questioning of class or functional differences in prerogatives of decision-making. Work could hardly be expected to escape the impulses of this groundswell. It is, of course, easy to exaggerate these manifestations. Some nervous ears claim to detect rumblings which presage the imminent collapse of society into anarchy and ruin, but reformers are more aware of the resistant qualities of tradition, habit, custom, and vested interest at all levels of the social hierarchy.* Nevertheless, manifestations there are, and the broad sweep of history over the past two centuries suggests that they strike the note of the future.

* The very different impressions that can be conveyed by emphasizing one selection of events rather than another are exemplified in Ferris 1972, and Daniel 1972. Ferris, an experienced journalist, presents one extreme: a dramatic, impressionistic account of recent industrial relations in Britain which draws attention to 'ugly scenes of violence and intimidation', 'crisis' in the unions, and 'the new militancy'. Daniel, an experienced academic researcher, in a highly critical review of the same book, offers us the other extreme by telling us, in effect, to keep calm and that nothing really untoward is happening. It is doubtful if either picture is adequate by itself as a basis for extrapolation.

It could be that the questioning of traditional assumptions extends eventually to the very fundamentals of our current modes of work organization. The argument was advanced earlier that the present universal acceptance by rank and file employees of such principles as, for example, that those in authority should receive higher pay by virtue of that fact alone, or that intrinsic rewards from work must be ignored when financial rewards are under consideration, owes something to their perceiving as natural laws what are no more than social conventions. Should there develop a growing awareness of the conventional – and therefore changeable – nature of social arrangements, aspirations might be generated accordingly and, along with them, a search for ways of mobilizing the power to realize them.

Developments of this kind would constitute signs of the crumbling of that pluralist perspective which has hitherto marked the mainstream evolution of employment relations. The system by which disputed issues are handled according to a set of established procedures and Queensberry Rules within an agreed social framework of highly unequal rewards, status and control would be losing legitimacy at the hands of one of the parties. We have already adduced as among the causes the social solvents referred to. No doubt we also have to suppose many employee groups as never having seriously internalized the pluralist perspective and its associated assumptions, even though they felt unable to challenge it and therefore had to submit to its conventions. Once nerved, however, by rising aspirations and awareness of a modicum of power lying to hand, they turn without overmuch hesitation to more radical patterns of behaviour.

Consequences for Industrial Organization

Were events to take these directions, management would find itself under pressure to negotiate the terms of collaboration on a narrowly contractual basis in a profoundly more comprehensive sense than is the practice now. Should society remain in its predominantly low-trust form, marked by competitive sectional struggles induced by major inequalities and institutions structured according to market values, the consequence might well be to make the existing type of industrial organization unworkable. We are envisaging the existence, in such a social setting, of free-floating employee groups whose contract-bargaining behaviour, uninfluenced by conventions masquerading as laws, by minority privileges camouflaged as functional necessities, and by changeable assumptions disguised as invariable facts about human nature, would be shaped solely by a particularist strategy of maximizing sectional advantage. This might make impossible even the minimum degree of cohesion, continuity, and flexibility necessary for large-scale operations under modern conditions.

We may set alongside this picture of the work organization as increasingly structured on contract the doubts expressed by Selznick as to whether contract can ever be an adequate basis for organizational effectiveness. He contrasts the notion of contract with the notion of 'association' in terms which echo the distinction between economic exchange and social exchange, between low- and high-trust relations. Modern contract, essentially 'a contract of limited commitment', presumes 'a world of independent, roughly equal actors who achieve their objectives by making determinate arrangements with predictable outcomes. . . .' Contractual arrangements tend to be 'specific rather than diffuse; they are determinate, not open-ended'.

These characteristics, he argues, 'strain against the reality of human association' seen as a going concern, a continuing relationship. 'Commitment to a going concern is diffuse, not specific; it is open-ended, not determinate.' Association 'bespeaks commitment, open-endedness . . . undermines predictability and proliferates obligations'. In human association, 'trust and continuity often have more practical worth than arm's-length reciprocity and limited commitment. In a cooperative system consensual specificity – detailed planning by prior agreement as to the obligations of each party – may do more harm than good. . . . A zeal for specifying obligations in advance tends to close relations rather than open them, undermines trust, and limits contributions.' The insistence on full specific reciprocity may thus be self-defeating. In the world of practical problem-solving, 'who needs whom' and 'who can do what' come to be more pressing bases of decision than 'issues of commutative justice'. The principle of *quid pro quo* 'is most effective when the independence of the parties outweighs in importance the union they have formed'. It is 'most compelling in the absence of a fuller social integration. As commitment to the social system deepens, so too does the idea that a social role is instinct with obligation, an obligation not wholly dependent on the dutiful conduct of others'. The specific reciprocity of contract 'lends legitimacy to retaliation as a way of life; undermines obligation by encouraging the view that one party is relieved from his duties whenever the other violates his own commitments; and makes rules vulnerable because, on grounds of reciprocity, any infraction becomes an occasion for questioning their existence. These tendencies are hostile to a form of organization that transcends immediate interests and encourages long-run cooperation.' Especially are these tendencies hostile, implies Selznick, to a form of organization capable of adapting flexibly to change. '. . . a fully planned relationship has a *static* quality. . . . It is difficult, in strictly contractual terms, to take account of a dynamic relationship, in which the needs and contributions of the parties may change, or to establish the capacity of the new entity to deal with new situations. When terms are "frozen", and interpreted as fully explicating the scope of the agreement, there is little leeway for adaptation and growth. A contract that forms a going concern must be, in some sense, a "living" document. In that case, however, the specificity of that agreement is less highly prized' (Selznick 1969: 3–32: 55–68: 145–51: 270–3).

Thus the modern corporation, increasingly seen as 'the dominant form of social organization', the 'dominant institution of the modern world' (Berle and Means 1967: 313), seems to be generating, jointly with the society which produced it, forces which seriously hamper its pursuit of the objectives which power-holders define for it. Increasingly, in a world of accelerating change, its success is said to depend on high-trust attitudes and behaviours on the part of rank and file. Yet given the low-discretion roles allocated to them they can only offer such attitudes and behaviours if they fully and actively legitimize and endorse their place in the total structure, the purposes of that structure, and the wider societal values which it embodies. Neither the organization nor the wider society, however, has been able to provide them with a frame of reference which leads them to offer this active legitimation (as opposed to passive acquiescence). They have found that neither the self-help exhortations of Samuel Smiles, nor the Social Darwinism said to justify the victor in his spoils, nor the social formula of the modern meritocrat (I.Q. + Effort = Merit; Young 1961) has disposed them to transcend the low-trust responses which low-discretion roles tend to generate.

The organization is thus, in this respect, hoist with its own petard.

Its very structure, and that of its containing society, seems likely increasingly to undermine its defined purposes. Extreme division of function; labour bought and sold as a commodity; contract defined as self-interested instrumental bargaining – so long as these could be combined with extreme inequalities of power, limited aspirations among rank and file, and traditional status concepts such as master-servant relations and the 'functional hierarchy of rewards', the foundations of privilege and control were secure. Power-holders were, and remain, well served. But the mainstream of concepts and principles which carried these notions also bore others which, reinterpreted in other hands, they were to find less convenient. Equality; citizenship; the principle of constitutional government; institutionalized checks against autocracy; the pursuit of self-interest untrammelled by ethical or social obligations; these and other ideas which were so ideologically important for the bourgeois revolution in weakening traditional values and institutions could not be kept indefinitely from the active consciousness of deprived groups, any more than the notion of choice in individual self-realization could be kept indefinitely from the active consciousness of women. Helped by cultural disturbances induced by the shocks of total war and by a certain shift in power relations consequent on collective labour organization, these values have been percolating down into the awareness and aspirations of those in the lower reaches of the social hierarchy. Too late the power-holders appeal for 'restraint', concern for 'the public interest', 'responsibility', and 'patriotism'. Too late they rearrange the image of the businessman as one fully alive to his diverse social responsibilities. Group self-assertion on an economic-exchange basis renders the viability of the organization increasingly problematic, and by the same token sharpens the defensive competition for rewards which we experience as inflation.

Yet even now the full implications of the system we are currently operating are masked by the fact that many occupational groups are only weakly organized or not organized at all; that women's emancipation is proving a far slower process than its pioneers imagined; and that convention, tradition, and ideology continue to engender quietest attitudes towards privilege. This is but one of many ways in which certain problems in modern industrial society – indeed in world society – fail so far to take on their full proportions only because major inequalities persist.

Low-trust market society as we know it, therefore, has maintained such stability as it has partly because large sections of its members have not yet (1) claimed the exercise of certain of its major rights or (2) demanded fully to participate in certain of its major values or (3) subjected certain of its basic conventions to critical examination. The first of these refers to that pressure group activity through which men conscious of shared interests assert their right to influence decision-makers. The second refers to those liberal values which assert the individual's right to such material, cultural, and spiritual resources as he needs to develop his personality and live in creative harmony with his fellows. The third has in mind those conventions of work organization, rewards, and status which it has suited the privileged to assert as immutable laws and which tend to be accepted as such by many of the less favoured. All three – including the spirit of rational and critical inquiry mentioned in connection with the third – are integral features of liberal-democratic market society. Were there any mechanisms by which the privileged could prevent them gradually becoming universalized there would be no grounds for predicting that instability is inherent in present social patterns and dynamics. There are no such mechanisms. Even if there were, major groups among the privileged would be likely to oppose their use, for their interests are bound up with promoting those very aspirations referred to under (2) which are part of the search for a happy and fulfilled life, and which so often stimulate action under (1) and (3). Since the forgoing argument has already suggested the likelihood of a long-term tendency towards universalization on all three counts, our proposition about the ultimate contradiction of low-trust market society is complete. Some, however, might wish to argue that no account has yet been taken of counter-trends. Is it possible to identify any developments in the field of work and its organization which might represent – and generate further – movement in a high-trust direction?

Counter-Tendencies towards High-Trust Relations

Postwar writings on organization structure, job design, and employee motivation have included many by such theorists as Argyris, Davis, Herzberg, and McGregor urging certain changes in the design and organization of work which they see as resulting in, *inter alia*, enlarged discretion for lower-level participants, both operative and managerial. The motive has not been to challenge the prevailing criteria of economic rationality but rather to argue that, in moving from the 'industrial' to the so-called 'post-industrial' era,* organizational 'effectiveness' increasingly requires a degree of personal involvement in, and commitment to, the job and the organization which is not generated among lower participants by the structures and methods of Scientific Management. This approach needs to be seen against the background of an increasing preoccupation among many organizational theorists with the problems of stimulating, organizing, and securing the acceptance of, and adaptation to, change. The offering of adaptive and creative responses to the growing state of flux in our economic, technological, and social environments is increasingly seen as a dimension of organizational efficiency which now ranks in importance with the engineer's or economist's criterion of maximizing the output from given inputs. In a world context of accelerating change, it is asserted, an increasing premium will be placed on flexibility, adaptation, problem-solving and creativity. These, it is said, are promoted most readily in situations characterized by high trust, open communications, and high personal involvement. Conversely, they are inhibited and impeded in situations of low trust, suspicion, and alienation. This is unexceptionable enough, though we must recall that our analytical framework does not directly equate high-trust relations with high-discretion roles. Occupants of low-discretion roles will offer some measure of high-trust response if they legitimize the organizational structure and their place in it. Given this high-trust stance there is no reason why they should not manifest creative responses if the occasion demands.

If it is accepted, nevertheless, that, beyond a certain point, division of labour is empirically likely to weaken the basis of association by generating a trend towards low-trust specificity, the way is open for managements for whom flexibility, adaptability, and problem solving are high priorities to try to evoke high-trust commitment by, *inter alia*, enlarging the discretion of the relevant groups of employees. Such a policy has in fact been pursued by a few companies, sometimes under the banner of 'job enrichment' (Davis and Taylor 1972), sometimes under the rationale of a more comprehensive

* Definitions of 'post-industrialism' are many: one favoured version can be found in Davis and Taylor 1972: 154–76.

philosophy (e.g. Hill 1971). Action research in Britain, America and Norway is tending to converge on the notion of the 'responsible, autonomous work group' (Davis and Taylor 1972). Much of this research has as its theoretical base the Tavistock concept of the socio-technical system, and seeks 'joint optimization' or 'best fit' between technology and social and personal variables (Herbst 1962, 1972). This approach, far from giving lower priority to economic rationality, 'states that when achievement of an objective depends on independent but correlated systems, such as a techological and social system, it is impossible to optimize for overall performance without seeking to optimize these correlative systems jointly' (Davis and Taylor 1972: 167). This trend is seen as according conveniently with the rising aspirations of the future, believed to be making their appearance already in some advanced countries, towards greater self-realization in work as in other spheres of life. This awakening quest for intrinsic satisfactions in work, achievable through enlarged discretion, is felt to be congruent with the growing need for adaptive, flexible organization patterns 'based on humanistic-democratic ideals' rather than on the 'depersonalized mechanistic value system of bureaucracy' and Scientific Management (Thomas and Bennis 1972: 218).

The possibility cannot be ruled out, moreover, that even where adaptability and flexibility are not high priorities, bolder managements may yet move away from Scientific Management patterns, as indeed a few have done already. If rising aspirations and growing awareness of the conventional nature of the institutional arrangements and assumptions which presently control them lead low-discretion groups increasingly to open up for negotiation many aspects which they now accept as given, management's cost-benefit calculations will be even more likely to undergo a change. The total costs of extreme division of labour, seen in their broadest sense, may come to seem disproportionate to its benefits. The strategy of the few companies mentioned earlier suggests that we may already be witnessing the earliest beginnings of such a trend. Work and jobs may, then, to some extent, come to be so designed as to offer marginally greater intrinsic rewards, not necessarily in response to explicit employee demand but because the costs of traditional low-level work patterns are becoming too high in terms of such responses as turnover, absence, wastage, accident, and sickness rates.

Counter-Tendencies towards High-Trust Relations

Current developments in advanced technology are often seen as rendering it easier for managements, in any case, to design work systems characterized by greater discretion, autonomy, and responsibility for work groups. Certain central themes recur. 'On the whole, these assertions suggest a sharp break with the past evolution of work, and the development of working conditions likely to be more satisfying to the individuals involved. More specifically, this golden era of work will bring safer and cleaner working conditions, a reduction in the physical effort required on the job, enlarged and more interesting tasks, increased professionalization of the worker, freedom from the immediate rhythm of the machine, and a greater sense of relevance to the total objective of the organization' (Shultz and Weber 1960: 192). In contrast with the earlier and traditional literature, which dwells on the fragmentation of work and destruction of skills, recent writing predicts a potential upgrading of the labour force and the creation of many new skilled tasks. This is usually viewed in conjunction with the undoubted tendency in advanced industrial countries for the proportion of the occupied population engaged in blue-collar work to fall relatively to the proportion engaged in professional, technical, and other white-collar occupations.

One prominent researcher in this field, L. E. Davis, writes that 'the most striking characteristic of sophisticated, automated technology is that it absorbs routine activities into the machines. . . '. It 'requires a high degree of commitment and autonomy on the part of workers. . . '. They 'must have a large repertoire of responses because the specific intervention that will be required is not known. . . . They cannot depend on supervision because they must respond immediately to events that occur irregularly and without warning. . . . They must be committed to undertaking the necessary tasks on their own initiative. This makes a very different world, in which the organization is far more dependent on the individual. . . . The major characteristics are those of planning, self control, self-regulation, i.e., of autonomy. . .' (Davis and Taylor 1972: 419–20).

A report initiated by Britain's Social Science Research Council (Sadler 1968), which reviews research into American and European as well as British experience, concludes that the effect of automation on the occupational structure is to intensify the existing trends. In manufacturing industry the groups which are increasing in relative numerical importance include managers, professionally qualified specialists, technicians, maintenance workers, administrative and clerical workers. Of decreasing importance is the labour directly involved in production, particularly at the unskilled level. These trends are towards higher-trust rather than lower-trust roles. Reporting a summary of the evidence concerning the effects of automation on working conditions, Sadler mentions the elimination of much highly repetitive work, greater responsibility, and more satisfying relationships with colleagues, technical service groups, and supervision (*Ibid*: 36–7). Research into the operator skills required refers to needs which point clearly to the more diffuse, discretionary contribution characteristic of high-trust situations. There is said, for example, to be a reduced need for 'sensorimotor' skills in favour of perceptual and conceptual skills together with 'qualities of character such as conscientiousness and sense of responsibility, and what have been termed "social skills", including the ability to work as part of an integrated team' (*Ibid*: 17). These pointers towards change in a high-trust direction are accompanied by evidence about supervision which strongly recalls the high-trust syndrome. A common conclusion is that 'the role of supervision changes from one of exercising discipline and control of manpower to one of providing technical leadership and guidance.' The supervisor is 'less concerned with hour-by-hour control and more involved with longer-term considerations affecting the operation of the plan'. His role 'as a service to the operator is reflected in the fact that in an automated plant interaction between supervisor and operator is more frequently at the operator's initiative'. Direct supervision declines in the face of the need for a more sophisticated system (*Ibid*: 30–1).

If we take experience in Britain, America and other advanced countries as our guide, then, our conclusion is likely to be, subject of course to empirical inquiry into each situation, that such changes could indeed in many cases promote a limited movement towards those more diffuse relations and obligations characterized here as high trust. Whether this movement is likely, however, to be sufficient to evoke from the employees concerned a stable identification with the company and bring to an end their collective pressures upon management decisions seems doubtful. Perhaps a more likely outcome is that described by Wedderburn and Crompton in their comparison of three chemical plants on the same site, one of which displayed the technology and control systems normally seen as characteristic of the new, automated advanced technology; and another the features of batch production and machine operation more characteristic of the older patterns. These differences in technology and control systems produced differences in the degree of discretion vested in work roles which were in turn accompanied by differences of attitude and behaviour. Yet overarching these differences was a consciousness common to all groups of being wage earners in a position of subjection and control. 'The fact that the degree of control over their particular work situation varied between the Works, did not mean that there was any variation in the extent to which the men felt they could exercise control over more general and universal aspects of their employment situation. . . . They were all . . . subject to the usual kind of social controls. They had to accept the work rules, work shifts and clock on. They were all affected by the nature of the wage effort bargain and by other issues of job regulation' (1972: 141).

The authors carry their point further. Referring to that group of workers most favoured in terms of discretionary job content, they define the work roles concerned as 'the paradigm of automation'. The occupants of these roles 'manifested very favourable attitudes to the job itself. They found it interesting, and . . . got on very well with their immediate supervision' (*Ibid*: 149). Are these the signs of that integration which some investigators claim to find among workers in advanced technology and predict as the predominant form of the future – that 'high degree of consensus between workers and management and an integrated industrial community in which employees experience a sense of belonging and membership' and where 'social alienation is absent'? (Blauner 1964: 178). Wedderburn and Crompton found little evidence among these employees of any increased identification with management or integration with the company. 'It was true that absenteeism, labour turnover, and the level of industrial disputes were lower . . . than elsewhere, but we found little evidence of positive identification with the firm. The men were as critical of management, and the "anonymity" of the site, as the other groups of workers, and they were as instrumental in their general orientations to work' (1972: 149). Evidence is given of their 'calculative involvement with the Company' and of their being 'as involved as other workers with their trades union' (*Ibid*: 150).

There are other reasons for treating with caution the predictions of a congruence between advanced technology and the requirements of humane, satisfying, and socially integrated work systems. Shultz and Weber, after examining considerable American evidence, warn that the impact of new technology on individual jobs is mixed. Some jobs in both the operator and maintenance categories have been enlarged, frequently as a result of the consolidation of tasks in an integrated production flow, but the skill requirements of many have apparently remained unchanged and at a level demanding little special training. Office automation frees some managers to spend less time on routine processing and more on matters requiring professional judgement, but downgrades others (1960: 202). In any case, the applicability and relevance of advanced technology for the economic system may well have been exaggerated by some of the more enthusiastic prophets. There may remain for the foreseeable future a significant range of activities which the designers of tasks, roles, and organizations deem as still requiring such structural modes as extreme division of labour, elaborate hierarchy, and other Scientific Management principles like close supervision, prescriptive rules, and rigorous control systems. One prominent writer in this field who in 1964 was predicting (and welcoming) the demise of 'bureaucracy as we know it and the rise of new social systems better suited to twentieth century demands of industrialization' was feeling the need by 1970 to revise this estimate. 'Rather than neat, linear and uniform evolutionary developments', he expects to see 'an erratic environment where various organizations coexist at different stages of evolution . . . both more centralization (in large-scale instrumental bureaucracies) and more decentralization . . .; both the increase of bureaucratic-pragmatic and of revolutionary-charismatic leadership; both the increase in size and centralization of many municipal and governmental units and the proliferation of self-contained minisocieties . . .' (Thomas and Bennis 1972: 97, 114).

Contributing to the likely survival of Scientific Management bureaucracy will be the positive conviction among many that it offers indispensable techniques for coordinating human action. The belief that its modes and principles, along with its implied concept of human nature, are the prerequisites of efficient organization remains widespread and deeprooted among managers and administrators. There is plenty of evidence that many of them see the abandonment of such modes and principles as profoundly threatening to their control and their personal security. Any argument which appears to justify the retention of conventional patterns is likely to be popular.

Other considerations prompting caution relate to certain crucial assumptions made by many of the observers who have predicted increasing social integration, legitimacy, and problem solving cooperation in this field. In contrast to the possibilities examined earlier, there has been a tendency to play down the diversity of interest groups mobilizing power to influence choices; to ignore the crumbling of authority and legitimacy in so many sectors of social life; and to assume as non-problematical the ultimate ability of organizational leaders to contain their possibly turbulent coalitions within the received conventional framework of institutions, values and principles. Other observers, however, have suggested different scenarios. As an example of these differences we may note the contrasting predictions offered with respect to those middle ranges of the occupational hierarchy which include not only the new 'white-coated' technicians but also engineers, scientists, operating managers, administrators, and specialists. Certainly, in Britain as in many other countries, an assessment of many of these groups in terms of their discretionary roles, ideology, and aspirations would probably predict the continuance of high-trust relations between them and top management. In certain industries of advanced technology, such as electronics, the emergence of large complex organizations employing scientists has sometimes been accompanied by 'a shift to less arbitrary less direct, and less dominating practices of authority' (Marcson 1961: 74). Marcson's study of one such company contrasts 'executive' authority with 'colleague' authority; the former being based on incumbency of position or office and issuing in directives and orders, the latter being 'shared by all the members of the working group' and issuing in rules established by agreement to which the individual voluntarily consents. This distinction is closely akin to that drawn by Gouldner between 'punishment-centred' and 'representative' bureaucracy – and indeed to many similar distinctions noted in Chapter 3 as constituting a theoretical convergence. It represents, of course, a shift from a lower- to a higher-trust situation and is deemed, in some situations of the kind Marcson describes, as desirable for effective collaboration, though more with respect to basic than applied research. Such changes affect, however, only relatively small groups, and that there is no inevitability about such technology promoting higher-trust relations within the management system has been demonstrated by Burns and Stalker (1961). In any case, Marcson suggests no more than the emergence, for these types of employee, of a new type of organizational model midway between the polar extremes of executive and colleague authority. Other groups within these middle or middle-upper occupational ranges might, given actual or likely encroachments on their discretion, lend themselves to the prediction that their work behaviour would move in the direction of low-trust responses. Thus one can envisage the possibility that, within these large and expanding middle ranges, the attitudes and responses of some groups would be broadening out towards more diffuse orientations, while those of other groups would be narrowing down towards greater specificity.

That some groups enjoying relatively high discretion may be so keen for more as to entertain radical sentiments towards existing patterns of industrial organization is suggested by arguments relating to the *cadres* in France. André Gorz, describing the events of May 1968, asserts that in many large factories 'engineers and technicians were the driving force behind the contestation of the management's authority, of the hierarchical division of labour, of differences in income, of the logic of capitalist profits. A fact which can hardly surprise since those who hold professional skill and intellectual autonomy are the first to become aware of the limitations which the pursuit of financial profit imposes on research, technical improvements and the full utilization of human creativeness. . . . The same occurred in medical and engineering schools. Young *cadres* and doctors . . . looked for a new definition' of their role (1970: 261–2. (For a much earlier statement of a somewhat similar theme see Veblen 1921). Such evidence is greeted eagerly by those who hope for a revolutionary alliance between manual workers, technicians, and operating managers, fostered by the high-trust relations between these groups which advanced technology is assumed to make possible. A leading exponent of this vision is Serge Mallet (1963), who visualizes this solidarity as becoming the basis of common interests and unified action against directors and top executives in a struggle for control. The events of May 1968 gave fresh stimulus to these hopes, leading one of their more recent expositors. Garaudy, to call for a combination of '*quantitative* claims (wage increases, shorter working hours, guaranteed national insurance scales, retirement age, etc.) with a new *qualitative* demand: that made by a working class which no longer accepts its exclusion from management or its passive integration into the system – a working class which refuses, in other words, to be denied its part in the decision-making upon which the future depends'. In this quotation the term 'quantitative' corresponds to 'substantive', as that word was used in Chapter 2, and 'qualitative' to 'procedural'. The combination of substantive and procedural demands could, suggests Garaudy, secure a conjunction between the working class and 'the technologists and cadres who are beginning to give forceful expression' to procedural demands. 'There can be no doubt that a primary role in that conjunction will be played by the engineers, the technologists, and the cadres. . . ' (1970: 65–6).

These may be very distant nightmares for power-holders in Britain and elsewhere. Nevertheless they suggest that any assumption of an automatic link between even relatively high-discretion work roles and identification with top management is invalid, thereby confirming once more the importance of mediating frames of reference, ideology, and aspirations. Taken along with other revisions of opinion and with such evidence as is offered by Wedderburn and Crompton, they cast some doubt on the proposition that technological and organizational developments are destined necessarily to promote a major enlargement of high-trust roles and relations.

Rearguard Actions against Low-Trust Behaviour

Among managements concerned to reduce low-trust responses yet unwilling to make structural changes the hope still survives that ways may be found of evoking high-trust commitment from lower-level employees without incurring the risks and possible costs of changing job definitions, authority relations, and control systems. Prominent among recent ideas is that of assimilating manual workers to 'staff status' by such means as the abolition of clocking in; their inclusion in pension and sickness benefit schemes; weekly or monthly payment in place of an hourly rate; and equalization of holiday entitlement and terms of notice (Wedderburn 1969). The *Industrial Relations Code of Practice* issued by Britain's Conservative government in 1972 recommends that 'Differences in the conditions of employment and status of different categories of employee and in the facilities available to them should be based on the requirements of the job. The aim should be progressively to reduce and ultimately to remove differences which are not so based.' An Industrial Society publication, *Applying the Code*, adds the gloss that 'Arbitrary distinctions in status and conditions of employment between white and blue collar employees help to create the barrier between "them" and "us" which increases conflict and mistrust. Equally, so long as one section of the workforce is treated as second class industrial citizens it is no use expecting from them a first class response' (Tolfree 1972: 14). There is little reason, however, for believing that such adjustment, unaccompanied by changes in the nature of work, produce qualitatively different behaviour, though they may well render employees less inclined to leave (which may in some cases be the only aim).

Other methods of attempting to reduce low-trust responses include the use of ideology. There can be no doubt that the conventionally received picture of business, work, and the managerial role which pervades the communications media seeks to place a burden of guilt and defensiveness upon individuals and groups who manifest low-trust behaviour. This picture is grounded in the pluralist interpretation of social structure now widespread. This provides the foundation for a view of the management role, increasingly fashionable within relatively sophisticated large scale business, as that of the disinterested social servant conscientiously searching for the best balance between the potentially divergent interests of employees, shareholders, customers, suppliers, government, and local community. This 'gospel of social responsibility', especially marked in postwar America, has been seen by some as a bid to restore the management legitimacy so keenly in question during the slump of the thirties, with its growth of liberal sympathy towards organized labour and distrust of the profit motive (Cheit 1964). Berle and Means, discussing the 'new concept of the corporation', argue that 'It is conceivable – indeed it seems almost essential if the corporate system is to survive – that the "control" of the great corporations should develop into a purely neutral technocracy, balancing a variety of claims by various groups in the community and assigning to each a portion of the income stream on the basis of public policy rather than private cupidity' (1967: 312–13). The new gospel is also making its way, for example, in Japan (Yoshino 1971: Chap. 4), and in Britain, where indeed early signs of it appeared after the First World War (Child 1969: 52–3). In a recent compilation of papers by British businessmen, industrialists, employers' spokesmen, academics, and clerics (Ivens 1970), some form or another of the social responsibility gospel – with variations, of course, in emphasis – is presented explicitly in the Foreword, Preface, Introduction, and six of the seventeen contributions, and implicitly in a further two. Nowhere in the book is an alternative rationale advanced.

The advantage of this ideology for the top manager of the large enterprise is that it encourages a view of him as the honest professional engaged in a perpetual struggle to reconcile conflicting pressures in his task of producing goods and services. The emphasis on his wealth-creating role rather than his profit-making role has, of course, been greatly fostered in many countries since the war by a deep pre-occupation with economic growth. This emphasis has been accepted even by Labour administrations which in Britain, for example, have given every outward impression of treating industrialists and business executives as fellow-professionals whom it would be naïve and old-fashioned to regard with class suspicion. Crosland comments on the gospel of social responsibility to the effect that 'part of it at least is genuine. . . .' He sees the trend as being in that direction, and those businessmen 'who most obviously express the change are coming to set the tone for industry as a whole' (1964: 18). In such an atmosphere it has not been difficult for those choosing to do so to present low-trust responses as indications of moral weakness, sectional greed, blind conservatism, or simply an inability to grasp the fact that times have changed. Most of the responses defined as 'management's labour problems' are open to being stigmatized in this way – absenteeism, high turnover, indifferent work, time wasting, clock-watching, obstructionism, resistance to change, the philosophy of 'couldn't care less', 'excessive' wage claims, and a suspicious refusal of any concession not instantly matched by one of equal worth from management. The very manner, therefore, in which we are encouraged to react to low-trust responses is one of moral condemnation, and those who so encourage us are, in all probability, unconsciously drawing upon a stock of interpretations, perceptions, and symbols that is profoundly ideological in nature. Thus can the ideology of a social system be used to discourage certain of its consequences deemed undesirable by its ruling members – in this case by holding up for disapproval those whose 'undesirable' behaviour is an outcome of the very nature of the system itself. They are exhorted to trust the company, become involved, collaborate constructively, remember the national interest, exercise restraint, respect the rights of others. Sometimes they are sufficiently imbued with the ideology themselves to feel defensive and unconfident about their actions, thereby becoming more open to appeals, even from their own leaders, for 'responsible' behaviour.

Lack of confidence can also play its part in rendering rank and file employees and even their leaders more susceptible to another ideological effect – namely that implicit in the distinction between 'industrial' and 'political' issues. This distinction plays an important part in Britain's system of social regulation. Certain types and categories of issues and claims are felt to be 'industrial' and to be appropriately dealt with by industrial decision-making processes – in which, of course, the unions and workgroup representatives play some part. Other types and categories are felt to be 'political' and to be reserved for the parliamentary arena. For most of the time, most of the trade union leadership has accepted and worked to this distinction. The exercise, by unionized groups, of their industrial power in support of claims or issues deemed political has been almost as predictably condemned and discouraged by higher union officials as by political leaders (of all parties).

The usefulness of the distinction is apparent for those who can safely predict that the political causes favoured by unionized groups are unlikely to accord with their own sympathies and interests. It ensures that the industrial power of unions or workgroups will not be used to support causes they do not approve. But in addition, even trade union and labour movement leaders who might personally sympathize with such causes are likely to feel that to use industrial power directly by non-parliamentary methods against the Party politicians would invite the politicians to use political power against them – to the possible detriment of their freedom to pursue what they deem their essential functions. Unless essential functions themselves are being threatened or inhibited in a way which cannot be adequately contested in the purely parliamentary arena, the distinction is likely to be observed.

Some leaders may, of course, not share the consensus about the substance to be given to the notion of 'essential functions'; about the meaning to be given to 'adequately contested'; and about the advisability of waiting upon the political process for an effective handling of their problems. Such disagreements have become apparent in the responses of Britain's unions to its Industrial Relations Act. There is another sense, however, in which the distinction between industrial and political issues can come under strain. Unionized work-groups may assert themselves forcefully (e.g. by occupying a factory in an attempt to prevent closure) in a manner which conveys to management the impression that new challenges are being presented to the established framework of institutions and principles within which they have been accustomed to operate. They tend to define such challenges as political in a pejorative sense which carries connotations of the illegitimate, the improper, and even the sinister. Taken up by the media, such connotations become items in an ideological armoury which can strengthen the self-confidence of those anxious to defend the *status quo*, and weaken that of the less militant among those challenging it.

This casts additional light on the distinction itself. Industrial issues turn out, on this usage, to be those which power-holders define as capable of resolution within the existing framework of institutions and principles. Issues which bring that framework into question are seen as political and condemnation is levelled accordingly. In so far as the term is used to discredit certain types of claim in this way the distinction is itself an ideological one. Should claims of this sort increase as part, for example, of a growing reaction against the use of labour as a commodity, the distinction is likely to be increasingly evoked but to have decreasing practical meaning, taking on the same empty legalistic status as the concept of full managerial prerogative.

Finally, the role of ideology enters into yet a further method by which some hope to limit the organized expression of low-trust responses. This is simply to oppose by various means the extension to unorganized groups of rights already enjoyed by the organized. A prominent example is employer resistance to the unionization of their white-collar staffs. Bain has shown that while between 1911 and 1961 their numbers increased by 147 per cent, compared with only a 2 per cent increase in manual workers, the degree of unionization among them has lagged considerably behind (1970: 11, 37). He offers convincing reasoning that 'One of the major factors impeding the expansion of union membership among white-collar workers is the refusal of most employers to recognize unions representing these workers' (1967: 1). He finds their most fundamental reason for this refusal to be fear of further encroachments on their discretion; of dissension among the staff and between staff and management leading to lower morale and divided loyalties; and of 'practices which tend to promote mediocrity' (1970: 138). The methods they use are described by Bain as peaceful competition and forcible opposition. The former include 'paying salaries equal to or better than those in unionized firms; granting salary increases during a union recruitment campaign; establishing welfare, profit sharing, and other benefit schemes; offering various types of rewards to "loyal" employees; giving speeches and interviews designed to convince employees that their interests can be better cared for by management than by a union; granting monthly staff status; and establishing company unions'. The strategy of forcible opposition employs such tactics as 'overlooking union members for promotion and pay rises, transferring active unionists from department to department, threatening to discontinue any "extras" presently being paid above the union rate, sending management officials to union recruitment meetings to note the names of those employees attending, and dismissing leading union members' (*Ibid*: 131–5). Both strategies may continue to delay white-collar organization, but hardly indefinitely. Legislation in the form of Britain's Industrial Relations Act (1971) includes provisions which can be invoked by groups seeking to unionize and win employer recognition. The Act will not survive the party-political struggle but no replacement is likely to exclude similar provisions.

The same Act can be adduced, however, as evidence of still another means by which some seek to contain what on recent signs appears to be a gathering momentum of organized low-trust responses. Reference was made earlier to the way in which, in substantial and apparently growing sections of Britain's industry, low-trust collective action among lower-level employees has become fragmented down from regulation covering the whole industry to regulation by separate self-defining workgroups. This development expresses a stronger and more impatient assertiveness by the groups concerned. Its consequences are experienced by managers as heightened instability in the social structure of the plant or company expressed in such forms as frequent challenges to their authority and policies, constant adjustments in individual and group rewards, low-trust obstructionism towards proposed changes in technology, organization or methods; and flouting of established procedures. The containment and if possible the reversal of this development has become a high priority among the relevant power-holders, as well as among some independent observers who see containment as serving principles of order (and perhaps social planning) which they value. The interests of the former, though not necessarily the judgements of the latter, find a keenly sympathetic resonance in provisions of the Industrial Relations Act through which it is hoped that trade unions may be coerced into imposing their will on membership groups and reintegrating them into a regulative structure more susceptible to managerial control (Fox 1973).

Strategies for Stability – High-Discretion Roles and Relations?

When we view these rearguard actions and counter-trends in the total context of industrial society and the forces at work within it, there seems little likelihood of the former stemming the overall trend towards low-trust relations and still less of the latter reversing it. Here and there particular groups of employees may be deterred from certain kinds of low-trust response, or even induced to take a more compliant view of their situation. Here and there particular groups may – provided such low-trust attitudes as they hold prove reversible – be led by technological or organizational change to adopt a marginally more diffuse perspective towards their work, supervision, and higher management. But the probabilities of the temper and tenor of the whole society being fundamentally changed by tactics such as these seem small indeed. Not only do they appear to be of minor scale by comparison with the trends to which they are opposed; they are in any case byproducts of the same drives towards efficiency, cost reduction, and 'more effective collaboration'. They are in no sense expressions of a different set of social priorities. What we have described as rearguard actions seek to suppress symptoms or change attitudes without modifying the fundamental structures of work roles and relations. Counter-trends represented by structural change which results, intentionally or otherwise, in higher-trust behaviour will be pursued only in so far as such change is seen as serving economic rationality, albeit defined in its fullest long-term sense.

For those who see the gathering tempo of low-trust relations as a movement away from, rather than towards, civilized values, logic might seem to suggest an answer which, however, in practical terms, is no answer at all. If the present situation is the consequence of an extreme division of labour which creates large numbers of low-discretion roles and a proliferation of relationships characterized by economic exchange, cannot it only be changed by a movement away from division of labour which restructures work and economic relations on a high-discretion social exchange basis? The daunting features of this solution extend further than the very severe reduction of living standards which it would certainly involve if applied on the necessary scale – a reduction which, it is worth noting, would affect medical and health provision, housing, welfare, and cultural amenities as well as those much abused symbols of consumer affluence: the car, television, and washing machine. For more socially taxing even than the state of reduced standards itself would be the attempt to move towards it. It is safe to say that the problems of social dislocation and adjustment involved in such a fundamental shift in the scale, values, and nature of institutions would be far beyond our present ability to cope with them.

Admittedly this prospect does not daunt some reformers. Indeed they may welcome large scale dislocation, whatever its origins, as providing the only circumstances in which new principles of social organization can be asserted in practical form. To this end they may encourage and perhaps try to foster the sources of dislocation currently at work in the hope of hastening what they see as necessary change of a fundamental kind. The adaptational and adjustment problems created by fundamental social reconstruction are immense enough, however, even on the assumption that a significant proportion of the people involved are clear that they wish to reject certain major features of their present society and are clear too about what they wish to replace them with. The problems become immeasurably greater if serious dislocations result only from individuals and groups striving to maximize their own participation in society's *existing* values. For the stresses and strains do not then result from a willed political act from which a willed, planned recovery might at least be hoped for. They are simply an unwilled byproduct which a few reformers hope to turn to advantage for their reconstructional ends. Human experience does not suggest this to be a fruitful context within which to promote the new Jerusalem. Bewildered and frightened men who fear losing their present social bearings and are conscious of no others to steer by are likely to turn to any strong leader who promises security. If these arguments are valid, then for reformers to calculate that such a situation will give them their best opportunity for creating a new heaven and a new earth is to take a somewhat naïve view of political probabilities. They would be likely, in the event, to find themselves elbowed aside by others with rather different priorities.

It is in this context that the particularistic nature of most work-group and union campaigns against management becomes important. Rarely do a majority – or even a significant minority – of the participants give any impression of being inspired in their challenges to management decision-making by a universalist opposition to the social and economic structure as such, though they often find it convenient to be led by men who are. Neither do pleas for justice or equality tend to carry the ring of a concern which extends to other groups equally deprived. Rather is the impression conveyed simply of a particularist concern with *this* management's decisions; with justice for one's own group in *this* situation. Were major dislocations to result from a multiplicity of pressures of this kind there would be little grounds for hope that the new would be inspired by nobler values than had informed the old.

In sum, then, a wholesale transformation of industrial society, structurally geared as it is to a complex set of interdependent institutions, expectations, and values shaped predominantly by the principles of low-trust economic exchange, would involve adjustments and adaptations totally beyond our power to cope with even given the (in practice inconceivable) condition of a mass political will. For good or ill, according to the point of view, there can be no reversion to the small-scale operations, handicrafts, and local markets which would constitute the most fruitful structural context for high-trust roles and relations.

Strategies for Stability – A Search for Social Justice?

For those unwilling to accept that existing social relations among men and groups within industrial societies represent the peak of civilized achievement this may seem a negative and pessimistic stance. There is still to be discussed in this context, however, a major feature of the theoretical framework which suggests a way of improving trust relations at least to the extent of enabling us to bring under control our more chronic problems of inflation and economic stagnation. It would leave the division of labour largely intact and thereby avoid the pains of material deprivation while also preventing the achievement of full high-trust relations. Even so it would require radical changes in values and institutions for its achievement.

We have to begin by recalling once more that no simple direct relationship exists between structural characteristics and human responses. Ideologies, frames of reference, and aspirations mediate to determine how the structural context is perceived. As we have had occasion to note several times, low-discretion roles and relations are not necessarily seen by the occupants in low-trust terms. Should they legitimize the structure and their place in it, they will perceive it in high-trust terms and behave accordingly. We have seen how managerial ideology seeks, *inter alia,* to induce the managed to extend this legitimation and high-trust response. That it tends increasingly to fail has been attributed to incongruence between the terms of the ideology, which appeals for willing compliance and loyalty in support of management's efforts towards the common good, and perceptions of the economic system by rank and file who see it as characterized by self-interest and as marked by a divergence between management's goals and their own.

Were 'social reality', as men perceive it, to be assimilated somewhat closer to that envisaged in the rhetoric of social democracy and the pluralist society, the possibility might begin to emerge of an economic system still based on extreme division of labour which nevertheless generated a higher level of trust than does the present one. Changes in men's perceptions of the society they live and work in can bring significant changes in how they respond to it. The fate of managerial ideology shows us, however, that to try to induce men to see their world through a frame of reference which does not tally with their observations and experience is unlikely to lay a firm foundation of confidence. At present, official exhortations, moral appeals, and coercive expedients to promote 'responsible' behaviour and restraint in the field of industrial relations are grounded in pluralist interpretations of society and a set of associated conventions governing patterns of decision-making and reward in work organizations. If our analysis is correct in suggesting that much of the apparent acceptance by employee groups of these interpretations and conventions is due to their present lack of the confidence and power to challenge them, time may shake that acceptance by remedying the lack. And even to the extent that the acceptance is indeed based on genuine conviction, it can surely be expected to weaken with the increase in sophistication, aspirations, and example set by those already sceptical.

What needs to be considered, therefore, is the possibility of a matching shift in institutions and ideology which would mitigate the operation of the low-trust dynamic without sacrificing the production methods to which individual and social expectations are increasingly and universally geared. Admittedly the continuance of extreme division of labour would probably mean that for many low-discretion jobs such improvement in trust relations as would be likely of achievement might have little significant effect upon their occupants' behaviour in the actual task processes themselves – at least in larger organizations. The division of labour may be proved, in many cases, to have created low-discretion work patterns of such anonymity that no conceivable frame of reference among their occupants could do much more than promote legitimation of a pursuit by management and government agencies of social objectives which all can respect. The lack of intrinsic satisfactions in work may be the price which many men have to pay for society's production of relative abundance – which constitutes the case for their receiving a specially generous share of it. But over and above the question of the motivation which men bring to their task activities is that of the general approach they bring to labour planning, social objectives, and the distribution of rewards. If higher-trust attitudes took no other forms than restraint in asserting claims for increased money income and the acceptance of some degree of labour and income planning they would mitigate what has been suggested here is the chronic expression of low trust which threatens the stability, growth, and planning of industrial society, namely inflation.

What kind of 'social reality' might engender such higher-trust perceptions and responses? This is hardly the place for a discussion of such issues as ownership, government intervention, planning and control. Certain points do need to be made, however, since they relate directly to the present analysis. If competitive self-seeking struggle is pushing us towards instability and considerable social tensions, we might mitigate our difficulties by pursuing a radical reconstruction which seeks to rally major sections of society behind shared purposes of social justice. To the extent that this succeeded, a division of labour supported in part at least by shared purpose would make possible higher-trust relations. Our analysis suggests that it would be a society which, *inter alia*, reduced suspicion and competitive power struggles by containing the problem of distribution within a set of egalitarian principles; which demonstrably prevented any group from overriding those principles; which manifested effective concern with the low-paid and deprived; which recognized that intrinsic satisfactions were part of the compensation for work; which ensured that low-discretion role definitions were not the means by which men were used to support and create privilege but the means for serving ends which they could respect; and which re-examined the numerous conventions governing decision-making and rewards in work organizations for their relevance and fairness.

The reason for seeking high-trust relations in any planning process which depends for success upon consent is obvious. Such relations do not exclude the challenge of plans by those affected; their submission of new information; their querying of the wisdom of means. But the shared purpose converts what would otherwise be power bargaining based on distrust into problem solving based on trust. During the 'working-through' process which clarifies available facts and probable consequences the participants trust each other and decide courses of action to which they commit themselves. Such a pattern of relations represents a high order of achievement in human affairs. It is not difficult to identify many spurious forms of it which owe any apparent success to a feeling among the planned that they are in the power of the planners and would be well advised to make the appropriate noises.*

It may be that higher-trust solutions are not within the reach of societies based on such elaborate division of labour as ours,whatever the pattern of ownership, control, rewards, and social objectives. Perhaps all hope of promoting a wider and more diffuse social

* A small-scale example can be found in some applications of 'Management by Objectives' – a method described in McConkey 1967. Applied in certain situations it can represent high-trust problem solving; in others it has been described by some middle managers subjected to it as a 'Do-It-Yourself Hangman's Kit'. Large scale examples can be found in the planning processes of totalitarian states.

fellowship is excluded by the fine-drawn specifications of so many jobs, institutions, and specialisms, with their elaboration of complex and delicately adjusted interconnections and their need to work to a formula of precisely predictable commitments and expectations. Perhaps there is simply no basis here for rank and file participants to feel involvement, responsibility, and diffuse obligation. Perhaps the centralized purposes of remote leaders, however noble, cannot project their spirit and sincerity through the many intervening layers of delegation, representation, multiple special interests, and fragmented perspectives which make consensus so elusive. Should this prove to be so, high-trust attempts to plan against instabilities will not serve. Since the need for planning will remain, the failure of planning-by-consent could lead eventually, after a stumbling by Western societies through crises of increasing severity, to authoritarian attempts at planning-by-power. At this point the uncertainties must overwhelm all further attempt at guesswork. Indeed they have become severe long before this. As was stressed earlier, the emergent nature of social change means that simple projections of currently observed trends are highly vulnerable to error. What can be said with some confidence, however, is that the degree of institutional and structural change which will be required if there is to be any hope of promoting the high-trust planning referred to is very considerable indeed. Western society would scarcely be recognizable. Moreover there would be needed a coherent radical ideology and analysis which replaced the prevailing pluralist interpretations and accompanying conventions.

Given this kind of shift in values, institutions, and social philosophy, advanced industrial society might enjoy a future in which aspirations to enjoy its major rights, values, and freedoms become universalized without generating serious instabilities. Without such a shift, these instabilities, along with the measures taken by powerholders to deal with them and the resistances to those measures, might well threaten the Western liberal rights and freedoms altogether – certainly all hope of universalizing them. The longer the delay in beginning this shift the less the likelihood of achieving it, for on recent and present showing Western society gives some signs of being increasingly dispersive. Dispersiveness and fragmentation in terms of intergroup sentiments there have long been; what seems noteworthy is the apparent increasing ability and readiness of groups to give practical expression to these sentiments in ways which threaten the precarious interconnectedness of an industrial society undergoing an accelerating pace of change.

But given that the shift would imply radical changes in institutions and policies, where is the political will to initiate and implement them? It certainly does not exist at present. But to say of Britain, for example, that the will for radical reconstruction inspired by a moral purpose cannot be mobilized by courageous leadership is to go beyond the evidence, for such a mobilization has never been tried. Whether any latent disposition that may exist for mobilization of this kind can survive a few more decades of intensifying low-trust stresses within a context of continuing inflation is another question. It would, in any case, be absurd to play down the difficulties and, indeed, to be optimistic about the chances of the labour movement tackling them. Such, however, is the long-term threat to community and fellowship with which the intensifying application of economic exchange presents us that a conscious mobilization against it cannot begin too soon. The effort is all the more worth making since in other respects industrial society has been accompanied by a widening of institutionalized fellowship in terms of health and welfare provisions of a wide variety of kinds. The limits of human sympathy which, in earlier times, might scarcely extend beyond the village now range much wider, and wealth enables sympathy to take practical forms. All the more reason, then, to consolidate and nourish this enlargement with new forms of institutionalized expression which bring fellowship to bear on the planning and distribution of the common product.

It should be emphasized, however, that this contemplated concern with strengthening and enlarging institutionalized fellowship goes much further and deeper than the type of concern manifested by industrial society so far. This has been directed chiefly towards relieving, healing, and supporting the casualties of the system and generally helping them to cope with their weaknesses, disabilities, deprivations, and wounds. It has not been directed towards changing the system in such ways as to reduce the number of casualties (some proportion of whom, of course, owe their misfortunes to purely random non-systematic causes). We thus have the irony that a growing number of high-trust jobs in so-called 'helping' professions or semi-professions like social work are being created to cope with the casualties of a predominantly low-trust society – casualties found mainly in the lower strata. The greater the efforts made by our acquisitive, competitive, and highly unequal society to counter some of its adverse effects upon the unfortunate, the more these efforts expand the ranks of middle-class professionals competing for status and rewards and acquiring a vested interest in the continuation and expansion of their own activity.

However, this is but one of many possible offshoots of the argument, which could only be pursued by enlarging the scope of this book far beyond reasonable limits. It hardly needs stressing, either, that the logic of trust analysis as applied to inflation cannot explore here its relationship to the vast theme of the international setting within which domestic inflation is but one strand in a complex of related factors. The increasing interdependencies of international trade, finance, and investment pose great problems for radical political change at the national level, as does membership of the European Economic Community for countries of Western Europe. The degree of dependence of modern economies on arms expenditure and on the rapidly changing technology with which it is associated is believed by some to threaten new sources of instability (Kidron 1970: 63–4), as also do the powerful forces generated by more general economic processes and expectations. These include, among many others, the seemingly uncontrollable tendency of capital, jobs, and people to converge upon massive urban-industrial concentrations which leave less favoured regions (in Britain, for example, those of Wales, Scotland, and Northern Ireland) vulnerable to social instabilities which take varied forms. 'In almost every country . . . [of Western capitalism] dormant and dead nationalisms, regional and linguistic movements are clambering out of the vortex, demanding the impossible from capitalism – an even distribution of wealth and power' (*Ibid*: 164–5). These features of the wider scene are mentioned in order that we can remind ourselves of the breadth and scale inevitably taken by any discussion of instabilities in Western society. Yet the theme of low-trust relations created by the division of labour does not thereby become swallowed up and disappear from view. Many of the instabilities derive from our failure to devise effective systems of planning, and it is not difficult to relate this failure to, among other things, the institutions and orientations characteristic of low-trust relations – not least those which render income and labour planning so crucial and yet so elusive.

9 · Conclusions

Throughout this book the high-trust relationship has been characterized as one in which the participants share certain ends or values; bear towards each other a diffuse sense of long-term obligations; offer each other spontaneous support without narrowly calculating the cost or anticipating any equivalent short-term reciprocation; communicate freely and honestly; are ready to repose their fortunes in each other's hands; and give each other the benefit of any doubt that may arise with respect to goodwill or motivation. Conversely, in a low-trust relationship the participants have divergent ends or values; entertain specific expectations which have to be reciprocated through a precisely balanced exchange in the short term; calculate carefully the costs and anticipated benefits of any concession; restrict and screen communications in their own separate interests; seek to minimize dependence on each other's discretion; and are quick to suspect, and invoke sanctions against, illwill or default on obligations. While we have been mainly concerned to explore the logic and dynamics of 'vertical' trust relations we also took note of the 'lateral' trust relations which grow out of them. They become important at a later point in this concluding discussion.

Meanwhile it is clear that the low-trust syndrome as we have defined it imposes limitations on human collaboration. Their severity varies with the task, technology, and aspirations of the participants, but no system of interdependence can be other than impeded in some measure by these wary arm's-length relations between superordinates and subordinates. The relevant power-holders in industrializing countries over the past two centuries have considered, however, that the costs of such limitations as they were aware of were outweighed by the benefits of the extreme division of labour from which the limitations sprang. So long as they could rely on holding a supervisory, planning, and managerial superstructure within a high-trust fraternity of shared values, status, and kindred expectations, they could see the system as viable. Hence the uneasiness as low-trust responses show signs of creeping up the hierarchy, and the strong rearguard action against 'breakaway' symptoms among supervisors and other white-collar staffs.

We have noted forces making for the intensification and universalization of low-trust responses, and saw that the projection of these tendencies towards their extreme form implies conflict of a more fundamental and radical kind than pluralistic interpretations of society are happy to accept. But we also noted certain counter-tendencies. Advanced technology may not necessarily reknit lower ranks into a somewhat higher-trust fabric than we know at present, but there are some signs in this direction. Technology may in some cases, therefore, marginally help power-holders by mitigating their difficulties in this respect, though it appears unlikely to eliminate them. What is evident, however, is that such conscious efforts as we are now witnessing towards reversing or modifying the Scientific Management approach are inspired by the same motivations as led to its adoption – namely economic efficiency, growth, or profit. High-trust relations are pursued, not for their own sake, but because they are thought to evoke commitment to managerial ends, improve performance, promote adaptability and receptivity to change, stabilize the labour force. On present showing we may expect a few of the more progressive and sophisticated power-holders to be increasingly alert to possibilities of changing technology or organization in a high-trust direction provided the benefits seem likely to outweigh the costs over the long period. In describing their motives as those of economic expediency we are not arguing that particular operational managers who may initiate and carry out such changes are necessarily acting under these motives. They may believe the changes to be desirable for their own sake, quite apart from the expected economic consequences. But whether they are allowed by power-holders above them to introduce the changes will depend on whether these can be justified in terms of economic or financial rationality. When, therefore, a manager who is carrying out change speaks and acts with obvious moral conviction he is likely to be doing so only under sanction from others who ultimately control his behaviour and perceive his policies to be congruent with their own goals. The fact that prudence normally deters them from making their position explicit causes the observer's attention to remain focused on the initiating manager and his moral convictions; a situation which may mislead those seeking insight into managerial goals in modern business. The crucial goals and criteria are those which inform the limits within which decision-makers are constrained to act.

Such considerations support the judgement that high-trust relations in work are at present a byproduct of decisions directed towards very different ends. They will remain so in any system, whether privately or communally owned, where prime importance is attached to maximizing the economic return on resources. Under the private profit system the pressures in this direction are of course very strong. The significance of public ownership is that, after removing this structurally induced disposition common to the controllers of resources, politically effective groups in society are free to make different choices. They may of course make the same ones. The ideology of Western-style economic growth now sweeping the world presents those who would have them choose differently with an uphill task. Public ownership is the necessary but certainly not the sufficient condition for any change in the primary objectives and methods of work organizations.

We are faced, then, with two different possible motives for moving away from organizational patterns which generate low-trust relations. The first springs from the argument that in a context of accelerating change where personal involvement and a willing creative approach to problem solving are at a premium, the promotion of high-trust relations through structural change offers long-term benefits outweighing any short-term costs. The argument may meet practical disagreement, and usually does, but at least the criteria being used are widely understood. The other motive has hitherto been the concern of a tiny minority. This is the conviction that high-trust relations are qualitatively superior and desirable for their own sake. As applied to work, this conviction takes the form of criticizing the extreme division of labour and its impoverishing effect upon men's personalities and the relationships between them. From the individual's subjective consciousness of work to groups and class relations, the critic of extreme division of labour can argue that it produces experiences and relations which fall far short, in qualitative terms, of the best within human reach. Implicit in many judgements of this sort is a conception of the individual as an autonomous moral agent, developing himself by making and accepting the responsibility for, and consequences of, significant choices, and in the process maintaining relationships of mutual trust and cooperation with others.

Measured by these standards, industrial society clearly pays a price for its mastery of nature. The price has to be paid, of course, not merely in the context of work. This book has sought to identify dynamics within the job situation which also operate within all trading, commercial, and business relations in industrial society and lead to the same kind and quality of interaction. We see pervading every aspect of human existence an ever extending network of commercialized relations – the offering of specific services in exchange for specific sums of money; the carefully calculated and jealously guarded reciprocation; the draining from the transaction of all expressive or other extraneous considerations; the quick suspicion of fraud or default; the ever increasing battery of State-initiated protections and penalties designed to control and punish the bad faith that otherwise increasingly accompanies the impersonal, specific contract. The argument of this book has been that these dynamics apply in exactly the same way to work relations and spring from the same basic thrust of the industrial and commercial order – the thrust towards extreme differentiation and specialization of function. This is the movement which, in rendering the relevant social relations ever more narrowly specific, squeezes out the reciprocal diffuseness of obligations which is the necessary condition of high-trust relations. It is the movement from social to economic exchange. There is no concern here, however, to mount a simplistic lament for 'the world we have lost'. Quite apart from other considerations, any implication that the profit and loss account of industrialization could be presented in those limited terms would of course be absurdly facile. Unquestionably the choices by power-holders of certain patterns of work organization as against other possible patterns have involved their own and subsequent generations in paying a price, but the gains for which the price was paid have to be seen in terms not only of cars, washing machines, and television sets, but also of the elimination of much poverty, material suffering, disease, and early death, not to mention the vast expansion of individual freedom, with its potentiality for creativity and happiness as well as for boredom and misery.

These truisms are mentioned only to lead up to the points that, except in so far as high-trust relations serve economic values, men are faced with a choice, and that rational choice implies some knowledge of the costs and benefits of alternatives. It has already been suggested that unless power-holders perceive high-trust relations as offering economic benefits which exceed costs they will prefer traditional patterns and policies. But events show increasingly that rank and file employees are not powerless and do not necessarily have to accept the choices of their masters. As yet, however, their preferences show no marked rejection of those choices. They demonstrate marginal disagreement about the distribution of the product and about the precise nature of some aspects of the productive process, but none about its essential characteristics of hierarchy and extreme differentiation of function. These are accepted as necessary conditions for the production of abundance. How far this represents a rational choice is debatable. Many are conscious of material need but have little or no experience of the intrinsic satisfactions of high-discretion work; they are increasingly socialized to raise their material aspirations but never to examine critically the quality of their work life and relationships. In these circumstances they are hardly likely to opt for lower material standards in exchange for intrinsic rewards of whose nature they are aware, if at all, only by repute. It is sometimes argued that with growing affluence diminishing returns will set in; that the pleasure derived at the margin of a rising material standard of life will decline relatively to the consciousness of being deprived of intrinsic satisfaction in work. The behaviour of middle and upper classes throughout the world are no help here, for they comprise those fortunate strata whose members receive ever larger financial rewards as they move ever upward in the high-trust fraternity of work. It would be prudent to bear in mind, however, that given the ingenuity of man in devising new mechanical delights, personal possessions, and status objects, the appropriate reference here may be not to the diminishing marginal rate of substitution but to the appetite which grows by what it feeds upon.

In sum, then, it is clear that there are many questions to ask when we try to assess the likelihood of those low-discretion employees who are relatively comfortably placed becoming prepared to sacrifice some material wellbeing in order to gain certain intrinsic rewards from work. Should their aspirations move in this direction, there seems no obvious reason to suppose that our present industrial system would be unable to adapt appropriately provided the adjustments sought were relatively marginal, though it is likely that even these would generate stresses of no small order. But marginal changes in job structure could be expected to produce only marginal changes in trust relations and it is conceivable that in time men might seek more than this.

In pursuing the implications of a more fundamental shift of preferences we have to enlarge our view to include the other dimension of trust relations – the lateral dimension which covers those in similar job situations within the organization. There emerged from the theoretical exposition in Chapter 2 a typology of four different combinations of vertical and lateral trust. First, at one extreme are the favoured who enjoy high-trust relations along both dimensions; second, at the other the deprived who enjoy them along neither. Third, in between are those in high-discretion roles who find themselves in low-trust rivalry with their fellows; and fourth, those who, though deprived of the intrinsic satisfactions of high-discretion work, derive the support, security, and fellowship of high-trust relations with fellow employees.

Which of these patterns would men be likely to choose, given knowledge of the alternatives? Some would opt for the third pattern; men specially confident of their own powers not infrequently relish competition, for fairly obvious reasons. It is difficult to conceive reasons why persons of average mental health should choose the second, and why prefer the fourth if the first is available? Lack of ambition; fear of responsibility; and the absence of talent are usually offered as possible reasons but these beg questions rather than answer them. Within a society and a culture where ambition is apt to be an individualistic thrust towards personal achievement, recognition, and success; where 'acceptance of responsibility' is often no more than the upward reach of the confident man who knows that his particular abilities can supply a particular demand; and where 'talent' refers to whatever abilities and aptitudes happen to be marketable within the currently prevailing economic arrangements, there need be no surprise that many fail to clear these definitional and practical hurdles, especially when to them is added the inequalities of life chances which so patently inhibit or frustrate aspirations. Social structures and work arrangements are, however, theoretically conceivable which would invite and promote high-discretion contributions in a setting where no premium was placed on individualistic ambition and self-assertion; where men ready to offer their involvement, judgement, and discretion were not deterred from so doing by the prospect of being drawn out to a fine point of 'success' or 'failure'.

Pursuit of this line of thought suggests that the reasons why some might choose the fourth pattern include not only those features of the existing social order which depress and inhibit aspirations but also those which render many high-discretion roles unattractive because they are perceived as being accompanied by characteristics collectively designated 'the rat race' – individualistic rivalry, jealousy, disproportionate valuation placed on personal success and recognition, the competitive tricks of one-upmanship, the jockeying for position, the dread of failure. To the extent that this argument is valid, we can say that those who would choose to forgo high-discretion work in order to enjoy high lateral trust relations would not have to make this sacrifice if offered the choice of work which offered high-trust relations in both directions. We thus arrive at the first pattern; the choice of many socialists down the ages. The arguments of this book have sought to suggest certain of the logical implications of their vision; implications with which, of course, they would not necessarily have agreed. These implications bear upon the nature of work; the values by which it is designed; the types of experience and relationship which it generates; and the ideologies which encourage men to seek from it rewards of one kind rather than another. To attempt to explore such further implications as what type of economy, society, and polity would be required to contain and express this vision would of course be a venture in its own right. All that can be said is that it would be profoundly different from the one we know now.

This alone will be enough to convince many that such theorizing is mere self-indulgence. Yet it may serve at least two useful purposes. First, it contributes, however imperfectly, to that process of social questioning by which we can convince ourselves that 'what is' need not mean 'what must be'; that there are alternative social patterns towards which we could move given the resolve. Second, it can help us to set up standards by which not only to judge what we have already created, but also to decide what to avoid in the acts of social creation which lie ahead. Most of these will be, not *macro* choices shaping whole social structures, but *micro* choices which though small in themselves can nevertheless between them affect the quality of society and its predominant culture – perhaps reinforcing the quality which currently prevails or on the other hand challenging it with different values. This illuminates the sense in which every act of choice can be important. Unless we have some insight into the probable consequences of different alternatives and are encouraged to evaluate them, choices will be made either in ignorance or in the light of evaluations made by others with whom we may or may not be in agreement.

This concluding discussion has included in its terms the possibility of men being prepared, given knowledge of choices and consequences, to sacrifice – where sacrifice was called for – the benefits of low-trust division of labour in exchange for the satisfactions of high-trust work roles and relations. In the previous chapter a more limited set of possibilities was examined – that the existing division of labour would remain and would be accompanied by increasing instabilities generated by, and further aggravating, inflation. Here it was suggested that there was no reason to assume as impossible the mobilization of a common purpose to strengthen fellowship, define and pursue social justice, and in the process bring inflationary pressures under some degree of containment. The low-trust dynamic would be mitigated at least to the extent of keeping alive some spirit of community. Even this would require a radical transformation in our institutions and principles. 'The task of the most advanced societies', wrote Durkheim, 'is, then, a work of justice' (1964: 387). Our definition of justice might not be his, but with the sentiment itself it is becoming increasingly difficult to disagree.

Appendix

Trust Relations and the Blood Gift

During the preparation of this book a study was published – *The Gift Relationship: From Human Blood to Social Policy*, by R. M. Titmuss (1970) – which explores the working, within a profoundly significant area of social policy, of a process closely akin to what has been described here as the low-trust dynamic. It concerns the 'procurement, processing, distribution, use and benefit in Britain, the United States, the U.S.S.R., South Africa and other countries' of human blood for medical transfusion purposes. Professor Titmuss's analysis will be used here, first, to illustrate the pervasive character of low-trust relations in industrial society as we know it at present and, second, to reinforce the argument advanced here that a consideration of trust relations should enter into our social awareness as one of the items in the profit and loss account of industrialization and in the evaluation of choices both past and to come. The theoretical framework within which Professor Titmuss presents his case will be modified in order to assimilate it to the framework used in this book, though not, it is very much hoped, in any way which misrepresents or does violence to his own arguments. Professor Titmuss must not, needless to say, be associated with the use made here of his study and the interpretation placed upon it.

The discussion of his theme might suitably begin by postulating a society within which there exists a reciprocated diffuse sentiment of fellowship sufficiently strong in certain respects to sustain a purely voluntary system of blood donation. Men give their blood to strangers whom they never see. It would not be convincing to present this as a purely utilitarian act on which a calculable return of equivalent nature is expected. We may assume donors, indeed, to hope devoutly that such a return will never be required. Yet it is not convincing either to suppose that the notion of reciprocity is absent. Relevant here is the comment of Nisbet quoted earlier in the discussion of social (as opposed to economic) exchange. 'Did the good samaritan come to my rescue because of his desire for gratitude? Such an ascription would be too simple. But were I to reward his assistance to me with chilly indifference or hostility a vital exchange relationship would have been ruptured' (1970: 65). What appears to make the flow of blood gifts possible is (a) a sentiment of fellowship on the part of the donor and (b) his perception that this sentiment is reciprocated by sufficient others to make it a significant reference point for his behaviour. He does not have to believe it to be shared by everyone. Neither does it have to be manifested towards him personally in terms of concrete acts. It is enough that he perceives the sentiment to exist and to take expression, when occasion demands, in acts of sympathy, support, caring, and concern for others. In other words, what is reciprocated is the sentiment itself, and it is the consciousness of this reciprocation which is the spring and the support of the concrete acts which are its practical expression. This is not to deny that the rare human being exists who is capable, given the support of exceptionally strong religious or ethical conviction, to continue offering support and concern in the face of a demonstrated refusal to reciprocate. Most of us, however, need evidence of a different kind. We find it impossible to sustain an outward-looking spirit of support and concern if we believe everyone else to be exclusively focused on their own interests which they calculate on a narrow *quid pro quo* basis. We cannot go on offering fellowship in the total absence of signs that sufficient others share our willingness to offer. In such situations the spirit withers. The space thus left does not remain empty. Into it move sentiments of wary watchfulness. If others are not feeling fellowship towards us, what *are* they feeling? Defensiveness and suspicion soon come to be seen as conditions of survival in a world where one is uncertain of the goodwill of one's fellows. Meanwhile, of course, others are observing one's own behaviour and reacting likewise, thereby confirming one's reading of the situation. The low-trust dynamic is under way.

The voluntary giving of blood is one expression, then, of a sentiment of fellowship which can be sustained by widespread perceptions that others share the sentiment and are also ready to give expression to it in this way. Such is the rapidly increasing demand for blood, however, that many countries have sought to enlarge the supply by offering money payments. Titmuss convincingly analyses the consequences. 'From our study of the private market in blood in the United States we have concluded that the commercialization of blood and donor relationships represses the expression of altruism, erodes the sense of community, lowers scientific standards, limits both personal and professional freedoms, sanctions the making of profits in hospitals and clinical laboratories, legalizes hostility between doctor and patient, subjects critical areas of medicine to the laws of the marketplace, places immense social costs on those least able to bear them – the poor, the sick and the inept – increases the danger of unethical behaviour in various sectors of medical science and practice, and results in situations in which proportionately more and more blood is supplied by the poor, the unskilled, the unemployed, Negroes and other low income groups and categories of exploited human populations of high blood yielders' (*Ibid*: 245–6).

How does this corruption of fellowship and withering of community come about? The short answer is that the commercialization of bloodgiving converts an act which springs from a social exchange relationship into an act of economic exchange. In a voluntary system, the gift rests on the donor's perception of a reciprocal, diffuse sentiment of fellowship. In a commercial system the transaction rests on no such support; requires no such ethical underpinning. It is one of narrowly calculated economic exchange – so much money for so much blood. The individual's moral self is not called for; comes under no appeal; is defined as largely irrelevant for this purpose. As was argued earlier in the context of alienation, the reduction to economic exchange drives out diffuse obligations and leaves only specific obligations which can be measured. Only obedience to the prescribed terms is required of each party, who is not required, therefore, to participate as a moral entity by deciding the nature and timing of his part in the exchange. In this sense the reciprocating act is deprived of its moral character. This attenuation of the ethical requirement has its effect, as we saw, even on that aspect of economic exchange which calls for honourable discharge of the measured terms. The diminished moral involvement weakens observance even here, creating thereby a tendency towards evasion, fraud, and deceit which has to be countered by a growing battery of controls and sanctions. In the light of these arguments it is no surprise that Titmuss found paid donors to be 'on average and compared with voluntary donors, relatives and friends, more reluctant and less likely to reveal a full medical history and to provide information about recent contacts with infectious disease, recent inoculations, and about their diets, drinking and drug habits that would disqualify them as donors' (*Ibid*: 151).

These are some of the consequences for blood donation when the sentiment of fellowship is replaced with a very different kind of nexus. The growth of a commercial system undermines the voluntary system by debasing the nature of the exchange. The manifest expression of fellowship institutionalized in the latter is perceived as being increasingly replaced by the calculative specificity institutionalized in the former. The downward spiral, as always, feeds on itself. Diminishing perceptions of manifest fellowship on the part of others increase the chances of withdrawal all round. The shrinking visibility of manifest concern diminishes the stock of latent concern. In other words, to pursue social policies which extinguish the visible expression of fellowship reduces the probability of men perceiving that such sentiments are shared by others, thereby increasing their own difficulty in retaining these sentiments themselves.

It is hardly necessary to labour the obvious affinity between fellowship and trust in order to demonstrate that we are caught up here in the same dynamic as is operative in the work situation. Men's labour is seen as a commodity to be bought and sold on the market. The extreme division of labour results in this commodity becoming, in many situations, subject to specific definition and equally specific reward. This movement towards economic exchange tends to displace the ethical involvement of the parties in their reciprocation, leaving not neutrality but wariness and suspicion. Where work systems of this kind prevail, the behaviour of those in the low-discretion roles is structured so as to minimize personal commitment and involvement in the task. They are perceived, and perceive themselves and each other, as being engaged in a largely calculative and contractual transaction. There is little in all this to generate and feed a rising reciprocation of fellowship and trust. Rather is it likely to produce a downward spiral into widening and intensifying distrust. In this major area of social life, then, men's behaviour becomes so structured as to minimize manifestations of the whole self in their work situation. This extinguishing of manifest diffuse commitment affects men's perceptions of the social motives of others. When fellowship, trust, and mutual commitment are not manifest, doubts arise as to whether they exist even latently and men feel the need to protect themselves. Their own doubts are, of course, cues for others.

It is integral to the analysis that these orientations do not predominate at the higher levels of the work organization. Those devotees of the market and its associated principles and behaviours who see it as the answer to all human problems provided it is applied unblinkingly and unswervingly enough still fail to grasp that even the modern economic system, to which it is assumed to apply *in excelsis*, continues to operate as it does only because the economic exchange of the market has not entirely taken over. Quite apart from the non-contractual high-trust aspects of business behaviour to which Macaulay (1963), for example, draws attention, there are the crucial sectors of managerial, administrative, professional, and specialist activity which could not be discharged except on a high-discretion basis which evokes a measure of personal involvement and diffuse mutual obligation on the part of those involved. The keen calculative specificity of reciprocation which characterizes purely market transactions is a contradiction in terms to these high-discretion relations. Any attempt to substitute such specificity for the relatively diffuse commitment among members of the high-trust fraternity would soon bring the modern work organization grinding to a halt. It is, in fact, the possibility of economic-exchange relations not only becoming universalized at lower levels but also moving up the hierarchy that helps to throw the indefinite survival of existing pattern into doubt. It will be recalled, of course, that we are talking in relative terms: trust is never totally absent from the factory floor and is always much qualified in the upper reaches. But the contrast of degree is great.

The principles of economic exchange continue, however, to be propagated with a conviction approaching that of religious faith. Its more fervent prophets direct their teaching far beyond the limits of the economy by urging its application to ever wider fields of social policy, through the extension of the market principle and the reduction of diffuse social sentiments of fellowship to specific individual exchanges of money and services. In Britain, for example, a publication in 1968 by the Institute of Economic Affairs, a favoured platform for disciples of this ideology, urged the payment of blood donors and competition for blood supplies (Titmuss 1970: 159).

The reason why it is so important to subject these and similar attempts to a careful examination of probable consequences is that every extension of low-trust relations increases the probability of a further extension. Low-trust situations habituate us to low-trust orientations, assumptions and responses, and make it more likely that when the need for the next decision arises we shall again make the low-trust choice. This preference comes to seem natural given the low-trust society to which men are becoming increasingly adapted. Conversely, each case of effective resistance to the reduction of social to economic exchange keeps alive a sector of high-trust relations which strengthens resistance to the next challenge. Strictly speaking, of course, the position is usually that these strategic choices are made not by us, but for us. We acquiesce out of ignorance of the deeper consequences and because we are indoctrinated on all sides in the virtues of the market and economic exchange. Sceptical vigilance of the kind brought to bear in *The Gift Relationship* is the necessary corrective.

References Cited in the Text

ADAMS, J. S. (1963) 'Towards an Understanding of Inequity' in *Journal of Abnormal and Social Psychology*, Vol. 67: 422–36.

ADAMS, J. S. (1965) 'Inequity in Social Exchange' in BERKOWITZ, L. (ed.) (1965) *Advances in Experimental Social Psychology*, 2. New York: Academic Press, 267–300.

AIKEN, M.; HAGE, J. (1971) 'The Organic Organisation and Innovation' in *Sociology*, Vol. 5 (1): 63–82.

ALDERFER, C. P. (1967) 'An Organizational Syndrome' in *Administrative Science Quarterly*, Vol. 12 (3): 440–60.

AMULREE, LORD (1929) *Industrial Arbitration in Great Britain*. London: Oxford University Press.

ANDERSON, P. (1967) 'The Limits and Possibilities of Trade Union Action' in BLACKBURN, R.; COCKBURN, A. (eds.) (1967) *The Incompatibles*. Harmondsworth: Penguin Books, 263–80.

ARGYRIS, C. (1957) *Personality and Organization: The Conflict Between System and the Individual*. New York and Evanston: Harper and Row.

ARGYRIS, C. (1964) *Integrating the Individual and the Organisation*. New York: Wiley & Sons.

ARGYRIS, C. (1972) *The Applicability of Organizational Sociology*. Cambridge: at the University Press.

BAIN, G. S. (1967) *Trade Union Growth and Recognition*. London: H.M.S.O.

BAIN, G. S. (1970) *The Growth of White-Collar Unionism*. Oxford: Clarendon Press.

BAIN, G. S.; PRICE, R. (1972) *Who is a White-Collar Employee?* in *British Journal of Industrial Relations*, Vol. X (3): 325–39

BAKKE, E. W. (1946) *Mutual Survival: The Goal of Unions and Management*. New York: Harper and Bros.

BAKKE, E. W.; KERR, C. (1948) *Unions, Management and the Public.* New York: Harcourt Brace & Co.

BARITZ, L. (1965) *The Servants of Power.* New York: Wiley & Sons.

BARNARD, C. (1946) 'Functions and Pathologies of Status Systems in Formal Organisations' in WHYTE, W. F. (ed) (1946) *Industry and Society.* New York: McGraw-Hill, 207–43.

BARNES, L. B. (1960) *Organizational Systems and Engineering Groups.* Boston: Harvard Business School.

BELL, D. (1961) 'Two Roads from Marx' in his *The End of Ideology.* New York: Collier Books, 355–92.

BELL, G. D. (1965) 'The Influence of Technological Components of Work Upon Management Control' in LITTERER, J. A. (ed.) (1969) *Organizations: Structure and Behavior* (Second Edition), Vol. 1. New York: Wiley & Sons, 441–5.

BELL, G. D. (1966) 'Predictability of Work Demands and Professionalization as Determinants of Workers' Discretion' in LITTERER, J. A. (ed.) (1969) *Organizations: Structure and Behavior* (Second Edition), Vol. 1. New York: Wiley & Sons, 446–52.

BELLAH, R. N. (1959) 'Durkheim and History' in NISBET, R. A. (ed). (1965) *Emile Durkheim.* Englewood Cliffs, N. J.: Prentice-Hall, Inc., 153–76.

BELSHAW, C. (1965) *Traditional Exchange and Modern Markets.* Englewood Cliffs, N. J.: Prentice-Hall, Inc.

BENDIX, R. (1963) *Work and Authority in Industry.* New York: Harper and Row.

BENDIX, R.; FISHER, L. H. (1949) 'The Perspectives of Elton Mayo' in ETZIONI, A. (ed.) (1962) *Complex Organizations: A Sociological Reader.* New York: Holt, Rinehart and Winston, 113–26.

BERLE, A. A.; MEANS, G. C. (1967) *The Modern Corporation and Private Property* (Revised Edition), New York: Harcourt, Brace and World Inc. (First published 1932).

BLACKBURN, R. (1967) 'The Unequal Society' in BLACKBURN, R.; COCKBURN, A. (eds.) (1967) *The Incompatibles.* Harmondsworth: Penguin Books, 15–55.

BLAU, P. (1964) *Exchange and Power in Social Life.* New York: Wiley & Sons.

BLAU, P.; SCOTT, W. R. (1963) *Formal Organizations: A Comparative Approach*. London: Routledge and Kegan Paul.

BLAUNER, R. (1964) *Alienation and Freedom: The Factory Worker and His Industry*. Chicago and London: University of Chicago Press.

BOTTOMORE, T. B; RUBEL, M. (eds.) (1963) *Karl Marx: Selected Writings in Sociology and Social Philosophy*. Harmondsworth: Penguin Books.

BRIGGS, A, (1961) *Seebohm Rowntree: 1871–1954*. London: Longmans, Green & Co.

BROWN, R. K. (1967) 'Research and Consultancy in Industrial Enterprises' in *Sociology*, Vol. 1 (1): 33–60.

BROWN, W. (1965) *Exploration in Management*. Harmondsworth: Penguin Books.

BURNS, T.; STALKER, G. M. (1961) *The Management of Innovation*. London: Tavistock Publications.

CAMERON, LORD. (1957) *Report of a Court of Enquiry into the causes and circumstances of a Dispute at Briggs Motor Bodies Limited, Dagenham* . . . London: H.M.S.O., Cmd. 131.

CAPLOW, T. (1964) *The Sociology of Work*. New York: McGraw-Hill (First published 1954).

CASTLES, F. G. *et al.* (eds.) (1971) *Decisions, Organizations and Society*. Harmondsworth: Penguin Books in association with the Open University Press.

CHADWICK-JONES, J. (1969) *Automation and Behaviour*. London: Wiley-Interscience.

CHAMBERLAIN, N. (1963) 'The Union Challenge to Management Control' in *Industrial and Labor Relations Review*, Vol. 16 (2): 184–92.

CHAMBERLAIN, N. W.; KUHN, J. W. (1965) *Collective Bargaining*. New York: McGraw-Hill.

CHARLES, R. (1973) *The Development of Industrial Relations in Britain 1911–1939*. London: Hutchinsons Educational.

CHEIT, E. (ed.) (1964) *The Business Establishment*. New York: Wiley & Sons.

CHILD, J. (1964) 'Quaker Employers and Industrial Relations' in *Sociological Review*, Vol. 12 (3): 293–315.

CHILD, J. (1969) *British Management Thought*. London: Allen & Unwin.

CLAY, H. (1929) *The Problem of Industrial Relations*. London: Macmillan.

CLEGG, H. A. (n.d.) *Purpose of the Unions*. London: National and Local Government Officers' Association.

CLEGG, H. A.; FOX, A.; THOMPSON, A. F. (1964) *A History of British Trade Unions since 1889: Volume 1, 1889–1910*. Oxford: Clarendon Press.

CLEGG, HUGH (1971) *How to Run an Incomes Policy*. London: Heinemann.

COATES, K.; TOPHAM, T. (eds.) (1970) *Workers' Control*. London: Panther Books.

COLE, G. D. H. (1917) *Self-Government in Industry*. London: Bell and Sons.

COLE, G. D. H. (1955) *Studies in Class Structure*. London: Routledge and Kegan Paul.

COMMONS, J. R. (1924) *Legal Foundations of Capitalism*. New York: Macmillan.

COSER, L. A. (1956) *The Functions of Social Conflict*. London: Routledge and Kegan Paul.

COSER, L. A. (1964) 'Durkheim's Conservatism and its Implications for his Sociological Theory' in WOLFF, K. H. (ed.) (1964) *Essays on Sociology and Philosophy*. New York: Harper Torchbooks, 211–32.

COTGROVE, S.; BOX, S. (1970) *Science, Industry and Society*. London: Allen & Unwin.

COTGROVE, S.; DUNHAM, J.; VAMPLEW, C. (1971) *The Nylon Spinners*. London: Allen & Unwin.

CROSLAND, C. A. R. (1964) *The Future of Socialism*. London: Jonathan Cape.

CROZIER, M. (1964) *The Bureaucratic Phenomenon*. London: Tavistock Publications.

CURTIS-BENNETT, SIR NOEL (1949) *The Food of the People; being The History of Industrial Feeding*. London: Faber & Faber.

CYERT, R. M.; MARCH, J. G. (1959) 'A Behavioral Theory of Organizational Objectives' in HAIRE, M. (ed.) (1959) *Modern Organizational Theory*. New York: Wiley & Sons, 76–90.

DAHRENDORF, R. (1959) *Class and Class Conflict in an Industrial Society*. London: Routledge and Kegan Paul.

DALTON, M. (1959) *Men Who Manage*. New York: Wiley & Sons.

DANIEL, W. W. (1972) 'Sliced Status' in *New Society*, 23 November: 468.

DAVIS, K. (1955) *Human Society*. London: Macmillan.

DAVIS, K.; BLOMSTROM, R. L. (1971) *Business, Society, and Environment*. New York: McGraw-Hill.

DAVIS, K.; MOORE, W. E. (1945) 'Some Principles of Stratification' in *American Sociological Review*, Vol. 10 (2): 242–9.

DAVIS, L. E. (1971) 'The Coming Crisis for Production Management: Technology and Organization' in DAVIS, L. E.; TAYLOR, J. C. (eds.) (1972): 417–29.

DAVIS, L. E.: TAYLOR, J. C. (eds.) (1972) *Design of Jobs*. Harmondsworth: Penguin Books. This volume comprises readings which all, in one way or another, argue the need for jobs to be redesigned so as to secure 'joint optimization' of both human and economic values.

DAY, R. C.; HAMBLIN, R. L. (1964) 'Some Effects of Close and Punitive Styles of Supervision' in *American Journal of Sociology*, Vol. LXIX (5): 499–510.

DICKENS, L. (1972) *UKAPE: What Future for the Professional Union?* Discussion Paper: Industrial Relations Research Unit of the Social Science Research Council, University of Warwick, Coventry.

DICKENS, L. (1972a) 'U.K.A.P.E: a Study of a Professional Union' in *Industrial Relations Journal*, Vol. 3 (3): 2–12.

DONOVAN, LORD (1968) *Report of the Royal Commission on Trade Unions and Employers' Associations, 1965–1968*. London: H.M.S.O., Cmd 3623.

DUBIN, R. (1958) *Working Union–Management Relations*. Englewood Cliffs, N. J.: Prentice-Hall, Inc.

DURKHEIM, E. (1964) *The Division of Labour in Society*. Glencoe: The Free Press (First published 1893).

ELLIS, N. D. (1969) 'The Occupation of Science' in BARNES, B. (ed.) (1972), *Sociology of Science*. Harmondsworth: Penguin Books, 188–205.

ENGELS, F. (1967) 'Socialism: Utopian and Scientific' (First published 1892) in *Engels: Selected Writings*, edited and introduced by W. O. Henderson. Harmondsworth: Penguin Books, 185–225.

ETZIONI, A. (1961) *A Comparative Analysis of Complex Organizations*. New York: The Free Press.

EVAN, W. M. (1961) 'Organization Man and Due Process of Law' in *American Sociological Review*, Vol. 26 (4): 540–7.

FERRIS, P. (1972) *The New Militants: Crisis in the Trade Unions*. Harmondsworth: Penguin Books.

FLANDERS, A. (1964) *The Fawley Productivity Agreements*. London: Faber & Faber.

FLANDERS, A. (1967) *Collective Bargaining: Prescription for Change*. London: Faber & Faber.

FLANDERS, A. (1968) *Trade Unions*. London: Hutchinson.

FLANDERS, A. (1970) *Management and Unions*. London: Faber & Faber.

FORSTER, SIR JOHN (1952) *Report of a Court of Inquiry into a Dispute between D. C. Thomson and Company Limited and certain work-people, members of The National Society of Operative Printers and Assistants*. London: H.M.S.O., Cmd. 8607.

FOX, ALAN (1958) *A History of the National Union of Boot and Shoe Operatives*. Oxford: Basil Blackwell.

FOX, ALAN (1966a) *The Time-Span of Discretion Theory: an Appraisal*. London: Institute of Personnel Management.

FOX, ALAN (1966b) *Industrial Sociology and Industrial Relations*. Research Paper 3, Royal Commission on Trade Unions and Employers' Associations. London: H.M.S.O.

FOX, ALAN (1971) *A Sociology of Work in Industry*. London: Collier-Macmillan.

FOX, ALAN (1973) 'Industrial Relations: A Social Critique of Pluralist Ideology' in CHILD, J. (ed.) (1973) *Man and Organization: The Search for Explanation and Relevance*. London: Allen & Unwin.

FRIEDMANN, G. (1961) *The Anatomy of Work: The Implications of Specialization*. London: Heinemann (First published 1956).

FRIEDMANN, G. (1964) *Industrial Society: The Emergence of the Human Problems of Automation*. Glencoe: The Free Press.

FRIEDMANN, W. (1972) *Law in a Changing Society* (Second Edition), Harmondsworth: Penguin Books.

GALBRAITH, J. K. (1962) *The Affluent Society*. Harmondsworth: Penguin Books (First published 1958).

GARAUDY, R. (1970) *The Turning-Point of Socialism*. London: Fontana Books.

GIDDENS, A. (1971) *Capitalism and Modern Social Theory*. Cambridge: at the University Press.

GITLIN, T. (1965) 'Local Pluralism as Theory and Ideology' in DREITZEL, H. P. (ed.) (1969) *Recent Sociology No.1*. London: Collier-Macmillan.

GLYN, A.; SUTCLIFFE, B. (1972) *British Capitalism, Workers and the Profits Squeeze*. Harmondsworth: Penguin Books.

GOFFMAN, E. (1952) 'On Cooling the Mark Out: Some Aspects of Adaptation to Failure' in ROSE, A. M. (ed.) (1962) *Human Behavior and Social Processes*. London: Routledge and Kegan Paul, 482–505.

GOLDNER, F. (1965) 'Managers: An Improper Subject' in *Proceedings of the Eighteenth Annual Winter Meeting of the Industrial Relations Research Association. December* 28–29, 1965 (Madison, Wisconsin).

GOLDSTEIN, B. (1955) 'Some Aspects of the Nature of Unionism among Salaried Professionals in Industry' in *American Sociological Review*, Vol. 20 (2): 199–205.

GOLDSTEIN, B. (1959) The Perspective of Unionized Professionals' in *Social Forces*, Vol. 37 (4): 323–7.

GOLDTHORPE, J. H. *et al.* (1968) *The Affluent Worker: Industrial Attitudes and Behaviour*. Cambridge: at the University Press.

GOLDTHORPE, J. H. *et al.* (1969) *The Affluent Worker in the Class Structure*. Cambridge: at the University Press.

GOODMAN, P. S. (1967) 'An Empirical Examination of Elliott Jaques' Concept of Time Span' in *Human Relations*, Vol. 20, No. (2): 155–70.

GOODMAN, P. S.; FRIEDMAN, A. (1971) 'An Examination of Adams' Theory of Inequity' in *Administrative Science Quarterly*, Vol. 16 (3): 271–88.

GORZ, A. (1970) 'What are the Lessons of the May Events?' in POSNER, C. (ed.) (1970) *Reflections on the Revolution in France: 1968*. Harmondsworth: Penguin Books, 251–65.

GOULDNER, A. W. (1955) *Patterns of Industrial Bureaucracy*. London: Routledge and Kegan Paul.

GOULDNER, A. W. (1959) 'Reciprocity and Autonomy in Functional Theory' in GROSS, L. (ed.) (1959) *Symposium on Sociological Theory*. Evanston, Ill.: Row, Peterson, 241–70.

GOULDNER, A. W. (1960) 'The Norm of Reciprocity: A Preliminary Statement' in *American Sociological Review*, Vol. 25 (2): 161–78.

GOULDNER, A. W. (1965) *Wildcat Strike*. New York: Harper and Row (first published 1954).

GOULDNER, A. W. (1971) *The Coming Crisis of Western Sociology*. London: Heinemann.

GRAVES, B. (1970) 'Particularism, Exchange, and Efficiency: A Case Study of a Construction Industry' in *Social Forces*, Vol. 49 (1): 72–81.

GRAY, A. (1946) *The Socialist Tradition*. London: Longmans, Green & Co.

GREENWOOD, E. (1957) 'Attributes of a Profession' in NOSOW, S.; FORM, W. H. (eds.) (1962) *Man, Work, and Society: A Reader in the Sociology of Occupations*. New York: Basic Books, 206–18.

GUEST, R. H. (1962) *Organizational Change: The Effect of Successful Leadership*. London: Tavistock Publications.

HABER, S. (1964) *Efficiency and Uplift*. Chicago: at the University Press.

HABERMAS, J. (1971) 'Science and Technology as Ideology' in BARNES, B. (ed.) (1972) *Sociology of Science*. Harmondsworth: Penguin Books, 353–75.

HAGEN, E. E. (1965) 'Some Implications of Personality Theory for the Theory of Industrial Relations' in *Industrial and Labor Relations Review*, Vol. 18 (3): 339–51.

HAGSTROM, W. O. (1964) 'Forms of Scientific Teamwork' in *Administrative Science Quarterly*, Vol. 9 (3): 241–63. For HAGSTROM (1965) see BARNES, B. (ed.) (1972) as under HABERMAS.

HALL, R. H. (1968) 'Professionalization and Bureaucratization' in *American Sociological Review*, Vol. 33 (1): 92–104.

HALL, R. H.; HAAS, J. E.; JOHNSON, N. J. (1967) 'Organizational Size, Complexity, and Formalization' in *American Sociological Review*, Vol. 32 (6): 903–12.

HARBISON, F. (1954) 'Collective Bargaining and American Capitalism' in KORNHAUSER, A.; DUBIN, R.; ROSS, A. M. (eds.) (1954) *Industrial Conflict*. New York: McGraw Hill. For other essays in the same volume which stress the 'stabilizing' effects of 'institutionalized conflict' see Chapter 1, 'Problems and Viewpoints', by the editors, and Chapter 3, 'Constructive Aspects of Industrial Conflict', by Robert Dubin.

HARMAN, W. (1969) 'The Nature of Our Changing Society' in THOMAS, J. M.; BENNIS, W. G. (eds.) (1972) *The Management of Change and Conflict*. Harmondsworth: Penguin Books, 43–91.

HAWKINS, K. (1972) *Conflict and Change*. London: Holt, Rinehart, and Winston.

HEATH, A. F. (1971) 'Exchange Theory' in *British Journal of Political Science*, Vol. 1 (1): 91–119.

HELLRIEGEL, D; FRENCH, W. (1969) 'A Critique of Jaques' Equitable Payment System' in *Industrial Relations*, Vol. 8 (3): 269–79.

HERBST, P. G. (1962) *Autonomous Group Functioning*. London: Tavistock Publications.

HERBST, P. G. (1972) *Socio-Technical Theory and Design*. London: Tavistock Publications.

HERZBERG, F. (1968) *Work and the Nature of Man*. London: Staples Press.

HICKSON, D. J. (1966) 'A Convergence in Organization Theory' in *Administrative Science Quarterly*, Vol. II (II): 224–37.

HILL, C. (1969) *Society and Puritanism in Pre-Revolutionary England*. London: Panther History Series.

HILL, P. (1971) *Towards a New Philosophy of Management*. London: Gower Press.

HILL, R. L. (1929) *Toryism and the People: 1832–1846*. London: Constable & Co.

HININGS, C. R.; LEE, G. L. (1971) 'Dimensions of Organization Structure and their Context: A Replication' in *Sociology*, Vol. 5 (1): 83–93.

HOBHOUSE, L. T. (1911) *Liberalism*. London: Oxford University Press.

HOBSBAWM, E. J. (1964) *The Age of Revolution 1789–1848*. New York: Mentor Books.

HOBSON, J. A. (1926) *The Evolution of Modern Capitalism* (Revised Edition), London: Walter Scott Publishing Co. (First published 1894).

HOPPER, E. (1965) 'Some Effects of Supervisory Style: A Sociological Analysis' in *British Journal of Sociology*, Vol. 16 (3): 189–205.

HOSELITZ, B. F. (1963) 'Main Concepts in the Analysis of the Social Implications of Technical Change' in HOSELITZ B. F.; MOORE, W.

E. (eds.) (1963) *Industrialization and Society*, Unesco-Mouton, 11–31.

HUGHES, E. (1952) Foreword to special issue on Work, *American Journal of Sociology*, Vol. LVII (5).

HYMAN, R. (1971) *Marxism and the Sociology of Trade Unionism.* London: Pluto Press.

INGHAM, G. K. (1970) *Size of Industrial Organization and Worker Behaviour*. Cambridge: at the University Press.

INKELES, A. (1960) 'Industrial Man: The Relation of Status to Experience, Perception, and Value' in *American Journal of Sociology*, Vol. LXVI (1): 1–31.

IVENS, M. (ed.) (1970) *Industry and Values.* London: Harrap & Co.

JANOWITZ, M. (1959) *Sociology and the Military Establishment.* New York: Russell Sage Foundation.

JAQUES, E. (1956) *Measurement of Responsibility*. London: Tavistock Publications Ltd.; Cambridge, Mass.: Harvard University Press.

JAQUES, E. (1967) *Equitable Payment* (Revised Edition), Harmondsworth: Penguin Books (First published 1961).

JEVONS, W. S. (1970) *The Theory of Political Economy*. Harmondsworth: Penguin Books (First published 1871).

JOHNSON, T. J. (1972) *Professions and Power*. London: Macmillan.

JUKES, M. (1970) 'Employers' Responsibility' in IVENS, M. (ed.) (1970) *Industry and Values*. London: Harrap & Co., 62–73.

KAHN, R. L.; BOULDING, E. (eds.) (1964) *Power and Conflict in Organizations*. London: Tavistock Publications.

KASSALOW, E. M. *et al.* (1965) 'A Symposium: Professional and White-Collar Unionism: An International Comparison' in *Industrial Relations*, Vol. 5 (1): 37–150.

KAWASHIMA, T. (1964) 'Dispute Resolution in Japan' in AUBERT, V. (ed.) (1969) *Sociology of Law: Selected Readings*. Harmondsworth: Penguin Books, 182–93.

KELLY, J. (1968) *Is Scientific Management Possible*? London: Faber & Faber.

KERR, C.; DUNLOP, J. T.; MYERS, C. A. *et al.* (1953) *Causes of Industrial Peace Under Collective Bargaining; A Final Report.* Washington D. C.: National Planning Association.

KERR, C. (1955) 'Industrial Relations and the Liberal Pluralist' in *Proceedings of the Seventh Annual Winter Meeting of the Industrial Relations Research Association.* December 28–30, 1954 (Madison, Wisconsin).

KERR, C. *et al.* (1962) *Industrialism and Industrial Man.* London: Heinemann.

KIDRON, M. (1970) *Western Capitalism since the War.* Harmondsworth: Penguin Books.

KLEIN, L. (1964) *Multiproducts Ltd.: A Case-Study on the Social Effects of Rationalized Production.* London: H.M.S.O.

KLEINGARTNER, A. (1967) 'The Organization of White-Collar Workers' in *First World Congress.* International Industrial Relations Association.

KOHN, M. L.; SCHOOLER, C. (1969) 'Class, Occupation and Orientation' in *American Sociological Review*, Vol. 34 (5): 659–78.

KORNHAUSER, A. (1965) *Mental Health of the Industrial Worker.* New York: Wiley & Sons.

KORNHAUSER, W. (1962) *Scientists in Industry.* University of California Press.

KURILOFF, A. (1963) 'An Experiment in Management : Putting Theory Y to the Test' in *Personnel*, November-December.

LANE, D. (1971) *The End of Inequality: Stratification under State Socialism.* Harmondsworth: Penguin Books.

LANE, T; ROBERTS, K. (1971) *Strike at Pilkingtons.* London: Collins-Fontana.

LASKI, H. J. (1947) *The Rise of European Liberalism.* London: Allen & Unwin.

LEE, J. (1924) *The Principles of Industrial Welfare.* London: Pitman and Sons.

LENIN, V. I. (1970) *What Is To Be Done?* London: Panther Books (First published in 1902).

LESTER, R. A. (1958) *As Unions Mature: An Analysis of the Evolution of American Unionism.* Princeton N.J.: Princeton University Press.

LIKERT, R. (1961) *New Patterns of Management.* New York: McGraw-Hill.

LITWAK, E. (1961) 'Models of Bureaucracy which Permit Conflict' in *American Journal of Sociology*, Vol. LXVII (2): 177–84.

LOCKWOOD, D. (1958) *The Blackcoated Worker: A Study in Class Consciousness*. London: Allen & Unwin.

MACAULAY, S. (1963) 'Non-Contractual Relations in Business: A Preliminary Study' in *American Sociological Review*, Vol. 28 (1): 55–67.

MACPHERSON, C. B. (1964) *The Political Theory of Possessive Individualism*. London: Oxford University Press.

MAINE, SIR H. S. (1931) *Ancient Law*. Oxford: at the University Press (First published 1861).

MALLET, S. (1963) *La Nouvelle Classe Ouvrière*. Paris: Éditions du Seuil.

MANN, F. C; WILLIAMS, L. K. (1960) 'Observations on the Dynamics of a Change to Electronic Data Processing Equipment' in *Administrative Science Quarterly*, Vol. 5 (2): 217–56.

MANN, M. (1970) 'The Social Cohesion of Liberal Democracy' in *American Sociological Review*, Vol. 35 (3): 423–39.

MARCH, J. G.; SIMON, H. A. (1958) *Organizations*. New York: Wiley & Sons.

MARCH, J. G. (ed.) (1965) *Handbook of Organizations*. Chicago: Rand McNally and Co.

MARCSON, S. (1961) 'Organization and Authority in Industrial Research' in *Social Forces*, Vol. 40 (1): 72–80

MARSHALL, A. (1898) *Principles of Economics*, Vol. 1. London: Macmillan.

MARSHALL, T. H. (1950) *Citizenship and Social Class*. Cambridge: at the University Press.

MARX, K. (1930) *Capital*. London: Dent. Translated from the fourth – and definitive – German edition published in 1890.

MARX, K. (1964) *Economic and Philosophic Manuscripts of 1844*. New York: International Publishers.

MARX, K.; ENGELS, F. (1967) *The Communist Manifesto*. Harmondsworth: Penguin Books (First published 1848).

MAUSS, M. (1954) *The Gift: Forms and Functions of Exchange in Archaic Societies*, with Introduction by E. E. Evans-Pritchard. London: Cohen and West (First published, in French, in 1923).

MAYO, E. (1949) *The Social Problems of An Industrial Civilization:* London: Routledge and Kegan Paul.

McBeath. G (1969) *Management Remuneration Policy*. London: Business Books.

McConkey, D. D. (1967) *How to Manage by Results*. New York: American Management Association.

McGregor, D. (1960) *The Human Side of Enterprise*. New York: McGraw-Hill.

McGregor, D. (1967) *The Professional Manager*. New York: McGraw-Hill.

McLellan, D. (1971) *Marx's Grundrisse*. London: Macmillan.

Meissner, M. (1971) 'The Long Arm of the Job: A Study of Work and Leisure' in *Industrial Relations*, Vol. 10 (3): 239–60.

Mészáros, I. (1970) *Marx's Theory of Alienation*. London: Merlin Press.

Miernyk, W. H. (1962) *Trade Unions in the Age of Affluence*. New York: Random House.

Miliband, R. (1969) *The State in Capitalist Society*. London: Weidenfeld and Nicolson.

Milkovitch, G. T.; Campbell, K. (1972) 'A Study of Jaques' Norms of Equitable Payment' in *Industrial Relations*, Vol. 11 (2): 267–71.

Mills, C. W. (1956) *White Collar*. New York: Oxford University Press.

Mills, C. W. (1959) *The Power Elite*. New York: Oxford University Press.

Moore, W. E. (1965) *The Impact of Industry*. Englewood Cliffs, N. J: Prentice-Hall, Inc.

Mumford, E. (1964) *Living With a Computer*. London: Institute of Personnel Management.

Nakayama, I. (1965) 'The Modernization of Industrial Relations in Japan' in *British Journal of Industrial Relations*, Vol. III (2): 225–36.

Naumova, N. F. (1971) 'Social factors in the emotional attitude towards work' in Osipov, G. V. (ed.) (1971) *Industry and Labour in the U.S.S.R.* London: Tavistock Publications, 261–9.

Nichols, T. (1969) *Ownership, Control and Ideology*. London: Allen & Unwin.

Nicholson, J. S. (1896) *Strikes and Social Problems*. London: Adam and Charles Black.

NISBET, R. A. (ed.) (1965) *Émile Durkheim*. Englewood Cliffs, N.J: Prentice-Hall, Inc.

NISBET, R. A. (1967) *The Sociological Tradition*. London: Heinemann.

NISBET, R. A. (1970) *The Social Bond*. New York: A. A. Knopf.

OLLMAN, B. (1971) *Alienation: Marx's Conception of Man in Capitalist Society*. Cambridge: at the University Press.

OSSOWSKI, S. (1963) *Class Structure in the Social Consciousness*. London: Routledge and Kegan Paul.

OWEN, R. (1927) *A New View of Society and Other Writings*. London: Dent and Sons (First published between 1813 and 1821).

PARKER, S. (1971) *The Future of Work and Leisure*. London: MacGibbon and Kee.

PARSONS, T. (1949) *The Structure of Social Action*. London: Allen & Unwin.

PARSONS T; SMELSER, K. P. (1956) *Economy and Society*. London: Routledge and Kegan Paul.

PARSONS, T. (ed.) (1964) *Introduction* to WEBER, M., *The Theory of Social and Economic Organization*. New York: Free Press.

PELLING, H. (1963) *A History of British Trade Unionism*. Harmondsworth: Penguin Books.

PEN, J. (1966) *Harmony and Conflict in Modern Society*. London: New York: McGraw-Hill.

PERROW, C. (1970) *Organizational Analysis: A Sociological View*. London: Tavistock Publications.

PHELPS BROWN, E. H. (1959) *The Growth of British Industrial Relations*. London: Macmillan.

PHELPS BROWN, E. H. (1962) *The Economics of Labor*. New Haven and London: Yale University Press.

POLANYI, K. (1945) *Origins of Our Time: The Great Transformation*. London: Gollancz.

POLLARD, S. (1968) *The Genesis of Modern Management*. Harmondsworth: Penguin Books.

POLSBY, N. W. (1963) *Community Power and Political Theory*. New Haven: Yale University Press.

PRANDY, K. (1965) *Professional Employees: A Study of Scientists and Engineers*. London: Faber & Faber.

PRATT, E. A. (1904) *Trade Unionism and British Industry*. London: Methuen.

PRESTHUS, R. V. (1958) 'Towards a Theory of Organizational Behavior' in *Administrative Science Quarterly*, Vol. 3 (1): 48–72.

PRESTHUS, R. V. (1961) 'Weberian and Welfare Bureaucracy in Traditional Society' in *Administrative Science Quarterly*, Vol. 6 (1): 1–24.

PRIBIĆEVIĆ, B. (1959) *The Shop Stewards' Movement and Workers' Control, 1910–1922*. Oxford: Basil Blackwell.

PUGH, D. S.; HICKSON, D. J.; HININGS, C. R.; MACDONALD, K. M.; TURNER, C.; LUPTON, T. (1963) 'A Conceptual Scheme for Organizational Analysis' in *Administrative Science Quarterly*, Vol. 8 (3): 289–315.

PUGH, D. S.; HICKSON, D. J.; HININGS, C. R.; TURNER, C. (1968) 'Dimensions of Organization Structure' in *Administrative Science Quarterly*, Vol. 14: 91–114.

PYM, D. (1968) 'Individual Growth and Strategies of Trust' in PYM, D. (ed.) (1968) *Industrial Society: Social Sciences in Management*. Harmondsworth: Penguin Books, 316–34.

REAGAN, M. D. (1963) *The Managed Economy*. New York: Oxford University Press.

RENNER, K. (1949) 'The Development of Capitalist Property' in AUBERT, V. (ed.) (1969) *Sociology of Law: Selected Readings*. Harmondsworth: Penguin Books, 33–45.

RHEINSTEIN, M. (ed.) (1954) *Max Weber on Law in Economy and Society*. Cambridge, Mass.: Harvard University Press.

RICE, A. K. (1963) *The Enterprise and its Environment*. London: Tavistock Publications.

RICHARDSON, R. (1971) *Fair Pay and Work*. London: Heinemann.

ROBERTS, B. C.; LOVERIDGE, R.; GENNARD, J.; EASON, J. V. (1972) *Reluctant Militants: A Study of Industrial Technicians*. London: Heinemann.

ROETHLISBERGER, F. J.; DICKSON, R. J. (1939) *Management and the Worker*. Cambridge (Mass.): Harvard University Press.

ROETHLISBERGER, F. J. (1942) *Management and Morale*. Cambridge (Mass.): Harvard University Press.

ROLL, E. (1945) *A History of Economic Thought* (Second Edition), London: Faber & Faber.

ROSOVSKY, H. (1961) *Capital Formation in Japan 1868–1940.* New York: The Free Press.

ROSS, N. S. (1958) 'Organized Labour and Management' in HUGH-JONES, E. M. (ed.) (1958) *Human Relations and Modern Management.* North Holland Publishing Co.

ROSS, N. S. (1969) *Constructive Conflict.* Edinburgh: Oliver and Boyd.

ROWNTREE, S. (1921) *The Human Factor in Business.* London: Longmans, Green & Co.

RUSHING, W. A. (1965) 'Organizational Size, Rules, and Surveillance' in LITTERER, J. A. (ed.) (1969) *Organizations: Structure and Behavior* (Second Edition), Vol. 1. New York: Wiley & Sons, 432–40.

SADLER, P. (1968) *Social Research on Automation.* London: Heinemann.

SCHACHT, R. (1971) *Alienation.* London: Allen & Unwin.

SCHEIN, E. H. (1965) *Organizational Psychology.* Englewood Cliffs, N.J.: Prentice-Hall, Inc.

SCHEIN, E. H.; BENNIS, W. G. (1965) *Personal and Organizational Change through Group Methods.* New York: Wiley & Sons.

SCOTT, R. (1955) *Elizabeth Cadbury 1858-1951.* London: Harrap & Co.

SEEMAN, M. (1967) 'On the Personal Consequences of Alienation in Work' in *American Sociological Review,* Vol. 32 (2): 273–85.

SELEKMAN, S. K.; SELEKMAN, B. M. (1956) *Power and Morality in a Business Society.* New York: McGraw-Hill.

SELZNICK, P. (1969) *Law, Society and Industrial Justice.* New York: Russell Sage Foundation.

SHEPARD, H. A. (1965) 'Changing Interpersonal and Intergroup Relationships in Organizations' in MARCH, J. G. (ed.) (1965) *Handbook of Organizations.* Chicago: Rand McNally and Co., 1115–43.

SHIRAI, T. (1965) 'The Changing Pattern of Collective Bargaining in Japan' in *British Journal of Industrial Relations,* Vol. III (2): 201–9.

SHULTZ, G. P.; WEBER, A. R. (1960) 'Technological Change and Industrial Relations' in HENEMAN *et al.* (1960) *Employment Relations Research.* New York: Harper and Bros., 190–221.

SIMMEL, G. (1964) *The Sociology of George Simmel,* translated and edited by K. H. Wolff. Glencoe: The Free Press (From works first published between 1902 and 1917).

SIMON, H. A. (1965) *Administrative Behavior: A Study of Decision-Making Processes in Administrative Organization* (Second Edition), New York: The Free Press; London: Collier-Macmillan (First published 1947).

SMELSER, N. J. (1959) *Social Change in the Industrial Revolution.* London: Routledge and Kegan Paul.

SMITH, ADAM (1904) *An Enquiry into the Nature and Causes of the Wealth of Nations* (Third Edition), London: Methuen & Co. (First published 1776).

SMITH, C. G.; ARI, O. N. (1964) 'Organizational Control Structure and Member Consensus' in *American Journal of Sociology*, Vol. LXIX (6): 623–38.

SPENCER, H. (1969) *The Man Versus the State*, Edited, with Introduction, by Donald Macrae. Harmondsworth: Penguin Books (First published 1884).

SPENCER, P.; SOFER, C. (1964) 'Organizational Change and its Management' in *Journal of Management Studies.* Vol. 1 (1): 26–47.

STINCHCOMBE, A. L. (1959) 'Bureaucratic and Craft Adminstration of Production: A Comparative Study' in *Administrative Science Quarterly*, Vol. 4 (2): 168–87.

STONE, L. (1972) *The Causes of the English Revolution: 1529–1642.* London: Routledge and Kegan Paul.

STRAUSS, G. (1963a) 'Professionalism and Occupational Associations' in *Industrial Relations*, Vol. 2 (3): 7–31.

STRAUSS, G. (1963b) 'Some Notes on Power-Equalization' in LEAVITT, H. J. (ed.) (1963) *The Social Science of Organizations.* Englewood Cliffs, N.J.: Prentice-Hall, Inc.

STRAUSS, G. (1964) 'Professional or Employee-Oriented: Dilemma for Engineering Unions' in *Industrial and Labor Relations Review*, Vol. 17 (4): 519–33.

STURMTHAL, A. (ed.) (1966) *White-Collar Trade Unions.* Urbana and London: University of Illinois Press.

TAIRA, K. (1964) 'The Labour Market in Japanese Development' in *British Journal of Industrial Relations*, Volume II (2) 209–27.

TANNENBAUM, F. (1964) *The True Society: A Philosophy of Labour.* London: Jonathan Cape (First published 1951).

TAWNEY, R. H. (1931) *Equality*. London: Allen & Unwin, 254–5.

TAWNEY, R. H. (1938) *Religion and the Rise of Capitalism*. Harmondsworth: Penguin Books (First published 1926).

TAWNEY, R. H. (1961) *The Acquisitive Society*. London: Fontana Books (First published 1921).

TELLY C. S. *et al.* (1971) 'The Relationship of Inequity to Turnover among Hourly Workers' in *Administrative Science Quarterly*, Vol. 16 (2): 164–72.

THOMAS, J. M.; BENNIS, W. G. (eds.) (1972) *The Management of Change and Conflict*. Harmondsworth: Penguin Books.

THOMPSON, J. D. (1967) *Organizations in Action*. New York: McGraw-Hill.

TILLET, A.; KEMPNER, T.; WILLIS, G. (1970) *Management Thinkers*. Harmondsworth: Penguin Books.

TITMUSS, R. M. (1970) *The Gift Relationship: From Human Blood to Social Policy*. London: Allen & Unwin.

TOLFREE, L. (1972). *Applying the Code: Notes on the Industrial Relations Code of Practice*. London: The Industrial Society.

TÖNNIES, F. (1955). *Community and Association*, with translator's Introduction by C. P. Loomis. London: Routledge and Kegan Paul (First published 1887).

TOURAINE, A. (1955). *L'Évolution du travail ouvrier aux usines Renault* (Paris: Centre National de la Recherche Scientifique), in WALKER, C. R. (ed.) (1962) *Modern Technology and Civilization*. New York: McGraw Hill, 425–37.

TRADES UNION CONGRESS (1966). *Trade Unionism: The Evidence of the Trades Union Congress to the Royal Commission on Trade Unions and Employers' Associations*. London.

TRIST, E.; HIGGIN, C.; MURRAY, H.; POLLOCK, A. (1963). *Organizational Choice*. London: Tavistock Publications.

TUMIN, M. M. (1953). 'Some Principles of Stratification: A Critical Analysis' in *American Sociological Review*, Vol. 18 (4): 387–93. This debate with Davis and Moore (1945) is reproduced in BENDIX, R.; LIPSET, S. M. (eds.) (1967) *Class, Status, and Power*. London: Routledge and Kegan Paul.

TURNER, A. N. (1955) 'Management and the Assembly Line' in *Harvard Business Review*, Vol. 33: September-October.

TURNER, H. A.; CLACK, G.; ROBERTS, G. (1967) *Labour Relations in the Motor Industry*. London: Allen & Unwin.

UDY, S. H. (1970) *Work in Traditional and Modern Society*. Englewood Cliffs, N.J.: Prentice-Hall, Inc.

VEBLEN, T. (1921) *The Engineers and the Price System*. Reprinted in 1963, New York: Harcourt, Brace and World, Inc.

VEBLEN, T. (1958) *The Theory of Business Enterprise*. New York: Mentor Books (First published 1904).

VEBLEN, T. (1964) *The Instinct of Workmanship*. New York: Sentry Press (First published 1914).

VOYSEY, E. B. (1919) 'The Human Element in Industry' in ALDEN, P. *et al. Labour and Industry: A Series of Lectures*. Longmans, Green: Manchester University Press.

WALTON, R. E.; MCKERSIE, R. B. (1965) *A Behavioral Theory of Labor Negotiations*. New York: McGraw-Hill.

WEBB, S. and B. (1902) *Industrial Democracy*. London: Longmans, Green & Co. (First published 1897).

WEBB, S. and B. (1920) *The History of Trade Unionism*. London: Longmans, Green & Co. (First published 1894).

WEDDERBURN, D. (1969) 'The Conditions of Employment of Manual and Non-Manual Workers' in *Social Stratification and Industrial Relations* (Proceedings of a Social Science Research Council Conference, Cambridge, 1968).

WEDDERBURN, D; CROMPTON, R. (1972) *Workers' Attitudes and Technology*. Cambridge: at the University Press.

WEDDERBURN, K. W. (1971) *The Worker and the Law* (Second Edition). Harmondsworth: Penguin Books.

WESTERGAARD, J. H. (1965) 'The Withering Away of Class: A Contemporary Myth' in ANDERSON, P.; BLACKBURN, R. (eds.) (1965) *Towards Socialism*. London: Fontana, 77–113.

WILENSKY, H. (1964) 'The Professionalization of Everyone?' in *American Journal of Sociology*, Vol. LXX (2): 137–58.

WILLIAMS, I. A. (1931) *The Firm of Cadbury: 1831–1931*. London: Constable.

WILLIAMS, R. (1961) *The Long Revolution*. London: Chatto and Windus.

WOLFF, R. P. (1965) 'Beyond Tolerance' in WOLFF, R. P.; MOORE, JNR., BARRINGTON; MARCUSE, H. (1969) *A Critique of Pure Tolerance*. London: Jonathan Cape.

WOODWARD, J. (1965) *Industrial Organization: Theory and Practice.* London: Oxford University Press.

WOODWARD, J. (ed.) (1970) *Industrial Organization: Behaviour and Control.* London: Oxford University Press.

WOOTTON, B. (1955) *The Social Foundations of Wages Policy.* London: Allen & Unwin.

WRONG, D. (1968) 'Some Problems in Defining Social Power' in DREITZEL, H. P. (ed.) (1969) *Recent Sociology No. 1.* London: Collier-Macmillan.

YOSHINO, M. Y. (1971) *Japan's Managerial System: Tradition and Innovation.* Cambridge, Mass.: M.I.T. Press.

YOUNG, M. (1961) *The Rise of the Meritocracy.* Harmondsworth: Penguin Books.

YOUNG, S. (1963) 'The Question of Managerial Preorogatives' in *Industrial and Labor Relations Review*, Vol. 16 (2): 240–53.

ZAND, D. E. (1972) 'Trust and Managerial Problem Solving' in *Administrative Science Quarterly*, Vol. 17 (2): 229–39.

Index